ENGAGING
TROUBLING
STUDENTS

ENGAGING TROUBLING STUDENTS

A CONSTRUCTIVIST APPROACH

SCOT DANFORTH • TERRY JO SMITH

 **CORWIN PRESS**
A Sage Publications Company
Thousand Oaks, California

For information:

Corwin Press
A Sage Publications Company
2455 Teller Road
Thousand Oaks, California 91320
www.corwinpress.com

Sage Publications Ltd.
1 Oliver's Yard
55 City Road
London EC1Y 1SP
United Kingdom

Sage Publications India Pvt. Ltd.
B-42, Panchsheel Enclave
Post Box 4109
New Delhi 110 017 India

Printed in the United States of America

Library of Congress Cataloging-in-Publication Data

Danforth, Scot.
Engaging troubling students: A constructivist approach / Scot Danforth and Terry Jo Smith.
      p. cm.
Includes bibliographical reference (p.) and index.
ISBN 1-4129-0447-1 (cloth)
ISBN 1-4129-0448-X (pbk.)
    1. Problem children—Education—United States. 2. Problem youth—Education—United States. 3. Constructivism (Education)—United States. 4. Classroom management—United States. I. Smith, Terry Jo, II. Title.
LC4802.D36 2005
371.93—dc22

                                                    2004007966

This book is printed on acid-free paper.

04 05 06 07 10 9 8 7 6 5 4 3 2 1

Acquisitions Editor:	Robert D. Clouse
Editorial Assistant:	Candice Ling
Production Editor:	Denise Santoyo
Copy Editor:	Liann Lech
Typesetter:	C&M Digitals (P) Ltd.
Indexer:	Pamela Van Huss
Cover Designer:	Anthony Paular

Contents

Acknowledgments

The authors and Corwin Press gratefully acknowledge the contributions of the following reviewers:

Ellen Brantlinger
Professor, Indiana University, Bloomington
Bloomington, IN

James Jackson
Professor, George Washington University
Washington, DC

Cindy Lensmire
Behavior/Learning Disabilities Teacher
Algoma Elementary School
Algoma, WI

James Paul
Professor, University of South Florida
Tampa, FL

Beverly Petch-Hogan
Professor, Southeast Missouri State University
Cape Girardeau, MO

Jay Shotel
Professor, George Washington University
Washington, DC

About the Authors

 **Scot Danforth, PhD,** is Associate Professor and Department Chair in the Division of Teaching of Learning, University of Missouri–St. Louis. He is a well-known leader in the growing area of Disability Studies in Education, a multidisciplinary field of educational research exploring disabilities as sociopolitical constructions and construing the disabled community as an oppressed minority group. He is also co-founder of the Disability Studies in Education Special Interest Group of the American Educational Research Association (http://ced. ncsu.edu/2/dse/). His research has explored the roles of professional and layperson discourses in the social and political construction of disability. Additionally, his publications have analyzed the historical and philosophical development of the field of special education. He has written a wide range of books and articles in the areas of special education teacher preparation, working with students with social and emotional difficulties, and classroom management.

 **Terry Jo Smith, PhD,** is Associate Professor of Special Education at National-Louis University in Chicago, Illinois. Before entering academia, she taught adolescents labeled emotionally/behaviorally disordered in urban settings for 10 years. Recently, she has been instrumental in creating a unique doctoral program at National-Louis University that draws on social and clinical models of disability with an emphasis on political, educational, and economic equity for people with disabilities. In addition, Smith is committed to activist teacher-research and working collaboratively with teachers in schools. Her research combines complex narratives of the lived experiences of schooling with social, psychological, and political analyses. She has published books and articles that focus on care and cruelty in the classroom, curriculum, and pedagogy, as well as an autobiography of her life as a teacher. A strong commitment to social justice for marginalized children fuels her research, teaching, and scholarship.

Introduction

Let us begin with a story about a 7-year-old boy named Chris. I (Scot Danforth, first author) was one of Chris's teachers at a special school for students considered to have emotional/behavioral disorders (E/BD). I had been teaching Chris for 3 months. I had also been working closely with the school staff and his grandparents to help this little boy deal with the suffering and challenges that confronted him.

Chris lived with his grandmother, grandfather, and his younger brother, James, in a modest home in a working-class neighborhood. His grandfather worked as a janitor for a middle school. His mother lived in a rooming house only half a mile from his grandparents' home. His father had left the family long ago, not to be heard from again.

Chris had lived with his mother until he was 5 years old. She was addicted to alcohol and narcotics. Her lifestyle was too unsteady, too irregular for her to raise her young boys. Knowing this, she asked her parents to take custody of her two boys. They agreed, believing that their home and their love were the best chance that Chris and James had in this world.

Chris had been moved to a self-contained "emotional/behavioral disorders" (E/BD) class within his neighborhood elementary school during the first grade. He was an angry, confused little kid who refused to follow the teacher's directions. When the adults got more demanding, he screamed, threw tantrums, kicked the principal in the shins, and raced like a wild man around the school. This behavior didn't change much in his brief stint in the special class. His first-grade record is filled with out-of-school suspensions for hitting teachers and the principal. By second grade, Chris had been sent to a more restrictive setting, the E/BD building where I met him.

In my experience, Chris was a delightful kid. He was funny, playful, intelligent, creative, and warm. He was also extremely sad. He often seemed to be brooding in a solitary fog, an encapsulated haze of anxiety and anger. He could break out of this haze for short periods of time to have fun, wrestle, tickle, or play a game. But he always seemed to return to that sad, hazy place.

One day, I asked Chris to draw a picture of himself. This was a way for Chris and I to discuss his life, how he viewed himself, and how he felt. He drew a boy with a large heart in the center of his chest. The fact that he drew a large heart was not surprising, for this was literally a boy with a big heart, big feelings, and a strong longing for love and warmth. What was striking was the fact that the heart was upside down. I asked Chris why he drew the heart upside down. He remained silent and looked away so that I couldn't see his face. So I interpreted to him, "Chris, is your heart upside down because you feel so sad?" I figured that this much was true. I was to find out soon that this child had more worries than I had thought.

He nodded.

I continued. "And I'm thinking that you feel so sad because you can't live with your Mom."

"She's sick." Chris had learned that his mother had a disease called alcoholism that sometimes interfered with her ability to treat him in loving ways.

Then I asked Chris if he might feel somewhat better if the many people in his life all loved him a lot. Not that we could ever replace his mother's love, but maybe the love of his grandfather, grandmother, brother, teacher, friends, and me could help him out some. He nodded and picked up the pen. He then drew a second heart, a smaller heart, inside the large one that he had already drawn. The second heart was right side up. It was smaller than and enclosed completely by the upside down heart, but it was right side up.

As he prepared to leave my room, Chris wrote "Bring this Wednesday" in big letters on the top of the picture. I was scheduled to visit his grandparents at home on Wednesday evening. He wanted me to show this to his grandparents and tell them about how he felt.

I didn't fully understand the significance of this until that Wednesday meeting. At that time, I sat down with his grandfather, a very rugged and silent man who rarely spoke or showed emotions. In our previous meetings, I had been extremely impressed with this man and his wife, an older couple who had raised their own children long ago and now found themselves spending their latter years raising their daughter's sons. I sat on the couch in the living room, and Chris's grandfather served me a cup of coffee. He sat next to me. His face quivered and his eyes welled with tears as he told me that his wife had been gone for 3 weeks, and he had not heard from her. Like her daughter, she was an alcoholic. She occasionally went on prolonged binges. With the two boys in the household, she did so by leaving the house for weeks on end. In fact, she often went on these drinking binges with her daughter. This time, both daughter and mother had run off together. Back at the house, her husband and the two boys were worried to tears, wondering if the two women were hurt or in danger, wondering if they would come back.

Chris's heart had been turned upside down long ago when his father left the family. It had been flipped again when his mother gave him up to his grandparents. And it continued to be flipped and flopped by the ongoing addictions and absences of his grandmother and mother. In the midst of all this abandonment and love unfulfilled, Chris's neighborhood elementary school had rejected him by suspending him repeatedly and ultimately sending him away to the E/BD school. It was amazing that this little boy didn't get in even more trouble at school given the difficulties he faced in his life.

Additionally, we should keep in mind the larger, socioeconomic context of Chris's experiences. His parents and grandparents struggled financially. His mother did not have the money or health insurance that would provide her access to the best drug rehabilitation treatment. His grandfather had health insurance through his employer, but that provided only very limited mental health coverage for Chris. The grandfather sought help for Chris at a local nonprofit mental health clinic that accepted payments through the federal Medicaid program. That community clinic provided mental health services for poor families. It was so overwhelmed with business that children and families could see a counselor only once per month, too infrequent for anything but superficial therapy. Medication (usually Ritalin) was the primary treatment for young children like Chris.

I had no illusion that Chris's school could somehow solve all these problems. But the professionals there could learn to understand these problems and play important roles in helping this boy and this family cope with very difficult life struggles. What were the school professionals doing to help?

At school, Chris was viewed by most of the teachers as an angry, resistant boy who needed to learn how to follow the rules and obey directions without mouthing back. Our school program consisted of a system of rewards and punishments—rewards for good behavior and punishments (or "consequences") for bad behavior—aimed at modifying Chris into a more compliant, obedient, agreeable boy. The school had a fairly elaborate system whereby students earned points for good and obedient behavior. These points were translated into status on a hierarchy of four status levels. Students who behaved themselves earned their way up the four levels over the course of months. Students who reached and maintained the top level for a month were considered ready to mainstream back to a regular education building. The basic idea was that if Chris changed his behavior and kept it changed, the school could transition him back to a less restrictive setting, a self-contained E/BD class in a regular building. Chris was supposed to try to earn his way back to a less restrictive setting by being good.

Chris didn't really try to earn his way back and didn't care very much about the rewards the school had to offer. His heart was too large and his troubles too deep for games like that. Often, he even seemed to relish the consequences, as if he somehow deserved the disapproval of the teachers, as if somehow he deserved more pain and sadness in his life. This was often taken by some of my fellow teachers as a further indication of how "disturbed" Chris was. "He's very E/BD," they would say, because if he was less E/BD, he'd "buy into the system." He'd go for the rewards and avoid the consequences and work toward earning back a spot in a regular education building. Only a severely E/BD kid would not do this.

During that school year, of the approximately 200 students we had in that E/BD school, fewer than 10 made it back to a general education building. Many of the teachers took this to mean that their students were very, very disturbed. This was full justification to continue with our important efforts to modify behavior with rewards and punishments. The program was good. It was the kids (and parents) who were screwed up.

TEACHING AS RELATIONSHIP

In our many years of experience as teachers and teacher educators, we have found this to be a common approach to the education of deviant, disruptive, and nonconforming students. We can't deny that if Chris only improved his behavior and maintained that improvement for a convincing amount of time, he would move one notch closer to the general education classroom. What we believe, though, is that an approach that focuses primarily on altering or controlling the behavior of the student is shortsighted and misguided. To be blunt, it misses the boat altogether.

What Chris needed was not just an improvement in his behavior. His problem was not merely that he misbehaved at school. The problems in his life were multiple, complex, and much deeper than that. Chris had been let down and wounded by dramatic losses and repeated instabilities in the most essential relationships in his life. This had occurred initially and powerfully within his family. This was continued by school professionals, who responded to his emotions and behavior with punishment, rejection, exclusion, and a systematic attempt to modify his actions rather than embrace him as a valuable person. He was heartbroken, heart-flipped, angry, sad, afraid, and confused.

At the very least, what he needed was to be surrounded by and fulfilled by a series of supportive relationships with people who cared about him deeply. What he needed was a variety of supportive people who could believe in him, accept him as he was, love him without condition, and help him express and cope with the many painful emotions that ran through his small body. These are the kinds of relationships that any child, adolescent, or adult needs in life. It is our belief that the primary goal of educational and mental health professionals should be to develop, arrange, and sustain relationships of caring, acceptance, and understanding for young people who face emotional and social challenges in their lives. This goal is not a supplement to good teaching, a side item on the menu that we toss in occasionally to add flavor. This goal is vital to and inseparable from good teaching.

Our valuing of the possibilities and promise of deep interpersonal relationships between teachers and troubling students is supported both by our own experiences and by decades of psychotherapy research. Psychiatrists and psychologists call the relationship between the therapist and the client the *therapeutic alliance* or the *working alliance*. The many decades after World War II were filled with research in which psychotherapists attempted to pinpoint the specific methods and techniques that were predictive of positive outcomes for clients. Researchers wanted to know what kinds of psychotherapy worked best. Instead of finding that a particular approach (such as psychodynamic or cognitive-behavioral therapy) stood above the rest, they found a common element within all forms of effective therapy. That common element was a respectful, valuing, and empathetic bond between therapist and client. Furthermore, researchers found that a central feature of this positive therapeutic alliance is an intentional and consistent focus by the therapist and client on discussing and developing the relationship they share. Ongoing collaboration on improving that relationship is vital to the success of the therapy itself (Gaston, 1990; Horvath & Greenberg, 1994; Horvath & Luborsky, 1993; Horvath & Symonds, 1991).

We believe that a similar bond—a pedagogical alliance—between teacher and student is similarly powerful when teaching students who struggle with social and emotional difficulties. No significant educational research base on this matter exists. We find the extensive psychotherapeutic research base to be compelling. Moreover, emphasis on building a pedagogical alliance fulfills our belief that human relationships are central to emotional well-being, happiness, and human fulfillment.

This book is devoted to the mission of helping new and experienced teachers actively develop nurturing, supportive, and even enjoyable relationships with students who are considered troubled and troubling. Although this goal of relationship seems simple, we must tell our readers up front that the task is uncertain, ever-changing, and filled with risk. There is no single method, no foolproof procedure, no scientifically validated series of steps for doing this. Teachers who engage in deep, valuing relationships with troubling students learn this delicate human art through years of practice, mistakes, reflection, suffering, and dialogue. Even then, a new student comes along who offers unforeseen challenges. Even then, a new student comes along whom we cannot understand, with whom we cannot connect. The challenge is unending.

Some teacher educators and traveling workshop gurus will espouse a system as the best way to be successful in teaching resistant and troubled youth. Although our tender and nervous teacher hearts yearn for a guaranteed way to be competent in the midst of messiness, we know better. There is no one way, no best system. There is only the goal of creating caring relationships and the fascinating journey we take with our students toward this goal. This book is a teacher's companion to that goal and that journey.

ABOUT THIS BOOK

The Bias of the Book

We do not claim to be neutral or objective in any way. Claiming objectivity and neutrality have been common ways for some researchers and purveyors of research to assert their beliefs and values in an indirect fashion, concealed under the cover and authority of social science. In a sense, a common bias has been to pretend to be, or try to be, unbiased. We don't believe that anyone can be objective and neutral. Each of us thinks, feels, and acts from a specific position in the world that is very partial, very limited, very fallible, and fully colored by human experience. The best we can each do is put our current beliefs and values out on the table for all to see.

The theoretical grounding for this book is a set of ideas called critical constructivism—basically, a combination of critical theory and constructivism. Within the umbrella of critical constructivism, we place and articulate our beliefs about educating troubling students in American schools.

Critical theory, briefly speaking, holds that our communities and our country are plagued by many forms of social injustice and economic inequality that bring tremendous suffering to children and families. These multiple forms of injustice and inequality tend to play out along the dimensions of social class, race, ethnicity, gender, religion, sexual orientation, and disability. The incredible array of difficulties that falls under generic headings like "behavior problems" or "discipline problems" occurs within schools and communities where human suffering and social inequality frequently go hand in hand. We view these behavior problems as inseparable from the depths of human suffering and the struggle for dignity and respect in a society where dignity and respect can often be difficult to find. Although the current tendency is to individualize these problems by diagnosing, labeling, and blaming the "disruptive" student, we view these problems as inseparable from the concrete, lived social contexts of the school and community. For us, the bottom line concerns in relation to all "behavior problems" are ethical and political. How can we find ways to live and learn together in mutual respect and peace? How can we do so within a society, community, and school rife with problems of economic and social inequality?

Constructivism is an approach to learning and teaching that assumes that knowledge is actively made rather than passively taken in. Traditional approaches to teaching and learning often assumed that knowledge resides in the artifacts of the curriculum—in the textbooks, the computers, and the teacher's mind. The job of the teacher was to effectively transmit that knowledge to the waiting students. A good student was a passive student who accepted the transfer of authoritative knowledge during the lesson, held on to it in his or her memory, and later demonstrated this knowledge on the examination.

A constructivist approach assumes that the minds and bodies of students are not empty slates on which the curriculum may be written. Instead, students bring their intellectual and emotional lives—the total of their experiences—to the classroom. These experiences are individual, familial, and cultural. When a lesson is taught, students bring all of their meanings and identities to the interaction with the course content. This interaction yields a wide variety of emotional responses and intellectual results.

Constructivism is an invitation to teachers to develop instruction that engages students in an ongoing dialogue of meaning, in a shared interaction that opens up channels of thought and communication. For the many students who resist and oppose the educational structures and activities provided by the school, a constructivist approach means not only that we ask the students to open themselves to the knowledge available within the curriculum, but that we make this act of opening up mutual, operating respectfully in two directions. The teacher opens up to hear, value, and accept the active contents of the student's experience, accepting the student's ways of knowing within the world. This allows for a negotiation leading to an exchange of ideas in both directions, authoritative knowledge for personal knowledge, school stuff for kid stuff. If we are asking students to engage the curriculum, we must simultaneously engage students in ways that support their emotions and thinking, in ways that value their experiences and cultural identities. We also must value the many ways that these students respond to and interpret the very thing we call the curriculum.

The Research and Scholarship Basis for the Book

In this book, we draw wisdom, knowledge, and support from the wide variety of intellectual and practical resources that have affected us as teachers, learners, and human beings. We draw from many academic fields, including psychology, philosophy, sociology, anthropology, education, and special education. The knowledge of these many disciplines are fully mingled with and flavored by our own lived experiences as teachers and students, brothers and sisters, parents and children. From the richness and depth of our lives, we bring forth lessons of thought, feeling, and action to bear on the pressing challenges of the moment.

Some books on teaching "disruptive" or "disordered" students assume that teaching practices should be supported by good social science research. We have been fully trained in the methods and procedures of quantitative and qualitative social science. Yet we do not believe that social science research stands above other kinds of available knowledge. It is our belief that social science provides an important source of knowledge for practitioners. Yet it is only one of many useful sources of guidance for teachers attempting to take ethical and practical action. A teacher in a given situation may draw guidance from a poem, a piece of literature, the words of a student, a spiritual belief, a lesson drawn from personal experience, the findings of social science, or a discussion with the teacher next door. All may be useful within the situation.

We have filled this book with a rich and valuable form of knowledge within the constructivist tradition: stories. Most chapters include one or more experiential stories written by us or by other teachers.[1] These narratives are richly textured and detailed. They are loaded with the ambivalent and antagonistic tensions of real teaching. We provide them as sources of wisdom and objects of discussion. Some stories provide examples of promising practices. Other tales tell of the very human struggles experienced by teachers, students, and parents.

While the experiences presented in this book are likely to be similar to those experienced by others, we do not pretend that these stories somehow cover all of the experiences of our readers. In fact, we encourage our readers to compare the experiential narratives in this book to your own experiences as children growing up, as parents raising children, as teachers working with students, and as human beings struggling to find love and fulfillment in a complicated world. We invite you to dig inside your own stories for the lessons you can cultivate there.

Our Focus on "Troubling" Students

It is very difficult in the current climate to write about students who experience significant social or emotional problems in schools without somehow creating a new diagnostic category, a new buzzword that fills the workshop circuit with lists of symptoms or characteristics. If we precisely define the students about whom we are talking in this book, the risk is that we, too, have joined in the diagnostic melee by creating just one more brand of pathology to hang on the necks of kids and families. We want to avoid that. Yet the risk in avoiding that consequence lies in not clearly defining the students about whom we are talking, leaving readers confused about our entire approach to working with "troubling" students. So we'll have to walk a tightrope in describing these students.

We have borrowed the term *troubling* from Nicholas Hobbes's (1982) classic book *The Troubled and Troubling Child*. Hobbes directed the focus of educators toward improving the quality of interactions and relationships between students and meaningful others (peers, teachers, parents, etc.). In dropping the term *troubled* from our description in favor of *troubling*, we are not at all downplaying the emotional life or human suffering of students. We choose the word *troubling* in order to attend to the wide range of students in public schools who behave in ways that teachers and administrators find troubling, concerning, problematic. This wide range includes students who resist and oppose school authority and norms in dramatic, loud, and violent ways; students who subvert the norms of schooling in humorous, sneaky, and manipulative ways; students who have great difficulty making friends and sustaining relationships; students who struggle to concentrate because of depression, anxiety, and fear; students who have been emotionally traumatized by violence and violation; students who feel deeply alienated and disengaged from the academic and social world of the school; and students who are withdrawn and isolated on the fringes of the social web.

These "troubling" students are educated in many school settings and placements: juvenile delinquency programs, mental health facilities, "behavioral disorders" schools and classes, substance abuse programs, alternative public school programs, special education resource classes, inclusion programs, and general education. Our goal is to speak directly to teachers who experience many forms and instances of "troubling" student activity each day in order to provide a useful practical and theoretical resource for teachers concerned with issues of classroom management and disruptive and deviant behavior.

Our approach focuses on building helpful, supportive, and trusting relationships with "troubling students." We make the assumption that teachers do not cure kids of internal psychological disturbances and mental illnesses. Teachers work in interactive and relational ways with students. These interactions and relationships can have a profound impact on the emotional well-being, learning, and whole life of a student. As teachers well know, there are times when it seems that their relationships with students fall far short of having the kind of positive influence for which they hope and strive. In the end, the role that the actions of a single teacher plays in the life of a student is greatly unknown. Students leave our classrooms and move on to futures about which teachers often know little. That being true, we take it as an article of faith that the most profound thing a teacher can do is to create a relationship with a student that communicates deep acceptance and love to that student. That relationship is the cornerstone of good teaching.

OUTLINE OF THE BOOK

We have divided the text into three sections. The first section (Chapters 1–3) deals with the broad concepts and underlying knowledge that provide the background support for our practical work as teachers. In this section, we explore critically the historical and theoretical development of programs and teaching troubling students.

Chapter 1, "Society, Schooling, and Childhood Misbehavior," looks back within the history of American education and the development of the mental health professions to explore the roots of current issues and dilemmas.

Chapter 2, "Introducing Critical Constructivism," critically examines behavioral theory and practice and offers alternatives to this dominant way of thinking about and dealing with child behavior problems in the public schools.

Chapter 3, "Creating a Participatory Classroom Community," explains the theoretical foundation for all of the ideas, practices, and programs that we discuss in the remainder of the book.

The second section (Chapters 4–6) offers a series of short chapters on the various dimensions of critical constructivist teaching. It is a sampling of the teaching practices that support the development of strong relationships and the construction of personally meaningful knowledge. Each form of teaching practice adds another array of tools to the artful complexity of the seasoned professional.

Chapter 4, "Adopting a Caring Pedagogy," focuses on the centrality and nature of the teacher-student relationship, explaining how a relationship of a certain quality is vital to good teaching.

Chapter 5, "Working Together," looks at how we can engage students in group experiential activities that capture their interest, promote greater learning, and build relationships among peers.

Chapter 6, "Reflective Teaching," explores ways that teachers attend to their own thoughts and feelings in order to develop improved practices with students, framing and reframing problems in multiple schemes in order to create more useful ways of thinking.

The third section (Chapters 7–11) examines specific programs and teaching practices that we find encouraging and hopeful.

Chapter 7, "Using Conflict Resolution as Instruction," explains the research literature and educational practice of teaching children and adolescents how to settle interpersonal disputes through peaceful negotiation.

Chapter 8, "Implementing the KEYS Program for Students With E/BD," is an in-depth description of a unique therapeutic program in St. Louis County, Missouri, whereby teachers provide additional social support for students who experience behavioral, emotional, and social difficulties.

Chapter 9, "Working With Families," examines the most promising ways of involving parents in the education of their children. In that chapter, we accept the insight and advice straight from parents as we hear three first-hand stories from parents of students labeled "emotionally/behaviorally disordered."

Chapter 10, "Considering Inclusive Education," explains why inclusive education is a worthwhile social goal and explores the complexities, difficulties, and successes of actively seeking that goal.

Chapter 11, "Honoring and Developing Ourselves as Teachers," is our chance to offer some direct practical advice for teachers about caring for one's own emotional well-being while struggling to help deviant and defiant students.

NOTE

1. When necessary, names have been changed to protect the identities of those individuals discussed in the narratives and case studies.

Part I

Conceptual and Historical Foundations

1

Society, Schooling, and Childhood Misbehavior

What seems self-evident in daily classroom experience–the disruptiveness of certain student behaviors and the sense that these behaviors somehow must change–has deep, tangled roots within schools and society itself. Beyond the initial, frustration-ridden impulse to call some students "bad" or "disordered" runs a host of complex issues about how our society raises and schools children. Examining these issues leads us to explore how we have come to view and treat challenging children, a journey that brings us inevitably to interrogate ourselves–to question who we are and what we think we are doing.

Deviant and disruptive student behavior is anything but a recent issue. The most difficult task a teacher has faced from colonial days through modern times is dealing with the disrespectful and rowdy behavior of students (Cremin, 1970, 1980, 1988). One-room schoolhouse teachers on the prairies of the early 1800s often complained of the overwhelming burden of managing 40 to 60 students of all ages and abilities in one large room. Central to this challenge was effectively withstanding the tradition of "turning out" the teacher, an age-old ritual in which the children attempted to cruelly persuade a new teacher to quit by placing numerous roadblocks and humiliations in his or her way (Cremin, 1980). It was common practice in many 19th-century schools for teachers or principals to settle conflicts with students with bare fists. Tyack

(1974) tells the story of one frontier principal who was reprimanded by local authorities not for fighting with a student but for losing that fight.

Occasionally, one hears nostalgic voices calling for a return to the "good old days" when children were as saccharine and obedient as Wally Cleaver; however, there is no historical evidence of any such times (Coontz, 1992). Teachers have always had to deal with troubling students. What has changed dramatically over time are the kinds of trouble; the social problems facing children, families, and schools; and the ways that schools and professionals have viewed those problems.

An exploration of the history of behavior problems in the American public schools allows us to take a broader view of the issues we are facing today, making our current perspectives seem less absolute and our current steps less surefooted. We can understand how behavioral difficulties have changed over time, how the problems of misbehavior in the schools have been linked to the difficult social issues of various time periods, and how changes in educational and mental health professions altered the way such problems were perceived and handled. In this chapter, we focus on student behavioral and social problems during the 20th century in order to understand how we have arrived at our current array of challenges.

AMERICAN SCHOOLS BEFORE 1900

> Here [the public school] children should be taught the usual branches of learning, submission to superiors and to laws, the moral or social duties, the history and transactions of their own country, the principles of liberty and government. Here the rough manners of the wilderness should be softened and the principles of virtue and good behavior inculcated. (Noah Webster, as quoted in Cremin, 1980, p. 265)

By 1900, public schools supported by tax dollars and serving white students were operating in virtually all regions of the country. Early public schools were founded by political leaders who envisioned an institution in which to pass on the values and beliefs of democracy to the young. This included preparation in the traditional European academic disciplines deemed necessary for proper citizenship. Additionally, this early idea of schooling embraced a distinctly Anglo-Saxon, Protestant brand of morality—a combination of work ethic and a fairly submissive orientation to religious tradition and civil authority (Cremin, 1970, 1980, 1988). To the 19th-century founders of public education and the educators of 1900, a vast portion of the mission of the public schools was the education of children as virtuous citizens.

Business and municipal leaders often encouraged the schools to bring virtue to families viewed as incapable of correctly raising their children. The schools could rein in the wayward and unclean children of the lower classes. The child in dire need of moral correction—according to the public schools of

1900—was poor, male, and either an immigrant or a rural transplant to the city. His parents worked as low-wage laborers for a factory, mill, or forge. They probably spoke a foreign language such as German or French. It is likely they were Catholic or Jewish. This "problem boy" either worked side by side with his parents or spent his days unsupervised on the city streets. Professional attention was devoted to softening the rough manners of this uncivilized child (Cremin, 1980; Katz, 1971; Nasaw, 1979).

TURN-OF-THE-CENTURY CULTURAL CHANGES

The American public schools at the dawn of the 20th century faced a host of serious problems arising out of dramatic, 19th-century changes in the social fabric of the country. By 1900, American society had become increasingly industrial. Between 1860 and 1890, the United States grew from a primarily agricultural nation into a world industrial power. Nasaw (1979) notes that although the United States trailed England, France, and Germany in industrial production in 1860, by the mid-1890s, the New England states alone outproduced all three of those nations combined.

Simultaneously, a great proportion of the American population shifted to the industrial ghettoes of the major cities. An agrarian, rural nation was changing into a modern form that combined industrial production and urban living. The booming factories of the large cities employed vast numbers of new arrivals, eastern and southern European immigrants as well as rural Americans fresh off the farm. The urban ghettoes quickly became the steaming holding tank of the industrial workforce, an overworked and underpaid labor resource with slim hope for economic advancement and individual achievement. These overcrowded neighborhoods often had no functioning sewer systems, no electrical service, no running water, and infrequent garbage collection. Most families lacked basic dental and health care. Disease, malnutrition, crime, and discontent brewed in the overpopulated, impoverished neighborhoods of the factory worker class (Addams, 1972, 1981; Katz, 1996).

The public schools in large cities such as New York and Chicago faced enormous challenges educating the children of poor immigrants. More than half of all students in major urban public schools were immigrants or the children of immigrants. Whereas English was the language of schools, most students spoke a foreign language at home (Richardson, 1989).

THEORIZING JUVENILE DELINQUENCY

Government officials and the public worried about the "youth problem" during the first three decades of the 20th century. Within the industrialized urban ghetto, juvenile delinquency was born. How juvenile delinquency was viewed and dealt with was very different prior to 1915 and after 1915. Before 1915, those attempting to solve the urban youth problem were radical childsavers—groups of primarily well-to-do, college-educated women who were the forerunners of the social work profession. The radical childsavers viewed juvenile delinquency as a complex social and political problem requiring intervention at many levels. Certainly, the energies of adolescent boys and girls required redirection toward more productive and healthy pursuits. But they were well aware that the delinquent youth they encountered were primarily immigrants who struggled to cope with the social prejudices, unjust laws, and economic inequalities of their new land. The problem was not merely an individual failure of an immoral child or the child-rearing failure of incompetent parents. The delinquent was just one aspect of a complex social puzzle (Jones, 1999; Richardson, 1989).

The radical childsavers worked on a number of political fronts to improve the lives of the urban poor: They worked to increase public welfare programs to support the poor; initiate mothers' pensions so that mothers could stay home and raise children instead of working; pass child labor laws outlawing or limiting the number of children working in dangerous factories; decrease the industrial laborers' standard work hours to permit parents time and energy to spend with their children; and increase the strength of unions to bargain for workers' rights and fair compensation. The childsavers knew that social and economic changes were necessary to alleviate the underlying stresses and obstacles facing poor families and neighborhoods. Their practical politics attempted to improve home, work, and community conditions for the immigrant poor, emphasizing education, nutrition, health care, recreation, and the interdependence of the community (Addams, 1972, 1981).

After 1915, efforts to solve the problem of juvenile delinquency took a dramatic turn, changing the focus from social and political problems surrounding youth to the defective character of the individual delinquent. With this change in theory came a shift in strategies. Many efforts turned away from political activism addressing the living and working conditions of poor, immigrant families and toward professional interventions to diagnose and change the maladjusted individual. The turning point was the publication of an enormous 800-page volume called *The Individual Delinquent* by a physician named William Healy (1915), an early leader in the development of child guidance clinics that offered mental health services to troublesome youth and their families. In his studies of delinquents in Chicago, Healy searched for the root factors that caused delinquency. He combined environmental factors and individual biology, what we would call nurture and nature, to explain that delinquency was a complex phenomenon with many causes but only one location: the defective character of the individual. To Healy, with his medical training emphasizing physical and mental disease, the proper way to address the problem of delinquency was the medical treatment of the individual child. Social change and political activism were irrelevant (Horn, 1989; Jones, 1999).

By 1921, Healy's focus on the individual had swept the imaginations of early mental health professionals. In that year, the influential Commonwealth Fund brought together leaders in the new field of juvenile delinquency for a conference in Lakewood, New Jersey. Conference participants did not even consider the social and economic conditions faced by immigrant families. The conference report deemed topics related to "poverty, variations in employment, migration to cities with consequent exposure to bad housing and other similar conditions" (quoted in Jones, 1999, p. 59) as irrelevant and therefore beyond the scope of discussion. Edith Abbott, a prominent social worker, was a lone critical voice, claiming that the Illinois Child Labor Law of 1917 had done more to decrease juvenile delinquency than all the mental health treatment offered by a well-known Chicago child guidance clinic. But her voice was ignored. Physicians, psychologists, and powerful funding groups like the Commonwealth Fund (a charitable arm of Standard Oil Company) followed Healy's lead. Juvenile delinquency was not a social and political problem. It was a medical and psychological problem of poor adjustment. What was needed were mental health professionals to help children become more adjusted to the conditions of their lives. The social change approach of the radical childsavers had been replaced by a professional mental health approach that denied the salience of social inequality in the lives of poor immigrant families (Horn, 1989; Jones, 1999; Richardson, 1989).

The juvenile delinquent was, virtually by definition, the disrespectful and dangerous child (typically a boy) of urban factory worker parents (Slawson, 1926). The helping professionals generally viewed this son as wild and menacing, a threat to the social order. Charles Loring Brace, the founder and long-time executive of the Children's Aid Society in New York City, "referred to the neglected children of the 'outcast poor' as the most threatening members of the 'dangerous classes' and conveyed the impression that unless immediate action was undertaken the more respectable classes would soon be overwhelmed" (Cremin, 1988, p. 276).

At the turn of the century, many viewed the public schools as the primary means of compensating for perceived weaknesses in the child-rearing practices of working-class families, approaches that reformers viewed as failing to instill the values of cleanliness, obedience to authority, and hard work. As Cremin (1988) describes, educators and helping professionals "never really trusted the mother" (p. 294). Mothers were frequently seen as ignorant or neglectful. The helping professions and the public schools focused their attention on cleaning up the troubling behavior of this new class of urban youth—lower-class adolescents who roamed the streets late at night, drank, spit, used foul language, gambled, performed sexual acts, frequented dance halls, and engaged in petty thievery.

Richardson (1989) explains why boys became the primary focus for professionals concerned with juvenile delinquency. The primary offense of the delinquent was truancy, or failing to attend school. Massachusetts enacted the first compulsory school attendance law in 1852. The last state to enact a compulsory attendance law was Mississippi in 1918. In the late 1800s and early 1900s, a girl who missed school was typically assumed to be at home helping with gender-appropriate domestic chores such as cleaning and child-rearing. In a sense, her very absence from school was preparing her for what most viewed as her future. On the other hand, boys who missed school were viewed as dangerous elements within their community, street criminals in the making. Therefore, truancy was viewed as a problem primarily involving boys and not girls. The professionals' preoccupation with the activities and offenses of boys was to continue throughout the 20th century.

THE NEW HELPING PROFESSIONS: SAVED BY SCIENCE

> Science would produce the experts who would serve the common good. (Cremin, 1988, p. 243)

The shift from viewing juvenile delinquency as a social and political problem requiring a wide range of social actions to an individual problem requiring treatment was one indication of the power of the new helping professions. The development of helping professions of a scientific nature occurred as a prominent response to the 20th-century social problems of immigration, urbanization, and industrialization. By 1900, scientific ways of viewing social issues and possible solutions had become increasingly popular in the media and the public. Educators who called themselves "progressives" espoused the need for educators to develop an expertise based in the new social sciences. Given the success of the physical or natural sciences, as evidenced in the development of the engines that powered factories and railroads, it was common to hope that the application of scientific methods to the social world would produce similarly fantastic improvements in society.

The human service professions such as psychiatry, psychology, social work, and education claimed scientific expertise in raising children of a moral and virtuous character. They believed that the problems of poverty and social deviance could be solved through the action of professionals whose practical expertise was based in this enlightened understanding. Universities would provide the research to unlock the social puzzles of modern life. Professionals would put this research into practice. By the early 1900s, the new social science-based professionals were applying their newly minted expertise within the public schools (Baritz, 1960; Cremin, 1988; Danforth, 1997).

Perhaps foremost among the turn-of-the-century educational reformers who claimed a scientific quality to their methods were the "administrative progressives" (Tyack & Hansot, 1982, p. 105)—turn-of-the-century schoolmen (early administrators) who claimed that schools should be run not by local politicians but by professional leaders who could make decisions through scientific means. Prior to the development of the professional administrator (and the science of management), schools answered directly to local political leaders—mayors, city councils, ward bosses, and so on. The new professional administrators said that they would pull the schools out of politics by managing them in an objective and unbiased way.

These early school administrators remained closely linked with the wealthy corporate leaders who served as their advisors and financed the political operations necessary to bring about the switch to the management of schools by professional administrators. The common value that both the business leaders and the educational administrators gravitated toward was industriousness, the old Protestant work ethic refashioned to meet the personnel needs of factory owners (Cremin, 1988; Tyack & Hansot, 1982). Business leaders influenced schools to prepare factory workers by altering the traditional academic curriculum with industrial education tracks, including special classes for poor, immigrant, and "backward" children. These early forms of "ability tracks" were designed to instill in working-class and poor students the limited aspirations and efficient habits needed for a life of manual, industrial labor with low pay and little opportunity for advancement (Katz, 1971; Tyack & Hansot, 1982). This was the beginning of the differentiated curricula that culminates today in both ability tracking and special education programs.

SOCIAL ILLS AND NEW
MENTAL HEALTH PROFESSIONS (1890–1945)

As the new mental health professions of psychiatry, psychology, and social work sought legitimacy for their fields, they often worked in conjunction with the public schools. The most prominent and powerful mental health field of both the early 1900s and today is psychiatry.

Before 1890, the field of psychiatry had been devoted to the development and management of institutions for lunatics (the mentally ill) and the feeble-minded (the developmentally disabled). Yet it had been viewed within the medical profession as unscientific and greatly ineffective. To many physicians, it wasn't even a branch of medicine.

By the end of the 19th century, psychiatry embraced the notion that a more scientific approach to the diagnosis and treatment of mental illnesses would allow psychiatrists to make a dramatic impact on social problems of the community. Although the psychiatric profession had demonstrated little or no success treating mental illness in decades of institution work, a new horizon for professional authority dawned. They would practice the "new psychiatry" (Grob, 1994, p. 129), a yet undeveloped but supposedly more scientific mode filled with great promise. They would apply this new curative power to the common social afflictions of the time: juvenile delinquency, prostitution, alcoholism, economic dependency, widespread syphilis infections, vagrancy, and the problematic adjustment of European immigrant groups.

Jettisoning their history as institution managers, these physicians used the promise of a new medicine of mental disease as a means to expand their professional authority beyond institutional walls. They would seek a medical approach to common social problems and suffering. In the early 20th-century rush of professionals to harness science to gain authority and expertise over social problems, psychiatry led the way (Grob, 1983, 1994).

The new mental health fields of child psychology and psychiatric social work derived much of their legitimacy from their close affiliation with the developing field of child psychiatry. Medicine was viewed by government officials, research funding foundations, and the American public as the most trustworthy and authoritative human service profession.

Ironically, as the less prestigious mental health professions (especially social work) hitched their stars to psychiatry in hopes of looking medical, the field of psychiatry itself struggled to be viewed by other physicians as a real branch of medicine. The 20th century brought a unique opportunity for psychiatry to step out of the institutions and into the limelight. Modern social problems were described by the media and the professions as dire. Horn (1989) captures the common sentiment in a 1926 editorial from a prominent mental health profession publication:

> It seems to be an accepted axiom nowadays that our young people are going to the devil. Press, pulpit, and publicist are agreed that youth is wild and getting wilder. The college boy and his flapper friend, it is charged, drink, pet, and are disrespectful to their elders; while the neighborhood gangster, aided by his youthful sweetie and stimulated by false course of heroin or cocain, robs and murders with casual calmness long before he is out of his teens. (p. 10)

If the times were supposedly troubled and dark, the professions spoke of optimism and light. The progressive mentality of the times put forth a new belief that social problems could be solved by forward-thinking, scientific workers. This combination of widespread social problems (or at least the public perception of such problems) and the promise of the new sciences of human psychology and behavior offered psychiatrists and other mental health professionals an opportunity to gain prominence as leaders in the business of solving social ills. Undoubtedly, these professionals gained tremendous prominence. How well they have been able to live up to their early ambitions of solving social ills is open to question (Grob, 1983, 1994; Horn, 1989; Jones, 1999; Richardson, 1989).

THE EARLY MENTAL HYGIENE MOVEMENT (1890–1930)

The creation of the mental health professions as a way of alleviating suffering and regulating deviance and nonconformity in communities—often called the mental hygiene movement—was launched by a book that spoke not of social change and society but of the cruelty of psychiatric institutions. Clifford Beers spent 3 years in a series of psychiatric facilities after attempting suicide. His groundbreaking book, *A Mind That Found Itself* (1907), was both a harsh critique of terrible conditions within mental hospitals and an eloquent personal testimony to the curability of mental illness. His criticism of institutions was raw and striking, but his story about the curability of mental illness was far more influential. If mental illness could be cured, then the work of psychiatrists and other therapeutic professionals could have a profound impact upon American society. Beers teamed up with prominent physician Adolph Meyer to found the National Committee for Mental Hygiene (NCMH), the driving force behind the mental hygiene movement in the pre–World War II years (Grob, 1983, 1994).

Mental hygiene was a vague concept that meant different things to different people. The movement concentrated on the idea that social problems in the community were manifestations of mental disease that could be prevented and/or treated by qualified mental health professionals. Psychiatry—and, to a lesser extent, social work, education, and psychology—could wipe out social ills at the root cause, the mental disease (Horn, 1989; Jones, 1999; Richardson, 1989).

In 1922, the NCMH set up the Division on the Prevention of Delinquency, an organization that quickly founded a number of "child guidance clinics" in major urban areas. The child guidance clinics were multidisciplinary field teams uniting psychiatrists, psychologists, social workers, and teachers to work with poor families in urban neighborhoods. They were often affiliated with the new juvenile courts that had been set up to deal with youth crime in a compassionate way. The courts frequently sent the young lawbreakers to the clinics for treatment rather than sending them to adult prisons. The child guidance clinics were the first attempt of the fledgling field of mental health to provide treatment to children and families in an effort to prevent or cure juvenile delinquency. Their motto, a familiar stanza to current-day professionals, was to "reach them earlier" (Ridenour, 1961, p. 35), treating would-be juvenile delinquents before delinquent tendencies had a chance to fully develop.

The child guidance clinics were the modern birthplace of child psychiatry and child psychology, spawning the development of a variety of treatment program options: residential treatment centers, juvenile court psychiatric clinics, school-based mental health interventions, and outpatient psychotherapy. Most important, the clinic placed medical doctors at the steering wheel of child mental health in the 20th century. Physicians successfully moved their authority and newfound expertise beyond the very limited confines of the 19th-century institutions to enter communities and schools (Horn, 1989; Jones, 1999; Richardson, 1989).

As the various mental health specialties developed into full-fledged professions, they built up their own knowledge bases about the problems of living, their own ways of describing and thinking about the troubles that their patients faced. This vocabulary and host of concepts drew greatly from Freud's psychodynamic psychology as well as other branches of psychology such as mental measurement (e.g., IQ testing). Just as architects had their own way of talking about and conceptualizing the physical arrangement of buildings, or engineers had a way of framing problems of design and utility, so, too, did the mental health fields create their own lingo and their own theories about the suffering, failures, and possible improvement of their patients. Beneath the increasingly complex jargon and theory ran a rather simple, everyday notion: The relationship between the therapist and the patient was both the place and the path of improvement.

THE LATE MENTAL HYGIENE MOVEMENT (1930–1945)

In the 1930s and early 1940s, the focus of the child guidance clinics shifted dramatically from the illegal behavior of the urban lower/working class toward the milder, typically legal misbehavior of the middle class. Treating immigrants who stole or vandalized gave way to treating the sons of businessmen who stayed out too late in the family car. The child mental health professions that had been launched as a means of taming the delinquent teenagers of the immigrant working class suddenly extended their expertise to include what was called "the problem child." The media, the mental health professionals, and the many new parent education groups defined the problem child as a normal, everyday child—not at all insane, feebleminded, or delinquent—who had taken a few wrong turns and needed guidance and correction. This middle-class child was predelinquent, displaying rather mundane behavior problems that required address before they bloomed into more serious concerns (Horn, 1989; Jones, 1999).

The change in child guidance clinic clientele occurred for a number of reasons. First, the child guidance clinics could not boast much success in curing juvenile delinquency. Although their diagnostic and treatment programs undoubtedly helped some youth and families, the problems of poverty and cultural dislocation facing new immigrants ran too deep for psychotherapy. Second, the mental health professionals and the media made great efforts to popularize the child guidance clinic approach to child rearing. Rearing children was not a matter of following maternal instincts and traditions, they claimed. It was a psychological matter requiring professional training. Magazine and newspaper articles by these new experts encouraged mothers to view themselves as inadequate and to view the mental health professionals as child-rearing authorities.

Finally, the radical modernization of American society put new stresses on middle-class families in the 1930s. The rapid pace of social and technological change that is very familiar to current-day readers had begun. The small, relatively private world of parents and children had been split open by the development of automobiles, the cinema, and the telephone, and also by liberalized sexual attitudes among the young. Middle-class parents felt that they were losing authority over their defiant adolescents. Mental health professionals served as mediators between adolescents seeking freedom and fearful parents baffled by their child's need to rebel (Horn, 1989; Jones, 1999).

PSYCHOLOGY, MEASUREMENT, AND DISORDERS

It was the school, the courts, the police, and the army which provided the psychology of the individual with those whom it would have to be able to construe as abnormal. (Gross, 1987, p. 229)

At this point, our story turns to the emergence of the field of psychology as a social force to define the moral problems (behavior problems) of children and adolescents in the 20th century. As the modern world became increasingly scientific, civil authorities who dealt daily with the deviant behavior of children— the schools, the police, the courts, and the early juvenile prisons and reform schools—looked to this new social science for authoritative knowledge about the children who crossed them. The moral themes of 18th-century rural Protestantism—the need for hard work and submission to authority and tradition—were assumed to be upheld by the institutions of civil authority. The new social sciences and the mental health professions refurbished this old religious morality in a new scientific form, stripping away the Christian references to Jesus and the New Testament while primarily upholding the same middle-class norms of behavior and attitude.

In the first four decades of the 20th century, psychology became a budding field of expertise concerning those who failed to comply with the rules and norms defined and enforced by the schools, police, and courts. Psychologists attempted to define the reasons why some children went morally bad while others remained normal and good. During that time, the emphasis of scientific study focused on the general question, "What is wrong with this individual?" Although a variety of factors may have contributed to the life and life conditions of the child, psychology assumed that the moral failing itself was within the individual who ran afoul of authority. If a child opposed or deviated from the social order as defined and defended by the school, the police, or the courts, that child was in some way lacking, deficient, or ultimately disordered (Gross, 1987).

PRE–WORLD WAR II SCHOOL PROGRAMS
FOR SOCIALLY MALADJUSTED YOUTH

Ignore children who are physically sick and they will probably die; ignore the mentally sick and they may starve to death; ignore the socially sick and they will spread the contamination of unrest and vice to vast numbers of their associates. (Heck, 1940, p. 19)

Conformity to the dominant social order is health: failure to conform is illness. (Carrier, 1983, p. 957)

Growth in special education programs in the public schools was very gradual during the early decades of the 20th century (Heck, 1940; Stullken,

1950; Winzer, 1993). For example, in 1929, special classes for disruptive students, often called "disciplinary classes," existed in only one out of every three states. Only 16 cities had special schools for delinquent children (Heck, 1940). Additional programs were called "industrial schools," which were early vocational training schools designed for working-class and delinquent youth (Winzer, 1993).

The public schools in the late 1800s and early 1900s were faced with the challenge of teaching and managing a student population of tremendous cultural, socioeconomic, and linguistic variety. Waves of immigration and the growth of the urban, industrialized poor brought many students to public schools that were unaccustomed to dealing with such heterogeneity. Ten million immigrants entered the country between the Civil War and 1900, mostly from England, Wales, Ireland, Germany, and Scandinavia. Another 15 million immigrants arrived between 1890 and 1914, mostly from eastern and southern Europe—Poles, Russian Jews, Ukrainians, Slovaks, Croatians, Hungarians, Romanians, Italians, and Greeks. Laws requiring attendance not only sent truant officers chasing after resistant children, youth, and families, but also forced schools to handle large numbers of new students who often did not fit neatly into traditional school structures and social habits.

Many school districts developed special classes and schools for remedial or immigrant children as a way of retaining the homogeneity and traditional practices of the general classroom. The new, segregated programs typically served as "dumping grounds" (Kauffman, 1976, p. 343) for the new students, who failed to fit the middle-class ideals of attitude, appearance, and behavioral style. These special programs took on a wide range of forms, each designated to a specific type of student. Many of these types parallel similar programs today. Schools for the blind, the deaf, and feebleminded (those with developmental disabilities) were direct forerunners to current special education programs. Supporting the construction of many of these types were the new mental measurements, such as the IQ test, that exploded into widespread use after World War I (Baritz, 1960; Winzer, 1993).

The educational and psychological descriptions of the socially maladjusted child of the early to mid 20th century continue the prior tendency of middle-class professionals to view the children of either the lower/working class or immigrants as morally deficient primarily because of incompetent parenting (Baker & Traphagen, 1935; Laycock & Stevenson, 1950; Slawson, 1926; Stullken, 1950) and economically deprived social conditions (Baker & Traphagen, 1935; Slawson, 1926; Stullken, 1950). It was common among psychologists and educators to conceptually link weaknesses in parenting skills with economic poverty, almost as if parents would have somehow provided more materially for their children if they were truly "good" parents. Poverty itself was often viewed as indicative of moral failure.

Although the conditions of poverty were often lamented as unfortunate, the professional descriptions of these children and their problems generally lacked a serious address of prevailing issues of social inequality in society at the time.

Political inequalities that stood as vital aspects of the social context of a child's life were absent from the educational and psychological discourse. The current practice of localizing complex social problems "in" a child who is said to psychologically carry that problem as a form of individual pathology had already captured the professional imagination (see Heck, 1940; Stullken, 1950).

AFTER WORLD WAR II: PSYCHIATRIC DIAGNOSES FOR CHILDREN

> The classification of mental diseases was an important part of the effort to substantiate the medical validity of psychiatry. (Richardson, 1989, p. 168)

After World War II, the field of child psychiatry still had much work to do to become a respected medical specialty. Child psychiatry (and the other mental health professions) still lacked a vital part of typical medical practice: diagnosis. Many psychiatrists and researchers had developed ways of classifying childhood behavior problems, but they had not yet been gathered up and formalized in a complete, authoritative way.

Throughout the 1950s, the Group for the Advancement of Psychiatry (GAP) worked to develop a formal set of diagnoses for childhood emotional and behavioral illnesses. This work culminated in the 1966 publication of *Psychopathological Disorders in Childhood: Theoretical Considerations and a Proposed Classification,* a complete manual of childhood mental illness (GAP, 1966). For the first time, mental health professionals could diagnose children with the same authority with which they diagnosed adults. This initial classification document was later incorporated into multiple editions of the *Diagnostic and Statistical Manual of Mental Disorders*, or the *DSM*, which is the backbone of diagnostic practice.

Richardson (1989) describes the development of childhood diagnoses as a boon to the status of mental health professions. Fields of research and practice that had always seemed soft and subjective suddenly had diagnoses that appeared as reliable as any medical disease diagnoses. In the decades to follow, the number and range of childhood diagnoses expanded dramatically. Gradually, the number of childhood disorders "found" among children, even so-called normal children, has proliferated greatly as the mental health professions and the American public have become increasingly accustomed to defining childhood difficulties as medical illnesses. Fears that childhood troubles could lead to adult failures ranging from unemployment to criminal activity to bad marriages have led to an enormous mental health industry of catching and treating problems early. Growing up in America has become a medical concern.

Since the 1970s, the field of psychiatry has emphasized the use of medications to alter behavior and mood. This was spurred by the pharmacological revolution that started in France in 1952, when physicians found that a medication called chlorpromazine produced a state of incredible calm, reducing agitation and overexcitement among psychiatric hospital patients. Soon thereafter, pharmaceutical companies played the primary role in the development and popularization of other psychiatric drugs. Initially, these efforts focused on severe conditions such as schizophrenia. Gradually, pharmacology found a market for drugs that alleviated the suffering of the "normal" population, the common depressions and everyday anxieties that plagued workers, parents, and even children. Living itself became a pharmacological concern (Shorter, 1997).

EMOTIONAL DISTURBANCE AND THE SPECIAL EDUCATION BOOM (1960–1980)

Conceptualizing the problem behavior of children and adolescents as a medical problem within the field of psychiatry set the stage for special education to do likewise (Carrier, 1983). After World War II, the field of special education worked to develop categories of disability that borrowed greatly from the field of psychiatry. Types of disability were "diagnosed" through the use of "objective measures" and "clinical judgment." The disabilities themselves were conceptualized as consisting of series of characteristics or symptoms manifesting underlying disorders or diseases. In true medical fashion, disabilities were documented in medical terms of "incidence" and "prevalence." Educational programs were framed as "treatments" or "prescriptions." The knowledge base of special education was crafted in the language of medicine, thereby borrowing the scientific authority of medical science.

Of particular note was the construction of the disability category called "emotional disturbance" (ED), the educational diagnosis for students with dramatically deviant or disruptive behavior. Nationally, in recent decades, less than 1% of all public school students have been labeled ED. Schools have dealt with misbehavior through a broad range of programs, punishments, interventions, and special schools. ED programs have become a central, consistent element within the framing of behavioral difficulties in American schools.

During the 1960s and 1970s, federal legislation spurred dramatic increases in both the number of students considered emotionally disturbed educated by public schools and the number of corresponding special education teachers for these students. Public Law 87–294 in 1961 supported the education of teachers for students with visual impairments. This law was expanded 2 years later to provide federal funding for the education of teachers for students with a wide variety of disabilities, including emotional disturbance. Although political activism and legislation on the state level brought about the rapid development of special education in most parts of the country during the 1960s, in 1972 more than 30% of the states had no laws mandating the education of students with special needs (by one definition or another, varying greatly across states) (Abeson, 1972). The federal government estimated in 1975, at the time of the passage of the landmark Education for All Handicapped Children Act (Public

Law 94–142) mandating special education across the nation, that 1.75 million children were being excluded from public education because of disability (Zettel & Ballard, 1979).

Whereas PL 94–142 brought about sweeping developments in all areas of special education by requiring local districts to provide an education for all children regardless of disability, it had a particularly large effect on the growth of public school programs for students considered emotionally disturbed. A 1980 study (National Rural Research and Personnel Preparation Project, 1980) found that PL 94–142 had brought about an immediate 478% increase in the number of students labeled ED in American public schools in less than 5 years. This sharp jump in the number of ED-labeled students in public education was a combination of the acceptance of this excluded group into the public schools and the new diagnosis of ED among many students who had been considered nondisabled prior to the implementation of PL 94–142.

The sudden five-fold jump in the number of ED-diagnosed students created a desperate need for new teachers. Universities and colleges across the nation scrambled to turn out teachers specially prepared for ED programs, typically self-contained classrooms and segregated schools. Federal funds poured into university research and professional preparation programs. The public schools clamored for teachers able to bring order to these newly created classrooms populated by students with histories of disruptive and aggressive behavior. The schools looked to the universities to send them teachers who could some-how keep a lid on these classrooms.

TEACHING METHOD NEEDED: NEO-FREUDIANS AND BEHAVIORISTS

Prior to the sudden boom in ED programs, the neo-Freudian or psychodynamic model of teaching troubling students held a prominent place in teacher education programs. Teachers of ED children were often educated as teacher-counselors, a dual role requiring the standard instructional abilities of a general classroom teacher and the psychotherapeutic insight and skills of a trained therapist. The neo-Freudian theory and practice (a mainstay of the mental hygiene movement) was a delicate social art that required a depth of theoretical understanding and years of supervised practice in clinical settings such as psychiatric hospitals, residential facilities, and therapeutic camps.

Many neo-Freudians were the disciples of Fritz Redl (e.g., Morse, 1993; Redl, 1966; Redl & Wineman, 1951, 1952). Redl devoted his professional life to translating the traditional theory and practice of psychotherapy into practices that could be used with children. Vital to this new application was the rejection of the traditional idea that children and adolescents could benefit from lying on the therapist's couch for 50 minutes twice per week in order to gain new insights into their confused psyches. Although the importance of having insight into one's own feelings and internal conflicts was not rejected, the couch was.

Working in residential programs in both Austria and the United States, Redl and his followers developed on-the-fly counseling techniques that could be used by teachers during the moments in the average day when children displayed raw emotion and aggressive behavior.

The central idea was that children and adolescents tended not to simply open themselves up to therapeutic intervention upon entering the therapist's office. Their emotional worlds opened up within the spontaneous course of daily events, within conflicts with peers and anxieties over academic learning. The neo-Freudians held that opportunities to "do therapy" occur as brief 2-, 5-, or 10-minute windows during the day—moments when self-esteem falters, anger flares, sadness overwhelms, anxiety freezes, or trust crumbles. Redl and his disciples believed that mental health and even education professionals could be trained to take advantage of these therapeutic opportunities—moments when young persons can receive and benefit from on-the-spot counseling.

The desperate need for ED teachers in the late 1970s combined with the public school's emphasis on authority and order turned the neo-Freudian emphasis on the subtleties of psychological insight into an anachronism and a perceived luxury. Schools had little patience for the heavy jargon, high-brow theory, and humanistic sensitivity of the traditional approach to working with ED students. What many schools wanted was a teacher with a firm hand, someone who could speak a direction from the front of the class in such a way that 10 angry boys did what they were told. This kind of order and authority did not call for counseling skills. It called for powerful techniques that could get students to behave in compliant ways whether they wanted to or not. It called for behavior modification.

The behaviorists (e.g., Brown, 1972; Patterson, 1965; Philips, 1968; Whelan, 1966) claimed that attempting to understand the inner psychic world of the child was a superstitious walk down a nonproductive pier. What they had to offer was behavior modification—a science of behavior and an applied technology for precise and sure change. To the behaviorist, human behavior occurs as a response to an external stimulus in the environment. The key to improving behavior lay not in therapeutic talk about issues and conflicts but in altering the external stimuli of the classroom to promote different behaviors from the students. Typically, this meant devising programs of incentives and rewards to encourage desirable behaviors.

The victory of behaviorism over neo-Freudianism within the field of ED was not due to the intellectual or practical superiority of behavioral theory and methods. Neo-Freudian theory was complex, language-heavy, and difficult to learn. Grasping the ideas and developing the subtle clinical judgment necessary to apply those ideas in practice with students took years of intense education, training, and ongoing professional development. Mastery of this theory-practice was only possible within a few elite, fully developed, university teacher preparation programs.

The rapid growth in ED school programs in the 1960s and 1970s brought about a parallel boom in teacher education. Universities high and low suddenly launched programs to prepare and certify the many ED teachers needed. In sharp contrast to the complexity and difficulty of learning the neo-Freudian approach, behavior modification as a program of systematic rewards could be taught quickly and easily to large groups of teachers. The theory—increase a behavior by rewarding that behavior—could be explained in half a sentence. The very simplicity of the behavioral approach made it the theory of the day in the new ED public school programs that desperately needed something to do and new university teacher preparation programs that desperately needed something to teach teachers to do.

Neither the neo-Freudian nor the behavioral school of thought questioned the way that schools had established the customary practice of locating complex social problems within the psychological or moral character of specific students said to be "disordered" or "disturbed" (see Kugelmass, 1987; Rhodes, 1977). Issues of race, social class, and gender were not raised as serious questions for examination within the profession (J. L. Johnson, personal communication, 2000; W. C. Rhodes, personal communication, 2000). As a result, ED as a disability category has remained an uncontested explanation for deviant or unruly behavior. That lack of critical analysis allowed ED programs to continue as segregated settings primarily for boys of working-class, lower-class, and/or minority group status, a state of affairs that still exists today (U.S. Department of Education, 1998).

In recent years, the overrepresentation of African American males in special education, especially in classes for students categorized as "mildly mentally handicapped" and ED, has been well-documented (e.g., Dunn, 1968; Harry, 1994; Patton, 1998). Less attention has been paid to the parallel overrepresentation of lower- and working-class students in special education and emotional/behavioral disorder (E/BD) programs (Danforth, 2000). Yet the predominance of ethnic minority and working-/lower-class males in ED programs is obvious. Wagner (1995), in an analysis of a large national data set, concluded that "students with disabilities in general and those with SED [serious emotional disturbance] were significantly more likely than students as a whole to be male, African American, and to experience a constellation of factors associated with economic disadvantage" (p. 95). One need not access a large national database to come to this conclusion. A day spent visiting the local E/BD programs in your local area will easily convince you that it is only a mild overstatement to say that in most school districts, ED is virtually synonymous with "angry black male" or "angry poor male." With only occasional exceptions (e.g., J. L. Johnson, 1968), the special education field of ED has neglected a serious address of social class and racial issues.

MISBEHAVIOR AND STUDENTS
FROM DEVALUED GROUPS

Different groups at different points in the social order tend to have their own typical forms of socialization and interaction and tend to use different preferred mental styles and forms of behavior in different social settings. . . . Educational practices tend to favor the preferred mental styles and forms of behavior of certain groups over others, the standard patterns of the dominant social groups. (Carrier, 1983, p. 961)

At the beginning of the 20th century, the public schools were troubled by the behavior of working-class and immigrant boys. At the beginning of the 21st century, the public schools are troubled by the behavior of working-class and African American (and, to some extent, Latin American) boys. Research evidence points to three primary ways that schools have dealt with these male students. First, working-class and African American males are punished with out-of-school suspensions at a disproportionate rate (McFadden, Marsh, Price, & Hwang, 1992; Rossow, 1984; Skiba, Peterson, & Williams, 1997). This indicates that many public schools are biased in the treatment of African American and working-class boys. At the very least, it demonstrates the degree of conflict between these males and the authority and order of the public schools. Second, schools that use systems of ability tracking place African American and working-class boys in lower or remedial tracks at a disproportionate rate (Bowles & Gintis, 1976; Chunn, 1987; Lee & Bryk, 1988; Oakes, 1985, 1990). Ability tracking is the practice of grouping students according to assessed ability level. Most public high schools operate a hierarchy of tracks, ranging from the college-bound classes for students assessed to be high achievers to remedial programs for those considered less academically able. These classes tend to be light on academic content while placing a heavy emphasis on compliance with authority (Oakes, 1985, 1990).

The third option, although not wholly separate from the institutional basis for the first two, deserves our more focused attention. As noted earlier, there is an overabundance of African American and working-class males in special education ED programs. We'll conclude this history by looking more closely at this specific way of handling this group of students within the public schools.

Although special education often seems like a separate education system with little relationship to the mainstream, it is helpful to view special classes and schools as a particular form of tracking within public education. In the case of ED classrooms and schools, we find "behavior tracking," which is an extension of existing ability-tracking structures in public schools after the passage of PL 94–142. Tyack and Cuban (1995), in their analysis of the history of educational reform movements, point out that programmatic and curricular reforms undertaken by public schools do not end up looking the way the reformers originally envisioned their projects. Instead, as the various structures, practices, and concepts of the new reform become part of the public school culture, many aspects of the reform tend to take on the shapes and colors of traditional schooling. The public school culture assimilates the new forms into the old forms, thereby enacting the "new" reform in a manner that often leaves the public school barely distinguishable from the way it used to be. Basically, if the reformers want to paint the classroom walls blue, and the walls are currently yellow, then chances are, the reform will leave the walls in some shade of greenish yellow.

When programs for students categorized ED were initiated in the late 1970s as part of the historic PL 94–142, ED programs did not merely attach to the edge of the public schools. They were developed as new elements within the public schools, where the long-standing tradition of ability tracking had historically isolated working-class and minority students from their middle-class peers. The overwhelming evidence from empirical research demonstrates the preponderance of working-class, poor, and ethnic minority students in remedial tracks (Bowles & Gintis, 1976; Chunn, 1987; Lee & Bryk, 1988; Oakes, 1985, 1990).

To this public school tradition of social sorting by class and race, PL 94–142 brought a new, powerful concept and terminology, the idea that an individual's poor academic performance or problematic behavior may be attributed to an underlying psychological disorder. This new individual pathology concept, the emotional disturbance or disorder, was woven together with the prior tendency of schools to segregate nonwhite minority and working-class children into special classes.

Whereas the traditional ability tracks sort and exclude students under the official justification of grouping by academic performance, ED classrooms and special schools sort and exclude students under the justification of grouping by behavioral performance. ED programs provide the tracks specifically designed to house students who engage in dramatic and frequent acts of opposition to school authority. In this light, ED classrooms may serve as a tool of social exclusion for economically disadvantaged and minority culture students who often conflict with the dominant cultural codes of student conduct embraced by school professionals.

Further complicating matters is the apparent ineffectiveness of most ED programs. While undoubtedly some teachers, classrooms, and schools provide quality support and instruction to students labeled ED, the overall picture of ED special education services is not impressive. Fifty-five percent of all students labeled ED leave school without a high school diploma (U.S. Department of Education, 1998). In comparison to students of other disability classifications, few students categorized ED are mainstreamed back into general education classes (U.S. Department of Education, 1998). There is little evidence that current programs and approaches to serving students considered ED in public schools are successful in helping these students improve their lives and futures (Knitzer, Steinberg, & Fleisch, 1990; Wagner, 1995).

In one of the most comprehensive studies to date, Greenbaum et al. (1998) looked at the psychological functioning and educational attainment of more than 800 adolescents and young adults who had been served by public school ED programs and mental health centers. They found that these young people were frequently involved in criminal activity and drug abuse while either dropping out of school or performing far below grade level in academic subjects. Given the complexity of the problems faced by students and families, we cannot claim that the ED programs cause these negative life paths or outcomes. However, we can admit that there is little reason to believe that current efforts in public schools contribute to improved academic, emotional, and social lives for kids called ED.

SUMMARY

The general purpose of this chapter has been to trace the American history of behavior and social problems of childhood in the public schools, the deep and winding roots of our current way of thinking about and dealing with child behavioral issues. The reason for doing this lies in the assumption that the conventions of current educational practices are the combined culmination of the historical development of the family, the public school, and the helping professions (psychiatry, psychology, social work, education). It took a long time and many twists and turns to arrive at our current place. Retraveling that path allows us to better understand where we stand today in relation to the social, political, and professional challenges that face us.

The public schools and the helping professionals of the 20th century tried to create a more moral democratic citizenry by molding and influencing children. The development of schools and the helping professions effected a shift in responsibility for child rearing, casting doubt on the traditional folk expertise of mothers by claiming that scientific expertise was necessary.

As the helping professions developed into full-fledged professions during the 20th century, they found themselves drawn toward both a moral purpose of serving children and families in need, and the rewards of professional prestige and power. Often, the moral purposes have been idealistic and unrealistic given political and economic realities. For example, the early child guidance clinics attempted to heal society of delinquency through methods of individual and family treatment while ignoring the economic problems and ethnic discrimination faced by lower-/working-class, immigrant families. Frequently, the professionals have displayed a middle-class, Anglocentric bias as they have developed goals and programs that did not fully value the perspectives and needs of the lower-/working-class, immigrant, or minority families with whom they worked. The professions have tended to view certain classes of people—immigrants speaking languages other than English, African Americans, the poor and working class—as morally suspect and as the causes of social disorder in communities and schools.

Currently, special education services under the "emotional disturbance" or "emotional/behavioral disorder" heading echo the historical biases and tensions brought about through the development of public schools and helping professionals. In recent decades, the theoretical victory of behaviorism over neo-Freudian psychology within the field of ED has reduced many public school ED programs to systems of behavior modification. The ED field has failed to seriously question the development of segregated ED classrooms and schools as a dumping ground for disaffected African American and lower-/working-class males. This is especially problematic given the apparent lack of success of most ED public school programs.

We may draw three specific lessons from this history that serve as challenges in current work. First, educators and other helping professionals have often focused heavily on developing and using authoritative knowledge. This effort has effectively amounted to building a knowledge base about students and families that we then say supercedes the knowledge of students and families about themselves. Our reasons for listening carefully to students and families have been unfortunately diminished by our own scientific knowledge. Second, educators and helping professions have often viewed social problems in a depoliticized way. Rather than becoming aware of complex dimensions of social inequality that surround so many troubling students, we have often defined the problem as an individual disorder needing treatment. This approach has allowed us to ignore the unequal and unjust social and political conditions that many of our students face in their daily lives. Finally, we find within our professional history a very hopeful and very old strand of wisdom. Mental health workers and educators since the early 1900s have been building deep, caring relationships with young people and their families. These relationships are vital to the helping task. We embrace and continue this tradition in this book.

CONSTRUCTING PERSONAL MEANINGS

1. Find a local administrator or teacher who has worked with troubling youth for 20 years or more. Interview this professional to learn about how programs, service, and ideas have changed over the years.

2. Find a local psychiatrist, psychologist, or social worker who has been doing psychotherapy with families and children for many years. Interview this professional to learn about how psychotherapeutic treatment and the problems facing families have changed over the years.

3. Conduct historical research on a local residential program for children considered ED that has operated for many decades. Many communities have programs with very deep roots in local charities and religious groups. Often, this kind of research involves reviewing old records and documentation as well as interviewing retired employees and administrators. Find out how the mission, practices, and service population of the institution have changed over time.

4. Use the university library to seek professional and/or popular publications on child behavior problems from the early 1900s. Many books on behavior problems and delinquency were written before World War II. Also, leading women's magazines such as *Ladies' Home Journal* published articles that translated professional beliefs into popular form for mothers to read.

5. Ask local school district and/or state administrators for data on race, gender, and social class (or socioeconomic status) among students labeled ED. Many areas collect data on race and gender, but very few have information on social class. They will have information on the number of students enrolled in free and reduced-price breakfast and lunch programs. That can serve as a means for finding students who live in poverty. Is the ED category in the local area and/or state disproportionately filled with minority and working-/lower-class boys?

2

Introducing Critical Constructivism

The question of how humans make meaning has tantalized philosophers, psychologists, sociologists, and educators for some time. This question is so fundamental to our existence that the ways in which we answer it can have a monumental impact on our relationship to knowledge, education, and each other. Constructivism is a broad set of interrelated theories that proposes that knowledge is at least as much a human construction as a discovery. With this emphasis on our active participation in constructing meaning comes added responsibility for the social impact of the knowledges we create. This understanding marks a loss of innocence in relationship to knowledge, because it can no longer be separated from power.

L ooking at the picture of an inkblot, one might imagine any number of interpretations. There is an understanding that what we see in an inkblot is, at least in part, our own making. Some interpretations may be more common than others, but it would be rare for someone to argue that his or her interpretation was "right" and someone else's was "wrong." At the bottom of it, an inkblot is only an inkblot, not an angel, nor a butterfly. Those are meanings we project onto the blot of ink. There is no way to determine which interpretation is the "best," although some certainly seem to fit better than others. In the process of interpreting an inkblot, there is conscious recognition of our projection onto it. We know, in part, that we are making with our mind what we are finding in the blot. Constructivist theories of learning and knowing assume that reality is much like this inkblot: The meaning is not inherent in the world, but in the interaction between our minds and the stuff onto which we project meaning.

In this chapter, we are going to look at several related theories of learning that conceptualize learning as an active, constructive process. First, we'll explore constructivism, with a focus on cognition. Next, we'll discuss social constructionism, where the focus is on the social nature of learning, and therefore interaction, language, and context are of central importance. Finally, we'll focus on considering how power is constructed, structured, and enacted within learning theories, learning processes, and learning relationships. It is focusing on dimensions of power that marks our theorizing as "critical." Together, these theories comprise our rendition of critical constructivist pedagogy. The emphasis in critical constructivist theories is not on "getting it right," memorization, or mastery of content. Rather, the focus of these theories is on the process of constructing meanings within social contexts, relationships, and languages.

BEHAVIORAL APPROACHES TO LEARNING

Historically, behavioral and constructivist theories have been presented as opposing schools of thought. Behavioral theories are popular in relationship to academic learning and addressing student behavior or classroom management. Behavioral theories hold that experts discover knowledge through scientific and objective processes. They encode this knowledge into languages, and then children learn the right "knowledge" through memorization and practice. The teacher's job entails breaking down complex bodies of knowledge to what is assumed to be their sequential component parts. Teachers create activities in which the students have opportunities to demonstrate the knowledge they are acquiring. Teachers give students feedback on whether they got it "right" or not. Teachers in this model take on roles similar to technicians. As Beyer (1992) explains,

> It has been commonplace, within the dominant traditions of schooling and teaching, to consider the teacher as a kind of technician. The

dominant activity of the teacher conceived in these terms involves the transmission of knowledge, values, and ideas, sanctioned by "experts" working outside the classroom. . . . Within this conception, teaching is largely a kind of application process, based upon a model of technical rationality ("for result X, apply strategies 1 and 2 in situation Y"). (p. 239)

Behavioral principles of reinforcement provide a "technology" to motivate students to engage in the learning process. Teachers motivate students by providing students with rewards, or reinforcements for participation and for "getting it right" (Fosnot, 1996).

Frank Smith (1998) describes a detrimental aspect of behavioral approaches to learning that are based on memorization of facts and are dependent on reinforcement. He tells us that much of this kind of learning is forgotten soon after taking the test. Reflecting on our own education tends to bear this out. When we separate learning from its social contexts and break it down into lists and facts, we often strip it of its overall meaning. It often loses its appeal and importance to us. Then, acquiring "it" becomes "hard work," and rewards and punishments are needed to motivate children to do "it." On the other hand, Smith (1998) points out that the vast amount of learning that occurs naturally through participation in social contexts, such as learning language, is rarely forgotten. This is the basis of constructivist theories of learning. They do not separate the social out of learning.

CONSTRUCTIVIST AND SOCIAL CONSTRUCTIONIST THEORIES

In the following pages, we will discuss two closely related theories, constructivism and social constructionism. Often, these theories are combined even though they emphasize different dimensions of the learning process. Constructivism emphasizes cognitive processes, whereas social constructionism focuses on the role of social interaction, social context, and language in learning. Both theories assume that learning is an active process in which new meaning is constructed in relation to existing meanings. Together, these theories form a foundation for the pedagogical approaches described in the rest of this text.

Constructivism and the Work of Piaget

Jean Piaget's theories of learning are central to constructivist thought. We will discuss some of the important tenets of Piaget's constructivist theory and then extend these as we consider some contemporary constructivist writers and theorists.

Piaget's early work was in the field of biology, and much of his subsequent theorizing about cognitive development is modeled on biological systems. The concept of equilibration, which is central to Piaget's theories of cognitive development, parallel what he believed occurs in biological systems. He noticed that the shape of pond snails changed to adapt to different environments. Piaget hypothesized that the change in shape resulted from changes in behavior necessary to survive in the different environments. Changes in environment required the organism to adapt in order to find balance or equilibration. Piaget viewed the organism as an indissoluble whole, so changes in behavior had an impact on changes in shape.

Piaget focused much of his attention on what he called cognitive structures—the fairly enduring forms that thoughts take in the mind. He suggested that cognitive structures were always under construction, always open to transformation. Cognitive structures involve holistic systems of meaning that structure experience. As Fosnot (1996) explains,

> Structural analysis of thought shows such patterns of organization, that is, ordering, classification, setting up correspondences and relations, coordinating contradictions, and explaining transformations by interactions, reversibility, and compensation, and so forth. In fact, the development of structures, according to Piaget, characterizes the growth process. Because of equilibration, the structure expands to include the "reach beyond the grasp" but also seeks organization and closure, keeping the structure always "under construction." (p. 18)

Piaget viewed humans as a whole structure in which cognitive, emotional, and physical development were inseparable constructs. Piaget theorized that development involves the ongoing effort to find equilibration, or balance. He proposed two complementary mechanisms, assimilation and accommodation, as fundamental to this process (Piaget, 1963; Piaget & Inhelder, 1969). *Assimilation* involves making sense of one's experience within the cognitive structures one has already developed. New information is stored within the categories, frameworks, and structures of thought that already exist for that individual. However, as the child develops, new situations arise in which the old cognitive structures do not prove adequate. The new information or perception doesn't seem to fit into the old way of thinking. In order to find equilibration in these situations, change must occur in the child's cognitive schema or structures.

In assimilation, the child organizes experience based on his or her existing cognitive structures. He or she makes sense of the world based on the categories and beliefs that he or she has already established. For example, a young child may develop a schema in which he or she calls all animals with four legs "dogs." Over time, the child is corrected, and new categories are learned. The child then adapts to this new information by creating finer distinctions in his or her criteria for mapping meaning onto four-legged creatures. This change in the child is called *accommodation*. According to Piaget, learning involves an ongoing process of assimilation and accommodation.

An important aspect of constructivist learning is the concept of viability within particular environments or contexts. These contexts are conceptual as well as physical. Von Glasersfeld (1995) suggests that viability takes the place in constructivist theories that truth occupied in traditional theories of learning:

> To a biologist, a living organism is viable as long as it manages to survive in its environment. To the constructivist, concepts, models, theories, and so on are viable if they prove adequate in the contexts in which they were created. Viability—quite unlike truth—is relative to a context of goals and purposes. But these goals and purposes are not limited to the concrete or material. (p. 8)

Environments or contexts are important in a constructivist view of learning. Learning makes sense in relationship to other meanings, surroundings, and one's position in the world. Unlike the traditional versions of knowledge, in which "universal" truths are sought, constructivists look at meaning within particular social contexts. This allows for multiplicity, variability, and change as a natural part of learning.

Social Constructionism

Social constructionism is a set of theories that is related to constructivism, but the emphasis is different. Constructionists emphasize the role of community, language, and social interaction in learning. Gergen (1995b) suggests three key assumptions of the social constructionist view.

1. *Meaning in language is achieved through social interdependence.* Gergen offers this assumption in purposeful contrast to the belief that language represents an external expression of the individual mind. Rather, the emphasis is on the importance of language as a social medium for meaning making. Our meanings are affirmed, denied, honed, clarified, changed, and so on by others with whom we converse. Learning language occurs within a social context as we learn what various words mean to other language users. Meaning is formed in a social agreement that a book is a book and not a chair. And although we may each contain variations on our understanding of any word, some degree of basic agreement in language is necessary for communication. These agreements are worked out continuously in interdependent relationships with others.

2. *Meaning in language is context dependent.* When meaning is seen as constructed in social interaction, it follows that various social contexts would contribute to diverse social meanings. As Goodman (1978) points out, we don't make meaning out of nothing, but out of other "worlds" of meaning that already exist. Children are socialized into meanings and languages that already exist. The history of meaning and social norms established within a particular context provide parameters for possible meanings.

3. *Language primarily serves communal functions.* Rather than seeing language as the bearer of truth, social constructionists see language as serving functions in the community. Even the most specialized scientific terms serve a social

function within the scientific community. However, the shift from language as the mind's accurate representations of the world to language serving a pragmatic purpose within the community has enormous implications for how we interact with one another, how we structure our social relationships, and how we conceptualize learning.

CONSTRUCTIVIST/CONSTRUCTIONIST PEDAGOGY

Whereas constructivists focus more on psychological processes and social constructionists focus more on social interaction, teachers need to attend to both. The following section distills some major pedagogical themes drawing from both constructivist and social constructionist theory. There are wide areas of agreement between these two approaches, along with some different emphases. However, for the sake of simplicity, we will use the term *constructivist* to encompass both approaches.

Although Sylvia Ashton-Warner didn't use the term *constructivism* in 1963 when she wrote *Teacher,* her classic text provides excellent examples of critical constructivist pedagogy. Ashton-Warner used the term *organic learning* to describe learning that emanates up from the lived experiences and inner life of the learner. Her book is based on her experiences teaching young Maori children in New Zealand. She became uncomfortable teaching the 5-year-olds in her class to read, write, and spell by imposing a vocabulary on them from outside. She saw the imposition of vocabulary as the imposition of culture. Rather, she wanted her students' first words to spring from their inner vision and to be "captions of the dynamic life itself" (p. 33).

Instead of using vocabulary words chosen by adults, Ashton-Warner (1963) allowed students to ask for the words they wanted to know. She insisted that, "First words must have intense meaning to the child. They must be a part of his being" (p. 33). From these first words come first sentences and stories, which become the basis of learning to read. Ashton-Warner's account is a poetic philosophy of learning based on her experiences. "I know all of this because I've done it," she tells us (p. 34). We'll use her words to frame each of the principles we sketch out below.

An Emphasis on Cognitive Structures

> Back to these first words. To these first books. They must be made out of the stuff of the child itself. I reach my hand into the mind of a child, bring out a handful of the stuff I find there, and use that as our first working material. Whether it is good stuff or bad stuff, violent or placid stuff, coloured or dun. To effect an unbroken beginning. (Ashton-Warner, 1963, p. 34)

Constructivists would not assume that when children memorize facts, what they demonstrate is "learning." Constructivist versions of educational practice are interested in learning as a process of development rather than an acquisition of "truth." Constructivists assume that learning involves an ongoing process of interaction between self and environment. Learning involves qualitative change in the learner's thinking, not simply an acquisition of more knowledge. Rather than focus on whether students get it right, constructivist teachers focus on trying to understand how students make sense of their texts or contexts. It is important for students to have opportunities to construct meaning and to share their constructions. This sharing gives the teachers an opportunity to try to interpret the students' understandings. It is necessary for the teacher to connect with the students' meanings in order to help mediate students' learning.

For teachers to learn with students, to learn from students how they are making sense of the texts and contexts in their lives, they must give students ample opportunities to express their sense making. Students should be encouraged to write their thoughts, tell their stories, and engage in dialogue around meanings. The classroom should be bursting with students' stories, theories, reasoning, artwork, and relationships. These become classroom "texts," the site of exploration, reflection, and learning.

An Emphasis on Connection

Ashton-Warner (1963) tells stories about the connection between her students and the words they choose. She first introduces Seven as a violent Maori child who asks for the word "bomb" for vocabulary. Then she tells of hearing a knock on the school door and answering it to find a barefoot Maori woman who has come to see Seven. She asks if Seven is this woman's son and is told that the woman raised Seven for 5 years, but sent him back to his real family so he could attend school. Ashton-Warner asks the woman where she raised the boy.

> "Way back on those hill. All by herself. You remember your ol' Mummy?" she begs Seven.

> I see.

> Later, standing watching Seven grind his chalk dust on his blackboard as usual, I do see. "Whom do you want, Seven? Your old Mummy or your new Mummy?"

> "My old Mummy."

> "What do your brothers do?"

> "They all hits me."

> "Old Mummy" and "new Mummy" and "hit" and "brothers" are all one-look words added to his vocabulary, and now and again I see some shape breaking through the chalk-ravage. And I wish I could make a good story of it and say he is no longer violent . . .

> "Who's that crying!" I accuse, lifting my nose like an old war horse.

"Seven he breaking Gay's neck."

So the good story, I say to my junior, must stand by for a while. But I can say he is picking up his words now. Fast. (pp. 37–38)

Constructivist pedagogy involves students in actively making connections between what they already know and what they are learning. Constructionist pedagogy encourages learning as a social engagement with others and within contexts. Students are encouraged to reflect on how their life experiences, prior "knowledges," beliefs, and values are affected by and affect the learning process. All learning involves self-learning. However, self is always in relationship to other selves in various environments, in various communities. Constructivist learning occurs through engagement, and language is the currency of engagement.

Constructivist teachers engage students in questions that help them make conscious links between themselves, their prior knowledge, and the new learning with which they are engaged. They might ask, What does this text or experience mean to you? What does it remind you of? How would you describe it? What is your reaction to it? Is it important to you? Is it something you want to pursue? Why or why not? Even in subjects like math, constructivists encourage students to describe their thinking and reasoning processes, making conscious the ways in which they approach a problem.

Social constructionism focuses on learning as a social process. Language, the currency of social exchange, is of primary importance in this pedagogy. Thus, the metaphor of a conversation has been used as means to help envision social constructionist forms of education (Gergen, 1995b; Stone, 1992). Rather than a top-down lecture, in conversation there is a reciprocal sharing that makes it impossible to guide exactly where the conversation will go. Rather than guiding students to a predetermined end, the teacher and the students engage in learning together. The teacher may have more access to certain "sanctioned knowledges" and have more responsibility to bring certain elements into the conversation. But this is not, by any means, the only important learning that goes on in a classroom. Students are encouraged to discuss ideas in groups, articulating and expanding their own knowledge in the give and take of conversation.

Teaching and learning need to occur within the context of respectful relationships. If teachers don't think it is important to understand the meanings students bring to school, which may well mean learning about the contexts in which their meanings make sense, then the possibility of conversational learning is reduced. When a student interprets a text or context differently from the teacher, explaining that interpretation will often involve stories about the student's life, relationships, and contexts. Teachers must be careful to respect the lives, families, and communities within which students situate their meaning making. Otherwise, teaching becomes a form of social oppression, and students often resist rather than compromise the integrity of the social groups with which they identify. Adriana Hernandez (1997) sums it up nicely when she says, "The motivation for engaging in a dialogue is love and friendship as opposed to domination and oppression" (p. 15).

Although we engage with students around texts, learning occurs in the conversations about texts, not solely "in" the texts. The text becomes one of many voices in the conversation, but it is not above question or revision. Texts may present a common focus for discussion, but each child is encouraged to bring his or her own social and historical knowledge to the table. Students often have access to contexts in which counterknowledges or alternative knowledges are enacted. Teachers are not the experts in all contexts, and there is no assumption that there is only one "real world." Diverse meanings, cultures, perspectives, and ways of representing learning are extremely valued in a social constructionist classroom, because this is what makes learning interesting and dimensional.

An Emphasis on Relationships, Contexts, and Cultures

Ashton-Warner (1963) tells us that one of the things that constantly confounds top-down forms of education is the children's social interest in one another. However, these very relationships form the foundation of her method.

> The children's interest in one another. It plays the very devil with orthodox method. If they'd only stop talking to each other, playing with each other, fighting with each other and loving each other. This unseemly and unlawful communication! In self-defense I've got to use the damn thing. So I harness the communication, since I can't control it, and base my method on it. They read in pairs, sentence and sentence about. There's no time for either to get bored. Each checks the other's mistakes and hurries him up if he's too slow, since after all his own turn depends on it. They teach each other all their work in pairs, sitting cross-legged knee to knee on the mat, or on their tables, arguing with, correcting, abusing or smiling at each other. And between them all the time is this togetherness, so that learning is so mixed up with relationship that it becomes part of it. What an unsung creative medium is relationship. (p. 104)

The classroom represents the most common context in which formal education is enacted. This social space is a significant aspect of the learning process. Bruner (1986) suggests that constructivist classrooms should be places where students can participate in meaning making within a "culture." The classroom provides a social context for engaging in the negotiation of meaning with others. Gergen (1995b) points out that this movement into conversational learning involves a diffusion of power in the classroom. Top-down processes such as lecture formats lose much of their appeal. Students are invited to participate (along with teachers, parents, board members, etc.) in creating meaning, choosing curriculum, and having input on decisions that affect the class. This does not negate the teacher's responsibility to his or her students to be in a position of authority in the room. However, the teacher's aim is for students to actively participate and take responsibility for their learning. This leads to very different classroom structures from "get it right" classrooms where students are socialized into obedience and disciplined when they don't comply. We will address these issues in depth in the next chapter.

Constructivist teachers want students to connect what they are learning to social interactions, social contexts, and social functions. This adds important dimensions to students' understandings. They have to understand not only meaning, but also the contexts in which meanings makes sense. This involves students in a study of cultures, as students begin to understand that there are many worlds of meaning. (Culture can be used broadly to include race or ethnicity, or more narrowly to speak about family culture or classroom culture.) Bruner (1986) believes that cultures are always in the process of renegotiation, and thus, students should be encouraged to become negotiators of classroom culture as means of social learning:

> The most general implication is that a culture is constantly in process of being recreated as it is interpreted and renegotiated by its members. In this view, a culture is as much a forum for negotiating and renegotiating meaning and for explicating action as it is a set of rules or specifications for action. . . .
>
> It follows from this view of culture as forum that induction into the culture through education, if it is to prepare the young for life as lived, should also partake of the spirit of a forum, of negotiation, of the creating of meaning. (p. 123)

Not only current meanings, but past meanings are considered multiple and open to negotiation as well. Students do not simply learn history, but learn to question "whose history, from what perspective?" Bruner (1986) tells us that "what is needed is a basis for discussing not simply the content of what is before one, but the possible stances one might take toward it" (p. 123).

When students feel an aversion to particular texts, they should be encouraged to delve into the differences (in background, social class, culture, gender, history, etc.) between themselves and the authors of the texts. Multiple views can be presented side by side. There is not just one "real world." We can disagree on what something means without feeling like someone must be wrong. In fact, disagreement provides the richest soil for learning, because those who disagree have opportunities to delve into the contexts, environments, cultures, institutions, beliefs, and languages that structure or affect their meanings. These questions open up space for students' voices.

The concept of *viability* in constructivist learning emphasizes that meaning occurs and makes sense within specific environments, contexts, or cultures. In today's society, students occupy many social environments. Students inhabit home environments, school environments, and various community environments. The media also represent extremely heterogeneous environments that affect students and teachers. The Internet provides students access to an endless array of virtual environments.

Today's youth find themselves navigating an increasingly complex array of social worlds and contexts. Constructivist pedagogy is viable in an emerging global society that includes an endless array of meanings, contexts, languages, and cultures. Adaptation involves an agility never required before (Gergen, 1995a). Rather than teach students the facts about the world, constructionist pedagogy engages meanings in relationship to various worlds. Trying to adhere to core "truths" or delineate "universal" knowledge in a global society involves a move to assimilate our complex worlds to structures they have clearly outgrown (Anderson, 1995). Education that seeks to prepare students for the complexity of contemporary society can no longer afford to indulge in rigid notions of static knowledge. Rather than seek the "one right answer," we need to ask, "right within what context, for whom, at what moment in time?"

GETTING "CRITICAL": LOOKING AT POWER IN EDUCATION

Although issues of power have been inherent in our discussion thus far, we have not addressed power explicitly. However, when we begin to assume that knowledge is constructed, many questions begin to surface. Whose knowledge have we been teaching and learning in schools? Whose knowledge is portrayed in the media? What mechanisms are in place that allow some knowledge to be heard and legitimized while others are silenced? If knowledge does not represent universal truth, then what does it represent? Who benefits from the versions of truth we privilege in our schools and other social institutions? Who is oppressed or denigrated by these sanctioned knowledges?

There have been many answers to these questions in recent decades. Members of some groups of people who have been, and continue to be, marginalized and oppressed within society have entered the dialogue of what knowledge is and how it is produced. They do not hesitate to declare that knowledge and power are inseparable, and therefore, teaching and learning are inherently political acts. Their daily experience within schools and society bears this out. Fine, Powell, Weis, and Mun Wong (1997) tell us:

> Scholars of multiculturalism, critical gender and race theory, and subaltern discourses have spent considerable energy centering the voices of those historically excluded and marginalized. Voices of those positioned at the "margins" or "on the edge" are being heard within and across all disciplines, contributing to a reformation of what constitutes "knowledge." While we do not mean to overstate the transformative success, it is indeed the case that significant challenge has taken place in academic canons and that these challenges at least partially reflect the intellectual and community-based movements of women and men of color, as well

as white women, gays, lesbians and bisexuals, persons with disabilities, and the working class and poor. As we make our voices heard in the academy, therefore, a single white coherent and male, heterosexual, and elite narrative no longer characterizes any of our fields. (p. vii)

Far from being neutral or objective, the academic knowledges we construct either enact or reject the racism, sexism, classism, ableism, heterosexism, and so on in our society. Versions of educational practice that seek to "get it right" have historically posited the knowledges of middle-class, white, heterosexual men as the "right" view of the world. Although this is being challenged on many fronts, this "right" view of the world remains embedded not only in our curricula, but also in our consciousness. Consequently, girls, children of color, children of low-income families, and children with disabilities have often found schools painful places where they cannot be themselves if they want to succeed. This can lead to a deep sense of alienation.

If we look back at educational practices of the past, deep-seated racism, sexism, classism, and ableism are often blatantly apparent. It is difficult to understand how teachers participated in practices that today seem cruel and inhuman. For example, Martinez and Smith (2000) describe the educational treatment of Native American children in the past:

> The boarding school system created in the 19th century had as its primary objective to "kill the Indian but save the man" (Lesiak & Jones, 1991). During this period in American history, Native American children were separated from their families to help them with the process of change. Upon their arrival at the boarding schools, children's physical appearances were immediately changed. Their traditional clothing was taken away and replaced with Western clothing and, in the case of boys, their hair was cut short. This was considered the beginning of the transformation. Forced to sleep on the floor on cold winter nights with a bare blanket to cover their frozen, malnourished bodies, children died of maltreatment and sadness. A policy of extermination had later become one of relocation and finally one of assimilation in post-Civil War years. (p. 68)

In this example, it is easy to see the cultural imperialism; the negation of a way of life; and the imposition of one culture's values, beliefs, language, behaviors, dress, and knowledge on another culture. One wonders how the teachers in these boarding schools could participate in such cruelty and consider it sound educational practice. Most likely, these practices were considered to be in the best interest of these children, done for their own good, to help them become productive American citizens. The educational system not only reflected, but institutionalized and thereby perpetuated, the prominent beliefs of that time.

The concept of *reification* helps explain how people can participate in cruel acts and believe what they are doing is for the "others'" own good. It helps explain how people can come to mistake their *view* of the world for the world *itself.* Berger and Luckmann (1966) use the term *reification* to describe a process by which we repress from consciousness our own participation in the construction of reality. They tell us:

> Another way of saying this is that reification is the apprehension of the products of human activity as if they were something else than human products—such as facts of nature, results of cosmic laws, or manifestations of divine will. Reification implies that man is capable of forgetting his own authorship of the human world, and further, that the dialectic between man, the producer, and his products is lost to consciousness. (p. 89)

This process of reification is much like what would occur if we projected an image onto an inkblot but mistook our interpretation for the true meaning contained *in* the inkblot. If we were certain our interpretation was "right," then all other interpretations would have to be "wrong." Thus, the common belief that Native Americans were uncivilized savages was projected onto them and then enacted in their brutal exploitation. To those who believed in the inferiority of the Native Americans, evidence for their beliefs seemed to be right before their eyes. In light of this belief, every difference between Native American customs and religion and Western customs and religion made clear how inferior Native American cultures were. Such a belief would be necessary to justify the widespread annihilation of a people. We look to history with horror at what others have done, and yet education that seeks "the one right answer" continues the process of reification today and easily becomes a vehicle for social oppression.

Politicizing Consciousness

Mistaking our view of the world for the absolute truth has the potential to lead to extremely oppressive practices while leaving us unaware of our impact. In Young's (1990) explanation of cultural imperialism below, we can see the role reification plays in constructing people who are different from the dominant group as deviant and inferior:

> Often without noticing they do so, the dominant groups project their own experience as representative of humanity as such. . . . The dominant group reinforces its position by bringing the other groups under the measure of its dominant norms. Consequently, the difference of women from men, American Indians or Africans from Europeans, Jews from Christians, homosexuals from heterosexuals, workers from professionals, becomes reconstructed largely as deviance and inferiority. (p. 59)

Radical constructivist and social constructionist theories call for a shift in consciousness and an explicit awareness of our participation in the meanings we project onto the world. This involves a politicization of consciousness. The major social movements (women's rights, civil rights, disabilities rights, and gay and lesbian rights) have begun to make visible how the reification process occurs, how it structures consciousness, how it becomes institutionalized, and how it functions to maintain social hierarchies.

Young (1990) describes how efforts for achieving social justice need to go beyond our conscious decision making, as is often the focus of traditional ethical theory. She suggests an ethic that involves taking responsibility for our unconscious actions, aversions, manners, and ways of speaking. She tells us, "The injunction to 'be just' in such matters amounts to no more and no less than a call to bring these phenomena of practical consciousness and unconsciousness under discussion, that is, to politicize them" (p. 152). Constructivist approaches for learning provide a foundation for social change by making conscious the ways in which knowledge is socially constructed. Participation in constructivist learning promotes a process of dereification by making conscious our partici-pation in constructing the truths that structure our social realities (Berger & Luckmann, 1966).

One focus in critical constructivist pedagogy involves an examination of how large social institutions such as government, schools, media, and economic structures enact, reflect, and maintain the reified social stratification within society. Often, schooling involves a conscious and/or unconscious cultural imperialism, and thus, an inevitable violence against many of the children we teach. Kohl (1994) describes the harm done:

> If a school curriculum denigrates one's ancestors, religion, and contri-butions to the history of the human race, and denies one's full dignity—that is, if it teaches the superiority of one segment of a democratic society over others—it is damaging to the minds and spirits of all children: those taught that their cultures are secondary and those given the false security of believing they are the creators of culture. (p. 95)

Kohl (1994) provides several examples of curricula that discount the social and cultural history of various groups of people. One example he shares involves the education of a group of children in a Texas school who were pre-dominantly of Mexican descent. Their textbook stated that the first people to settle Texas came from New England and Virginia. The children and their families felt insulted by this text. Were their ancestors not "people"? This and many other slights had the community and the children depressed. They were continuously being assaulted with texts that denigrated who they were, histo-ries that denied them, and images of excellence that did not include them.

Traditional methods of teaching and learning often set up extremely diffi-cult situations for many groups of students. For example, when students see images of themselves and their social groups depicted in curricula in ways that they find disrespectful, they often resist schooling. In an educational system based on "getting it right," there is no room for them to construct meaning based on their own understandings of history, prior knowledge, or experience, and there is no legitimate way to protest. They are often given the option of conforming to an education that does not respect them or their families, or facing the consequences.

THEMES IN CRITICAL CONSTRUCTIVIST PEDAGOGY

We will focus on four interrelated themes of critical pedagogy: *desire, identity, institutional oppression,* and *teaching for social justice.* The term *desire* is used to focus attention on feelings, dreams, and bodies—aspects of our being that traditionally have been not only ignored, but also denigrated in educational settings. The term *identity* involves the social meanings attributed to various aspects of our embodied being, as well as our personal interpretations of these social meanings. *Institutional oppression* covers the ways in which racism, sexism, classism, heterosexism, and ableism are often embedded in institutional practices, policies, and structures. We will consider identity and institutional oppression together, because they involve, inform, and enact one another. Finally, *teaching for social justice* involves an explicitly political agenda of teaching in which learning involves participation in social action aimed toward circumstances of greater political equality and freedom for all persons. The following case study provides an excellent example of critical constructivist pedagogy that will help us develop the themes below.

A Critical Case Study

Linda Christensen (1998) is a high school teacher who enacts critical constructivist pedagogy with her students. She has been working with students for more than 15 years, helping them to use writing as a means to find their voice, tell their stories, and engage in conversation. She has successfully taught students to use "writing to take the power out of their pain" (p. 39). However, she found that this is not enough. She needed to get beyond the individual human level with her students, to "get at the social roots of our feelings of alienation and inadequacy, as well as our possibility for joy and resistance" (p. 41).

Christensen tells the story of helping her students understand the broader social and political contexts of standardized tests. This exploration evolved out of the personal experiences of her urban students, who were viewing their difficulties with testing as personal deficiency. Each student wrote about her or his experiences, good or bad, of taking a high-stakes test. They shared their stories in class and began to realize that they weren't alone. Once each student began to realize that this was not an individual, personal problem, Christensen had them explore the racist history of achievement and aptitude tests. The students were shocked when they found, for instance, that Carl Brigham (creator of the Scholastic Aptitude Test) had written an article in a journal in which Hitler had been published and had argued for "stronger immigration laws to protect the 'contamination of the American intellect'" (Christensen, p. 43). Brigham named many groups from which Americans needed to be protected, although he emphasized "especially—Negroes." Students began to make connections between past and present, with one student writing: "This struck me because even though slavery has been over, they still enslave us differently so we will still be seen as dumb." From this, the students began an analysis of the items on standardized achievement and aptitude tests. This analysis continued, and students looked at studies of relationships between income levels and achievement. Christensen (1998) tells us the impact that this critical inquiry had on the students:

> After scrutinizing the test, the students concluded that Brigham's grandchild didn't measure their intelligence nor would it predict their success in college. When the test became demystified, when it was no longer a bogeyman, when the kids saw it as an obstacle, ETS (Educational Testing Service) no longer held the same kind of power over them. (p. 45)

Many of Christensen's students became very engaged in their school learning that year, some for the first time in their lives. They expressed that they had begun to question everything, rather than simply accept what they were told. This is critical constructivist pedagogy.

Desire

> Trained in the philosophical context of Western metaphysical dualism, many of us have accepted the notion that there is a split between the body and the mind. Believing this, individuals enter the classroom to teach as though only the mind is present, and not the body. . . . The public world of institutional learning was a site where the body had to be erased, go unnoticed. (hooks, 1994, p. 191)

Feminists have worked hard to establish that the body is a social and political site. We are em-bodied, and this flesh we inhabit is the site of pain and pleasure. Our bodies are the places in which our lives are lived out and that mark us, to some degree, as having gender, race, sexual orientation, (dis)ability, and age. The families and social situations into which we are physically born, and physically connected, deeply and profoundly affect our experiences of self and world. It is within bodies that we feel pain, pleasure, joy, and passion. Schooling has often served as a place to cut us off from these vital aspects of ourselves while our dispassionate minds learn the "facts" about the world.

To say that something is subjective often implies it is not to be trusted. Traditionally, women and girls, and people of color, have been associated with the subjective world, and thus their participation in the public sphere, the logical realm of white men, has often been denied or constrained. Entry into these public spheres has often been at the price of denying and diminishing one's embodiment, passions, and feelings.

Schools are often places where students learn that what they feel is not important or that it is "bad." This easily translates to feelings that *they* are "bad." Kelly (1997) describes the interchanges between bodies, desire, knowledge, and power in schooling, and how these converge in constructs of identity through schooling:

> The notion of mind/ing bodies bespeaks most accurately and succinctly how the intersection of knowledge, power, and desire craft identity as the cultural project of schools. Schooling, then, is "a mode of social control" (McLaren, 1994, 173), a means by which to produce particular forms of subjectivity and elicit particular forms of participation in social life. These controls are affected through the management and domestication of desire. (p. 1)

Education should be a place where all students are able to learn how to make their hopes and dreams come true. Kelly (1997) describes desire as "the shape our dreams and identities take in the social" (p. 2). Given the social worlds and the bodies in which we live, what are we allowed to dream? Critical educators are interested in the ways that schooling shapes desire, shapes the dreams and possibilities that embodied students carry in their hearts, souls, and flesh.

How schooling, curriculum, discipline, literacy, and social relationships in schools make students, their families, teachers, and administrators feel are important aspects of critical education. Feeling pain, dis-ease, anger, and humiliation, for example, are often our bodily reactions to oppressive policies. However, if students are socialized to ignore their bodies, desires, and feelings, and if expressions of such are denied, shamed, or punished, then oppressive policies and practices can continue unhindered. Listening to our bodies, expressing our emotions—even when they involve dis-pleasure—are critical aspects of critical pedagogy.

In the case study described above, it was the pain and humiliation that students in Christensen's class felt in relationship to standardized tests that signaled a need for critical inquiry. Trisa, one of Christensen's students, summarized their learning. She wrote: "[Tests] caused us to feel nervous, made us feel stupid, conditioned us to testing and to being told what to do without questioning, made us compete against each other, fostered an 'I'm better than you' attitude, appeared fair, but made us internalize the fault" (Christensen, 1998, p. 42).

It is the pain of social oppression that makes it worth fighting against. It is the anticipated pleasure of an embodied participation in schooling that fuels the passions for educational change. The body, the emotions, the desires of teachers and students are the sites of education, identity, and politics. To silence these is to silence the reasons for change and alienate us from our own existence.

Critical constructivist educators seek to help students heal the mind/body split that schooling has traditionally sanctioned and deepened. How schooling and all it entails makes us feel, how it quenches or quells our desires, is of critical importance. The importance is not simply so we can be in touch with our feelings, but so we can begin to connect how we feel, what we desire, and what we feel aversions to, to what others feel, and to larger social and institutional structures. To discipline the body, to silence its messages, to shame its desires, and to do this systematically, for years on end as a by-product of schooling, shapes our consciousness in ways that make us feel ashamed to resist our own oppression. Unbinding that shame and silence from our schooled bodies is a powerful move toward creating impassioned students who are free to work toward a more socially just society.

Identity and Institutions

Important to developing critical consciousness is understanding the connections between peoples' personal lives and institutional inequality. Each of us has a social identity which reflects various aspects of human diversity. For example, race is one aspect of a person's social identity. It might be black, white, Native American, Asian American, biracial or racially mixed and so forth. Some aspects of our social identity are typically constant, such as race and gender. Some, like class, religion and language may change over our lifetimes. Others, like age, are guaranteed to change. (Schniedewind & Davidson, 1998, p. 16)

Identity has emerged as a concept that often replaces the concept of self in constructivist thinking (Gergen, 1995a; Zweig, 1995). Whereas the self traditionally has been thought of as a stable, autonomous, essence of being human, identity involves the social meanings of selves within multiple and changing contexts. Identities are multiple, such that one person can be a mother, a daughter, a sister, a lawyer, an activist, a troublemaker, a liberal, a Hispanic, a Catholic, and middle class, all at once. Identities are considered political, in that social power is often conferred in relationship to some social identities and not to others. Schniedewind and Davidson (1998) tell us that "Given the many aspects of our social identities, most of us experience some benefits and pay some prices because of institutional inequality" (p. 17).

The term *identity* has been used to imply the interaction between our subjective experience and the larger social structures that serve to help shape those experiences. Identity involves our sense of who we are and who "others" are. Identity is not something each one of us determines by him- or herself. Nor are our social identities rigidly fixed. Aspects of social identity have social meanings before and beyond us. For example, what it means to be female, gay, African American, Hispanic, disabled, or an adolescent involves social constructs that we do not determine alone and that, in part, determine us.

Identity, desire, and institutional oppression are related processes that all come together in pedagogical practices. Adriana Hernandez (1997) describes these connections:

> Any pedagogical practice is about the production of subjectivities. A transformative feminist pedagogy should disclose how subjectivities—particularly gendered—are being constructed and/or represented outside and inside the school setting, and enhance the development of "compound identities." A pedagogy of difference not only has to assert students' multiplicity of voices, but also deconstruct them, see how they have become what they are, challenge problematic sexist and racist assumptions within them, and reconstruct them. (p. 20)

The production of students' and teachers' identities is embedded in almost every aspect of schooling. Curriculum, pedagogy, testing, discipline policies, norms of behavior, and concepts of what teaching and learning are all contribute to the production of social identities in both subtle and overt ways. When students read history, the identities of the various groups of people involved in the historical events described are being constructed in the process. Kelly (1997) describes the role curricula can play in constructing students' identities:

> Through the institutional base of schools, curriculum serves as a planned means by which some discourses are legitimized and others marginalized or silenced. Such curriculum positions teachers and students in particular (and regulatory) ways in relationship to specified forms of knowledge, through both their absence and their presence, and to specific notions of knowledge-production. As such, curriculum is itself a process and a practice active in the production of subjectivities, of knowing subjects—school subjects—whose engagement with curriculum is relational, that is, based on relations of power into which subjects are (re)positioned differently and inequitably. (p. 18)

Identity, as an embedded theme of critical constructivist pedagogy, involves continuous reflection on how texts, contexts, policies, and practices within schools represent and construct the social identities of selves and others. As such, encouraging students to inquire into their own social identities legitimizes their own desires, experiences, and feelings in relationship to the institution of schooling. As students become sensitive to the ways in which aspects of their own social identities have been constructed, they can begin to understand how other forms of social identity are constructed and maintained as well. Once students begin to question the social constructions of identity to which they are related through their embodied experience, they can begin to question how identities different from their own have been constructed. Schniedewind and Davidson (1998) describe the process:

The similarity in the dynamics of oppression on members of different social groups opens up the possibility for empathy and common understanding. While a white man with a physical disability hasn't experienced racism, he may be able to empathize with a person of color if he makes the connection with his discriminatory experiences rooted in ableism. We can help students make these kinds of connections in our classrooms and schools. (p. 27)

This quote contains the hope of what can be accomplished through a pedagogy that critically addresses issues of identity that are at once personal and social. The personal involves a kind of learning that can be transformative as students begin to understand the social and political dimensions of their own identity. This provides a basis to learn from others about the complexity of their social worlds. The intent is that students might be able to expand their own worlds as they learn from others. Hernandez (1997) writes about such a process:

From a pedagogical perspective, this concept of world as lived in the first person seems to me very important because it makes more visible the living multiplicity of voices, of representations, of experiences, that make people "world" travelers. Traveling as a relational shift from having one subject position to having a different one according to the world or worlds inhabited at the time, not only helps us to get to know and understand others but should be applied to do so. (p. 21)

This concept of a pedagogy that promotes "world traveling" moves us into the hope for working toward greater social justice, which is also a central value of critical constructivist pedagogy. This sharing and critical reflection allows students to begin to recognize both similarities and differences in their worlds and others. This allows for an understanding of difference and an appreciation for diversity that goes way beyond tolerance.

Although it is critically important for students to learn to value and embrace human diversity, this alone is not enough. Individuals do not maintain the social inequality in society, institutions do. Institutional structures involve the social institutions that "regulate" social life. School, media, government, and economic structures are prime examples. Critical theorists focus on institutional structures because of the important roles they play in creating and maintaining possibilities and constraints of groups based on social identity.

In Christensen's (1998) account of her students' critical inquiry into the institutionalized practice of standardized testing, the students began to see the broader social structures that shaped their identities. This shifted their focus from an uncritical acceptance that the tests were fair measures of their own deficiency to a realization that "the test was biased toward the privileged and functioned to segregate students on the basis of social class" (p. 45).

Teaching for Social Justice

Critical constructivist approaches to teaching and learning encourage active engagement in the learning process, social responsibility, and social action. Teaching for social justice involves an explicitly political agenda. This is contrary to the position that traditional versions of education espouse in which objectivity and neutrality are considered ideals. Critical constructivists assume all teaching and learning are political, whether those that engage in them are conscious of this or not. Reification often contributes to our political agendas being concealed even from ourselves. Teaching for social justice involves making our political agendas conscious and explicit. Ayers (1998) sums up the heart and soul of teaching for social justice:

> Education, of course, is an arena of hope and struggle—hope for a better life, and struggle over how to understand and enact and achieve that better life. We find ourselves living in the midst of cruelty and oppression; we uncover a long story of domination, oppression and catastrophe; we come to believe that we can become makers of history—not merely the passive objects of the great drama, but actors and catalysts and full subjects in the action. At that moment we realize that no teaching is or ever can be innocent—it must be situated in a cultural context, an historical flow, an economic condition. Teaching must be toward something; it must take a stand; it is either for or against; it must account for the specific within the universal. (p. xviii)

Critical constructivist teaching involves an agenda toward greater social justice and should involve real opportunities to work for change. This involves both personal and institutional change. Exploring and participating in change strategies and social activism, and building equitable communities, are central to critical constructivist education. The classroom provides a place for creating a democratic community. However, because it is embedded in larger institutions and broader communities, opportunities abound to go beyond the classroom in participating in collective efforts toward social change. Schniedewind and Davidson (1998) summarize what they believe is possible in educating for social justice:

> We also recognize that what we do in schools alone won't change society. By practicing democracy on a small scale students: a) experientially understand what democracy is; b) develop insights about what democracy can be when practiced on a broader scale; c) become knowledgeable about the sources of inequality and approaches to change; d) act to create those changes. These are important first steps.
> In addition to educating students, we can all be involved in broader efforts to foster social equality. Along with our colleagues, students, parents and administrators, we can examine our schools for practices and policies that may maintain discrimination, such as tracking and

hiring practices, and work to change them. We can become involved in community based projects and national organizations committed to social justice and share these efforts with our students. (p. 33)

Teaching for social justice may seem like a risky proposition for many teachers who have been raised to believe education should be a neutral enterprise. Teachers need to assess their school contexts, be sensitive to the social and political dynamics, and learn to be wise about how they enact their social justice teaching. Teaching for social justice is an unfolding process in which teachers and students learn as they go.

Most teachers go into education because they want to make a difference in the lives of children. Teaching for social justice takes this commitment to deeper, more satisfying levels and involves children in making a difference in their own lives and those of others as well. Teachers know how important it is to make a difference in the world, and they want their students to have opportunities to engage in this kind of meaningful learning and work.

SUMMARY

We began this chapter with a brief discussion of behavioral approaches to learning. Then, we introduced the reader to constructivist and social constructionist theories of learning. Constructivist theories focus more on cognitive processes, such as assimilation and accommodation, whereas social constructionist theories emphasize social interaction, context, and language. Critical constructivist theory adds in an emphasis and awareness of power. Major themes of critical constructivism include desire, identity, institutional oppression, and teaching for social justice.

Engaging students in critical constructivist learning allows them to actively engage in learning that is personally meaningful to them because it includes them. Students are encouraged to learn about themselves, their worlds, and others and their worlds. The process of constructivist learning occurs in the context of social interaction, in conversation, dialogue, engagement, and sharing. Diversity is the richest source of critical constructivist learning. Social justice is the inherent goal.

CONSTRUCTING PERSONAL MEANINGS

1. Reflect on your own education. What class in your own history was the most constructivist in nature? What was it like? What do you remember from the class?

2. Think about the three most interesting learning experiences you have ever had. What made them interesting? How were they structured? How can you help create this kind of learning for your own students?

3. Think about your own social identity. What are the identity markers you would use to describe yourself? How do these various aspects of your identity affect you as a student and a teacher?

4. What issues of social justice are most important to you? Inquire into local and national groups that address those issues. This can be done by phone, mail, or Internet, or in person. Find out what you and your students can do to help.

Creating a Participatory Classroom Community

Terry Jo Smith, Scot Danforth, and Suzanne Nice

The classroom is a complex social space where a group of individuals meets, sometimes for many hours, with the intention of learning. Within a critical constructivist framework, that social space is of utmost importance. It not simply a container for learning, it is the substance of learning. It is composed of lives in dynamic relationship. In those relationships, in that social space, learning occurs through interaction and dialogue. To silence the voices is to constrain the learning and alienate the students. So why do many classrooms feel constricting? To answer this question, we need to look at the fundamental beliefs that guide our practice and think deeply about how we want to promote the social, emotional, and academic development of students.

The attention given to the social dimensions and organization of classrooms often goes under the heading of "Classroom Management." However, there are assumptions in the word "management" that we find troubling from a critical constructivist perspective. The metaphor of management implies an active teacher role and a passive student role. The major responsibility for order falls on the teacher and his or her abilities to control the activities of the classroom. Classroom management strategies often provide technologies by which to manage students' behaviors. We prefer to think of the classroom as a complex and variable participatory community. Rather than technologies, we will talk about relationships, processes, and social meaning.

In the previous chapter, we emphasized the social nature of learning in critical constructivist pedagogy. Within this framework, it doesn't make sense to separate the social and academic dimensions of classroom life. In fact, it is the weaving of lives and texts, of histories and knowledge, that is a source of meaningful learning and transformation in critical constructivist pedagogy. Because all knowledge is considered social knowledge in constructivist thought, classroom management approaches that separate the everyday workings of the classroom from academic learning run counter to the underlying assumptions of constructivism.

Top-down approaches of classroom management still dominate schooling, often deeply embedded in institutional cultures. It is common for teachers who engage in constructivist pedagogy to find their approaches in conflict with top-down school discipline processes and policies. We believe constructivist teachers need to be clear about the differences between constructivist and top-down approaches in order to most effectively navigate potential pressures to engage with students through a curriculum of control. In this chapter, we will focus on the social dynamics of the classroom with the assumption that most teachers will have to grapple with institutional cultures that expect teachers to be absolute authorities in the classroom while being passive recipients of dictates sent from above.

We will begin this chapter by looking at tensions between top-down and constructivist pedagogical approaches. Next, we'll provide an overview of behavioral methods and assumptions because they form the foundation of most top-down classroom management methods in use today. Then, we'll address social, emotional, and moral dimensions of the classroom, comparing and contrasting constructivist and behavioral views. We'll complete the chapter with several principles and processes that can help create a participatory classroom community.

FUNDAMENTAL DIFFERENCES IN APPROACH

The differences in constructivist and behavioral approaches, when whittled down to basics, involve fundamentally opposed beliefs about how human beings best learn, as well as how power should be enacted in learning processes. John Dewey and Paulo Freire, two of the most revered educational philosophers of the 20th century, have both addressed these fundamental differences.

In 1938, John Dewey asserted that "The history of educational theory is marked by the opposition between the idea that education is development from within or that it is formation from without" (p. 17). The distinctions he draws between "progressive education" and "traditional education" speak to essential differences in constructivism and behaviorism. Dewey (1938) writes,

> To imposition from above is opposed expression and cultivation of individuality; to external discipline is opposed free activity; to learning from texts and teachers, learning through experience; to acquisition of isolated skills and techniques by drill, is opposed acquisition of them as means of attaining ends which make direct vital appeal; to preparation for a more or less remote future is opposed making the most of opportunities of present life; to static aims and materials is opposed acquaintance with a changing world. (pp. 19–20)

Paulo Freire (1970) described the top-down, authoritarian type of education as a "banking model" in which the students become receptacles for the teacher to fill. In this approach, students are prized for how meekly they allow themselves to be filled. Freire sees a basic contradiction between top-down educational processes and the active inquiry processes essential to developing critical consciousness. This contradiction is played out in the teacher-student relationship. Freire (1970) asserts that we will never solve this contradiction by using the banking concept.

> On the contrary, banking education maintains and even stimulates the contradiction through the following attitudes and practices, which mirror oppressive society as a whole: (a) the teacher teaches and the students are taught; (b) the teacher knows everything and the students know nothing; (c) the teacher thinks and the students are thought about; (d) the teacher talks and the students listen—meekly; (e) the teacher disciplines and the students are disciplined; (f) the teacher chooses and enforces his choice, and the students comply. (p. 73)

Freire (1970) says that it is no surprise that the banking system "regards men as manageable, malleable human beings" (p. 73). He concludes that the banking concept of education interferes with more active learning, developing students who passively accept the world as it is rather than becoming actors in changing it. This serves the purpose of the status quo, while diminishing the capacity of people, especially oppressed people, for participating in the kinds of social change that could lead to greater social justice.

Currently, educational pedagogy based on principles of behavioral theory most clearly embody the top-down, banking system approach decried by Dewey and Freire. These behavioral approaches have become so thoroughly entrenched in education and in pop culture that they are often considered common sense (Kohn, 1993).

Teachers who want to transcend top-down, behavioral approaches will have to tease out what it is about these practices that is problematic. They will need to be able to conceptualize and articulate their departure from commonly accepted practice. Dewey used the word "opposed" to describe the relationship between these two approaches. Constructivist teachers often live these oppositions in their everyday lives in schools.

In the next section, we'll provide an overview of the principles of behavioral modification. We do this because behaviorism is extremely common in schools, and constructivist teachers will most likely find themselves in some conflict with it. We provide this overview in order to compare and contrast behavioral and constructivist approaches in this chapter. We will not address behavioral approaches from a supposed position of neutrality. We have strong preferences for critical constructivist pedagogy because we believe it leads to a deeper, more meaningful type of education and nurtures the development of active, critical thinkers. We find classroom management systems that involve little or no input from students to be lacking in the very educative processes we hold dear as critical constructivists.

THE PRINCIPLES OF BEHAVIOR MODIFICATION

The principles of behavior modification are relatively simple to learn. They involve analyzing and purposefully manipulating the events that occur before and after behavior as a means to shape behaviors in desired ways. These methods are based on the principles of classical conditioning developed by Pavlov (1906) and the principles of operant conditioning developed by Skinner (1971). Both theorists developed their theories in relationship to experiments with animal behavior and applied them to human behavior. Taken together, the theories of classical conditioning and operant conditioning provide the basis of many of the classroom management approaches used with children today.

Behaviorists look carefully at classroom environments and events and try to eliminate or reduce the antecedent events that might trigger undesirable behaviors. This is based on principles of classical conditioning, articulated by Pavlov (1906). He realized that if he rang a bell before he let his dogs eat, after a few times of pairing bells and food, the bell alone was enough to make his dogs salivate. Salivation in relationship to food is a natural reflex, but salivation in relationship to the ringing of a bell is known as a conditioned reflex. Those who are involved in constructing and maintaining environments for troubling children often spend time trying to determine what in the immediate environment triggers undesirable behaviors in students.

This approach leads to a purposeful structuring of the environment to best elicit desired behaviors. More often than not, teachers try to eliminate things that trigger undesired behaviors. A student who becomes distracted from doing his or her work when sitting by a window might be moved to a different area in the classroom. Two children who argue after being seated near one another might be moved to opposite sides of the room. In these examples, structuring the environment to reduce harmful triggers seems like common sense, but the extremes to which this is taken with resistant children often leads to very restrictive environments. We have seen classrooms in which students are isolated from one another as much as possible, not allowed out of their seats, and given extremely routine tasks in order to reduce possibilities for disruptive behavior.

The other important focus in behavior modification involves the relationship between behavior and the consequences that follow behavior. The important emphasis is whether or not the behavior is followed by a pleasant or an aversive experience. Rats that are shocked each time they push a lever learn not to push it. Rats who are fed each time they push a lever learn to push it more. These are principles of operant conditioning. As B. F. Skinner (1971) explains,

> A much more important role is played by behavior which weakens harmful stimuli in another way. It is not acquired in the way of conditioned reflexes, but as the process of a different process called operant conditioning. When a bit of behavior is followed by a certain kind of consequence, it is more likely to occur again, and a consequence having this effect is called a reinforcer. Food, for example, is a reinforcer to a hungry organism; anything the organism does that is followed by the receipt of food is more likely to be done again whenever the organism is hungry. (p. 25)

In addition to reinforcers that are experienced as pleasurable and thereby increase the likelihood of repeating the behaviors that precede them, reinforcers can also be aversive. In behavioral methodology, aversives are also used to modify behavior. Skinner (1971) explains that

> negative reinforcers are called aversive in the sense that they are the things which organisms "turn away from." . . . Escape and avoidance play a much more important role in the struggle for freedom when the aversive conditions are generated by other people. Other people can be aversive without, so to speak, trying: they can be rude, dangerous, contagious, or annoying, and one escapes from them or avoids them accordingly. They may also be "intentionally" aversive—that is, they may treat other people aversively because of what follows. Thus, a slave driver induces a slave to work by whipping him when he stops; by resuming work the slave escapes from the whipping (and incidentally reinforces the slave driver's behavior in using the whip). (p. 26)

According to behavioral logic, aversives can be used as punishment, to extinguish a target behavior, or as a negative reinforcer (as in the example above) in which the intention is to increase a behavior (work) through the threat and use of the whip when the behavior stops. The removal of the whip—taking away something that is aversive—is used to increase a desired behavior.

ELEMENTS OF BEHAVIORAL ANALYSIS

Behavioral principles can be used with groups or individuals. Behavioral analysis is used when responding to problem behaviors and in efforts to shape more desired behaviors. Behavioral analysis involves a systematic process of identifying target behaviors (those the teacher considers problematic and wants to extinguish), as well as an analysis of the antecedents and reinforcers. Charles (1996) describes this procedure:

> Analysis involves clarification of the behaviors that are causing concern, specifying what is wrong with them at present and deciding exactly what they should be like in the future. Analysis should also focus on antecedents, conditions existent in the classroom that may be contributing to the problem, and consequences, the system of rewards and punishments presently used, or that should be used, to motivate and guide student behavior. (p. 37)

Once a teacher has identified target behaviors as well as antecedents and reinforcers that might be influencing the behaviors, he or she sets up a system of rewards and punishments in an effort to shape the behaviors of students.

CLASSROOM MANAGEMENT SYSTEMS

Behavioral principles are often used with an entire class or school through the institution of a classroom management system. Although there are many variations, the rules-rewards-punishment (RRP) model is very common in schools around the country. The approach begins with rules, includes rewards, but also incorporates punishments for breaking the rules. Charles (1996) describes the basic elements of RRP.

> Rules, few in number, are established, understood, and put on written display. The teacher explains that compliance with the rules is expected. Students who follow the rules will be rewarded in various ways: they will receive praise if appropriate; they will receive laudatory notes to take home to parents; or they will earn points that count toward a larger reward, either for themselves or the whole class.
>
> Students are also clearly informed about what will happen if the rules are broken. They realize it is their prerogative to break the rules but that if they do so, they will simultaneously choose the consequences (mild punishments) attached to rule breaking, which will be involved immediately in accordance with procedures that have been described fully and carefully. (p. 35)

Charles's description is presented with a tone of certainty that often accompanies behavioral theory. It seems one need only set the plan in motion, and from there, everything works like clockwork. The central concerns of critical constructivist pedagogy—such as issues of culture, identity, multiple social meanings, teacher/student relationship, desire, critical thinking, and the value of collaboration and negotiation—are absent in these descriptions.

WHAT ARE WE EDUCATING FOR?

Often, behavioral practices are justified by teachers, who say that they "work." Alfie Kohn (1993), a leading critic of behavioral approaches, asks us to question what we mean when we say a behavioral approach "works." He simplifies behaviorism to one fundamental principle: "The best way to get something done is to provide a reward to people when they act the way we want them to" (p. 3). He says a core concept is, "You do this and you'll get that" (p. 3). This principle is apparent in large doses in most schools, and Kohn points out inherent limitations in this approach: "Rewards do not generally alter the attitudes and emotional commitments that underlie our behaviors. They do not make deep, lasting changes because they are aimed at affecting only what we do" (p. 41).

Kohn (1993) prompts us to think more deeply about our long-term objectives. It is easy to get swept up in an institutional culture and simply do what is expected without thinking through what we are trying to achieve. This seems particularly true when it comes to the ways in which classroom communities are formed and governed. Kohn asks critical questions:

> If your objective is to get people to obey an order, to show up on time and do what they're told, then bribing them or threatening them might be sensible strategies. But if your objective is to get long-term quality in the workplace, to help students become careful thinkers and self-directed learners, or to support children in developing good values, then rewards, like punishments, are absolutely useless. In fact, we are beginning to see, they are worse than useless—they are actually counterproductive. (pp. 41–42)

Charles (1996) states in his description of the popular rules-rewards-punishment system that "the teacher explains that compliance with the rules is expected" (p. 35). Compliance is what classroom management approaches are *for* or *about*. Although this may seem advantageous in the short run, the long-term impact of such practices is rarely contemplated. However, critical educators such as Freire and Dewey, who are concerned with the social development of students as moral agents and critical thinkers, equate top-down education methods with the production of passive citizens, unable to actively participate in democracy. Freire (1973) contends that education should be a practice of freedom rather than simply adaptation. He asserts that participants need to have opportunities to affect the context in which they learn:

> *Integration* with one's context, as distinguished from *adaptation,* is a distinctively human activity. Integration results from the capacity to adapt oneself to reality *plus* the critical capacity to make choices and to transform that reality. To the extent that man loses his ability to make choices and is subjected to the choices of others, to the extent that his decisions are no longer his own because they result from external prescriptions, he is no longer integrated. (p. 4)

Often, classroom management techniques are based on attempts to get students to adapt to the school and classroom culture. However, Freire asserts that education as a practice of freedom involves students at the level of participation in transforming classroom culture. This is an essential difference in critical constructivist and top-down approaches.

MORAL DEVELOPMENT

An important question for educators to ask involves the distinction between "shaping" students' behaviors and promoting their moral development. Lawrence Kohlberg (1967, 1984), a developmental psychologist, developed a hierarchical schema of moral development through which he believes children evolve. This hierarchy of moral development has three levels (see Table 3.1). Each level has two stages. Notice how the first level, known as the premoral level, echoes the behavioral themes presented above.

Thomas (1992) explains that in the first stage of the Preconventional Level, referred to as the Obedience and Punishment Orientation, a child judges whether an action is good or bad based on whether it results in a punishment. Doing the "right thing" is equated with avoiding punishment. This judgment does not involve the human meaning of the act, just its consequences. The second stage of the Preconventional Level is referred to as the Naive Instrumental Orientation. This stage involves actions based on what "pays off" for the child, not on a sense of justice or loyalty. Thomas describes the motivations that are characteristic of the Preconventional Level as follows: "A person follows society's rules of right and wrong but in terms of the physical or hedonistic consequences (punishment, reward, exchange of favors) and in view of the power of the authority who imposes the rules" (p. 501).

The second level of moral development in Kohlberg's schema is the Conventional Level and involves conformity to the expectations of the family, group, or nation. The third level is the Postconventional Level, in which moral behavior is first defined in terms of individual rights but advances toward universal principles of justice.

Behavior modification is the systematic enactment of the Premoral Level of development. This is particularly problematic in light of Kohlberg's beliefs about how moral development is fostered. Kohlberg believed that children's moral development is a result of both the child's genetic inheritance and the child's environment. Because the environment is what is affected by the use of behavior modification, we will focus on that aspect here. Kohlberg theorized that the environmental aspects affecting children's moral development are "(1) the child's opportunities to learn social roles and (2) the form of justice in the social institutions with which the child is familiar" (Thomas, 1992, p. 503).

The behavior modification systems commonly used in schools, according to Kohlberg's schema, do not involve moral reasoning at all. Drummed into students' heads all day is the morally bankrupt message of "behave and you'll be rewarded." If the form of justice in social institutions affects moral development,

Table 3.1   Kohlberg's (1967, 1984) Levels of Moral Development

Level	Stage	Social Orientation	Defining Features
Pre-Conventional (Premoral)	1	Obedience and punishment	Follow norms set by authority figures
	2	Naïve instrumental	Act in own self-interest
Conventional	3	Good boy/girl	Seek approval of others
	4	Law and order	Abide by laws and rules
Post-Conventional	5	Social contract	Seek welfare of others as inseparable from own welfare
	6	Principled conscience	Follow universal principles of justice for all

as Kohlberg has suggested, then classrooms provide promising opportunities to promote moral development. In particular, a classroom culture that is based on the concept of a community has the potential to promote moral development that involves rights and responsibilities, as well as relationships between the individual and the group. We are deeply concerned by the long-term impact of classrooms that operate on premoral principles.

GILLIGAN'S THEORY OF MORAL DEVELOPMENT: A CARE ORIENTATION

Carol Gilligan (1977, 1982, 1988) has effectively challenged Kohlberg's justice orientation to moral development as being incomplete. Kohlberg's theories adhere to a view of healthy child development in which the child becomes more and more autonomous, or independent, as he or she develops. Gilligan (1988) has described another aspect of normal development that involves a healthy attachment to others rather than the independent, autonomous self idealized in Kohlberg's theory. Both the ability to become independent and the ability to forge lasting bonds are healthy aspects of moral development. Without diminishing the insights of Kohlberg's theory, Gilligan's (1988) work has added another dimension of moral development that is concerned with care:

> From the perspective of someone seeking or valuing care, relationship connotes responsiveness or engagement, a resiliency of connection that is symbolized by a network or web. Moral concerns focus on problems of detachment, on disconnection or abandonment or indifference, and the moral ideal is one of attention and response. (pp. xvii-xviii)

Noddings (1984) tells us that when we operate from an ethic of care, we can't make decisions about how to respond to others based on principles alone. Rather, we must enter into dialogue with others to find out what they need. We need to provide children opportunities to care for others as well as be cared for themselves. In a care perspective, fostering caring classroom relationships is imperative for moral development. There is concern that in classroom environments where the main emphasis is on earning rewards, relationships suffer. Kohn (1993) tells us:

> Rewards also disrupt relationships in very particular ways that are demonstrably linked to learning, productivity, and the development of responsibility. They have these effects both with respect to horizontal relationships (those among peers) and vertical relationships (those among people whose status is different, such as teacher and student, parent and child, supervisor and employee). (p. 54)

According to Kohn, rewards rupture horizontal relationships by setting up competition and by causing jealousy among peers. When students have their eyes on the prize, they tend to discount the importance of cooperation with others. Often, in an attempt to overcome this problem with horizontal relationships, rewards are given on a groupwide basis. However, this sets up other difficulties, because children who "ruin it for the group" are often the target of anger and retaliation from classmates.

The vertical relationships, or those between students and teachers, are even more strained by the use of behavior modification. Most teachers want to establish a caring relationship with students that will allow the students to trust them. They want students to come to them to talk about problems as well as feel safe to own up to their mistakes. This important goal is undermined by the continued emphasis on the teacher in the role of rewarder and punisher. Kohn (1993) describes the unfortunate dynamic:

> This is precisely what rewards and punishments kill. If your parent or teacher or manager is sitting in judgment of what you do, if that judgment will determine whether good things or bad things happen to you, this cannot help but warp your relationship with that person. You will not be working collaboratively in order to learn or grow; you will be trying hard to get him or her to approve of what you are doing so you can get the goodies. (p. 57)

Piaget and DeVries

The work of DeVries and her colleagues (DeVries, 1997, 1998; DeVries, Haney, & Zan, 1991; DeVries & Zan, 1994) provides further insight into how the ways in which we construct classroom cultures affect students' moral development beginning at very young ages. DeVries has conducted studies in which she has looked at the moral development and behavior of very young students in relationship to the interaction styles of teachers. Her work illustrates the conflict between behavioral approaches and moral development described above. In summarizing Piaget's beliefs about moral development, DeVries

(1998) discusses two types of morality that are developed in relationship to two types of adult-child relationships. The first, morality of obedience, is developed in relationships with adults that are based on coercion or constraint. This type of relation is called *heteronomous*, which means it is regulated by others. DeVries (1998) describes the impact of these types of relationships on moral development:

> In Piaget's view, following the rules of others through a morality of obedience will never lead to the kind of reflection necessary for commitment to the internal or autonomous principles that typify moral character. Piaget warned that coercion socializes only the surface of behavior and actually reinforces the child's tendency to rely on regulation by others. That is, coercion has three possible effects: Mindless conformity, rebellion, or calculation. By "calculation" I refer to following adult rules only when under surveillance and not following them when away from adult observation. (p. 41)

According to DeVries (1998), the second type of adult-child relationship that Piaget describes is called *autonomous* or *cooperative*. This type of relationship involves mutual respect. He believed that when adults abstain from imposing unnecessary control and coercion, children are able to develop moral feelings and convictions. DeVries tells us that a teacher who operates from a cooperative stance with students "considers the child's point of view and encourages the child to consider others' points of view" (p. 41).

DeVries (1988) researched the impact of these two relational styles on students' ability to solve interpersonal conflicts. She collected and studied more than 6,000 interactions between children in three kindergarten classrooms in lower-income urban neighborhoods. The three classrooms were selected based on the nature of classroom management styles used by the teachers. One classroom, which DeVries called the "Boot Camp," was characterized by heteronomous relationships between students and teachers. Another classroom, named the "Community," was characterized by cooperative relationships between teachers and children. The third classroom, known as the "Factory," was a mix of these two styles. Her research showed significant differences in how the children in these classrooms interacted with one another. DeVries describes the results:

> Children from the Community were more actively engaged with one another. They had more friendly, shared experiences and not only negotiated more, but negotiated more successfully. Community children used a greater variety of different strategies and resolved twice as many conflicts as children from the Boot Camp and the Factory. Boot Camp children tended to resolve conflicts by overwhelming the other physically or emotionally and, in general, related in less complex ways. Moreover, children from the Community used significantly more strategies reflecting consideration for the other's point of view and efforts to achieve mutually satisfying interactions. (p. 44)

The conclusion that DeVries draws from her extensive research is that teachers may not be aware of the type of interpersonal development their classroom atmosphere promotes. She believes that teachers who interact with students through top-down, behavioral methods set up a socio-moral atmosphere that is detrimental to students' moral development. She suggests that this is the case in most schools.

WORKING WITH KIDS WHO ARE HURTING

A very clear pattern is beginning to emerge from the most recent studies of children identified by the school as having serious emotional and behavioral problems. Around half are children from poor families, often single parent families. Their lives have been difficult; some studies suggest that as many as one-half have been victims of sexual or physical abuse. The pervasiveness of these patterns is stunning, posing both treatment and educational implications that, to a large extent, neither the schools nor mental health have confronted. (Knitzer et al., 1990, p. 17)

Although we are concerned about the impact of behavior modification practices on human relationships in general, we are particularly troubled by the impact on students who are suffering or grieving. Often, the most distressed children end up in special programs in which top-down practices, compliance, and control are pervasive characteristics of the curriculum and environment. This is true in special schools for students labeled Emotionally/Behaviorally Disordered, in schools in low-income areas, and in programs for at-risk students. Often, the students with whom behavioral modification is used in its most extreme forms are students who have had, and continue to have, extremely difficult lives.

The behaviors that have been typically associated by psychologists with grieving or extreme suffering in children are the same behaviors targeted for extinction in behavior modification systems. Grief is a natural, human reaction to personal experiences of loss. We are not talking only about grief that occurs after the death of a loved one. We are referring to a wide range of losses that students can encounter in their lives, such as the loss of innocence that comes with sexual abuse; the loss of trust that comes with abandonment; and the losses that occur when parents get divorced, are in abusive relationships, are physically sick or die, are addicted to drugs or alcohol, or are going through extreme traumas. Grieving can also come in relation to living in dangerous, high-crime neighborhoods where students see others die, go to prison, suffer police brutality, and encounter high rates of joblessness and addiction. Grieving can come from the loss of hope.

Lagorio (1993) tells us that children often respond to grief differently from adults. She describes several areas of a child's functioning that may be affected:

Cognitive—preoccupation, disorganized thinking, decline in academic performance, worry . . . , confusion.

Behavioral—acting out, withdrawing, truancy, overeating or under-eating, daydreaming.

Emotional—guilt, fear of intimacy, anger, sadness, loneliness. (p. 4)

If we think of troubling student behaviors as signs of grieving rather than signs of disorder or disrespect, the commonsense approach is one of support and understanding. The expressions of grief, whether in sadness, anger, or even agitated denial, are all natural and healthy parts of healing, yet these very same behaviors are often the target of behavior modification. Unlike hungry rats in a maze, children who have suffered tragedies in their lives have much more complex sources of pain gnawing at them. It is not so simple to alleviate their discomforts with a candy bar or a promise of a movie on Friday.

Alice Miller (1986, 1990a, 1990b), writing from a psychodynamic perspective, proposes that society pays a great price when we do not allow children to experience, own, and express their anger and hurt. Miller makes a convincing case that when children are given no legitimate means by which to express their feelings, and when the manipulative motives of adults are disguised and denied, anger is often channeled into violent reactions. As Miller (1986) writes,

A person who can understand and integrate his anger as part of himself will not become violent. He has the need to strike out at others only if he is thoroughly unable to understand his rage, if he was not permitted to become familiar with this feeling as a small child, was never able to experience it as part of himself because such a thing was totally unthinkable in his surroundings. (p. 65)

When children are punished for showing anger, rather than learning to understand and integrate anger, the anger does not get resolved, but repressed. From a psychodynamic position, punishing students for expressing the way they feel is a pathological response to a child's pain. How much more so when this response is embedded in a system that ignores the child's inner states altogether?

DIVERSITY, RESISTANCE, AND BEHAVIOR

In addition to the individual social and emotional history of each child, broad social issues and group experiences also need to be taken into account in the classroom. In recent years, a strong critique of schooling has emerged from several different social movements. Because of the ongoing work of critical educational theorists, there is a growing awareness that education in the United States functions to justify and fortify existing social hierarchies. There is a growing recognition that school is often a painful experience for students who do not fit the norms that reflect white, heterosexual, middle-class values.

Several critical theorists (Brantlinger, 1993; Giroux, 1983; Kohl, 1991; MacLeod, 1995; McLaren, 1985, 1993, 1994) have suggested that students of color and students living in poverty often actively resist the inherent cruelty and oppression of schooling. Herb Kohl (1991) wrote an excellent essay on resistance called *I Won't Learn From You,* which describes this phenomenon in convincing detail. He named the resistance of marginalized students "not-learning." He describes the origin of this resistance:

> Not-learning tends to take place when someone has to deal with unavoidable challenges to her or his personal and family loyalties, integrity, and identity. In such situations there are forced choices and no apparent middle ground. To agree to learn from a stranger who does not respect your integrity causes a major loss of self. The only alternative is to not-learn and reject the stranger's world.
>
> Students who have been marginalized in society and school often protest in the form of not-learning. Often, this not-learning results in limitations on students' opportunities for future success in school and work. Resistance often takes on the forms of behaviors we see in troubling students. (p. 29)

The signs of not-learning are evident in large numbers in E/BD programs, at-risk programs, correctional educational facilities, and many inner-city schools. Not-learning may take the form of not-learning to read, not-learning to "behave," or not-learning to conform. Too often, schools respond to resistance by attempting to coerce children to "behave," as if the healthy response to oppression is conformity and compliance. However, as Kohl (1991) has pointed out and Skinner (1973) has made exceeding clear, resistance to painful situations is both a normal and a healthy response.

The pain of existing social hierarchies for marginalized students is often difficult for those who have more privilege to understand (Delpit, 1993). The overrepresentation of students of color and poor students in special programs for troubling students is not surprising in relationship to resistance theories. A narrow focus on rules and behaviors eclipses social and political dynamics and thereby works to reinforce the white, middle-class values embedded in most school systems. This is not necessarily a conscious effort to oppress marginalized groups, but often the well-intended efforts of people who mistake their own cultural norms for universal truths. Lisa Delpit (1993) makes a similar point with regard to cultural differences. She contends that we are often unaware of the differences in the worlds of meanings that we and our students carry inside of our heads. She tells us:

> We all carry worlds in our heads, and those worlds are decidedly different. We educators set out to teach, but how can we reach the worlds of others when we don't even know they exist? Indeed, many of us don't even realize that our own worlds exist only in our heads and in the cultural institutions we have built to support them. (pp. xiv-xv)

Proponents of social justice champion teachers who are trying to understand the worlds inside their students' heads. Delpit (1993) tells us this requires trying to see with the student and reflect on one's own behavior from the student's perspective.

> To do so takes a very special kind of listening, listening that requires not only open eyes and ears, but hearts and minds. We do not really see through our eyes and hear through our ears, but through our beliefs. To put our beliefs on hold is to cease to exist as ourselves for a moment— that is not easy. It is painful as well, for it means turning yourself inside out, giving up your sense of who you are, and being willing to see your- self in the unflattering light of another's angry gaze. It is not easy, but it is the only way to learn what it might be like to be someone else and the only way to start the dialogue. (p. 47)

The kind of dialogue that Delpit proposes is central to constructivist teach- ing. It is important for constructivist teachers to understand how students are constructing the meanings they bring to texts, the classroom, and life. It is only then that teachers can truly engage with children to negotiate the social mean- ings of the classroom.

LIVING THE CONFLICTS OF PRACTICE

Often, new teachers are presented with textbook versions of behavior modifi- cation and begin their teaching feeling confident they have the tools they need to "manage" classroom behaviors. Below, the journal entries of a first-year teacher in her second month of teaching in a tough inner-city school capture the difficulties teachers often encounter when trying to apply behavioral "inter- ventions" with students who are experiencing significant social and emotional stress.

> S's mother came in today screaming and shouting and smacking her daughter. I HAD to call home the day before since S was tormenting other kids. She takes the pushpins out of the walls when I'm not look- ing and pokes kids . . . she tells the kids that their mothers are whores, has told classmates to "suck my dick" and regularly swears at other kids. . . . Her mother said that if her daughter didn't beat up C (who had allegedly thrown a basketball at her face the day before), she would— and she would go to jail if she had to. The girl is an unfocused menace in class but she loves to read and is eager to tell us what they did at library. Even when I yell at her, she gives me a hug, handshake, high five, and kiss before she goes home. She's so needy. These, to me, seem to be the signs of emotional abuse. Always worried about some marks on her—cigarette burns on her arm, strange marks (like a belt or other

big object) that struck her abdomen? Will tell the counselor. . . . The whole family has a bad reputation at the school amongst teachers, staff and students.

Reading this part of the teacher's journal, one realizes that the behaviors that are deemed so inappropriate in relationship to school rules may make sense within the broader contexts of a student's life. As disruptive as this student's behaviors are, as this teacher surmised, they are likely the signs of and reactions to abuse. Plus, this student's behavior is not out of line with her parent's nor the norms of the tough inner-city neighborhood in which she lives. The child's mother encourages her daughter to fight. This is not unusual, because children who do not learn to fight can be easily victimized in some inner-city environments (Canada, 1995). Yet the fighting that may help a child survive in her neighborhood keeps her at odds within the school.

This teacher sees the parent striking the child in her presence. The complexity of troubling behavior is so apparent in this description. Yet initially, this teacher resorts to what she has been taught in her education courses and to the heavy-handed, top-down approach that is the norm in her school. In spite of all the reasons this child might act the way she does, the teacher reasons how she might shape this student's behavior through reinforcement. She writes,

> May try special behavior plan with her next week—good from 9 till 11:30, get a sticker; good during lunch and bathroom breaks—another sticker; well behaved from 12:15–2:30—another one. Maybe smaller increments are necessary for behavior modification.

To us, this approach seems like an absurdly simplistic and cruel response to this child, and yet we have seen this type of response thousands of times in our work in schools. Giving an abused child stickers to be compliant in school seems both doomed to failure and insensitive. Later in the week, this same teacher turns a critical eye on the behavioral practices in which she had been trained and is expected to use. She writes,

> The behaviorist principles have been instituted in my classroom and every day I come home sadder and angrier. Not a single lesson plan has been completed and I feel the kids are learning nothing, except some core "School Values." I am starting to doubt my entire role in such a school community. If virtually no one believes my students will go to college, and the greater society has already written off my little ones as poor, black, ghettoized, what can I do by making them keep their antsy little bottoms implanted on the seats of this prison? Students like S, the bully who has not a single friend in our class, or M, whose father is in prison and gets in the middle of a fight every day, what good are these ridiculous school policies? . . . One school rule after another is at odds with their out-of-school reality. The community I have been trying to

build continues to be sabotaged as the kids compete for the right answer for a measly Tootsie Roll.

The frustration this teacher felt was echoed by nearly every one of the first-year, inner-city teachers in her education class. As these teachers began to get a glimpse of the worlds in which their students lived, the school policies and behavioral methods began to seem extremely inadequate.

In her journal, the teacher reflects on how at odds the school and community values are. She recognizes that students' behaviors and her own behaviors may be interpreted differently by her students and their families. This recognition gets at some of what we mean by realizing that the meaning of behavior is socially constructed. This places a responsibility on teachers to get to know their students and their families in order to understand their meanings, and to reflect on their own meanings as well. It is best to assume that students' behaviors make sense to them and seek to understand the beliefs, experience, logic, and values to which they adhere.

SYSTEMIC CHANGE

One of the broadest examples of systemic change from top-down to child-centered classrooms has been undertaken by H. Jerome Freiberg and his colleagues. Freiberg (1999a, 1999b) has developed a nonbehavioral model called Consistency Management and Cooperative Discipline (CMCD). This model has been researched extensively in controlled studies and has been used with more than 40,000 students and teachers. It has been implemented on a large scale in whole districts.

One of the major trusts of the CMCD program is to involve students as partners and stakeholders in the classroom. The emphasis on building a cooperative community happens at all levels of instruction and classroom management. Freiberg describes the difference between this approach and a behavioral orientation as the difference between being a tourist and a citizen. Tourists don't have an investment, a sense of ownership, or strong ties with people. Citizenship requires participation, responsibility, and the development of deeper relationships.

CMCD focuses on instruction and discipline and sees these two as "two sides of the same coin." The CMCD model involves five themes: Prevention, Caring, Cooperation, Organization, and Community. Prevention stems from an understanding that sometimes, student misbehavior is a healthy reaction to an unhealthy environment. Creating an environment in which students share ownership and responsibility is conducive to preventing the types of protests that are often labeled as misbehavior. Caring involves honoring students by listening to them, involving them, and sharing oneself with them. Cooperation involves the building of trust as students learn to take ownership in the classroom. Organization involves students in the everyday running of the classroom.

Students apply for classroom jobs. Jobs are rotated so that all students have opportunities to take leadership roles. Community involves building relationships in the classroom, school, and surrounding community. CMCD focuses on building up the very things Kohn (1993) has suggested that behaviorism breaks down: trust, communication, intrinsic motivation (ownership of the process), cooperation, and involvement.

The CMCD model has been, and continues to be, extensively researched. The results have been very encouraging. In summarizing the results of research on the program, Freiberg (1999a, 1999b) reports an increase in student and teacher attendance, significant increases in student achievement, and significant reduction in discipline referrals. In a 4-year study of seven elementary schools in which CMCD was implemented, the number of behavioral referrals declined from a total of 1,017 the year before the program was implemented to 265 during the third year.

In addition to empirical studies on CMCD, qualitative studies were conducted that elicited teachers' and students' impressions of the program. One teacher described the emphasis as "I think it teaches responsibility, kindness, and respect, and those are the things they need to learn" (Freiberg, 1999b, p. 78). Judy Kirby, an English teacher for 25 years, describes the difference before and after implementing CMCD:

> It is early May. I look at my fifth-hour class and marvel at the climate of cooperation in a room full of 30 14-year-olds, hungry ones at that. They aren't disagreeing, sleeping, being insubordinate, or indifferent. They are enjoying learning and one another.
>
> Last year, I spent all my time trying to control my students. This year the students know they matter. The negative attention-getting has stopped— there is no longer a need for it. They belong. (Freiberg, 1999b, p. 75)

One has to wonder, when whole schools and school districts move away from top-down behavioral approaches into a collaborative model and show dramatic decreases in behavioral problems and increases in cooperation, learning, and engagement, what is happening to our kids in the more restrictive behavioral programs? Are we creating situations that engender resistance and opposition? Are we structuring relationships between human beings in ways that create oppression, anger, and pain?

CONSTRUCTING CARING CLASSROOM COMMUNITIES

It is important to make conscious the assumptions and principles one takes into teaching and classroom management. This has been the purpose of the above discussion. Our hope is that it will help teachers clarify what they are doing and why, as well as give you criteria by which to evaluate your own classroom community. In the following pages, we become much more practical in our approach and suggest several processes and practices for creating a participatory classroom culture. However, there are no formulas. What we offer are processes, principles, and some possibilities.

Many different factors affect how teachers promote the social, emotional, and moral development of students and construct a participatory community within the classroom. This is an evolving, dynamic process. The challenges of first-year teachers are often different from those of veteran teachers. Each group of students, each teacher, each classroom, and each school have different challenges and possibilities. We do not offer formulas or one right answer. Instead, what we hope to encourage are reflective, collaborative processes that allow for the emergence of a caring community that learns, loves, laughs, and creatively solves problems together. We'll use excerpts from a case study of a gifted constructivist teacher to offer a glimpse of how one veteran teacher establishes a caring learning community in a first-grade classroom.

AN EXEMPLARY CASE STUDY

The following portrait of the pedagogical practices of a teacher named Dee is based on the dissertation research of Suzanne Nice (2003). Nice is a school psychologist who works therapeutically with students in an elementary school. Nice began to notice that some teachers in the school were exceptionally gifted in relating to students who were experiencing social and emotional difficulties. She became curious about what these gifted teachers did in their classrooms that allowed them to work so effectively with troubling students.

Her dissertation study involved extensive observations and interviews of three exemplary teachers, but the case study of Dee Grant is the centerpiece of the study. Dee is an experienced, talented, and caring constructivist teacher who has continued to learn from and with her students for more than 20 years. She is recognized by teachers, administrators, students, and parents as an exceptional teacher. We will focus on issues related to how Dee thought about and nurtured the classroom community and how that community provided a context for supporting even the most troubled and troubling students. In excerpts from the study, Dee's words will be represented in italics.

Nice (2003) describes the physical environment of Dee's room and how it is an enactment of Dee's philosophy of teaching:

> As the students enter the classroom they are entering an environment that has been carefully prepared for them. As I enter the classroom, I have two impressions. The first impression is a feeling of warmth. The room has a cozy and inviting feel. The second impression is books, books, books. . . .
>
> There is a picture of the entire class with a calendar of the school year. Each person's birthday will be noted and highlighted on the poster. On

the right wall of the entrance way are photo albums of the class that sit on top of the bookshelves. There are black letters on the glass to the right of the door that say, "We are all one family under the sky."

Inside the doorway is a bulletin board that is titled "Random Acts of Kindness." There are books mounted that support that concept. On the back wall of the classroom the words "The Family" are mounted in wood letters. As each student walks into the room on the first day of school, they will see their name on this wall. Later, the wall will contain pictures of the class engaged in various activities or examples of students' work. The front of the classroom also has letters that state "We Are Family." Below these are words or phrases that reflect Dee's philosophy and that will be actively taught to the students. These statements are:

> Believe in yourself.
> Make a list of five things you are thankful for every day.
> Act with kindness. Helping others is the best way to help yourself.
> You never run out of love. You can give lots of it away and still have plenty left over for yourself.
> Each morning take time to imagine the person you want to be.
> Spread respect and tolerance.
> A positive attitude is contagious.
> No learning ever goes to waste.
> Become someone you can be proud of.
> Anything worth doing is worth doing well.
> Your best effort is in itself its own reward.
> At day's end ask yourself what have I learned today.

What is missing from this classroom is a list of class rules. Dee does not post group rules that relate to listening, raising your hand, etc. Instead, she posts materials related to the attitudes or behaviors that she wants to promote in her class. . . .

Over the months and years that I have been observing Dee, I have begun to view the physical environment of the classroom as an extension of her philosophies. The physical environment is a visual representation of the personal relationships that will develop as the year progresses. Thus, the ecological environment of the classroom is reflected in the physical environment. (pp. 92–94)

As a constructivist researcher, Nice wants to get at the beliefs and philosophies that provide the foundation of Dee's work. Nice describes her interpretation of this process and then asks Dee to describe the theoretical influences on her teaching.

Dee's personal beliefs have driven how she sets up instruction, the physical environment, and her daily interactions with students. However, this is a reciprocal arrangement, because the results of daily events influence how she modifies her theories and instructional practices. Dee's teaching practices are guided by constant self-reflection and self-critique that serve as an ongoing process connecting her beliefs to her practices. Dee discussed the development of ideas that would shape her teaching practices.

When I got here in 1980 I read a book by Donald Graves about writing. I picked that book up and was influenced by it. In college I was always into Carl Rogers. One of the most important things a teacher can be in the classroom is a genuine person. If you're mad, you're mad. If you're happy, you're happy. If you're a grouchy person and come everyday as a grouchy person then the kids will know that. But above all be genuine. So I had those whole things in my mind in college. I had decided to be a facilitator more than a teacher. Because there's a difference about being a facilitator. My goal is to show—is to expose kids to things and then let them go off. (Nice, 2003, p. 96)

Working with first graders, Dee recognizes that these processes need to be taught and practiced before students can enact them on their own. However, her goal is to prepare students to take ownership of their learning on all fronts. Thus, Dee teaches the students a process to use in literature circles and then describes what happens:

I love the idea of reciprocal teaching. When the kids go to literature circle the four steps are in there. Summarizing, questioning, clarifying and predictions. The kids use those four things and they run their own literature circles. If there is something they need to clarify, they write it down. They know how to make predictions. Then they summarize. If they have just read two chapters, they can tell me in the least amount of words what those chapters were about. (Nice, 2003, p. 115)

The same philosophy goes into preparing students to take ownership of the social processes in the classroom as well. Nice (2003) explains that

when the students are having problems or do not know what to do, Dee has also spent an intensive amount of time during the first month of school teaching the students a six step problem solving process. She will reinforce this and discuss the process throughout the school year. The students will have explicit instruction and multiple opportunities to practice. This process can be used for work completion assistance, conflict with a peer, or any problem that arises. Dee identified the following process that she teaches the class.

The first step is to determine what needs to be decided. That's what I have to tell some students in particular. Most of the time when you're getting ready to do something wrong you already know it. That's when they need to go into the problem solving process. After determining what needs to be decided, determine what your choices are and you always have choices. If a student tries to tell me that another student did something too, well okay, what does that have to do with your choices? After you determine what the choices are you have to think about the choices. The fourth step is to choose the best alternative and fifth step is to do it. And then the last step is to think back over your decision. If you don't feel good about something that you did, if you hurt somebody's feelings, if you find yourself in trouble, then you didn't make a good decision. Don't repeat it. (pp. 108–109)

In addition to directly teaching students processes they can use in problem solving, Dee provides students with abundant opportunities for discussion and participation in the social dimensions of the classroom during class meetings. She explains,

I never schedule class meetings and I don't have a formal process. I tried that stuff, but it didn't work for me. When something happens, we stop what we are doing and go to the rug to talk about it. And the kids know we are going to talk about what is happening. Another thing that I like is that the rug is not a place where we just talk about problems. I do my reading aloud there. . . . We do our literature groups there and we do our math groups there. Everything happens there, but there is not a set time for a class meeting. At the beginning of the year I do it every day. We talk about all kinds of things. If a student walks around alone at recess and doesn't have anyone to play with, then we talk about that on the rug. If there are problems at recess then we talk about that. There are certain things that I just don't let go. Such as peer relationships. I never let that go. Even if the lunchroom lady comes to me and says that it is solved, I still don't let that go. And the reason for that is that the kid who got hurt—I need to let that kid know that I know this has happened. So that the next time a kid has a problem that kid feels like he can come to me. . . . I think those kinds of problems are so important to talk about. So even though it might take 30 minutes to work it out, I never let anything go that has to do with peer relationships. (pp. 121–122)

Dee also uses literature that addresses students' social and emotional issues and as a means to help students conceptualize the classroom as a family. Another practice that she uses involves the word of the week. The word of the week often refers to a concept she wants to teach the children in relationship to their social and emotional development. In the following excerpt, Nice (2003) describes how Dee weaves social learning with academic learning in a seamless and effective manner.

During a whole class math lesson on learning to tell time, Dee congratulates a student who was able to accurately display 8:30 on a clock. She says, "Very nicely done. Very nicely done. Let's clap for that boy." She talks about how difficult understanding time can be. After they all clap, Dee brings in the word of the week, which is self-esteem. Different students give definitions of self-esteem. She then asks the class about last week's word, which was attitude. They talk about how self-esteem and attitude connect, and then Dee connects this to the student who has just shown 8:30 on the clock. She talks about his effort and attitude toward learning to tell time and how the positive experience relates to self-esteem. (p. 125)

The holistic nature of Dee's pedagogy does not separate the social from the academic. She facilitates the creation of a classroom community that is fashioned after a family. This context, as well as her insight into children, her openness to learn from them, and her deep love for her students, come together to form a classroom culture in which even the most troubled and troubling students are able to engage and learn in meaningful ways. The following excerpts contain Dee's explanation of how she worked with Alan, a boy with a history of aggression and noncompliance, when she was his second-grade teacher.

I could see that Alan had a tendency to be a bully and the biggest weapon was his secrecy. Alan needed to have a lot of control. He was big and strong and it was very easy for him to bully the others and the other students never wanted to say anything that he did. Although I don't use punishments, there were a couple of days when he seemed so angry that I knew it wasn't safe to send him to recess. I just had a little voice that said when he goes to recess he is going to get that kid. He couldn't let anything go. So everything we did was out in the open. Every little thing he did I said everybody, we all know he did this and this is what we are going to do as a class. At first, it was the class and Alan. And then slowly he just sort of creeped in. It just didn't pay off for him anymore. He was a smart kid and wanted to learn—so that was his ace in the hole. I think that the schools made a lot of mistakes with him. There were family problems and he had trouble since preschool. In some ways I could relate to Alan and he sort of picked up on that. He was a very angry kid. And my feeling about that is that I don't know what is going on in that home, but maybe he has a right to be angry. I always tell the kids the story of me and growing up and my mom died. I told the whole story and I think that made a big impact on him. I didn't call people when there were problems, I just dealt with them myself. I told him it was between you and me. If he physically punched a kid or something then I would have to call, but I wasn't on the phone every week. Slowly but surely he began to come around. I never forced his work because he was so smart that he already knew most of the stuff in second grade. As far as I was concerned he was part of our family. The kids didn't like him and nobody wanted to sit by him, but we used the words of the week and the six steps. (pp. 136–137)

At the end of the day, I told him that he could make the decision. I could hug him, shake his hand, or do nothing. He said do nothing. So I gave him his space. . . . Whenever he said something or did something to another student we would talk about it and eventually he just came around. Whenever there was a chance that I could stick up for him, I did. One day he wrote in his journal, Ms. Grant taught me the six steps and I'm learning how to make better decisions about my behavior. I was shocked. That happened in two months time and I wouldn't have expected that to happen until May. He types this up and inside my body I'm just jumping up and down. I am so happy, but don't show this because Alan does not like emotion. I didn't have everyone clap for him because I knew that wasn't the right thing to do with him, but I was thrilled he wrote it. I think that's how I gained his trust. (p. 138)

When I talk to Alan I often talk to him like I talk to an adult. We spent weeks talking about the word reputation and what it means to have a reputation. I told him that you have to have a sense of yourself and you can't be worried about everything that everybody thinks about you. But it is also not true that it doesn't matter what other people think about you. I told him that people have seen him be mean to other students and talk back to people. I told him he had a bad reputation at school. We had all of these conversations one-on-one. When the other kids were working we would just sit at the computer and talk. Then we would talk about it indirectly in group. I would confront him if he said mean things to others in a group or during a game. We spent a lot of time talking to each other and little by little he came around. (p. 139)

In this story, we see the integration of many of the processes and practices Dee has developed in her class. She is a teacher who knows her students well and considers their history, feelings, and needs. She is able to support Alan while making sure the class is safe for all of her students. She uses the concept of a family to include Alan and support his development. She does not punish, post rules, or use predetermined classroom management strategies. We see a much deeper, more authentic learning occur in this classroom, where students are taught to solve problems and participate in their own learning.

GETTING STARTED

We shared the troubled reflections of a first-year teacher in an inner-city school earlier in this chapter, as well as the reflections of Dee, a veteran teacher in a middle-class school. These teachers are certainly at different places in their careers and bring different lives to the classroom. They are also teaching in very different institutional cultures. Assuming that many of the people who are reading this text may be new teachers, this section addresses thoughts on assessing an institutional culture to determine role expectations for teachers. This is not an activity that should be done only by new teachers at the beginning of a school year, but should occur as part of an ongoing, reflective process as teachers evolve and grow. However, the urgency for a new teacher to understand the institutional culture may be greater.

At the beginning of a school year, teachers have a number of factors that need to be considered when planning how to initially approach establishing the classroom community. The overall institutional culture must be appraised to understand what the expectations of others will be. Although every school has a range of teaching styles and philosophies within its walls, there are established norms and acceptable practices. Schools differ drastically in some respects. In the United States, the socioeconomic class of the student is often one of the major deciding factors in the social structure of schools. Unfortunately, the more marginalized students and their families are, the more often top-down approaches are used. Sometimes, drastic differences occur within one school or one institution. This is well documented in Brantlinger's (1993) study of one high school, in which low-income students and high-income students experienced a very different school. Thus, a teacher's role expectations may be further defined by the cultural and socioeconomic status of the groups of students he or she teaches.

Based on the critical constructivist assumption that meaning is contextual and socially constructed, a new teacher needs to learn about the meanings in the institutional culture in which he or she has entered. Are teachers expected to be tough disciplinarians? Is punishment heavily used? Are parents involved in the process? The following questions might be helpful guides to such an inquiry. These are not only questions to use in framing one's observations, but also questions one can pose to other teachers and administrators as a means of gathering important information for developing a classroom community.

How do administrators interact with teachers in my school? Are there dialogues or one-way conversations? (Faculty meetings are often a good place to observe the dynamics between administrators, teachers, and staff.) Do people feel free to ask questions or present alternative points of view?

Are there mandated, school-wide classroom management systems in place? If so, does the system involve input from students? Is the system based heavily in rewards and/or punishment? Is there any aspect of the system that involves reflection, dialogue, or negotiation?

How do teachers talk about students and their families in this school? What kind of advice would they give a new teacher for working effectively with students? Who are considered the "best" teachers? What kind of classroom culture do they promote? What advice do these teachers have on classroom "management"?

What is the relationship of the community to the school and other social systems? Are parents involved and welcome at the school? What is the relationship between the police and the community? To what kinds of community dynamics are students privy?

This list of questions is by no means exhaustive. However, how these questions are answered will have considerable implications for how the teacher might *initially* address issues of setting up the classroom culture. Unfortunately, what often happens is that teachers become acclimated to the institutional culture without critically reflecting on the impact of the culture on themselves and their students. The more conscious teachers can be of their own values and assumptions as well as those of the students, teachers, and administrators within the school, the more they will be able to intentionally work toward creating a classroom culture that fosters social, emotional, moral, and academic development.

It is equally important to understand students' expectations and ideas of what school is and what it should be. This should be addressed as early in the school year as possible. Often, teachers will look through students' cumulative files to get a sense of the students' histories, but that is only one story. As is always the case in constructivist learning, it is important for the teacher to try to understand how students make meaning, and this is just as pertinent in relationship to the social meanings of the classroom as it is the meanings in academic texts. Students bring their histories into the classroom in the form of expectations, and this is a powerful aspect of classroom culture.

Teachers can elicit students' experiences, beliefs, values, and expectations in relationship to school in a number of ways. Teachers can have students discuss or respond in writing to questions such as the following:

- What makes a good and/or bad classroom?
- If you were the teacher, how would you run the class?
- What should happen to kids who break school rules?
- Do you like school? Why or why not?
- What is the best (worse) experience you've ever had in school? Why?

Students' past experiences in school, the particular mix of students in the classroom, and the teacher's style have enormous impacts on classroom dynamics. Each year, creating classroom cultures has different challenges and different possibilities, and it follows different courses depending on many different dimensions. It is important that teachers actively learn from students, teachers, administrators, and families about family, community, and institutional cultures. This kind of learning should be ongoing throughout the school year.

NURTURE A PARTICIPATORY CLASSROOM CULTURE

It is not just that the child must make his knowledge his own, but that he must make it his own in a community of those who share his sense of belonging to a culture. It is this that leads me to emphasize not only discovery and invention but the importance of negotiating and sharing—in a word, joint culture creating as an object of schooling and as an appropriate step en route to becoming a member of the adult society in which one lives out one's life. (Bruner, 1986, p. 125)

We understand that teachers are the adults in the room and fully recognize that there are decisions they must make and responsibilities they must shoulder. However, students should be involved in the creation and ongoing maintenance of the classroom culture. This is how students learn to become responsible members of a community. Their participation allows them to take moral responsibility and feel ownership in the classroom. This participation should evolve to deeper levels throughout the year and as children develop. This parallels the objectives of parenting in which the child's ultimate independence is the goal that is worked toward from the time the child is born and evolves with the child's development.

Dee's first-grade classroom is an excellent example of a participatory culture. Many people might question that first-grade students can handle so much ownership of their social and academic learning. However, Dee recognized that students need to be directly taught processes for participation, have opportunities for practice, and have a lot of adult support.

Nancy Schniedewind and Ellen Davidson's (1998) book, *Open Minds to Equality: A Sourcebook of Learning Activities to Affirm Diversity and Promote Equity*, provides excellent activities and processes to help establish a caring participatory classroom. They present activities on getting acquainted, developing listening skills, building group process skills, sharing feelings, and developing skills for creative cooperation. These are important aspects of learning to consider and explore with students that can provide the foundations of a dynamic, exciting, and enjoyable classroom community. A participatory classroom culture doesn't excuse teachers from the responsibilities of teaching, but it does change the nature of teaching and learning, the nature of classroom relationships, and the nature of participation for everyone involved.

CREATE PROCESSES THAT ARE FLEXIBLE AND RESPONSIVE TO STUDENTS' LIVES

Initially, when teachers hear that we are not in favor of behavioral practices, they sometimes worry that we are advocating a classroom environment where "anything goes." They say that society has rules, and if you break them, you pay the price. They believe that it is the teacher's responsibility to teach this to students by consistently enforcing the rules through a series of rewards and punishments, because this is what happens in the real world in relationship to the legal system. However, what seems to be missing in many classroom management systems that emphasize rules, rewards, and punishment is acknowledgment of students' rights and a system of due process. In addition, laws are always open to interpretation and changed when they are no longer relevant. The legal system is a fluid and dynamic system in which the public participates in various ways. Behavior modification systems are more consistent with the processes that occur in prisons, once someone has been convicted and lost his or her rights.

Rather than set up a system devoid of opportunities for reflection, participation, negotiation, and compassion, we suggest that teachers and students set up dynamic systems and processes that don't limit the teacher or students to predetermined punishments and rewards. The following example of a process that can be used to set up a classroom constitution emulates the real-world model of the legal system in the United States. It may be a particularly useful model in schools that require teachers to use a rule-based classroom management system.

We believe that classrooms should have guiding principles, but we believe that these should be established with regard to students' rights and responsibilities. The guiding principles may be called rules (if the institutional culture requires it) or agreements. Like the U.S. Constitution, the rules of the classroom should be open for revision. Rather than begin with the rules, teachers and students can first establish the rights each individual should have in the classroom. A bill of rights for the classroom can be written and posted. Students and teachers have rights, such as the right to learn, to express themselves, to feel safe, and to have fun.

The next step could involve responsibilities. Together, students and the teacher can think about what each person would need to do in order to create the kind of classroom he or she envisions. For example, students not only have the right to learn, but they have a responsibility to learn. They must do something to make it happen. The responsibilities of citizenship can be created and posted in the classroom. Responsibilities can involve everything from participating in learning to keeping the classroom clean. These documents should also be open to revision.

After rights and responsibilities are established, the class can engage in a process to create rules to ensure students' rights. This process allows students to see that rules are there to protect them and their classmates and not simply as a means of control. Once rules are established, the class can decide on processes that will be followed when rules are broken. Rather than focus on rewards and punishment, opportunities to make amends, apologize, and compensate others should also be established. However, these should never be imposed, but offered as options. Depending on the circumstances, there should be options and room for negotiation and judgment. There doesn't always have to be a consequence. Participating in the process may be enough to help students learn to do things differently. These processes, rather than a prescribed system of reinforcement, allow students to learn and grow in relationship to their behavior and what it means to be a responsible member of a community. Conflict resolution, the topic of Chapter 9, is an example of a classroom process in which students have primary ownership in resolving conflicts that arise.

Once a classroom constitution has been written, it can be revisited and amended, and it can evolve as the classroom community evolves. In addition, this document can serve as a means to explain your classroom governance approach to new students, parents, and administrators. This approach has many of the same elements one finds in many classroom management systems, but avoids many of the pitfalls. Students are involved throughout. Many opportunities for insight, communication, and learning are involved. There are rules, but instead of rewards, there are rights. There may be consequences, but these are determined in relationship to processes that lead to deeper understandings.

The approach outlined above is only one possibility for establishing a participatory classroom culture. Being fashioned after our legal system, it reflects principles of democracy and will often satisfy the expectations of a top-down institutional culture because, *on the surface,* it contains some of the same elements as behavioral classroom management systems. This is by no means the only way to conceptualize a participatory classroom culture.

Dee established a classroom community around the concept of a family rather than a legal system. A family metaphor allows Dee to interact with her students in a much less formal way. Instead of posting rules, she posts sayings that embody the attitudes and values she wants to nurture in her classroom.

WORKING IN TOP-DOWN BEHAVIORAL ENVIRONMENTS

When institutional cultures are more inclusive, collaborative, flexible, and friendly, establishing a participatory classroom community will be supported by the overall culture of the school. This is not to say that everything will be easy, but the teacher's main energy will not be spent defending his or her practices to colleagues and administrators. When schools are more authoritarian, top-down, behavioral, and structured (inflexible) constructivist teachers often encounter institutional pressures and requirements that work counter to their values and beliefs. These pressures can range from being overwhelming to being mildly annoying. However, it is safe to bet that most teachers will encounter some tensions between top-down and constructivist pedagogy.

In this section, we'll address some of the ways in which teachers might navigate within the constraints of a top-down system. It is important to realize that the most difficult environments for teachers to work in are also often the most difficult environments for students to learn and grow in. When constructivist teachers leave restrictive schools so they can be better supported in their work, they exercise a liberty that the students in those same schools don't have.

If there is a mandated classroom management system in place in the school, it is probably advisable for a new teacher to begin the school year using that system or one that resembles it on the surface, such as the one described earlier. This is not to say that teachers should passively accept everything they are told to do with students. It is simply a means of starting with what is there and then working with students throughout the year to build an authentic learning community. No matter what system or approach a teacher starts with in the beginning of the year, it should be used with an attitude of critical reflection, flexibility, and openness toward change.

Students should be included in ongoing, critical reflection on the dynamics of the classroom culture. If a teacher feels conflicted with using a particular system, it can be insightful for the teacher and students to discuss those conflicts. It benefits students to understand that teachers have to make compromises and actively work out their own position in the school. A teacher who feels conflicted about punishing a student according to school policy might say to the student, "I am required to give you a detention for walking out of the classroom, but I feel uncomfortable doing that. I'd much prefer to understand why you walked out and work together to find solutions in the future." Even if the teacher gives the student the detention, he or she has communicated concern for the student and opened doors for problem solving. The incident could be used as a reason to have a class meeting to brainstorm options for what students can do when they are feeling angry or frustrated. Although teachers may feel constrained to use a mandated program, it does not preclude creating, simultaneously, deeper collaborative approaches. In fact, as the example above indicates, a top-down system can provide the impetus for doing so.

If teachers want to establish a deeper, more meaningful approach, they will need to establish collaborative and communicative processes. The evolution of a classroom culture is not usually accomplished by instituting abrupt change, but by establishing processes with the students that will allow for growth and development of a participatory learning community. As we mentioned earlier, these processes often have to be taught and practiced before students can participate effectively.

One of the important things to work toward when one is required to use a behavioral approach involves finding ways to move from nonverbal, symbolic action to using words to construct meaning. For example, many behavior plans use tokens, a point system, or some other numeric system as a means to respond to students' behaviors. Students have little input, and there is little insight into behavior. Any rule-governed, automatic system that has little need for dialogue silences both teachers and students. The important thing is to encourage dialogue in which students and teachers can honestly discuss issues rather than simply follow the dictates of a system. Ultimately, the objective is to move beyond top-down behavioral approaches and for students to think about, reflect on, and take responsibility for their behaviors and their development.

One example of beginning with a behavioral program and moving into a constructivist one involves the work that Terry Jo Smith, the second author of this text, did as a behavior specialist in a very top-down middle school. She worked with the students labeled emotionally/behaviorally disturbed and their teachers. When she was hired, a behavioral system had been in place for many years. The teachers had never been exposed to any other approach and were adamant about using this system. Although extremely uncomfortable, Smith realized that she couldn't change the teachers' minds in a day.

Rather than trying to set up a whole new approach that ignored the teachers' wishes and would have certainly provoked their resistance, she simply added one "consequence" to the behavioral system. Smith added the option of the student writing a paper to help her understand the student and the event that led to the behavioral referral. Given the other options of suspension, detention, or a phone call to parents, most students eagerly took the writing assignment. For those who couldn't write, she let them dictate it to her and then rewrite it in their own handwriting.

Smith assured students she sincerely wanted to understand why they were having difficulty. She told them she needed to understand how they saw things and what affected their behavior so she could work with them and their teachers to make school better for them. Adding this option slowly began to change the culture of the department. At first, teachers were unhappy with the option, feeling it wasn't punishing enough. However, Smith began to encourage the students to give the teachers parts or all of their writing, and the teachers began to gain a better understanding of the students and their worlds.

Students began to find reasons to write because they had found a space to have a voice, to be heard, and to think through their difficulties. Many of the most troubled students used writing and the dialogues that sprung from their writing in very therapeutic ways. The following quote from a student named Dennis, who used his personal journal as a means of transformation, captures the sense of importance many of the students gave to their writing as the school year advanced.

> Well, I hope your happy because its four-twenty A.M. I woke up at four fifteen and instead of going back to bed I stayed up and wrote because you made it to where I love to write. Now, every time I find something to write about, no matter what time, I will do it, because you turned me around from hating to do something good like writing, to loving to do something great . . . and now I want to write every second of every minute, of every hour, of every day, of every year, of every generation. (Duplass & Smith, 1995, p. 146)

In addition to their own personal insight, learning, and empowerment, often the students' writing affected the teachers' attitude toward the students and interpretations of classroom events. The antagonistic relationships that existed when punishment was the major response to "problem behaviors" were significantly changed, and behavior problems decreased. The teachers who had at first been reluctant to move away from a punishment-based system eventually defended it to the assistant principal. By the end of the year, two of the four teachers had discontinued using the behavior system altogether.

Working within the constraints of a behavioral system is by no means an ideal situation. Hopefully, as a teacher establishes him- or herself within the classroom and the school, he or she will have increasing freedom to modify it, transcend it, or at least minimize its prevalence. The important thing is to realize the freedom one does have. Just because a behavior system is in place doesn't mean that the more collaborative processes can't also be established. Teachers, like students, need to have voice and choice in what they do. Over time, the behavior system will become less and less important as meaningful relationships develop, spaces for classroom dialogue are established, and students begin to feel a sense of ownership and acceptance within the classroom culture. For this to happen, teachers need to be open, flexible, and willing to learn from and with their students.

CREATING PROCESSES FOR DIALOGUE, LEARNING, AND NEGOTIATION

There are many different ways to nurture the dialogue that is central to a collaborative classroom community. We believe that the most critical component of teaching all children, but especially those who are troubled and troubling, is the quality of the relationship between teachers and students. We have spoken extensively on this issue in Chapter 4 on Caring Pedagogy and Chapter 6 on Reflective Teaching, so we will not go into much detail here. We believe that teachers' attention, care, and encouragement should be unconditional. The safety and security that come when students know they are cared about and valued provide the foundation for all other learning.

Teachers should not assume that students feel safe and cared about. Students should have many opportunities to provide feedback to the teacher on how they are treated in the classroom and whether they feel safe, respected, and listened to. One way for students to provide feedback might involve students making a report card for their teachers, touching on areas of instruction, fairness, and students' perceptions of care. Students should have ways to provide feedback to teachers that are anonymous as well, because many students may not feel safe critiquing an adult. In addition to these formal measures, teachers should listen closely when students are angry with them and try to understand from the students' perspective why that is. Most teachers believe they are caring, fair, and supportive of students' learning. However, students' perceptions are more important than their own in this regard and need to be solicited to help teachers develop in more caring ways.

Teachers need to take the time to get to know each of their students. We saw in Dee's account of working with Alan that she had many one-on-one conversations with him. She found time to do this when other students were working. Often, teachers worry about the time this takes away from others, but once students begin to take ownership of their learning—the way Dee described with literature circles, for example—teachers' time is freed up from continuous management and instruction. This allows teachers more opportunities to talk with individual students. Finding time to talk to all students is important, but especially students who are troubled and troubling. These children will often find ways to get teachers' attention anyway, so it is better to focus this on positive conversations.

In addition to encouraging and opening dialogue with students, classroom meetings can be used to discuss issues that pertain to the whole class. This is a critical way to build the bonds of classroom community. Classroom meetings can be more or less structured. Often, this depends on the teacher's experience and style. It is important that all members of the classroom, teacher and students, feel free to bring topics to the discussion. Dee used classroom meetings for a variety of purposes, from discussing social issues to planning classroom parties. She didn't want classroom meetings to always be about problems, and she made sure that the group came together to discuss many issues.

Parents as well as students need to feel welcome in the school and classroom. They need to feel like they can talk with teachers about issues without feeling judged. They need to feel safe to ask questions, provide feedback, and make suggestions. If parents feel cut off or disrespected, students may feel conflicted about alliances between home and school. In addition, teachers who want to understand their students within the contexts of their lives can gain valuable insights from the people who have lived those lives with children. Chapter 9, on working with families, will address these issues in depth.

INTEGRATE SOCIAL, EMOTIONAL, AND MORAL LEARNING IN EVERY ASPECT OF CLASSROOM LEARNING

It is common to see classroom management and discipline written and spoken about as if they are separate from teaching and learning, curriculum, and subject matter. In this text, we propose pedagogical approaches instead of isolated behavior strategies. Pedagogy involves the whole teaching and learning process—including curriculum (broadly conceptualized), learning processes, theories, methods, and assumptions. We suggest pedagogical approaches that promote and nurture social, emotional, and academic growth. We encourage teachers to utilize curriculum, literature, role-playing, social studies topics, current events, and writing as important, integrated ingredients in helping students reflect on and gain insight into their own behaviors, their relationships with others, and the roles they play in the classroom and community.

If students are having difficulty with controlling anger, then they should watch films and read stories and other literature on anger. They should be given encouragement to write about their anger, reflect on its sources, and think about ways to deal with it. If students are living in dangerous neighborhoods, then they should read autobiographies by people who grew up in similar circumstances and who offer insight for how to survive the pressures they feel. Teachers need to pay attention to the issues students face and the tensions that surface in the classroom, and look for appropriate curricula that will allow students opportunities to think through their lives, reflect on themselves, and envision new possibilities.

Dee's classroom involved many curricular processes that helped students conceptualize the social and moral issues they faced. The word of the week, the slogans on the wall, and the concept of a family were taught directly to students and integrated into the social life of the classroom. The six steps and literature response processes were also taught to the students so they could actively participate in their own learning. The literacy processes of reading, writing, and speaking all involved compelling social meanings rather than simply drills and memory. Students were learning to read, write, speak, and solve problems as active participants in a classroom culture.

Pedagogy that addresses the whole child provides teachers opportunities to learn a tremendous amount about and from students. They can learn about students' hopes, fears, dreams, and desires. They learn about the contexts in which students are engaged and the topics that interest them. They learn how students think and perceive their worlds. All of this helps teachers engage students in meaningful learning and makes teaching and learning an incredibly enriching experience.

SUMMARY

Constructivist approaches to creating a participatory classroom community are based on fundamentally different beliefs about learning and development from those of top-down, behavioral approaches. These fundamental differences often lead to tensions in practice for constructivist teachers. The main objective for top-down classroom management is compliance. Although top-down approaches may help teachers gain control in the classroom, there are concerns that such approaches stifle moral development, repress authentic emotions, and eclipse the social and political sources for students' behaviors.

Constructivist approaches value the students' active participation in creating the classroom community. Children are taught the skills and processes they need to take ownership of their learning. The social and academic dimensions of the classroom are seamlessly interwoven. Curriculum, literacy, and the lived experiences of the classroom affect and involve one another. Children are engaged in academics, planning, maintenance, and problem solving in their classroom. They are given ample opportunities to discuss important issues with their teachers individually, with one another, and with the full class.

Teachers may experience pressures within top-down institutional structures to use mandated classroom management systems. Although teachers may feel constrained to comply with these dictates, there are ways to modify these systems that mitigate some of the limitations. Constructivist teachers can use the mandated system as the focus of critical reflection and problem solve with the students ways to work beyond the silencing of voices it engenders. Teachers can create opportunities for dialogue and participation. They can also create management systems that have some of the same surface components of behavioral systems, such as rules, but are flexible and involve student input at every phase.

There are no recipes for how to create a participatory classroom community because every student, teacher, classroom, and school is different. In participatory classrooms, these differences matter. Teachers need to carefully consider the social norms of the school and community, as well as the expectations and beliefs of the students in determining how to initially approach the class to set up guidelines and processes. We presented two possible metaphors, the "constitution" and the "family," that might guide teachers' thinking. We also acknowledged that teachers might be constrained to use a mandated system. No matter with what process or system a classroom begins, it should begin with an attitude of openness and reflection and a willingness to evolve and develop.

It is this responsiveness, this willingness to engage and create something together, that is the heart of a constructivist classroom.

It is important to realize that developing trust; getting to know students; reflecting on one's own values and beliefs; and nurturing a classroom community that is conducive to learning, taking chances, and social and emotional growth doesn't happen in an instant. Engaging troubling students is a complex, multifaceted process, not a technology. Be patient.

CONSTRUCTING PERSONAL MEANINGS

1. Interview three teachers about their approach to classroom management. Ask them to explain both theory and practice. Reflect on which principles and practices you would consider using in your own class.

2. Discuss your hopes and fears about classroom management with several colleagues or classmates. Discuss what you think will be your greatest challenges and your greatest gifts.

3. Reflect on your own schooling. How would you describe the norms and methods of classroom management in the various schools you attended? What are the practices you want to emulate? What are the practices you hope to never emulate?

4. Pick three metaphors to describe how you envision your role in classroom management (e.g., police officer, parent, mediator). Describe why you picked these metaphors.

Part II

The Pedagogies
of Constructivism

4

Adopting a Caring Pedagogy

The most important thing in life is to learn how to give out love, and to let it come in. . . . Let it come in. We think we don't deserve love, we think if we let it in we'll become too soft. But a wise man named Levine said it right. He said, "Love is the only rational act."

(Morrie Schwartz, as quoted by Albom, 1997, p. 52)

There are some who say that if you care enough about your students, that will make you a good teacher and you'll be able to teach any student. But that's ridiculous. Having strong feelings toward a group of kids won't make you teach any better, and it won't make those kids learn any better. There has to be more than strong feelings. If caring matters as much as we think it does, it has to be something much more than a bundle of strong feelings. It has to be a way of being.

In her writings on caring, Nel Noddings (1984, 1992) calls for a radical change in the purpose of American education. Rather than purely or primarily seeking academic skills as demonstrated on standardized tests, Noddings asks us to view our mission as one of developing moral citizens who care deeply about others and themselves.

> If the school has one main goal, a goal that guides the establishment and priority of all others, it should be to promote the growth of students as healthy, competent moral people. This is a huge task to which all others are properly subordinated. (Noddings, 1992, p. 10)

Noddings emphasizes that the cultivation of empathy, social concern, and responsibility among children does not conflict with goals of academic development. Learning academic, practical, and vocational skills is obviously important. But more important in the lives of children, families, and communities is the nurturance of a quality of caring and caring relationships.

Noddings does not individualize morality by talking about increasing the virtuous character of individuals (e.g., Bennett, 1995). To Noddings, morality is not an individual attribute or characteristic that can be measured and increased through training in social skills or a moral development curriculum. We become moral citizens by taking part in and living within relations of care—connections that bind us, support us, and improve us. Morality is social, an enacted concern for the well-being of self and others that occurs within interpersonal interactions and lasting connections. Therefore, Noddings's emphasis is not on arranging for lessons that drill children on some sort of moral skills. Her emphasis is on the difficult-to-define yet crucial process of developing and maintaining caring relations between individuals. Specifically, in schools, this means the relationships between teachers and students and between students and their peers. Noddings challenges teachers to not only *feel* a sense of caring or *believe* that caring about students is important. She challenges us to *live* an ethic of care in our day-to-day interactions with our students and help our students take on more of an ethic of care in their own lives.

What is caring? Noddings (1992, p. 15) rather stiffly defines a caring relation as a connection or encounter between two human beings—a carer and a recipient of care, or cared-for. It is an interaction or connection in which the carer accepts the cared-for for who he or she is while holding the cared-for's best interests as the highest priority. This connection may be brief or lasting. An enduring relation that exists and deepens over time has the greatest impact and is the most meaningful in the lives of children. Such a relationship is characterized by what Noddings (1984, 1992) calls *engrossment* and *motivational displacement*. These two terms help us move beyond Noddings's initial definition.

Engrossment is when we offer ourselves completely in attending to another, listening and supporting fully. We are fully receptive, taking in the words and perspective of another, receiving the cared-for with all of our person. Literally, engrossment means "written in large handwriting." At the moment of encounter and interaction, whether we are giving directions to a stranger on the street or assisting a child with a mathematics problem, engrossment is a bodily, emotional, and mental act of perceiving another in large letters written across the sky. At that moment, those letters are enormous. That person written in the sky makes up the totality of our focus. The carer is in a state of complete and gripping attention to the cared-for.

Motivational displacement describes the way that the purposes and needs of the cared-for become the complete goal of the carer. This occurs with great intensity and focus at the moment of interaction. In the example of the child struggling with a mathematics problem, we feel ourselves leaning inward toward the child in order to feel and receive the child's frustration and doubt. We listen carefully to his or her words to understand the difficulty. We attend carefully to the child's demeanor and facial expressions, and the tone and movements of the body. We attend to the child's anxiety and doubt as well as his or her strength and competence. Whatever other motives, intentions, and concerns we might have at that moment are displaced by the student before us. We take in the child's needs and situation, and we pour back our support, our total presence, and our aid. We respond to the student's needs with full attention, concern, and effort. We could say that all of who we are is available to that student.

EIGHT THEMES OF CARING

Tarlow (1996) conducted research on caring relationships at schools, in families, and in volunteer agencies. Based on interviews, she found eight basic concepts that make up caring relationships: time, "be there," talking, sensitivity, acting in the best interests of the other, caring as feeling, caring as doing, and reciprocity.

Time

"Time is a necessary, latent force underwriting all caring activities" (Tarlow, 1996, p. 66). Although students and teachers generally understand that the very structure of school places limitations on the amount of time teachers can spend with individual students, both groups highlighted the importance of spending time together in the formation and maintenance of a caring relationship. For example, high school special education teachers explained how helpful it was for them to work with the same students for 4 years. This allows students and teachers to develop a familiarity and trust that is unlikely when a student sees a teacher only 50 minutes a day for 1 year.

"Be There"

"He was always there and it didn't matter what it was that you needed him for" was the way one student described his teacher. Caring involves "being there" for someone, being physically present and emotionally available when needed. Teachers who were there for their students were attentive and poised, watching their students closely and following the ups and downs of their lives with great interest. They knew how to be prepared for and respond with unconditional support in a time of need.

Talking

Talking serves as both a means and an end in caring relationships. Talking about mundane and serious matters alike served as a means to intimacy, a way of developing a relationship. The primary activity in which caring lived and breathed was talking. It also was an end in itself, a satisfying way of enacting the relationship, confirming the bond, and being companions in the moment. Additionally, an absence of talking was viewed as problematic. When one partner in a relationship stopped talking or struggled to express him- or herself, the other partner often viewed this as a difficulty within the relationship.

Sensitivity

Sensitivity is not described as a personal characteristic but as an action that takes much time and effort. Teachers involved in caring relationships with students tune in to the moods and needs of their students. They take the time to understand and empathize with what is going on in their students' family and peer friendship lives. They attend closely to the subtle and overt shifts in the emotional and interpersonal drama of their students' lives. Sensitivity can be demonstrated in a wide range of teacher actions, from firmly confronting a student who is acting irresponsibly to consoling a student who is feeling down.

Acting in the Best Interests of the Other

Teachers who act in their students' best interests are able to set aside personal needs and even school institutional priorities in order to attend to the needs of the individual students. Often, this required that the teacher view the current situation faced by the student in light of a biographic time line projecting into the future. Actions taken today were often seen as enabling and empowering a student to live in a more self-reliant, successful way in the future. This typically involved actions of providing emotional support, serving as a positive role model, and relating to the student in an honest and non-manipulative way.

Acting in a student's best interests also required limitations on teachers' actions. Sometimes, teachers had to hold back, refraining from doing too much. Often, this meant refusing to interfere or assert control in order to allow students the freedom to make choices and then learn from both their successes and their failures.

Caring as Feeling

Tarlow (1996) found that teachers and students described caring as both a feeling and an activity. Sometimes, teachers and students become connected in very deep ways that stir intense emotions. Such relationships can be filled with empathy, concern, hope, and love. In this study, two male teachers cried as they told stories about students they had loved dearly (see Paul & Smith, 2000).

Often, the teacher actions we describe as caring are fueled by powerful emotions and by a desire to give to and connect with students.

Caring as Doing

"The dominant conclusion of this research is that caring means doing for others. . . . The essence of caring was benevolent activity in behalf of another" (Tarlow, 1996, p. 73). Some students and teachers used the words "caring" and "teaching" as synonyms, suggesting that giving to students in the variety of ways we call "caring" is inseparable from the moral challenge and social role of teaching. Teaching, if done in the best way possible, is caring. In this vein, teachers underscored the fact that caring is an ongoing process that takes hard work. At times, it is very routine and taken for granted. But often, it requires creativity, innovation, and spontaneity.

Reciprocity

Tarlow (1996) found that both teachers and students often described caring relationships as a mutual exchange. In her analysis, all of the previous aspects of caring contributed to this final one, to a dynamic interplay involving giving and receiving by each participant. A negotiation of selves occurs through which the needs, wants, and feelings on both sides are somehow balanced. When reciprocity was not honored, when the feelings and effort were not returned in mutual fashion, teachers and students expressed disappointment. Yet frequently, even when reciprocity occurred in an uneven and inconsistent way, relationships continued and survived. The balance need not be perfect. Caring relationships often persevere through many frustrations.

RECEIVING CARE: THE STUDENT'S ROLE

Although students often give back, we must acknowledge and accept that teacher-student relationships are usually unequal. Noddings (1984, 1992) explains that although the teacher serves primarily as caregiver and the student receives the care, the student does play an active role. A caring relation inevitably involves two people who must both participate. Teachers who exhaustingly care, care, care all day long but do not feel like their students are really receiving that care know the frustration of a one-sided relationship. It is not that the student should give back in the same way, for that would create a mutual, mature relationship that is more suitable for two adults. A teacher-student relationship tends to send the caring more often from the teacher to the student than the reverse. But the student's role in this relation is one of actually and actively receiving the care. The caring relation is completed and fulfilled when the student takes in the teacher's attention and concern.

How does this happen? How does the student receive the caring? Typically, caring occurs in the many mundane interactions throughout the day, so students need not offer big "thank yous" or send gifts and cards. Generally, the student receives or accepts the caring and responds. If a student is struggling with math, he or she allows the teacher to assist by participating in a discussion about the problem and then by adjusting his or her efforts in a new attempt to solve the problem. By doing this, he or she recognizes that the teacher has behaved in a caring way. The student responds to that caring by demonstrating that the teacher has made a difference to him or her.

For teachers of resistant, depressed, or troubling students, this can be a problem. Although it may seem simple that a student who is offered some sort of help would just receive that assistance and recognize the helpfulness of the teacher, teachers often find that some students are reluctant to accept our care. Some students do not trust us. We are school authority figures, the same kind of professionals that they may have battled or dodged in the past (or the present). It may have been school authority figures who misunderstood them time and time again, who blamed them, punished them, failed to listen, or sent them off to a special class or school. In fact, the teacher offering the care may be simultaneously the same person who manipulates the student with rewards and punishments. The student operating on the weakened side of this power relation often will not trust the authority figures enough to allow a caring relation to develop.

Cultural differences can serve as barriers to trust in the classroom. Ethnic minority and/or working-class students often find their teachers to be of a different cultural group, a group that frequently misunderstands and devalues the values, styles, and activities of the student's culture. Faced with middle-class, white teachers such as the authors of this book, these students often defend by erecting tall walls, which are high barriers to trust and caring relations in the classroom.

Some students have been harmed in terrible ways by adults. They have suffered sexual or physical abuse at the hands of adults who were supposed to love them and keep them safe (see Miller, 1993). In most cases, the very adults who perpetrated the abuse were simultaneously behaving in loving and caring ways. The alliance of abuse and love, of cruelty and caring, can be very confusing to a child or adolescent. When other adults offer love and caring, will that come with abuse and cruelty, too? Is that the way the deal works? These issues can be very confusing to students who have been traumatized by sexual or physical abuse.

Additionally, we educators bring all of our own psychological baggage into the interactions. Our own issues with trust, control, personal boundaries, and intimacy arise in our every interaction with students. What parts of ourselves will we offer to our students? On what terms will we offer these parts? To some students or to all? What do we expect in return? What will we do if we do not get what we expect in return?

The relational world is a quagmire filled with traps, quicksand, and sudden drop-offs. This why we must remember that caring relations cannot be created from a recipe or formula. Such relations do not merely consist of a list of approved behaviors that teachers should memorize and adopt. The entire enterprise is uncertain and subject to change at any time. Additionally, each relationship has a flavor and a tension of its own. Knowing how to be caring with one student is not necessarily ample preparation for creating such a relationship with another student.

Let us read two stories about relationship in public school contexts. The first is a story about one teacher (Danforth) attempting to be caring to a 9-year-old student named Katie. The second story is written by Talley Hahn about her work with adolescents in a therapeutic day program in Chicago. After the story, we will tease it apart to understand more about the nature of caring in this specific relationship.

THINKING AHEAD: RELATING TO THE STORIES

The purpose of the teacher stories in the following sections is to flesh out the main concepts and practices of this chapter within a particular teacher's practice, within a specific situation. The concepts and practices play out quite differently depending on the situation, the students involved, and the teacher. As you read each of the teacher stories in the upcoming sections, it will be helpful to keep a small list of questions in mind.

1. In what ways do you think this story enacts the main themes or ideas of this chapter?

2. Putting yourself in the teacher's place, what do you think you might have done differently? The same? Why?

3. What troubles you about this story?

4. What brings you hope in this story?

5. What surprises you?

6. What insights, values, beliefs, and processes do you think the author was trying to convey through this story?

7. What stories of your own does this story remind you of?

STRONG AS AN ELEPHANT

One morning before school, I was sitting in my classroom preparing for the day. I was the teacher in a single-classroom day treatment program for preadolescent children considered to have serious emotional disturbances—or at least that's what we called it in our official jargon. Through the door walked Pam, the program social worker, with a tiny girl with dirty blonde hair. I immediately pictured her jumping rope and laughing. That's what I thought she should be doing. But she wasn't. She shuffled in slowly with her eyes downcast and her mouth hardened into a deep frown. She seemed like she was living inside of a dark cloud. Pam introduced us and left this new student, Katie, with me. I tried to talk with Katie, get to know her a little bit before the other students started to arrive. She was silent and sad, as if the life had been siphoned out of her.

I had read her file. She was 9 years old. I knew that her parents had gone through a very bitter divorce, and that the conflict between the parents raged on now, 2 years later. I knew that Katie split time between each of her parent's homes. She seemed to be the family member carrying the grief and sorrow of the broken family, of the marriage deteriorated to bitterness, of the ideal family cracked wide open and spilled out on the ground.

After trying unsuccessfully to get Katie talking, I settled back in my chair and just stared at this sad girl seated before me. Howard (1991) teaches us that life stories often go awry, take a bad turn, spin into a ditch, or break into pieces; our task is one of story repair, of helping someone put things back together in a livable way so that the story can go on. In doing so, we, the professional helpers, bring our own broken, ailing, and half-repaired life stories into the fray. We step forward into the life story of another, seeking to bring about healing and reparation, while simultaneously experiencing the broken-ness and lost-ness and uncontrollable-ness of our own life stories. I looked at Katie's cloud-darkened face. I could not recall ever seeing such pure and deep sadness in a child. It hurt me just to see such grief in such a small child.

She sat down next to me. "Katie," I leaned forward as I addressed her. She looked up to me slightly with hollow eyes. "Sometimes we call that lousy feeling you have 'depression.' It means you feel lousy and sad, and the feeling just doesn't seem to go away. Know what I mean?" She nodded and whispered, "Yeah."

"This school is where kids and families come to get help with their problems. Different kids and families have different problems. You're going to come here 5 days a week for a while. We'll do school work. We'll do fun stuff. We'll get to know each other pretty good. And little by little, you'll begin to feel better. Pam and Carol and I and the other kids are pretty good at helping depressed girls feel better. And one day, not too long from now, you'll tell me that you don't feel so lousy and sad anymore. At least, not all the time. Does that sound OK to you?" Katie nodded. She was intrigued, and she probably wondered how this rough magic was going to work.

Over the next 8 weeks, Katie did improve. Her parents finally realized that they were using Katie as a foil for their anger with each other. They stopped talking about each other to Katie and began communicating, even if only minimally, with each other. In our days spent together, Katie was the joyful jump-roper I had envisioned. But she was also tough as nails, a real scrapper who could hold her own with the rough-and-tumble crew of boys I had in the class. She could push in the lunch line and pinch and scratch as well as anyone I've ever seen. She had a strong spirit that came out in both her playful laughter and her intense anger. Somehow, that tiny frame carried a world full of burning rage and deep hurt. When it came bursting forth in her words and actions, I was simply amazed that a hurricane could be stuffed into the body of a little girl.

One morning she simply refused to do anything. I tried talking to her, but she refused to talk. She simply put her head down on her desk and did no schoolwork all morning. But she wasn't lifeless and resigned in her inactivity. She was seething. She rolled over on her desk and groaned and complained like an insomniac enraged at the slow-passing night. When it came time for recess, I decided to do something I typically did not do. I decided to provoke her. As her classmates lined up to go outside, I pulled her aside and told her that because she hadn't completed any schoolwork all morning, I was not allowing her to go outside for recess. Boom! That was it. She screamed and pounded her fists on the wall. She ran at me and kicked at my shins. I grabbed her arms to hold her off so I wouldn't be kicked. She wriggled away and moved back out of my reach. Standing there, too mad to know what to do, she started crying. Tears ran down her face, and she wailed so loud that I was sure her classmates must have heard her outside. I stepped forward to console her, but she put up her arms in defense and backed away. I took a step backward. She slid down the wall and curled up in a ball on the floor, still crying with tremendous force and energy. I followed her lead and sat down on the floor to be with her while she cried.

Katie cried with all her might for 10 minutes. I sat there on the floor, watching her silently. Then her tears began to dry up, and her sobs softened down to gentle murmurs. I looked at my watch. The class would be coming back inside in 5 minutes. Without a word, Katie got up and walked to her desk. She pulled out her math book and started working on her assignment. I went to my desk and pretended to do paperwork while I watched her out of the corner of my eye.

Katie worked silently for the rest of the morning, catching up on much of what she had refused to do earlier. After about 45 minutes, I walked over to her desk and knelt down. She didn't look at me. She kept working. I said, "You come in every day and work so hard. And today you were so upset, but you wouldn't talk to me. And you wouldn't do any work. So I decided to keep you in from recess. I didn't know that was going to make you feel so bad."

"Well, it did," Katie commented sharply.

"I know. I was surprised. I've never heard you scream so loud. You almost broke my eardrums." I put my hands over my ears for emphasis. Katie looked up and cracked a slight grin.

"I was the loudest?"

"Absolutely. Louder than an elephant screaming for peanuts." Katie grinned a little more. That became our little joke after that. Katie was the little girl who was as loud as an elephant. Later on, we changed it to "strong as an elephant." Katie liked that, and it fit her as she became stronger and more confident over time.

I really don't keep many photos. I have never even owned a camera. I do have a photo of Katie riding on top of my shoulders. She is smiling from ear to ear. It is very much a little girl's smile. But I see more than that in her smile, for she had suffered too much too early to ever smile the smile of a little girl. She was experienced and worn deep and hard like leather beyond her years. And she carried the power of an elephant in her tiny frame.

CARING FOR KATIE

What strikes me (Danforth) first about this story is my own intuition. I recall having a full, very intuitive sense about this child, about her dignity and strength, about her ability to find her way through the darkness. I sensed that my role was to light an occasional lamp along the way and allow Katie to come into her own strength, grow into an awareness of her own ability to cope with difficult situations and use her talents and anger to her own best interests.

I could feel Katie's emotions better than I could explain them. I adjusted my own stance and my approach to her based on what I felt and thought was going on with her. In this, I had to trust not only Katie, but also myself and my understanding of this child.

My sense of trust and my belief in Katie's capabilities can be seen in the way I did not impose myself on her. When she came flying at me with her feet kicking at my shins, I held her off with my hands. But I let her go quickly when she pulled back from me. I knew that I didn't want to be kicked, and also that she didn't need me holding her to control her. I defended myself briefly, and she backed away and stopped being violent. Then, when I stepped forward to console her, she very directly communicated that she wanted some physical distance between us. I heard this message and accepted that she was best able to define what she needed from me at that time. I settled into a position of silent support at a distance that she considered safe.

By my very presence, I made it clear to her that I was with her. Yet I tried to neither comfort her nor stifle her with my words. I knew that she didn't need my words. I sensed that all she needed was me being there for her and with her. At that time, I thought to myself that I could talk to her later. She was a tough little kid who didn't like sentimentality. Mushy and sweet words were not the stuff on which Katie built her identity. Her edges were hardened solid, and I had to respect that.

When I spoke to her later, I wanted her to know that I hadn't intended to spin her into such a painful place. I hadn't intended to bring about such intense suffering. I didn't want to overdo it by apologizing. I didn't feel like I had done anything wrong. But I did want to tell her that I meant no harm. She accepted this and received my care. And when she laughed at my little jokes, she was again receiving my caring energy. I also took that as a sign that all was well between us. We could go back to our usual, jovial style of relating to one another.

Finally, I question my decision to provoke her with a punishment. I had never kept anyone in from recess for any reason. My class simply did not work that way. Recess was not a privilege to be earned or lost. It was a guaranteed right, something we all deserved and enjoyed. Taking it away from Katie surprised me as much as it did her. When the words came out of my mouth, I knew that I was desperate to send her a message that something was very wrong. I can't say that provoking Katie in that way in that situation was necessarily right or wrong. There is no clarity or certainty in giving care. At best, we make errors and we learn from them. In this case, Katie's seething anger came flying out, as if my provocation had poked a hole in her balloon. Then, thankfully, she trusted me in the midst of being outraged at me. That trust was born and cultivated over the prior weeks as Katie and I built a solid relationship of humor, playfulness, and concern. I had cared for her each day, and she had received that care each day. When the whole village seemed to be on fire and the building was falling down around her shoulders, she somehow remembered that trust, and our relationship sustained us through the crisis.

DIGGING IN: MAKING THE STORY PERSONAL

Perhaps the most powerful lessons we can take from a story take place when we allow ourselves to reflect and connect in a deeply personal and emotional way with what happened. We can often do this by placing ourselves in the roles of the teacher or the students, connecting those roles to the rich experiences of our own lives.

1. What do you think of the notion of "story repair" discussed in this story? In what ways did this teacher enact story repair?

2. The author said, "It hurt me just to see such grief in such a small child." How do you think you are or will be able to allow yourself to care deeply for children who are hurting without being overwhelmed by the sadness of their young lives?

3. What do you think the effect may have been of the teacher telling the little girl that she will start to feel better pretty soon?

4. Do you think your own intuition on how to work with hurting kids can be trusted? Why or why not?

5. If you were the teacher, how would you interpret and respond to Katie's crying, screaming, and attacking you?

6. What aspects of this teacher's behavior did you think were respectful? Not respectful?

7. Do you think there may ever be therapeutic value in provoking a student?

THE AFTERSCHOOLERS

(The following segment is written by Talley Hahn, a special education teacher who has taught in various settings in Chicago. This story is set in a therapeutic day school for adolescents considered E/BD.)

I cried. I cried until I had no tears left and then I sat and felt empty inside. That is how I felt after I made the decision to leave my school. I had worked with the same kids for four years and some of them had still not graduated. Some of them were the reasons I had fought the administration. I fought to keep them in the school. And others I knew would return one day and I would not be there.

Still, I knew it was time to move on. I guess I cried because I cared, because I knew that as much as I might not have liked the business of education, I had loved the students. When I look back, my time spent with Jerry and John was one of the first challenges I faced. I am not sure what made them pick me, whether it was that John had last period class with me, or that my room was the most inviting, but they made my room the hanging-out room after school. John was the black version of that old TV hero McGyver. He avidly read adventure magazines, carried a heavy-duty backpack filled with all kinds of gadgets, one of which was a mirror he could use to flash a search helicopter to help them find him. This might make sense if I was teaching in a rural area, but I was teaching in the projects of the South Side of Chicago! John did not fit in. Jerry was his closest friend. Jerry was a tall, lanky, nineteen-year-old black man. He avidly played basketball and wrote poetry, so he as well, though in different ways, did not fit into his neighborhood. John always sat and wrote in my class after school. Occasionally he would throw in a comment here or there, but Jerry, Jerry spent his time pacing my room, looking around and talking through his many problems. Through the years, Jerry spoke to me of his dating life, his relationship with his Mom, and friends.

Right before I left this school, Jerry had run into serious trouble. He was missing several days of school a week, but one day he landed in my room again. As I sat at my desk and he paced the ancient creaky floor of our 100-year-old building, he told me a story. He explained how the girl he had been dating had gotten pregnant, his mother had kicked him out of the house, and he was trying to work and finish school to support his child. He explained that there were many nights that he had slept in the park down the street from school, because he had nowhere to go. I was shocked and I did not know what to do. My heart wanted to offer him a place to stay, but I did not, I just kept listening. He told me other stories that day, but what shocked me was that he was telling me at all. I asked him why, and he said he needed someone to know what was happening. He needed to sort it out in his head.

These conversations continued after school, the days he was able to make it. One day, though, was different from all the others. Jerry came in, and explained to me that something had happened on the basketball court by his house, and that he was looking to exact revenge. He meant to kill someone. I knew it did not make sense to me, but I did not tell him that. He paced, I listened and he told the very sad and angry story of his life at that moment. By this time, his baby had been born and he was off the street, living with his Grandmother who lived below his mother, in the same building. He finally finished telling the tale, and asked me, with his head hung low, and his eyes, eyes of steel focused on the floor, what I thought he should do.

I knew the answer right away. Nothing. It was hard, though, at that moment to tell him that. I had to help him find a way to challenge his anger, to exact revenge in a different way. At the same time, I was faced with a moral dilemma. Do I tell anyone? Deep in my soul I knew the answer: No.

Many people will say I did the wrong thing, but I view my caring relationship with Jerry as one that was confidential. I always told him that there might come a time when I would need to tell, but that I would be honest with him and let him know. This was not that time. Looking at Jerry, I knew how angry he was, and the fact that he had a plan laid out in his head concerned me. I also knew Jerry, though. I knew if I was to tell someone, that person most likely would not know Jerry, and would not really see him. They would not see the poetry he wrote, the moves he made on the basketball court, or the tears that fell from his eyes so many times in my classroom. All they would see was a young black male who did, or was going to, commit a crime.

So I told him to think of his Grandmother's love for him, what her reaction would be when he was caught. I told him to write. Write it all down in poetry. Jerry was convinced he would not be caught, though, and could not listen to me or John. This conversation continued over the next few weeks. It was a new semester and Jerry was attending regularly, trying to get out by August. We would talk about his anger every day; John would throw in his comments, and thank God that he was not the only one talking sense to Jerry.

Our conversations continued, and Jerry and John both graduated. I never will know what Jerry's decision was, but I know that I showed compassion and caring to him by listening. Other teachers would ask me why I let "The Afterschoolers" take my time after school. As teachers, we had no break, no lunch, or even bathroom time. Why would I let these two boys hang out in my room until all hours talking?

The answer was simple. They chose me. They needed something in that room. Whether it was me, my ears, my time, what I will never know. I do know, though, that they continued to come to school, which for these two boys was a feat. I know they both graduated as well. If hanging out in my room after school helped that happen, then I am glad I took the time. It was such a small concession; the least I could do was respect their desire. We all know it takes a lot to ask someone to care about you. It also takes an awful lot to care about another human being.

As teachers, we are often taught about the laws regarding contact with students. So much so that often we are scared to care. We are led to believe that caring can cause problems. And it does. It tears you up inside when you get close to another human being and you experience their pain and anger. What

I see, though, is that allowing yourself to care, saying that it is worth the cost, shows the kids that you are right there beside them. It shows that you want them to succeed, and you will offer up yourself for that goal. We say all the time that we want our students to succeed, but do we show them? Do we take the time to find out who they are? Do you stop, and spend that extra minute with a student you may not know that well? Do you eat lunch with the kids? Whom do you talk to on field trips, students or other teachers? These are all signs that our students look at, and believe me, they know who really does want them to succeed, and who does not. They look at these little things, and then they choose. They choose the teachers to really believe and trust, and that makes all the difference in their lives.

I am not sure why John and Jerry chose me, but they showed me that caring is not something you do; it is something that you are. When training new teachers in my classroom, I have often been asked the question, how do you do what you do? I listen, and I care. I never mastered how to teach this to other teachers, other than watching other caring teachers. The one piece of information I do pass on is that BD students will always know if you do not really care, or if you are trying to "play" them. Be honest, with your students and yourself, as to what you can do. Those who see you as caring will find you, just as Jerry found me, and I was honored that he picked me. It has shown me how important it is to take the time to care about our students. The education will always come, but without the caring, much of the education will be lost.

DIGGING IN: MAKING THE STORY PERSONAL

Perhaps the most powerful lessons we can take from a story take place when we allow ourselves to reflect and connect in a deeply personal and emotional way with what happened. We can often do this by placing ourselves in the roles of the teacher or the students, connecting those roles to the rich experiences of our own lives.

1. How comfortable would you be knowing some of the difficult details of students' lives?

2. How would you decide what to do when/if a student confides something that leaves you concerned for his or her safety or someone else's?

3. Do you think this teacher did the right thing by not telling anyone about Jerry's talk about getting revenge?

4. Why do you think some of the other teachers in the school questioned the extra time this teacher spent with her students? Do you think you would spend time beyond the school day with students?

5. What do you think about this teacher's notion of the students "choosing" her?

6. Have you ever chosen someone to teach you or in whom to confide? On what basis?

7. What is it about you as a person that might entice students to choose you?

TIPS FOR TEACHERS

1. Make a list of five obstacles to building caring relationships with your students. Choose what seems to be the least difficult obstacle. Specifically, what can you do to partially or completely overcome that obstacle in the next week? Try it out.

2. Name one student to whom you often say negative or critical statements and rarely say kind or supportive statements. Don't worry about whether the student seems to deserve it. Go out of your way tomorrow to say kind or supportive things to this student three times, five times, eight times, or more.

3. Often, it is helpful to learn the art of caring from those who know best. Based on your experience, which teacher, staff member, or administrator in your building is the most skilled at connecting with troubling students. Make a point to spend time talking to this professional in order to learn more about how this person does what he or she does.

4. Hold a weekly (or more often) class meeting to engage your students in a discussion about the quality of relationships that exist in your classroom. Ground rule: No blaming of individuals allowed. The discussion must be about how "we" cooperate, work together, treat one another, enjoy one another, and resolve conflicts with one another.

5. Spend one lunch per week with a student with whom you do *not* share a trusting and caring relationship. Do not set this up as a reward to be earned or lost. Do not use the lunch time to discuss the student's misbehavior or problems. Intentionally spend the time just getting to know the student in a relaxed, conversational way. For young students, you may want to have some games handy.

SUMMARY

In this chapter, we have examined many dimensions of caring relationships between teachers and students. Caring is not an add-on, an option, a layer of frosting that might be used to coat the pedagogical cake. It is not a method, something we try out to see if it "works." Caring is a central journey within good teaching, an ongoing mission in the development of self and community. When we value ourselves and our students as human beings needing love, we embrace caring as vital to teaching itself.

In our stories, we have painted caring as complex, uncertain, rewarding, and intuitive. We have depicted teachers struggling to be caring with students who struggle right back. Each side of the caring bond presses for intimacy and safety, connection and comfort, interdependence and independence. At times, it can seem that finding one another is a stumble in the dark, a slim chance. This is especially true with students (and teachers) who have experienced traumatic emotional pain, those who cover and hide, who defend against both the joy and the suffering that intimacy can bring.

Throughout the mystery and the difficulty, these stories tell of teachers who are open to learning how to better love their students. In this context, we might imagine love as not only many-splendored but many-faceted. Finding the way to give and receive love with a particular individual is often a journey of idiosyncracy, of trying to find the peculiar, right way for these two persons to love one another. We can certainly cull lessons from prior relationships with other students, and we can be fortified by the importance of our goal, yet our learning about connecting with an individual resides within the unique character of our interactions with this one person. Our vocation is one of finding a way, making a way. At every uncertain and promising step, we listen fully to the wisdom of that student, and we listen to the wisdom of our own inner voices. Hearing and honoring both, we love and learn again.

CONSTRUCTING PERSONAL MEANINGS

1. Write a story about a student with whom you connected in a caring way. Take the time and effort to write the story in full detail. Examine the story to find the challenges and turning points in the relationship, and the times when the actions of you or the student further cemented the bond.

2. Write a story about a student with whom you failed or struggled to connect in a caring way. Take the time and effort to write the story in full detail. Examine the story to find the reasons why this relationship did not develop into the caring relationship for which you'd hoped. Is there anything that you wish you had done differently?

3. *Stories out of School: Memories and Reflections* on *Care and Cruelty in the Classroom*, by James L. Paul and Terry Jo Smith (2000), contains a procedure that offers useful and personal learning. Think back to when you were a young student. Think of a teacher whom you knew loved and cared for you very deeply. Write a letter to that teacher, expressing your feelings and recalling your memories. Then, do the opposite. Think of a teacher whom you felt did not love you or care for you, someone who treated you with cruelty and disdain. Write a letter to that teacher, expressing your feelings and recalling your memories. These letters are often made more powerful if presented and discussed in a group.

5

Working Together

Sometimes, we view ourselves as pouring knowledge from a big pitcher into the brains of students—or trying to. But constructivist teaching calls us to engage with people and learning opportunities, to bring together young people in a meaningful way while connecting young minds and hearts with academic content and skill development. How can we arrange for experiences when this can happen?

The two most common teacher complaints about students considered troubling are that (a) they are frequently off-task, not doing their assignments, and not sufficiently engaged in academic work; and (b) they don't get along well with their peers, interacting in negative or disrespectful ways. There are many emotional, human reasons why academic disengagement and socially disruptive behavior go together. Many students have difficulty handling the powerful and difficult emotions—fear, sadness, anger, frustration, boredom—they feel while participating in educational groups.

Some students fear being exposed as poor readers or unable mathematicians. The average classroom places academically struggling students in difficult emotional positions all day long by highlighting weaknesses. Frustration and feelings of inadequacy are daily events that confound attempts to build a positive concept of self. For these students, preserving the self and saving face in the context of a devaluing academic environment is often crucial. Taking on the role of a "bad guy" or "tough guy" may be greatly preferred to seeming and feeling stupid.

Many students fear social rejection or ridicule by peers for reasons that go beyond academic struggles. Group interactions require a complex array of active skills, including judgment, tact, self-confidence, and specific linguistic skills. Finding and maintaining a sense of balance and personal boundaries within close friendships is an ongoing challenge. Some students may lack experience with close friendships or with participation in cooperative groups. Or, they may feel uncomfortable or inadequate negotiating the complex dynamics, confused about how to behave and unsure of what to say. The entire social experience of the classroom may seem overwhelming and unrewarding.

Yet the same social context that provides a painful and frustrating minefield is simultaneously a place offering the greatest possibility of reward and growth. On the other side of rejection is social acceptance. On the flip side of feelings of inadequacy are feelings of support and love. Converse to fear and anxiety are friendships of enjoyment, ease, comfort, laughter, camaraderie, and fulfillment. The goal for the teacher is to arrange for a social climate within the classroom where acceptance, support, love, and fulfillment are more common occurrences than rejection and disappointment. This goal is a tall order, something to be worked on and toward every day.

In this chapter, we will address both academic and social problems through the facilitation of group experiential activities. Our focus is the task of creating and guiding lessons that engage students in learning activities that they find personally engaging while also facilitating the development of supportive social groups that encourage the growth of social and relational skills. Each activity is a double lesson, a lesson expanding the students' academic knowledge and skills *and* a lesson developing the students' emotional and cognitive capacities for friendship and cooperation with peers. These conjoined lessons will be experiential, building forward from the students' current storehouse of cultural and personal knowledge into a new realm of activity and interaction that creates new knowledge, awarenesses, and skills.

First, we will explain *experiential learning,* an approach to teaching that intentionally offers students learning activities that connect with and extend from their own life experiences. Experiential learning assumes that knowledge and understanding are by-products of human experience—aspects of what people actively think and feel as they go through an encounter or event of personal significance. Second, we dovetail experiential learning with *cooperative learning,* a group approach to instruction that both furthers the individual's development of knowledge and provides a helpful format for students to learn important social skills. Dovetailing experiential learning with cooperative learning amounts to creating rich opportunities for students to work together, helping them to advance both as learners and as friends. The goal is ambitious—to hook the students on ideas and on one another at the same time.

Third, we will briefly examine the interpersonal workings of group dynamics. As educators who lead small and large group activities, we are aware of the fact that the group plays a powerful role in influencing the attitude and behavior of an individual student. A given student seems almost completely different in different groups or classes. We also know that simply placing troubling students in activity groups does not mean that harmony will blossom like a thousand daisies. The act of working together stirs emotions and sets the stage for interpersonal tensions and conflicts. A skilled teacher facilitating experiential group activities must deal with a wide range of complex relationship issues that arise within the life of the group. Psychologists have spent many years studying the interpersonal dynamics that occur within groups. We will tap into this wisdom as a source of guidance. After that, we will explore real experiential activities by presenting two stories of teachers working with groups, the first a group of preadolescent youngsters and the second a group of adolescent students.

LEARNING THROUGH EXPERIENCE

John Dewey (1916) taught us that students will not be truly engaged in a subject if the reason to learn something is simply because it must be learned, it will be on the test, or the adults say this is what we are studying this week. Some students will apply themselves to their lessons with great effort under these conditions. A second group will work at about half velocity, going through the motions in order to stay out of trouble. A third group will simply withdraw or refuse to engage in learning because the adults implore that they have to. This group will critically point out what Dewey told us long ago, that learning cannot be imposed upon students, that we teachers cannot forcibly stuff an academic subject into their experiences or their consciousness. Often, these students will simply spit it back out, unchewed and undigested.

Dewey (1916, 1938) taught that education is the process of engaging with students in activities that tap into and extend their experiences, that envision and animate subject matter learning in and through the thinking, feeling, and actions of the students.

As teachers, our job is to carry around a variety of sizes and shapes of firewood, looking to offer fuel when and where we see the fires already smoking, when and where we see curiosity and interest ripe for development. Our task is to fan these flames at their base, to meet the learner where his or her heart and mind are active and alive.

But we do not just stoke the fires of the engines, because a vehicle propelled without adequate direction might wander aimlessly. We also provide intelligent guidance and emotional support as the engines fire and the wheels seek direction. Whereas the students bring their own valuable experiences to the lesson, the teacher brings a different kind of crucial experience. He or she is the tour guide who has been on similar journeys before, who knows about academic knowledge and the resources that are likely to be helpful along the way.

Part of the teacher's skills is a sensitivity to and appreciation of the rich experiential world of the students. The skilled teacher is a student of not only biology or history or mathematics, but also the lives of his or her students, knowing full well that good teaching involves daily exploration of both the academic and the human realms. The skilled teacher is acutely sensitive to the learning and thinking that the students are already doing. He or she envisions intellectual journeys that wind together this personal brand of thinking and thinking that we would call "academic." What are the students already thinking about, talking about, and interested in? What new topics might spark their interest? How can we bring materials, resources, and guidance to these topics and interests in such a way that the students' thinking, talking, and interests are expanded, broadened, deepened, and developed? What kinds of experiences can we arrange and facilitate that will help this to happen?

COOPERATIVE LEARNING

The extensive literature on cooperative learning will provide us with some guidance as we learn how to facilitate group learning experiences. Cooperative learning is simply the instructional use of small groups. Students work together to maximize their own and each other's learning.

The essential ingredients of cooperative learning are positive interdependence; face-to-face, promotive interaction; individual and group accountability; interpersonal and small group skills; and group processing (Johnson, Johnson, & Holubec, 1993).

Positive interdependence occurs when group members perceive that they are linked with each other in such a way that one cannot succeed unless everyone succeeds. Therefore, group goals and tasks must be designed and communicated so that students understand that they sink or swim together. Positive interdependence highlights the fact that (a) each group member's efforts are required for group success, and (b) each group member has a unique contribution to make to the joint effort because of his or her resources and/or role and task responsibilities.

The second basic element of cooperative learning is promotive interaction, preferably face-to-face. Students need to do real work together in which they promote each other's success by sharing resources and helping, supporting, encouraging, and applauding each other's efforts to achieve. There are important cognitive activities and interpersonal dynamics that can occur only when students promote each other's learning. This includes orally explaining how to solve problems, teaching one's knowledge to others, checking for understanding, discussing concepts being learned, and connecting present with past learning. Each of those activities can be structured into group task directions and procedures. Doing so helps ensure that cooperative learning groups are both an academic support system (every student has someone who is committed to helping him or her learn) and a personal support system (every student has someone who is committed to him or her as a person).

The third basic element of cooperative learning is individual and group accountability. Two levels of accountability must occur within cooperative lessons. The group must be accountable for achieving its goals, and each member must be accountable for contributing his or her share of the work. Individual accountability exists when the performance of each individual is assessed and the results are given back to the individual in order to decide if that student needs more assistance, support, and encouragement in learning. Group accountability requires an assessment by the teacher, peers, or the group itself of the quality of work produced by the group.

The fourth basic element of cooperative learning is teaching students the necessary interpersonal and small group skills. Cooperative learning is more complex than individualistic learning because students have to engage simultaneously in task work (learning academic subject matter) and teamwork (functioning effectively as a group). Social skills for effective cooperative work do not magically appear when cooperative lessons are employed. Instead, social skills can be taught to students just as purposefully and precisely as academic skills. Leadership, decision making, trust building, communication, and conflict management skills empower students to manage both teamwork and task work successfully. Because cooperation and conflict are inherently related (see Johnson & Johnson, 1995a, 1995b), the procedures and skills for managing conflicts constructively are especially important for the long-term success of learning groups (D. W. Johnson, 1991, 1993; Johnson & Johnson, 1994).

The fifth basic element of cooperative learning is group processing. Group processing exists when group members discuss how well they are achieving their goals and maintaining effective working relationships. Groups need to describe what member actions are helpful and unhelpful and make decisions about what behaviors to continue or change. Continuous improvement results from the careful analysis of how members are working together and determining how group effectiveness can be enhanced.

Dealing With Group Dynamics

Group dynamics is a term used to describe the entire range of interactions among the members of a group of students; the way that they talk to, play with, connect with, and conflict with one another over time. We might say that an individual child or adolescent is one thread within the woven pattern of a classroom or neighborhood peer group. Although the thread has individuality, a color and texture all its own, it is simultaneously an inseparable part of the large group fabric. Additionally, to extend that metaphor a bit, we notice that the fabric is always dynamic or changing, always being altered in the moment. Group dynamics is the daily weaving and reweaving of the fabric, the always changing movements and tensions within the group that greatly influence the feelings, thoughts, and actions of individuals. In holistic logic, the group makes the individuals as the individuals make the group.

Group dynamics greatly influences the emotional and social development of each individual within a group. All groups consist of more than the sum of the individuals included within. All individuals within a group are influenced and swayed in their attitudes, emotions, and abilities by the activities of the group. To some extent, we learn and mis-learn about our character, our potential, and our value as human beings within the groups that we inhabit (Brendtro & Wasmund, 1989; Kysmissis & Halperin, 1996; Lavin, Trabka, & Kahn, 1984; Siepker & Kandaras, 1985; Vorrath & Brendtro, 1985; Yalom, 1995).

GENERAL GUIDELINES FOR DEVELOPING POSITIVE GROUP DYNAMICS

Our goal for all students who participate in experiential groups is that they will learn the social attitudes and skills that enable them to initiate and develop supportive and nurturing friendships with others. As teachers, we help our students learn these lessons by organizing and facilitating group dynamics in which mutual support and valuing of both self and another is the norm. Teachers attempting to cultivate positive learning groups should keep in mind a list of four basic guidelines.

1. *Make relationships an explicit focus in the group.* Create times to discuss the quality of the interactions between group members. This is often easily done as part of a regularly scheduled evaluation meeting in which the group assesses its work. How well have group members been working together? How well have group members been listening to one another? How well have group members been treating one another? Bringing these questions to the forefront places these concerns on the cognitive front burner so that group members actively think about them during the activities. Asking these questions also gives the group members a chance to discuss obstacles and difficulties, setting the stage for problem solving and improvement. Finally, these questions help the individuals to see the group as a group, as a social unit to which each belongs and to which each is, in some sense, responsible.

2. *Serve as a constant model of acceptance and compassion.* In order for group members to learn how to be accepting of others and compassionate despite interpersonal conflicts or the problematic behaviors of their peers, the teacher must be accepting and compassionate. The goal is to be constant in viewing the students and him- or herself as valuable and worthy of love. Even when the teacher is confronting a student about a specific behavior or incident, the message within and throughout should be that even this incident does not diminish the student in the teacher's eyes. The teacher provides a consistent example of how an individual can make a positive contribution to a group. When the teacher fails in this difficult goal, the teacher should be honest with students about how he or she has fallen short and how he or she will work on doing better. It is best to be honest about both how important and how difficult this goal is. This is a very difficult challenge for anyone who doesn't wear a halo and walk on clouds. The act of viewing students as worthy of love depends greatly on an underlying act of viewing oneself as worthy of love. For the great

proportion of us who were raised with some element of shaming, degradation, or even abuse, finding a way of viewing ourselves as inherently acceptable and lovable is an ongoing challenge. Seeing one's own internal struggles to accept and love oneself as the underlying basis for learning to love and accept students is a helpful start to taking on this very personal challenge.

3. *Consistently support all emotions as valid and natural.* Feelings of any kind—anger, fear, sadness, joy, anxiety—are valued. The safe, nonviolent expression of all feelings is supported. Feelings are never wrong. They are often difficult and painful, but they are not wrong. Also, feelings and behaviors are not the same thing. If a student feels angry, that is legitimate. If that student punches a friend out of anger, that behavior is a different story. We teachers always support the validity of feelings while we help our students look closely at the value and effect of their actions.

4. *Whenever possible, frame problems as belonging to the entire group rather than belonging to any single individual.* The general message is that we are all in this together, all connected and working together to makes things better for all. In saying this, we do not mean to imply that an individual is not responsible for his or her own actions. What we are emphasizing is the power of a cohesive, concerned group to help individual members of the group by sharing in the task of problem solving.

Now let's look closely at two examples of students working together. The first involves a group of preadolescents and the second involves a group of adolescent students. Although the two accounts and the two teaching styles differ, each is a good example of cultivating cooperation and unity within a group learning experience.

THINKING AHEAD: RELATING TO THE STORIES

The purpose of the teacher stories in the following sections is to flesh out the main concepts and practices of this chapter within a particular teacher's practice, within a specific situation. The concepts and practices play out quite differently depending on the situation, the students involved, and the teacher. As you read each of the teacher stories in the upcoming sections, it will be helpful to keep a small list of questions in mind.

1. In what ways do you think this story enacts the main themes or ideas of this chapter?

2. Putting yourself in the teacher's place, what do you think you might have done differently? The same? Why?

3. What troubles you about this story?

4. What brings you hope in this story?

5. What surprises you?

6. What insights, values, beliefs, and processes do you think the author was trying to convey through this story?

7. What stories of your own does this story remind you of?

THE PLAY IS THE THING

I wanted my students (self-contained E/BD class for grades two through five) to not only learn how to write but to become comfortable with writing as a habit of expression. I required my students to write a story every morning as the first activity of the day. They usually spent about a half an hour working on it. Often, they wrote a story and drew a picture to go with it. For students who struggled in writing a story, I encouraged them to draw the picture first and then write about the picture. For some children, it seemed like working out ideas in a visual depiction came more naturally than developing those ideas in words. Then the words followed fairly easily.

After we had been writing stories for a month, I thought that we would add a social skills dimension to the morning story ritual. After completion of the stories, I asked students to stand in front of the class and read their stories to the class. In this activity, we worked on both the skills of public speaking and what it means to be a respectful listener. The students learned how to stand tall and speak clearly when presenting. They learned how to look like they were paying attention even if the story bored them silly. These results were not unsatisfactory to me, but I wasn't really thrilled with the whole exercise. The kids were pretty stiff and robotic as presenters, and the listeners looked like an ad for the benefits of medical sedation. The entire activity lacked energy and vitality.

One of the things that I have learned time and time again as a teacher (for most lessons must be repeated before I learn them) is how students will go to great lengths to combat boredom. If I organized an activity that had all the flavor of salt-free saltines, they would very quickly add a wide range of hot and spicy toppings to that dull educational cracker. It was up to me, I found, to be open to the input of the kids, to their creativity in response to my boring teaching.

In this case, my idea about how we present our stories was the boring cracker that the students wanted to invigorate with their imaginations and energies. It all began on a Tuesday morning when a boy named Fish (short for his last name, Fisher) brought in a backpack loaded with action figures—Ninja Turtles and Power Rangers. When it came time for his presentation of his story, he pulled a desk up to the front of the class. He placed the various action figures on top of the desk and began the drama. He used the action figures as puppets in his play. He hid behind the desk and read lines from the script that he had prepared. Although his head was focused down to the script pages spread out on the floor, his arms reached up to the desktop to maneuver the characters around the set. He altered his voice from high to low, squeaky to husky, animating each character with a separate vocal identity.

I looked out at the students in my class, the usually sleepy-eyed group of listeners. Their faces were alive and their eyeballs were glued to the desktop drama. Personally, I could hardly follow the story. Each of the action figures—characters in and of themselves—was an actor playing the role of another character within the drama. It was difficult for me to keep track of who was who.

But my students were fascinated. And when the play was over, they started asking Fish questions about the play. How did he think of it? Why did he use this action figure as the bad guy instead of that one? Did he want to do the play again with some help because it was so hard for one person to speak all those roles? It turned into a discussion about writing plays. The students agreed that plays were more interesting than stories because you could act them out and play different parts.

The next morning, we discussed the two options, reading aloud a story just as we had been doing or writing and producing a play as a group. The students opted for a combination of the two. Only one other student really felt able to write a full script the way that Fish did. So we agreed that Fish and Cindy would write dramatic scripts, and everyone else would work on their usual stories. After the scripts and stories had been written, Cindy and Fish would be the directors of their own plays. The other students would be the actors appearing in both plays.

When Cindy and Fish finished their scripts, one student ran to the copying machine to make enough copies for everyone. The eight students gathered together on the floor behind the single desk that served as a stage at the front of the class. I was left as the only member of the audience. They would perform for me.

First would come Fish's play. He passed out the scripts and gave each peer a part. They whispered directions and questions back and forth, trying to sort out exactly how the scene should be presented. They discussed using action figures and various hand puppets we had in the classroom. They wanted the handheld actors to fit the roles. I laughed to myself at the frantic whispering, their attempt to not let their audience of one in on the rehearsal session. Of course, I sat 8 feet away listening to every word.

Everyone had trouble reading Fish's handwriting, so he literally had to take the entire group through every line. This was a great help to Danny, a fourth grader who was not able to read well enough to read the script aloud. Danny's attention during Fish's rehearsal reading of the script was fiercely focused. When Fish finished the reading, Danny asked questions to make sure that he knew what his character was doing. He wanted to understand the story and the context in great detail. I understood this better when it came time for him to speak his lines. Rather than speaking his lines word for word, he improvised similar lines that basically fit into the story line. He wanted to know the gist of the story so that he could handle his role without reading.

When the group finally presented Fish's play, I could not follow the story at all. The students' voices were often muffled and incomprehensible. Frequently, the wrong action figure bobbed his head when it wasn't his time to speak.

Siskel, Ebert, and Roper would have panned the drama, three thumbs down. But what I observed did not occur so much on top of the desk/stage as below it. I watched seven young children with hand puppets, action figures, and many pages of script jockeying about under a tiny student desk. Their little knees and heads and torsos were bumping and moving about as each tried to keep pace with the script and speak the right lines at the right times. I saw Fish whispering directions and his classmates scrambling around on all fours in order to act out the final death scene with the Ninja Turtle and the villain alligator hand puppet. With tremendous intensity, working in the tightest of quarters, eight students who often could barely form a line to go down the hallway to lunch were able to pull off a complex dramatic performance. And when they finished, and I had clapped and shouted "Bravo!" too many times, they immediately went to work on planning out the performance of Cindy's script.

So why did this group come together so well for this activity?

The group activity grew out of and extended their own interests and their own lives. What the students arranged for themselves through the play production activity was a way to tell the stories of their lives. If a psychoanalyst had sat in that audience, he or she would have realized that the stories enacted by the students were expressions of their worries, fears, frustrations, and hopes. They expressed their lives in those plays. Angry fathers ended up as bad wolves. Overbearing mothers were played by mother hens. The action figures were much-needed heroes who, time and again, swept into treacherous territory to save the day.

My role in the process, while seemingly that of a passive audience member, was significant. I certainly provided encouragement to my students. I also helped to facilitate many of the discussions in which the students organized themselves for the mission. I helped them to see that there would be different jobs or roles that could be handled by different people. Not everyone had to write or direct plays. The production also required actors and set designers and acting coaches who could help peers understand their parts and select the right hand puppet. I helped them to see this production as a sequence of steps starting with the writing of the script and culminating in a performance.

Perhaps the most important thing that I did was give them permission to indulge and pursue their interests in an academic setting where student interests are often secondary. This involved my giving the students permission to race ahead of me, moving in front of my supervision, moving beyond the immediate sphere of my control.

For me, the hardest part about giving permission in these ways and playing the follower role was setting my personal boundaries in such a way as to allow the students room to work, create, interact, and claim ownership of what they were doing. The original idea that I had, the plan for students to simply write stories and read them in front of the class, was purely my activity. The students stole it, ran off with it, wrote their names on it, and changed it to fit their identities and needs. I had to trust them enough to allow them to revise my plan into their plan, knowing that they would transform it into something of greater personal relevance and meaning, knowing that they would tune it to the rhythms and concerns of their own lives. Trusting them meant backing off, staying in my own emotional space, not jumping in every time I saw a possible problem, not allowing my own need to be helpful or be in charge get in the way.

There was a strange moment when I sat back watching my students huddled under the desk, trading enthusiastic whispers back and forth with great urgency, when I felt like they didn't need me at all. I usually felt that my students had a great need for me to provide emotional support and guidance. I usually felt like the necessary hub of the wheel. At that moment, as I leaned back in my chair and watched the rehearsal taking place in front of me, I knew that sometimes my students needed me to get out of their way. They needed me not to be the hub of the wheel all the time, not to be the captain of the ship all the time. I would have to dim my own light so that others could have room to shine.

DIGGING IN: MAKING THE STORY PERSONAL

Perhaps the most powerful lessons we can take from a story take place when we allow ourselves to reflect and connect in a deeply personal and emotional way with what happened. We can often do this by placing ourselves in the roles of the teacher or the students, connecting those roles to the rich experiences of our own lives.

1. As a child, adolescent, or even as an adult student, have you ever experienced a time when a teacher or leader allowed you (and others) to take great control of a project or activity? What was that like for you? How did that teacher or leader do it?

2. This teacher says that his students "needed [him] not to be the hub of the wheel all the time, not to be the captain of the ship all the time." In your own experiences working with children and adolescents, when have you been able to allow the students greater control When has this been difficult for you to do? Why?

In the following section, special educator Rebecca Cima-Bardosy tells stories about working on cooperative activities with her students. Ms. Cima-Bardosy teaches at Benet Lake School, a residential treatment facility for adolescents with severe emotional and behavioral problems. She primarily teaches high school students. Her courses differ from year to year, but generally she teaches high school science, history, math, and literature.

RAIN FOREST DELUXE

The most memorable group project for me was when I asked my environmental biology class to build me a rain forest. I asked that each of my students pick one animal and one plant from the rain forest and recreate it. I wanted them to do some research on their plant and animal and explain its importance directly or indirectly to us humans. I only knew that I wanted to teach about the rain forest and decided that the best way to do that was to turn our classroom into a living model of the rain forest. My budget was limited, so I offered the class one large roll of white paper, two gallons of green paint, a box of scrap material, 10 yards of yellow and brown felt, all the newspaper they wanted, and flour for papier-mâché. We had a few bottles of tempera paint (primary colors only) to recreate all the wondrous colors of the rain forest.

Carl had shown some artistic talent in the classroom, so I declared him the official Art Director and then looked at him and asked if that would be okay. I didn't want him to refuse, but I have to admit that that was terribly manipulative on my part.

The whole project took just over 2 months. We started in January and had our open house in March. As the teacher, my role consisted of helping students locate research material, conducting mini-lessons on the ecology of the rain forest, and brainstorming alternative approaches to making certain items. The rest was in the hands of the students and Carl.

I want to describe Carl for a minute so that it is clear what this project meant to the class and to Carl. Carl is a student that our psychologist said was the "sickest kid" she had ever met in all her 18 years as a psychologist. It was true that Carl was a violent individual who spoke of violent thoughts and drew violent images. He had been an enforcer in the gangs and maybe would be again. His father had been horribly abusive mentally and physically as he was growing up, until the day that Carl became physically abusive back toward his father. Violence had become a part of Carl's existence as a manner in which to both live and survive.

Carl was also a promising artist, whom the art therapist said was the most talented artist she had ever encountered. To me, Carl was one of the most straightforward, honest students with whom I had ever worked. I really enjoyed and respected him for this honesty. The rest of the staff did not enjoy him nearly as much as I did and would refer Carl to me in times of crisis. He was not very patient with his peers, or himself, for that matter. He would at times become very paranoid and feel that the world was out to get him. He looked intimidating, and the students reacted in such a way as to give him a good deal of distance, especially on days when he was more agitated.

I guess I chose Carl to be the art director because I wanted him to become more connected with his peers and the classroom, and not so much for his artistic talent, because at the time I really did not appreciate his incredible artistic talent. I did not want Carl to refuse my offer and retreat into his own little world, so I made the proclamation that he simply was the art director. Carl was an inspiration to the class. He was patient with his examples and his ideas. He was demanding of the class to stay focused on the project. There were many meetings and many denials for requested supplies, which led to more meetings to problem-solve building trees, animals, and plants with the material at hand.

Often, as the teacher, I felt left out of the daily events of creating the rain forest. I had allowed my students to take over the classroom, and it was wonderful, but boring on my part. I made my own plant and animal so that I could feel connected to the process. My own behavior changed, and I found myself intentionally annoying my students so that I could get some of the attention back. All of this was incredibly enlightening for me and gave me a glimpse of what my students feel when they feel unconnected and bored. I wandered the classroom during project time quizzing my students on various facts about the importance of their species of animal or the rain forest in general. They all knew the answers.

The rain forest was an unqualified success. We had an open house and invited parents, administration, and anyone we could think of to show off our achievement. There were lots of oohs and ahs, and we felt good. My mother came. She comes to all our events. "Perfect attendance," my students call my mother. Mom went up to Carl and said she heard he was responsible for pulling this whole thing together. He told her that it was her daughter that was behind this whole project. What did I do? I asked my students to build me a rain forest and they did.

We kept the rain forest up until the end of the year, until the rest of the staff could no longer stand it, and they took it down one weekend saying that it was falling down and becoming "dangerous." I regretted not having the students tear down the rain forest themselves as a final act of creating the glory and destruction of the rain forest as I had originally planned. But once the rain forest was up, I wanted to keep it there forever as a monument to what we, as a class, had accomplished. I was sorry when the forest was gone and immediately set about putting blank paper on the wall, wondering what wonderful new creation my next school year would bring.

The majority of my teaching revolves around projects. Sometimes the students work in small groups, and sometimes they work individually. I generally encourage my students to work in groups if they normally work alone and vice versa. Sometimes we create big monsters like the rain forest, and that really needs a coordinated effort from everyone. Sometimes I want my students to produce a project all on their own so that they know that they did it all by themselves.

I often mix up the curriculum with the theory of multiple intelligences, and when it comes to the projects I ask my students to show me what they have learned through each of the multiple intelligences (Gardner, 1983). One of those intelligences is called "interpersonal," and I have always enjoyed the strategies that my students have used to demonstrate that part of the project. Sometimes they invent a game and teach the subject by having their peers and me play it. Sometimes they write a play and have us act it out. Without fail, there are moments of frustration and confusion. The rain forest project taught me that my students can and will find the answers with what we have.

Often, when students are really confused, they will come to me and ask me what they should do. I usually turn the question back and ask them what they think they should do. What do you want to do? How can you do it? My directions are left intentionally vague because I do not want to limit the imaginative powers at work. If a student gets really stuck, I send him or her to fellow students to ask for ideas and help. This has led to wonderful brainstorming sessions and long "conferences" on the hows, whats, and whys of the project at hand. My job becomes the task of running interference between my students and other adults who just hand over answers. I would never let my students fall between the cracks, as has happened so much in their past, but I want them to know that they can come up with the solutions on their own and that their solutions have real value. These self-created solutions belong to my students, and no one can ever take that process away from them or own it as they own it. We do it together as teacher and student, student and student, and all the combinations in between.

DIGGING IN: MAKING THE STORY PERSONAL

Perhaps the most powerful lessons we can take from a story take place when we allow ourselves to reflect and connect in a deeply personal and emotional way with what happened. We can often do this by placing ourselves in the roles of the teacher or the students, connecting those roles to the rich experiences of our own lives.

1. In this story, the teacher chooses Carl—a young man who had much experience as a leader of a negative group—as the leader of the project. He rises to the occasion, demonstrating skills and attitudes far beyond his bad history and reputation. Have you ever seen a negative leader take such a positive role in a group? Why would that happen? Also, why might this strategy backfire on the teacher?

2. This teacher says, "Often, when students are really confused, they will come to me and ask me what they should do. I usually turn the question back and ask them what they think they should do. What do you want to do? How can you do it? My directions are left intentionally vague because I do not want to limit the imaginative powers at work." Have you ever experienced a teacher who turns the students' questions back on them? Have you ever done this with your students? Why would a teacher intentionally do this?

TIPS FOR TEACHERS

1. If you are not accustomed to or skilled at facilitating group experiences, try it out first on a very small scale. Start from a small success and build from there. Put together a group of three or four students that you know you can count on. Hold a meeting with them to discuss and plan the

activity. It is helpful for you to enter this discussion with a preliminary list of possible activities that you think would work well. After you've experienced success with a small, highly trusted group, you can branch out gradually to more challenging groups and activities.

2. Find a teacher in your building or district who is very skilled in facilitating group activities. If possible, observe this person in action. Pick his or her brain for advice. It is helpful to have some guidance and mentorship as you develop your skills in a new area.

3. Keep a balanced but optimistic attitude toward your students. You must be realistic about what they are able to do. Be aware, though, of allowing students' bad reputations to limit your expectations. At some point, we must support our students in taking new risks that are reasonable and offer a fair chance of success. Without some risk, there can be no growth . . . for students or teachers.

4. For students who are not very accustomed to working together in groups, it will be helpful to hold a group meeting prior to starting the project. The purpose of the meeting is to discuss how the students will work together and treat one another. You might lead the group in creating a short list of rules (five or fewer) for behavior in the group. The group might create a short list of interpersonal goals that describes how they want to work together. Lists such as this make it very clear what group members expect from one another.

5. Some activities work best if certain students take specific roles. One student might be the leader. A second might be the head researcher who looks up information in the library or on the Internet. A third might be the art director, coordinating the artistic activities. Make sure that the students both accept and can handle their roles. Also, avoid always assigning the same students to the same roles in each project. Whenever possible, have the students be involved in role definitions and assignments.

SUMMARY

In this chapter, we have explored cooperative ways to develop and nurture learning that is a natural extension of the students' thoughts, feelings, and interests. We have presented experiential group activities as a format for the co-construction of meaning within groups. Teachers who work with troubling students know that lessons that lack personal relevance and salience are likely to be rejected. Our challenge here is to bring materials, resources, and guidance to students' areas of interest—what they already care about—in such a way that the students' thinking is expanded, broadened, and deepened.

We have looked closely at the five basic ingredients of cooperative learning: positive interdependence; face-to-face, promotive interaction; individual and group accountability; interpersonal and small group skills; and group processing. According to researchers, these aspects are essential to success. Additionally, we examined group dynamics, which is the way that individuals interact and relate to one another within a group. The group can have a profound influence on the attitudes and behavior of individual members.

In our stories, we have shed some light on the promise and problems of facilitating group experiences with troubling students. An obvious benefit is that students who may have difficulty building trusting relationships or working productively with peers are offered a supportive opportunity to practice and learn these skills. In our experience, this approach is far superior to teaching students social skills in isolated lessons that lack the reality of a live social context. Skills taught in isolation tend to fall flat in real life. Skills taught in context are employed immediately and become tangible within the student's experience with others.

Cooperative activities are often difficult to do because students are asked to do precisely what many of them have had trouble doing—work together in a peaceful way. Some students lack social skills, or they lack confidence in those skills. Some habitually perpetuate destructive conflicts with peers. Some students have been educated in segregated programs that "divide and conquer"— programs that offer students little freedom or opportunity for social interaction. Working together is new and strange to these students.

Ultimately, we have found that leading group experiences with students is ongoing, challenging negotiation requiring great sensitivity and flexibility. We are called on to listen closely to the cultural and personal rhythms that pulse through our students' veins, hearing and honoring the stories, themes, and topics that course through their lives. We are often called on to follow rather than lead, a challenge that requires us to reel in our controlling and helpful tendencies. By pressing our ears to the living heartbeats of children, following their imaginations and interests, and valuing the learning that they are already pursuing, we put ourselves in a place of tremendous opportunity. We are then able to arrange, plan, support, and guide. We are then able to use our pedagogical skills to challenge our students, encourage them, and help them further develop their own thinking.

Coupling a focus on cultivating instruction through students' interests with a cooperative approach allows us even greater opportunities. We may then engage in strengthening the sense of group identity and unity among the students while we pursue lines of learning that students feel are personally meaningful and relevant. Coming together as people and as friends, and learning together as co-creators of knowledge, go hand in hand.

CONSTRUCTING PERSONAL MEANINGS

1. Write a story of a time in your own life when you felt like a learning experience—within formal schooling or beyond school boundaries—that

you shared with one or more others helped to bring you closer together. How and why did this experience bring you closer to one another?

2. Write a story of a time in your own life when you felt like a learning experience—within formal schooling or beyond school boundaries—that you shared with one or more others *did not* help to bring you closer together. In fact, the experience created distance, unresolved conflict, and hurt feelings. How and why did this experience fail to bring you closer to one another?

3. Observe your students closely for a week, watching for subtle and not-so-subtle signs of their interests, of the topics and concerns about which they are already thinking and talking. Be aware that much of this will be seen during what is often called "off-task" time. Some of these interests may seem to be inappropriate (sex, violence, drugs, seemingly nonacademic matters). What are those interests? How can these interests serve as the foundations for cooperative projects?

4. Find a good mentor. What teacher do you know, in your building or elsewhere, who can provide you with guidance, coaching, and support as you learn to teach through cooperative activities? Who does this well and can help you learn, too? Talk to that person and arrange for your own learning.

6

Reflective Teaching

Teaching is a complex and dynamic engagement with other human beings. Far too often, teaching is trivialized by teaching theories and methods that ignore the complexity of lives. Teachers can consciously and purposely work to unearth the multiple theories, beliefs, and values that guide their day-to-day practice. Ongoing reflection is a door to continuing professional development and to a deeper personal relationship to one's students, one's work, and one's self. Given the time pressures on most teachers' lives and institutional cultures that don't always promote critical reflection, teachers will have to make a concerted effort to create a space for reflection. However, such an endeavor holds the potential to transform teaching from being a job one performs to being a vocation one lives.

"In my classroom, I do what works."

"How do you know what works?"

"Oh, I can tell."

"How?"

"I just watch and see what happens. If it works, it works."

Although it is important to watch closely and to take notice of how things work or don't work in the classroom, there are deeper questions that lie beyond this limited beacon of classroom practice. Kohn (1993) asks us to reflect further and ask what something works for and at what cost. For example, Kohn points out that behavior modification works if what we want is blind compliance, but not if we desire for children to become self-reliant, creative, and caring human beings. In the dialogue above, we can see that the word "works" seems to stand like an enormous stop sign in the road of inquiry and discussion. Beyond this sign lies something that is not often questioned or examined. Beyond the sign is reflection.

Reflective teaching is the opposite of resting comfortably in the assured knowledge that one's teaching practices are beyond question. Reflective teaching is critical doubt in action, continuous examination, an always open questioning concerning the value and effects of one's own teaching practices. Rather than closing the door to self-exploration and critique, reflective teaching takes the door off its hinges so that everything about one's work with children is open to self-examination, digging, wondering, and ultimately changing and improving.

Reflective teaching involves an intentional act of looking back at ourselves, our experiences, our students, our school cultures, and our policies and pedagogical practices. Reflection means that we pause to look *at* the place we usually look *from*. It involves intentionally shifting our gaze from others in order to look *back* onto ourselves. Reflection also involves shifting our gaze from the present and/or future in order to look back over our work, our day, our week, or our career. In both time and space, reflection involves a turning around and looking back.

Reflection takes very different forms for different people. In this chapter, we will consider aspects of pedagogy that embody reflective practice. These include means of consciously reconstructing or representing our teaching and learning experiences so that we can look back on them, and also transforming our teaching through a process of reframing. These are interrelated processes that allow us to continuously learn from our work, our colleagues, and our students and their families. We will conclude the chapter with two portraits of reflective teaching in action that illustrate how reflective teaching is an ongoing process of discovery and adventure.

(RE)CONSTRUCTING OUR WORK AND OUR "SELVES"

> Like everyone else, we teachers tell our stories. . . . Our stories are never neutral or value-free. Because they are always embedded in space and time and people, they are necessarily infused with values, forever political, ideological, and social. Our stories occur in cultural contexts, and we not only tell our stories, but in a powerful way our stories tell us. Interrogating our stories, then—questioning and probing our collective and personal myths—is an important pathway into exploring the meaning of teaching. (Ayers, 1992, p. 35)

In order to reflect on what we experience in classrooms each day, we must find a means to re-present or reconstruct the experience. Classroom experience as it is lived is at times chaotic, occurring on multiple levels of consciousness and through various means of communication at once. Describing any moment in the classroom involves an endless variation of possibilities. Within each individual, there are many possible stories and stances. As a classroom teacher, one can easily describe a given event from several different, and often contradictory, possible viewpoints. For example, a conflict among students may be seen as exhibiting poor social skills from a behavioral stance, whereas the same disagreement may be viewed as involving an honest and healing dialogue from a psychodynamic perspective. A teacher who knows both of these theoretical perspectives may see it both ways. And formal theoretical perspectives are only one type of interpretive frame we bring to "seeing our work."

How each teacher makes sense of schooling is as unique as the individual teacher. One's professional training plays some part, as do the social norms of each school. However, each teacher, like each student, walks into school each day with his or her whole lifetime of experiences—some conscious, some not—that act as interpretive frames for making sense of the complex interactions that comprise the context of schooling. Each teacher brings beliefs, assumptions, values, fears, and hopes into the classroom and school, and these become the ingredients in teachers' stories.

On a simple level, this means that some students "push our buttons," touch our most emotional spots because of some connection between the student and our own history or makeup. Looking deeper, we notice that we view our students through our own lenses—through our own interpretive and emotional stances—and those lenses are the result of everything that we have been through in our lives. Being aware of our own lenses helps us to work with students with fairness and understanding. Being aware of our own lenses is a way of being responsible for our feelings, thoughts, and actions as we work with students.

One way to become aware of our lenses is to create representations or stories of our experiences, knowing full well, as Ayers (1992) points out in the previous quote, that "we not only tell our stories, but in a powerful way our stories tell us." When we describe events in our classroom or an aspect of our teaching, what metaphors do we use? How do we represent our students, their parents, ourselves, our colleagues, and/or the system? Are we always complaining, depicting students as "problems"?

The temptation for many teachers is to view the "problem" student as the inevitable source of whatever uncomfortable feelings we may have. If we feel irritated, angry, annoyed, or disgusted with a student, then the student must be the reason why. We reason that he or she is the one with the problem, or maybe even a "disorder" that makes him or her irritable, angry, annoying, or disgusting. Viewing the student as the problem distracts us from looking deeply at ourselves and taking responsibility for our own contribution to the situation. We respond to students not simply based on what they do, but based on our own interpretation of what they do. That interpretation is laced with the contributions of our own world, our own beliefs, hopes, emotions, ambivalence, and conflicts.

Reflecting on the stories we tell about classroom life, as well as the stories our students, their parents, our colleagues, and our administrators tell, provides an avenue to understanding what we "bring to the picture." It also gives us opportunities to change our contributions, interrogate our assumptions, and understand ourselves and our students at deeper, more satisfying levels. However, just as classroom experience is temporal, always fleeting, so are our stories of classroom life. Our conversations about our work leave no trace once they are uttered, and therefore do not allow us to do some of the deeper, more systematic analysis that reflective teaching sometimes requires.

Teachers' Journals

As chroniclers of our own stories, we write to create ourselves, to give voice to our experience, to learn who we are and who we have been. Our diaries become the stories of our journeys through life, stories that are both instructive and transforming in the telling and the listening. (Cooper, 1991, p. 111)

Journaling is a means of transforming experience into words, images, stories, and accounts that have permanence. This is indispensable for reflective teaching and living. Journaling allows us to capture our experience and then gives us the opportunity to walk away for a while and come back to look again upon what we have captured. Often, on the second look, we see our own hand and heart in what we have written. We may realize we were angry or afraid. Or, we may look back at a time when our fingers joyously wrote about a breakthrough in our teaching or our students' learning, and we see how much we love the people and the process. Journaling, as Cooper describes above, is a way of creating ourselves and of learning who we are and who we have been. We create a text and, in the process, learn about ourselves, the creator.

Teachers' journals can be used to think through difficult situations in more complete ways than is possible while one is engaged in teaching itself. It allows us to clarify issues, to make conscious our feelings, values, beliefs, and tensions in our work. It allows us a canvas to paint portraits of our students, events, and ourselves as teachers. To write about a student who is troubling us, to wonder on paper about the complexities of our students and ourselves, allows us to develop deeper and more elaborate and dimensional representations of the relationships that comprise teaching.

Although we may share our journal entries with others as we see fit, journaling always involves the option of total privacy. This allows us to explore areas of our teaching where we feel vulnerable or afraid. It also allows us great flexibility in what we write. We can write our true feelings about a student, for instance, without worrying what anyone will think of us and with the full understanding that tomorrow we might feel differently. We do not have to present a coherent, sensible self in our journals, as we often try to do in dialogue.

We can be multiple and contradictory. In fact, multiplicity, paradox, and contradiction are often rich sources of personal learning in journaling.

In addition to providing priceless insights into ourselves, journals allow us to chronicle our students' lives in the classroom over time. Writing our impressions of students' progress, difficulties, and learning allows us to see not only how they have changed over time, but also how our opinions of them change over time. Journals allow us to trace the development of our relationship with students across the year. They allow us to look back at where we've been and better understand where we're going.

The emphasis here is to look both inward and outward as we work with students. Looking outward means carefully watching and listening to our students so that we can learn about their lives and their needs, their difficulties and their abilities. Looking inward means settling back at the end of the day or week to journal or reflect on our own feelings and ideas. This means digging inside our lives to see how we bring our deepest emotions to our interactions with students. As we look at the students before us, we also look in a mirror of our own construction. What about ourselves do we see? What about ourselves do we see influencing our work with our students?

Framing and (Re)framing Meanings

Telling stories of classroom life in conversation and in journals provides an avenue to see not only our students, but how we re-present them or reconstruct them in language. This not only deepens our understanding of our students and ourselves, but actually creates our understandings, and as such is a worthy undertaking. However, reflection offers us a truly transformative opportunity by not only helping us "see what is there" but also providing a means to change what we see, how we see, and ultimately what we do.

The concepts of "framing" and "(re)framing" help us understand the transformative potential of reflective teaching. Framing is the mental act of gathering up salient features and elements of the situation at hand and arranging them within a conceptual scheme that provides order, direction, and possibilities for action (Schön, 1983, 1987, 1991). Although each of us frames experiences differently based on our individual interpretive frames, it is the ability to shift our frames and try out other possibilities that leads to exemplary teaching and lifelong learning.

A teacher can often come to new understandings by reconceptualizing the situation in different ways. Different reconceptualizations call for different actions and stances. We call this (re)framing because the teacher is framing or constructing or seeing the situation in a certain way at first, and then he or she intentionally tries out new ways of seeing the situation as he or she inquires and attempts to further understand what to do. The teacher frames or defines the situation in a certain way, constructing the issue conceptually and practically given his or her own life history, beliefs, education, and values that he or she brings to the matter and the requirements interpreted from the situation itself.

Situations can be framed in many ways. No single way is ever the only way or necessarily the best way. Often, we have ways of framing to which we are accustomed or with which we are comfortable. Likewise, some ways of framing seem odd or foreign to us. The key to remember is that how a situation is framed inevitably opens up some doors for action while closing off others. It helps us see very well in some directions and not so well in others.

Shifting Metaphors

One way to begin to access the frames we use to interpret our school experiences is to look at the metaphors we use to describe our work, our students, and our educational systems. Metaphors provide a means to conceptualize our teaching roles in ways that allow us to get at our fundamental beliefs. Tobin and LaMaster (1992) have described how our guiding metaphors influence our teaching behaviors. For example, a teacher who uses the metaphor of "police officer" for teaching most likely sees his or her role as one of "keeping the peace" and/or "enforcer of law and order," whereas a teacher who conceptualizes her teaching role as "mother" most likely sees nurturance as central to what she does with students. These different metaphorical conceptualizations lead to different types of teacher behaviors.

Tobin and LaMaster (1992) suggest that teachers can reconceptualize their teaching roles through directly reflecting on and changing the metaphors they use to guide practice. They tell us:

> Teaching can be defined in terms of roles undertaken by teachers. And just as metaphors are at the basis of all (or most) concepts, so the metaphors used to make sense of the main teaching roles can be the focus for reflection and change. The power associated with changing these metaphors is that changes in metaphors lead to reconceptualized roles and associated beliefs. Further, a focus on metaphors at this level of generality enables teachers to consider whether or not there are significant conflicts between the way they conceptualize and what they believe about their roles as facilitators of learning. (p. 134)

Metaphors provide teachers with a reflective device that can help us access our underlying beliefs. Beyond this, metaphors can be shifted and changed. Tobin and LaMaster (1992) provide an example of working with a first-year teacher to identify the metaphors she used to describe her role as teacher, classroom manager, and assessor of student performance. The teacher was asked to reflect on the assumptions in each of her metaphors. The contradictions in her roles and beliefs became apparent. Then, the teacher was asked to imagine new metaphors for each of these roles. As she reconceptualized her roles, dramatic changes in her teaching became apparent to her students and colleagues. Tobin and LaMaster suggest that one doesn't have to go through and change teacher beliefs one by one, but one can change the guiding metaphors and affect whole sets of beliefs. They state, "The futility of attempting to change beliefs one at a time became clear as the potential of using metaphors about roles as a master switch emerged" (p. 135).

Teachers can interrogate their guiding metaphors in order to begin to make conscious their assumptions about their roles, themselves, and their students. In addition, teachers can ask students to identify metaphors that describe the teacher's, the student's, and the student's family's roles in schooling. These metaphors can then be switched or changed in the conscious process of (re)framing practice. This is an effective means of teacher reflection.

Theoretical Frames

At least some of the frames we bring to bear on our work are, in an academic sense of the word, theoretical in nature. They are the theories we have learned about in our teacher training and through other avenues of academic learning. One way for a teacher to begin to reframe his or her seeing and interpreting of students' lives and behaviors would be to begin to explore various theoretical orientations. In addition to theories of education, psychological, sociological, anthropological, and philosophical theories provide alternative theoretical frames that open up the possibilities of our seeing differently.

Theoretical frames are often presented as "the truth" in our own education, rather than as social constructions. This can act as a means of shutting down further theoretical exploration. However, when we begin to look at different theories side by side, as Rhodes and Tracy (1975) did in their classic, multi-volume text, *A Study of Child Variance*, we realize that each theoretical perspective is based on a set of beliefs or assumptions that leads to different interpretations and interventions. Teachers who feel dissatisfied with the theoretical frames they have been taught can transform their own teaching by exploring different theoretical stances and applying them to their work with children.

Socioeconomic and Cultural Frames

Culture and social class provide additional sources of framing. We often mistake our own cultural frames as "the truth" (Young, 1990). When we are not challenged by other perspectives, our habitual way of cultural framing is often invisible and unconscious. When we begin to engage with others who have different cultural frames, we can be somewhat perplexed with their differences in attitude, social behavior, values, and beliefs. It is far too easy to equate the world we live in with the "real world" and treat others as somehow inferior. The tendency is to try to change our students to come into line with what feels comfortable to us, while not considering and valuing the child's cultural frames and experiences.

Several cultural theorists (Delpit, 1993; Kohl, 1994; MacLeod, 1995; McLaren, 1985, 1993) have carefully documented how students often resist our efforts to change their behaviors, values, language, beliefs, and attitudes to come into line with our own cultural mores. The difficulty exists because most of the cultural norms that have been institutionalized into educational practices, policies, and curricula reflect white, middle-class norms. Thus, students of color and low-income students often feel a deep sense of alienation within schools. Kohl (1994) points out that these students may reject the school's and/or teacher's world as a means of maintaining the integrity of their own social and cultural identity:

> Not-learning tends to take place when someone has to deal with unavoidable challenges to her or his personal and family loyalties, integrity, and identity. In such situations there are forced choices and no apparent middle ground. To agree to learn from a stranger who does not respect your integrity causes a major loss of self. The only alternative is to not-learn and reject the stranger's world. (p. 6)

The problem with the cultural frames we bring to teaching, and those that are deeply embedded in institutional culture, is that they are often invisible and unconscious. Few teachers set out to be insensitive to the cultural frames of their students and are therefore perplexed at students' resistance. Even teachers who share similar economic and cultural backgrounds with students often internalize the dominant norms and believe, consciously or unconsciously, that students must do the same in order to succeed. If teachers have not reflected deeply on their own economic and cultural frames, they will not be able to help students navigate the treacherous socialization process involved in schooling in ways that allow them to maintain the dignity of their own social, cultural, and familial identity.

Reflection on cultural and economic frames is difficult to do unless one engages with others who hold different cultural and economic worldviews. Anthropologists have learned that an engagement with people from other cultures allows them to not only learn about those people and cultures, but also look back at their own culture through different eyes. Tatum (1997) tells us that in the United States, white people often don't identify culture as part of their core identity; rather, they equate their cultural frames as being universal or "normal." People of color, on the other hand, almost always include race and/or ethnicity within their descriptions of self. For teachers who have lived white, middle-class lives with little exposure to people of other cultures and social classes, reflection on cultural and economic framing is much like a fish becoming aware of water.

Shifting our cultural frames involves learning about and from other cultures and people from different social and economic backgrounds. Often, our students and their families provide wonderful opportunities for us to reflect on our own cultural frames. The key is to notice when students and families resist us or disagree with us, either passively or assertively, and to ask them to help us understand the way they see things. The most important aspect of this ongoing communicative process is careful, respectful listening. A belief that social realities are socially constructed, multiple, and paradoxical allows teachers and students to understand that people can disagree without someone having to be right or wrong. This fundamental belief creates the space for openness and learning.

Another important source of learning to appreciate economic and social frames involves reading books, watching films, and attending art and cultural events that emanate from cultural and economic frames different from one's own. Spending time in social contexts that do not reflect and reify white, middle-class values provides opportunities for us to become sensitized to various social, economic, and cultural lenses. Spending time in a homeless shelter, befriending people with severe disabilities, or frequenting cultural events in which one is an ethnic minority allows teachers opportunities to become familiar with students' cultures and reflect back on their own. Watching the TV shows students watch, listening to their music, and reading their popular magazines also offer opportunities to connect with students through aspects of popular culture to which they are drawn.

(Re)framing our experiences of teaching and learning in relationship to culture and social class involves a deep process of consciousness raising. The more aligned we are with the dominant white, middle-class culture, the more we will need to intentionally engage in a reflective process that involves expanding our own social and cultural horizons. This process allows us to experience what many marginalized students feel when confronted with the white, middle-class culture of most schools. We begin to feel like the very foundations of our identity are thrown into question. However, engaging in such a process is the key to becoming sensitive, respectful, and supportive of our students as they confront images of self and other in curriculum and school culture. We do not lose our selves in the process, but expand our selves to a broader array of meanings. This deep personal learning will make us not only better teachers, but better human beings.

Institutional Frames

Each school comprises a unique institutional culture that is affected by many interrelated factors. The surrounding neighborhoods, the social and cultural makeup of the school, the administrative style and policies, and the school's own history all affect the institutional culture. Beyond this, the school district and the rules and regulations that provide the parameters for policy and practice provide powerful sources of framing and (re)framing. The school or district discipline code that prescribes penalties for certain infractions holds a powerful influence over how teachers and students make sense of various behaviors. Academic standards work much in the same way, by prescribing criteria for what is to be considered excellent, good, poor, and substandard work, as well as what knowledge is considered legitimate. Often, because these various rules and regulations are formalized, they are not questioned and therefore become the unexamined and privileged frames for interpreting school life.

Troubling students are often interpreted through these institutional frames in ways that cast them into roles of damnation. Teachers, following an ethic of conformity, often feel like it is not their place to challenge the rules and regulations of the school or district (which are often presented as being beyond question). Kohl (1994) uses his own learning as a teacher to explore how institutions work to shape the behaviors of students and teachers. He emphasizes the importance of getting to know his students and their parents outside of school in order to gain insight into the role the institutional culture plays in students' school behaviors and attitudes. His experience with students and their families beyond school led him to reflect on and reframe his interpretation of the school culture and his students' identities. Kohl describes his reframing as "creative maladjustment" in an essay in which he admonishes teachers to learn how to question, subvert, and, when necessary, resist the mandates of the institutional school culture when they do not serve the best interests of students:

I had to maladjust myself to the notion that the demands and the structure of schooling were normal and the students were problems if they did not adjust. This meant examining the nature of the life I was expected to lead as a teacher and sorting out what was sensible and beneficial for my students from procedures simply meant to keep things under control. This meant learning to recognize practices and texts which were racist and sexist, as well as coming to understand the mechanisms for tolerating professional incompetence and for marginalizing children who are outspoken or different. This had to be done while I was figuring out how to teach well, and I had to be creative about it if I wanted to keep my job. I had to develop the skills of creative maladjustment and integrate into every aspect of my teaching the idea that school was not always worth adjusting to and that my students were often right to resist the education that was being forced upon them. (pp. 133–134)

Teachers working with noncompliant or struggling students often find themselves in situations where they must creatively maladjust to school policy and practice in order to work in the best interests of their students. This is risky business, as Kohl points out, where teachers must be careful not to jeopardize their jobs. Many teachers worry that they are somehow doing something immoral if they do not submit to every mandate, even when it is clearly not in their students' best interests to do so. Teachers who blindly conform to the dictates of institutional culture will require their students to do so as well.

Ultimately, most teachers go into teaching because they are dedicated to children rather than school systems. (Re)framing that runs counter to institutional practices often requires teachers to go back to their deepest passions and values about teaching children. Although this can be a frightening endeavor, failure to do so when institutionally sanctioned practices disrespect students' integrity, identity, culture, or personal history makes us complicit in institutional cruelty. This is not why we become teachers, and a failure to interrogate these practices and resist them causes great harm not only to students, but also to the teachers who find themselves defending a system rather than advocating for children.

Children's Frames

The final source of framing and (re)framing that we will discuss involves the differences between how children and adults view the world. Noddings (1991a, 1991b) tells us that as adults, we have the capacity to both see the child and see with the child. Having been children ourselves at one point, we have a tacit understanding of childhood. Plus, we have all been students and remember the times we felt both cared for and disrespected within school contexts (Paul & Smith, 2000). It is amazing how readily we expect children to change their behaviors when many of us struggle with changing our own. Not only do teachers sometimes forget that children are children, we sometimes expect that they are capable of feats we do not expect of ourselves.

In spite of our own struggles, we often expect children to miraculously change how they act. We do not take into account their limited experiences, their own cognitive development, or the nature of the situations and contexts that have affected their behaviors. Adults who have experienced a painful breakup of a romantic relationship may avoid dating or commitment for some time out of fear of being hurt again, and yet we assume abused children should trust us without hesitation no matter what their histories with adults have been. This is not because we are uncaring, but largely because of professional training that focuses on changing behavior rather than understanding lives.

Children living in difficult situations in school, neighborhood, or home usually do not have the ability to change the situations in which they find themselves. And yet, we take the person with the least power (student) and expect him or her to do the most changing. Often, we do not ask children how they see things or what they are feeling or thinking. Children's perceptions of situations can help us understand the conceptual, experiential, and cultural frames that they bring to a situation, and yet we often spend our time trying to teach them the "right way" to act, think, and be without understanding their own logic and meanings. Ultimately, this leads to children feeling discounted and teachers making decisions without adequate reflection on students' interpretive frames.

It is important to engage in pedagogy and classroom processes that give students ample opportunities to share their view of the world and the classroom. Through writing stories and journals; drawing pictures; discussing readings, events, and processes; and answering teacher-made surveys about how they perceive the classroom, the teacher, and the school, students should have extensive opportunities to help their teachers shift their frames to see with them. Attempts to understand a child within his or her own interpretive frames allow teachers incredible insight into students' lives and worlds. It allows teachers to become flexible as they move from teacher perspectives to student perspectives and back again. In addition, when students feel they are being heard, seen, and respected, they often feel freer to learn from the person involved. It is important to stay open to each student's story and not diminish the importance of students' feelings, beliefs, and experiences.

In the remaining pages of this chapter, we will take a close look at the reflective work of two teachers, one teaching at the elementary level and one at the secondary level. These two examples will provide us with an understanding of the variation and individuality of reflective practice.

THINKING AHEAD: RELATING TO THE STORIES

The purpose of the teacher stories in the following sections is to flesh out the main concepts and practices of this chapter within a particular teacher's practice and within a specific situation. The concepts and practices play out quite differently depending on the situation, the students involved, and the teacher. As you read each of the teacher stories in the upcoming sections, it will be helpful to keep a small list of questions in mind.

1. In what ways do you think this story enacts the main themes or ideas of this chapter?

2. Putting yourself in the teacher's place, what do you think you might have done differently? The same? Why?

3. What troubles you about this story?

4. What brings you hope in this story?

5. What surprises you?

6. What insights, values, beliefs, and processes do you think the author was trying to convey through this story?

7. What stories of your own does this story remind you of?

MR. WATERS: REFLECTIVE TEACHING AS (RE)FRAMING

In our first example, we will analyze the ongoing development and use of (re)framing in relation to professional practice within the case of one elementary school teacher dealing with a problem situation involving a boy categorized as having an emotional/behavioral disorder (E/BD). As Schön (1983) has observed, reflection often takes place when a teacher runs into a turn of events that catches him or her by surprise, a situation when one of his or her usual ways of dealing with a social or behavioral issue does not bring the expected and desired results. The teacher then finds him- or herself questioning not only his or her actions but his or her way of framing the problem.

This case is drawn from an action research project undertaken by a teacher in a graduate course. *Action research* is a flexible process of teacher inquiry that encourages teachers to utilize and further refine their skills of reflection within a specific experiential course of events, helping teachers to mine personal experience for modes of useful knowledge (Cochran-Smith & Lytle, 1993; Elliott, 1991; Kincheloe, 1991).

Reggie Waters is an elementary school teacher who used action research to help him figure out how to deal more effectively with David, a fifth grader whose behavior had become increasingly disruptive and oppositional in recent weeks. As we follow this process of inquiry, we'll notice that he frames and reframes the problem three different times. He uses each problem framing as a working hypothesis, a starting place for gathering information and thinking about what to do. Each time, he discards a framing when he concluded that it fails to sufficiently inform and guide his practice. Finally, he finds his third problem framing to be a highly useful way of thinking in relation to this problem. He elaborates from this conceptualization and builds a fairly full theory to guide his action. Here is an overview of the three frames he considers.

- Problem framing #1—The reasons why David is misbehaving reside in his life history.

Mr. Waters: "If I want to help David behave better, I have to understand him as a whole person. I have to know more about his life and the problems he's had in the past."

- Problem framing #2—A teacher with sufficient skills can help David behave better.

Mr. Waters: "I will take a close look at my own practices as a teacher to see what I am doing right and what I may need to change in order to improve my skills."

- Problem framing #3—The power struggles between teacher and student continue only because both parties keep the battle going.

Mr. Waters: "I learned to give him [the student] some power."

Mr. Waters's initial way of seeing the problem draws heavily from his professional training and his own common sense. He decided that in order to help David, he would need to understand David's life in a more complete way. Essentially, he figured that there must be something in this boy's social and educational history that will explain his current behavior. Mr. Waters decided to compile a case study emphasizing those aspects of David's biography that would seem to be connected with the current problematic behavior.

Mr. Waters consulted school records and interviewed David's parents and other teachers to put together a biographic case study of this one boy. He asked David if he could interview him, but David declined. This biographic portrait combined information about David's family history and current home life with a narrative account of his development in relation to social history, academic learning, social skills, friendships, and relationships with school authorities. Mr. Waters traced David's ups and downs with particular emphasis on school behavior issues.

Mr. Waters found that David had been adopted, had a history of paranoid schizophrenia in his biological family, and had himself been diagnosed with Oppositional Defiant Disorder and Attention Deficit Hyperactivity Disorder. His adopted mother reported instances of verbal and physical aggression. David's behavior at school during his elementary years was similar to his behavior at home. Academically, David seemed to have average skills in all subject areas.

After completing this biography, Mr. Waters reflected that this activity did not help him to specifically understand his own interactions with David. He then decided to turn his analytic eye from the problematic student to his own professional thinking and action. He reasoned that his own behavior may have affected David's behavior. Additionally, he noted that it would be much easier to seek a solution that involved changing himself rather than trying to change David. Mr. Waters then reframed the problem toward a goal of analyzing his own weaknesses and strengths in dealing with David.

Mr. Waters felt that although he typically could reach and befriend troubled students, his efforts with David were falling short. Thinking back over recent behavior problem incidents, Mr. Waters theorized that he and David tended to come into conflict over minor matters, an embattled pattern of interpersonal conflict that kept the teacher and student from developing a positive and supportive relationship. Mr. Waters decided to take daily field notes for 4 weeks documenting all his conflicting interactions with David.

During the data collection, Mr. Waters reflected on what was happening and his own role in the conflict. He drew his analytic frame from readings in a university graduate course on processes of constructive conflict resolution (Johnson & Johnson, 1995a, 1995b). Conflict resolution researchers often theorize a conflict involving two persons as a shared dilemma, a problem held in common and contributed to in some fashion by each disputant. Responsibility for resolving that conflict falls to each side of the dispute.

Mr. Waters developed a picture of the typical scenario, a model of the average conflict incident he encountered with David. Generally, David broke some minor school or class rule. Mr. Waters confronted or redirected David in an effort to bring him back in line. David responded with a question or comment indicating that he didn't think he should have to behave in a different way. Mr. Waters responded by arguing back at the student. Soon, the student and teacher were verbally debating the issue. The debate always grew to be much larger and more heated than the original problem that prompted Mr. Waters's intervention in the first place. These heated feelings only set the stage for future conflicts. Furthermore, Mr. Waters noticed that he typically placed the sole blame for the struggle on David. This blaming left David feeling very angry at his teacher.

Mr. Waters viewed these power struggles in the light of his concept of a positive and useful relationship between teacher and student. That relationship concept involved a certain degree of trust, mutual enjoyment, respect, and affectionate feelings. He considered such a relationship necessary to a teacher working effectively with and helping a student. He began to question the negative impact of the power struggles on their relationship. After one notably exhausting struggle, he predicted, "If we found ourselves in another power struggle that day, we might have damaged our relationship beyond repair."

Mr. Waters began to notice and take responsibility for his own part in creating and maintaining the power struggles. He saw that he often attempted to make David feel guilty for not following his directions. Also, he observed that he tended to provide David with no real options other than doing the one thing that his teacher was demanding. David often reacted to this kind of controlling approach by becoming defensive, by digging in his heels and refusing to cooperate.

At the conclusion of the action research, Mr. Waters came to a number of important lessons he learned about avoiding future power struggles with David:

> First, I learned to pick my fights. If what he is doing is not a big deal, then don't make a big deal about it. . . . Second, I learned that I shouldn't just tell him what to do without explaining to him why I want him to do it. If he knows where I'm coming from, he will be more likely to do what I ask. Third, I learned to give him some power. I always try to give him choices when I ask him to do something. If he feels like he is in control of the situation, then there will be no power struggle.

In this case, we see Mr. Waters dealing with questions concerning the authority of his teaching role and the quality of his relationships with students. He is a third-year teacher whose prior uses of authority primarily consisted of giving directions to students who complied or at least seemed to comply with his wishes. David presented a novel situation by directly denying his authority, catching Mr. Waters off guard and provoking him into a position of questioning his own use of authority.

At first, Mr. Waters's mode of thinking forestalls reflection, failing to open up serious questions about his use of authority by continuing to apply his customary authority stance to the novel situation. When he sees that the relationship between himself and David is in jeopardy of permanent damage, a loss that Mr. Waters views as personally and professionally unacceptable, he is jolted out of his usual authority role and opens up to critical examination. He begins to refashion his model of the interactions between himself and David to involve a negotiation between two parties, each having some input into the matter. This is a dramatic alteration of the professional role for Mr. Waters that can be drawn on in future situations.

DIGGING IN: MAKING THE STORY PERSONAL

Perhaps the most powerful lessons we can take from a story occur when we allow ourselves to reflect and connect in a deeply personal and emotional way with what happened. We can often do this by placing ourselves in the roles of the teacher or the students, connecting those roles to the rich experiences of our own lives.

1. In this story, Mr. Waters gradually shifts from viewing a single student as the source of a problem to viewing the problem as shared between himself and the student. Have you ever made this interpretive shift in viewing a student or situation? When? How did it change your approach to the problem?

2. Consider a power struggle you have had with a student or a child. How was it resolved? What lessons can you learn from this experience?

A PORTRAIT OF REFLECTIVE TEACHING, WRITING, AND BEING

The following journal entries are written by Craig Ahern, a middle-level special education teacher. He loves learning and is particularly interested in constructivism as philosophy and educational practice. At first, Craig struggled with the open-endedness of constructivism. He wanted to pin down answers. But as time went on, Craig began to enact constructivism in very authentic and personal ways. He began to try on different lenses in his writing and his teaching. His opinions became less certain, opening up space for change.

The first piece expresses Craig's conceptualization of reflective writing and how it has allowed him to become a more conscious, empowered person. The second excerpt is a sample from an entry in Craig's teaching journal. He uses the journal as a tool to help him understand the activities taking place around him and the thoughts and feelings that flow through his consciousness, and as a catalyst for personal and professional growth.

Craig's Reflections on Reflection; Writing on Writing

As I begin to write in my reflection frame, I allow the words to flow from myself onto the page. I don't want to spend time thinking about what I am going to write because it brings in hesitations and self-doubts. It is as if I am revealing and creating who I am at the same time. As I begin following my words to the paper, I wait for self-discovery later on to explore who I was at that given moment. Therefore, I do not delete anything, and I allow the paper to become the evidence of how I am feeling at the present time. There are times when I feel that I want to censor what I write because I am afraid of what other people will think. However, if I do that, I am no longer true to myself, no longer creating who I may become. There is a certain freedom within this way of writing. In essence, I am my own helper and not only heal but create who I am through my writing. I give myself the power to explore within the inner recesses of the mind while pulling this out into my everyday world. As I continue to write, I find there are really no borders between the inside world and the outside world. As I become aware that I have the ability to explore these possibilities within the outside world, I look for different possibilities in what I see. The way I saw things before begins to go within the background, and what I did not know was there comes into focus. I have entered a new world I have literally created and that becomes curious for me to explore.

I am soup with the world. Inseparable, we're blended like a soup having endless possibilities. I want my writing to have anger, sadness, happiness, and all the emotion, because these are the spices of my life soup that give me meaning and flavor. I want to actively leave an imprint of who I am. As I begin to give myself tolerance for my own flow of ideas, I begin to give others acceptance of their ideas and creating as well. As I add the ingredients of thinking within my soup, I begin to find my writing taking on a whole different level of creative meaning. I no longer feel that my thoughts are the dominant figure, but have become the background to the foreground of my feelings. For me, thinking was always the foreground, and I have chosen to reverse this figure-ground to bring life back within my life. For me, life without emotion left a world without passion.

Reflecting on One Day in the Life of a Teacher

(In the following excerpt from Craig's journal, italics are used to denote a shift in reflection from the "outside" world of school events to the "inside" world of Craig's thoughts and emotions. The italics mark off the feelings, thoughts, and wondering that stirred inside of Craig.)

I was cautious of Eddie when he arrived today at school since I wanted to let him know I meant business. I no longer wanted to play the victim with him. I was ready to pounce on him when he came into school. I was not willing to give him any benefit of the doubt. I was emotionally raw when it came to Eddie and I was afraid that if I did not pull him back in, I would lose him.

George's parents came in and wanted to talk about yesterday's incident. The students were doing morning work when they entered the room with George. I went out in the hallway to discuss with them how George spit at the playground supervisor. His Dad told me that he knew that George had done wrong in the past, but he believed that this detention was not justified. He wanted me to know that George told him he did not spit on the supervisor and that George was an honest child. I told him that I was not there but had to rely on the lunch room supervisor's story. I told him that her story had more authority than George's since it was from a teacher. I told them that the decision was made based on the decision of another staff member and I had to go along with that decision since it was above my head.

George's mother seemed to interrupt his father a lot.

George's mother spoke about how George has built up a reputation. I agreed. Even as we talked, George was having a conflict with both Eddie and Josh. I stuck my head in the room and told them all to get back to work. I noticed George was armed with two pencils, defensively pointing them in the direction of Eddie and Josh. When I went back to talking with George's parents, Eddie left the room and I did not try to stop him. I finished up with George's parents, then I went searching for Eddie after talking with my assistant about what went on when I was outside the room. She said Eddie took the initiative to leave the room without any permission.

This made me angry at him because he was taking this too far. I wanted to let him have it.

Gym time came shortly, and as we were lining up the stairs Eddie was coming down the stairs. He got first in line and began bragging about skipping class.

I was becoming furious at him when I dropped them off for gym.

I left them in gym and was quickly pulled aside by the principal who asked me about George's parents. I told him what I told them and he was irritated that I allowed the parents to get off with the comment that George was telling the truth. As far as he was concerned the playground supervisor's story should not have been questioned. I told him I was with the kids and I didn't want to argue with the parents and let it go at that. I also spilled about his fight within the room yesterday. I told him that George grabbed me when I stopped the fight and how I had presented this to George's parents as further justification for the detention. The principal was becoming overwhelmed. I continued about Eddie purposely not coming to class and bragging about it to the other students. I pointed out that this might lead to me sending Eddie to the office with my aide if he continues to be a loose cannon.

I was filled with emotions and was releasing these emotions with words in a conversation with the principal. Later, I became angry at myself, thinking I had revealed too much.

I went to the gym to confront Eddie. I was going to have a showdown with him and tell him what I felt about him skipping class. As I got to the gym, the class was nowhere in sight.

I thought to myself that Eddie was damned lucky.

I went to the social worker's office and told her I might need her to see Eddie. I was worried that he might blow since he was pushing the limits. I told her of my choice to be firm with him.

My story was bullshit because I was the one who was going to blow and I transferred it onto Eddie. I was doing everything I try to forbid my students to do at times. I was trying to solve my problems through intimidation. In all truthfulness I do not know what I would have done if I had seen Eddie. Probably I would have been tactful. However, I will never know because he was not there and I was able to fantasize how lucky he was for not being there.

My assistant told me that she feels everyone except Glen has been following Eddie.

I became angry at how much power he really had and how powerless I felt. I wanted the students to like me and be influenced by me. I was beginning to have all of the feelings that make me feel alive with these kids. I feel like I have an investment and feel helpless at how easy all of it can be taken away. This is the core of teaching, where my heart and soul is into the kids and I feel extreme pain and love for these kids as if they were my own.

When I entered the room after gym I asked Eddie to come out in the hall to talk with me. In spite of my fantasies to "let him have it," I talked to him about his leadership skills and how others looked up to him. I told him I needed his help. He agreed and reentered the classroom. He continued operating with the same amount of freedom but became much more responsible and stopped creating problems at that moment.

I had been frozen in my anger in the morning, whereas he was able to go on to the next situation. I was only able to help him when I became unfrozen and was able to put it behind me and pretend that we were really starting over.

I decided that I was going to try group work with science but they didn't want to so I ditched the idea. We all read the work together while I discussed the section in more detail. Some of them got out of their seats to check and help the others, which was fine. They finished ten minutes early and I gave them time on the computer. After that, we went on to social studies. I paired them up to work in groups. They didn't want to work in the groups I assigned them. Eddie became leader and said that he and Josh had to work in different groups because they always work together. Finally after five minutes of problem solving they had worked it out to where Eddie worked with Carl, Don worked with Josh, and George worked with my assistant. They worked at different levels filling in the resource chart.

When we got ready for lunch, I asked everyone to help George during lunch to stay out of trouble and they agreed. I asked George also and he told me he really wanted to try and accomplish recess without fighting. Later, when one of the yard teachers entered the building I had asked her how George was doing at recess, she said that he was laughing and playing with four girls. When recess was over and George neared the building, I ran out to him and told him that I was proud of him. I hammed it up and it was contagious. Josh hugged me and I told them that everyone did great team work.

The end of the day came and I told the kids that every teacher deserves a great day. I told them I had a super day and hoped they did also. There were many successes and I told them I was really proud of them. Josh hugged me again. Eddie started hugging others but then turned it into bear hugs.

I love this great group despite all of the different emotions I have experienced today. They have surprised me and helped me come out of my shell in so many ways.

DIGGING IN: MAKING THE STORY PERSONAL

1. At one point, Craig realizes, *"I was trying to solve my problems through intimidation."* Look closely at your own practices. Do you use intimidation in an effort to change students' behavior? If so, how? What else might you do that would be both more respectful and more effective?

2. In this story, Craig notices that his strong love for and desire to teach his students set the stage for his many feelings of disappointment and frustration toward those very students. When have you felt frustration and disappointment toward your students or others in your life? How do you cope with these types of frustration and disappointment?

TIPS FOR TEACHERS

1. Read teacher autobiographies as a means of enjoyment and to provoke reflection on your life as a teacher.

2. Ask your students to write a piece telling how they would describe you to a new student. Tell them to be completely honest. Note your surprises, joys, and disappointments in response to their depictions.

3. Decide what you would like to accomplish in your professional development each year and determine means to evaluate your own progress.

4. Keep artifacts from teaching such as class photographs, videos, copies of students' work, and so on. This will provide rich fodder for reflection over the years.

SUMMARY

Reflective teaching requires us to represent the way we see things. These representations occur in the stories we tell in dialogue and in journals. Looking back at the way we depict our classroom experiences provides glimpses of classroom life and our own thinking and beliefs. Beyond the opportunities our teacher stories provide for reflection are the possibilities of transforming our teaching through (re)framing. There are several ways to (re)frame our work. First, we can examine and switch the metaphors we use to conceptualize our roles. Second, we can (re)frame our interpretation of the classroom by bringing different theories to bear on our interpretations. Third, we can learn about diverse social, economic, and cultural frames in order to understand our students better and to make our own cultural framing more visible and conscious. Fourth, we can interrogate the practices of institutional culture in order to move beyond a blind conformity to school policy. Finally, we can provide students with ample opportunities to share their perspectives and frames with us, so we can learn to see with the child as well as help the child see with us.

Reflective teaching involves actively cultivating an openness to ourselves and the world. Reflective teaching helps teachers understand that there are multiple ways to construct a situation, a student, our roles, our classrooms, and our schools. Reflective teaching provides teachers with continuous opportunities to learn and grow as human beings. As we learn to move around a situation, trying on different frames, we become more flexible, tolerant, and respectful, and, in the process, allow our students to do the same. This is a far more lofty and lasting goal than doing what "works," and it makes the process of education vastly more dimensional, enjoyable, and meaningful.

CONSTRUCTING PERSONAL MEANINGS

1. Keep a personal journal. After you have compiled a few weeks' worth of entries, read back over what you have written. What can you learn about the ways that you habitually construct your students, your self, and your work with students?

2. Find a critical friend, a colleague who will agree to talk with you on a regular basis and provide constructive criticism that provokes you to look more deeply at your teaching.

3. Interpret acts of student resistance as acts of constructive criticism. Rather than attribute the problem to the student, ask yourself, What is this student's resistance communicating to me? How does this student construct this situation? What might this student want or need?

4. Disrupt your cultural security. Go to a restaurant, church, bar, or other social place where the cultural norms (including language) differ markedly from your own. Make it a practice to periodically or even frequently socialize with persons from different social classes, religions, ethnic/racial groups, sexual orientations, and nationalities. Use these cultural self-disruptions as opportunities to broaden your own awareness and sensitivity.

Part III
Programs and Practices

7

Using Conflict Resolution as Instruction

Schools must become more conflict-positive. They must become places where conflicts are encouraged; where students have the opportunity to resolve their disputes themselves, in mutually satisfactory ways, without having to engage the attention of a teacher; and where the same set of negotiation and mediation procedures are known to and used by everyone.

(Johnson & Johnson, 1996, p. 334)

JUST MY LUCK, A CONFLICT

The idea of liking and encouraging conflict seems crazy. With our most troubling students, it often seems like the students' job is to create turmoil and unrest, setting fires here, there, and everywhere. And the teacher's job is to rush around in harried fashion with the fire extinguisher, putting out existing blazes and soaking matches in the hands of the fire-starters whenever possible. It sounds like an impossible act of mental gymnastics to view our students' problems in getting along with others or in coping with emotionally difficult situations as useful opportunities for learning and growth. Leading researchers on conflict resolution Johnson and Johnson (1996) advise us to do just that, to embrace social conflicts as occasions ripe with educational potential. Rather than spending the school day running away from problems (and any experienced teacher realizes that problems will hunt you down and find you anyway), we can take a current predicament as a prime opportunity to teach the students how to handle things in a better way. Rather than attempting to solve social conflicts *for* our students by intervening in an authoritative way, a common practice that only teaches students to be helpless and dependent in the face of interpersonal difficulties, we can take the immediate conflict as one of those infamous teachable moments.

In this chapter, we proceed from the assumption that troubling students, if provided with sufficient emotional support and guidance, can learn to deal with social conflicts in more peaceful and cooperative ways. We do not pretend that providing this support and guidance guarantees that students enveloped in daily lives of violence, confusion, cruelty, and suffering will necessarily and immediately embrace peace, calm, and mutual respect. The challenges of teaching peace are enormous in a society saturated with violence and abuse.

We do not deny the difficult and even overwhelming realities facing special and general education teachers. What we promise is that the processes of conflict resolution we will explain in this chapter provide an ethical, practical way of working with students who frequently engage in aggressive, abusive, or violent behavior. We believe that violence is not remedied by violence, nor cruelty by cruelty, disrespect by disrespect. A courageous and hopeful path embracing practices that enact and teach peace in the face of violence, cruelty, and disrespect is the most ethical choice we know.

How can we help our students learn to deal with interpersonal conflicts in peaceful and constructive ways rather than violent and harmful ways? How can we help our students deal with conflicts in ways that help them become more emotionally strong, socially skilled, morally concerned, and relationally bonded to their classmates, friends, teachers, and family?

We will first examine the rich social psychological literature on conflict and conflict resolution. This will help us get a grasp on the nature of conflicts between individuals and between groups. It will help us to understand the difference between conflicts that are resolved in destructive, harmful ways and conflicts that are negotiated and resolved in ways that further relationships, cultivate peace, and provide crucial opportunities for personal growth. We will provide case examples of constructive, destructive, and mixed constructive-destructive conflict processes that are stories from our own experiences working with kids. Then, we will look at the specific ways that schools and teachers can teach students to mediate, negotiate, and compromise. These ways consist of both cultivating a social climate of cooperation and utilizing more formal processes of mediation. Finally, we hear first-hand accounts from a teacher who uses conflict resolution processes in her work with students experiencing social and behavioral difficulties.

RESEARCH AND THEORY ON
CONFLICTS AND CONFLICT RESOLUTION

Morton Deutsch spent the better part of six decades researching and thinking about processes of conflict and the resolution of conflict (e.g., Bunker & Rubin, 1995; Deutsch, 1949, 1973, 1990, 1994; Deutsch et al., 1992). He was a social psychologist who completed countless experimental studies examining the types of conflict in which people engage and the external conditions that support peaceful resolution or explosive escalation. He also researched the effectiveness of various approaches to teaching people the necessary knowledge, attitudes, and skills to resolve conflicts through mutual negotiation and agreement. He concluded that conflicts generally can be divided into two specific categories, *destructive* and *constructive*. He also theorized that the social conditions that surround, define, and influence how a conflict is perceived and handled by participants can be divided into two basic categories, *competitive* and *cooperative*. Conflicts occur in either condition, but the ways conflicts are dealt with tend to be different. In this section, we will explain all four of these terms. We will explain how competitive social situations tend to promote destructive conflicts, and cooperative social environments tend to promote constructive conflicts. We'll start off by defining conflict and work forward from there.

According to Deutsch (1973),

> A *conflict* exists whenever incompatible activities occur. The incompatible actions may originate in one person, group, or nation; such conflicts are called *intra*personal, *intra*group, or *intra*national. An action that is incompatible with another action prevents, obstructs, interferes, injures, or in some way makes the latter less likely or less effective. (p. 10)

Adapting this definition to our purposes, we can see that school-based conflicts involve episodes in which the actions of one party (student, group of students, teacher, etc.) and the actions of another party (student, group of students, teacher, etc.) are opposed in such a way that they cannot both occur. Heads bump, and goals and wants collide.

Destructive conflicts result in outcomes that are not satisfactory to any of the participants. Often, the situation escalates into a firm stand-off or an embittered, ongoing feud that leads to violence or other side battles. Central to the destructive conflict is competition. If a conflict is viewed by the disputing parties as a competition, it is assumed that a satisfactory outcome for one party (person or group) depends on an unsatisfactory outcome for the other party. This is also called a zero-sum game or a win-lose situation. Only one side can win; the other must lose. The goal of each participant is to end up in the winner's circle, thereby placing the opposition in the loser's column. This approach is typical of war and court trials (Deutsch, 1973).

Constructive conflicts result in outcomes that are satisfactory to all participants. When a conflict is handled in a constructive way, both parties get some or all of what they want or need. Sometimes, needs and wants are redefined to create new goals and new alliances. A constructive conflict is called a *win-win situation* because both sides emerge sharing a mutual victory. The well-being of one party is assumed to be intimately linked to the well-being of the other party, allowing for a compromise solution. This approach to handling conflicts is common in negotiated agreements between a workers' union and management or two countries who agree upon a plan of peace (Deutsch, 1973).

There is a dramatic difference between the social conditions of cooperation and the social conditions of competition. Cooperation involves some degree of *interdependence*—a lived sense that the fate and well-being of conflicting parties are connected. The happiness and health of one is assumed to be positively linked to the health and happiness of the other. The fulfillment of one requires the fulfillment of the other.

Although a competitive social arrangement does not guarantee a destructive conflict, it tends to work in that direction, moving against the peaceful, cooperative resolution of conflicts. Conversely, although a social setting/situation filled with cooperation does not guarantee a negotiated, mutual resolution to a conflict, it tends to support such a positive result. The reason is that individuals are greatly influenced by the kinds of social situations—the external factors, environmental arrangements, systemic ecologies, relational climates—that surround their decision making. These social contexts present the unwritten rules of the game, which are the behavioral norms, habits, and codes used by a given group in a given place. The same person may handle conflicts very differently in a cooperative setting in comparison to a competitive setting. Table 7.1 shows the processes of cooperation and competition side by side to explain how each influences an individual's communication, perception, attitudes, and approach to conflict.

SETTING THE STAGE FOR CONSTRUCTIVE CONFLICT RESOLUTION: CULTIVATING COOPERATION IN THE CLASSROOM

At this point, the reader is probably pointing to the entire middle column of Table 7.1—the cooperative side—and saying, "Yes, that's what I want to see in my classroom. How do I do that?" Here is where we turn to what is called *Deutsch's crude law of social relations:* "the characteristic processes and effects elicited by a given type of social relationship (cooperative or competitive) also tend to elicit that type of social relationship" (Deutsch, 1990, p. 245). What this means is that cooperation is achieved only through cooperation. The ends cannot be separated from the means. If the goal is to cultivate a classroom or school setting in which cooperative, socially concerned actions are the norm, the only way of getting there is through those same actions. This means that cooperation cannot be coerced or demanded by an authority figure who enforces cooperation through the use of power, punishments, and rewards. Cooperation involves

Table 7.1   How Do Students Tend to Behave in Social Processes of Cooperation and Competition?

	Cooperation	Competition
How do students communicate with one another?	Communication tends to be open, honest, and trusting. Each student wants to listen to and be informed by the other.	Communication tends to be distorted or shut down. Each student wants to discourage or mislead the other.
How do students feel about one another?	Students tend to feel an increased sensitivity to similarities and common interests shared with others. Differences are minimized or set aside.	Students tend to feel an increased sensitivity to differences. Dissimilarities are heightened and turned into sharp, moral distinctions ("You are bad; I am good.").
What attitudes do students hold toward one another?	Students tend to be trusting, friendly, and helpful to others.	Students tend to be suspicious, hostile, and exploitative to others.
How do students handle conflicts with one another?	Conflicts between students are viewed as shared problems to be solved by collaboration. Attempts to influence others are limited to negotiations and gentle persuasion.	Conflicts between students are viewed as problems to be solved by complete victory of one side over another. Conflicts are often escalated in scope. Attempts to influence others are coercive and forceful.

NOTE: Based on Deutsch (1949, 1973, 1990).

respect for the perspective of other persons, sensitivity to their needs, empathy for their feelings, and concern for their well-being. Building cooperation by way of cooperation involves actively living these values in working with students while encouraging and teaching the same at every step.

Much of the work of cultivating the social conditions supporting cooperation comes down to the development of a healthy classroom and school climate consisting of the following eight elements (Deutsch, 1973, 1990):

1. *Trusting relationships*—The glue that holds a teacher and a group of students together in a way that encourages cooperation and sharing is trust. Students will work together to resolve difficult issues only to the extent that they trust their teacher and one another. Without trust, one would be foolish to negotiate a problem or settle a dispute with a handshake agreement. Conversely, a peacefully resolved problem can help to build trust between people who previously viewed one another with suspicion. New breakthroughs

in resolving conflicts peacefully and mutually nurture the development of trust, building friendships between students who previously had remained distant from and suspicious of one another.

2. *Open communication*—Trust and cooperation depend on the ability, opportunity, and safety to openly express feelings and ideas with one another. When the lines of communication are open, allowing each to speak honestly and directly without fear or suspicion, then alliances and allegiances are fostered and strengthened.

3. *Readiness to help others*—We could also call this empathy or social concern. When individuals feel and believe in their interdependence with others, then reaching out to aid a peer or teacher is barely separable from helping oneself. This is the nature of community as we envision it.

4. *Sense of commonality*—Often, what divides students comes down to deeply seated beliefs about "people like me" and "people not like me." Differences in race/ethnicity, gender, social class, nationality, religion, sexual orientation, disability, and neighborhood are often translated into identity markers creating the beloved "us" and hated "them." These social walls can be powerful in dividing students into isolated cliques. Furthermore, some individuals sequester themselves into an island of one by believing that no one is like them, that no one can truly understand. Cultivating cooperation involves helping students to honor human and cultural differences while emphasizing what is shared and common across those differences. Students who find reason for common ground and a shared communal identity are more likely to work and live in cooperative ways.

5. *"Power with" instead of "power over"* (Kriesberg, 1992)—Power and responsibility go hand in hand. When we place students in positions of low power—those times when we wield power over them and coerce compliance—students hold little ownership for their actions or investment in the consequences of their actions. Sharing power with students places them in positions whereby they are supported in accepting responsibility for their actions and in making decisions in their own lives.

> Requiring students to obey rules out of fear of punishment reduces student self-regulation. . . . Allowing students to be joint architects in matters affecting them promotes their feelings of control and autonomy, higher level moral reasoning, and ultimate self-regulation of behavior. . . . The more students are given responsibility for regulating their own and their classmates' behavior, the more autonomous and socially competent they can become. (Johnson & Johnson, 1996, p. 323)

6. *Creative thinking*—Many social conflicts perpetuate due to cognitive inflexibility and emotional rigidity. People trapped in ongoing feuds often lean on old problems as if they were familiar friends without whom they can't live. Such traps often rely on simplistic, black-and-white forms of thinking. Novel

thoughts and fresh ways of seeing can create new opportunities for change and growth.

7. *"Cooperative commitment"* (Deutsch, 1973, p. 364)—Whether spoken or unspoken, a cooperative commitment is a shared sense of unity, "all for one and one for all" or "we are all in this together." Sergiovanni (1992, p. 103) calls this a "covenant," an agreement made by all members of a group or class concerning the rights and obligations of each community member, a social contract outlining what each individual owes to others and what the groups owes to each individual.

8. *"Benevolent misperception"* (Deutsch, 1973, p. 364)—People who share close and successful relationships—long-term partners, family members—tend to see their loved ones (to some extent) through proverbial rose-colored glasses. They often perceive the actions of loved ones in a positive light. Of course, this does not mean the denial of large and important problems such as patterns of abuse. It simply means attributing positive intentions in unclear situations, seeing a loved one as basically good and trustworthy.

In the next three sections, we'll present stories from our own work with troubling students. The first will demonstrate a social conflict handled in a destructive way. The second is an example of a constructive conflict. After each example, we will briefly examine the reasons why the conflict was resolved in a destructive or constructive manner, emphasizing the influences of cooperative and competitive contexts in the incident. We present these two clear types of incidents for purposes of demonstration. Many conflicts are mixtures of constructive and destructive.

DIVIDE AND CONQUER: AN EXAMPLE OF DESTRUCTIVE CONFLICT

I (Danforth) was teaching an E/BD self-contained class for students in grades two through five. Our single class was a day treatment program for young children located in a psychiatric hospital. At the time of this example, the class consisted of six students, five boys (Lloyd, Reggie, Chaz, Danny, and Johnny) and one girl (Sherry). All were fourth graders except Danny, a second grader who was wide enough, round enough, and surly enough to hold his own against the older guys.

"Can we line up for lunch, Mr. D?" Johnny asked. The big white clock on the wall was nearing noon. The word "lunch" drew every little head upward in anticipation. They had been working so hard all morning, I thought.

The students had gotten very competitive lately over who was doing the best and the most schoolwork. They had come up with the idea that the best worker gets to lead the line. So, they always wanted a lunch line so that someone could win the morning competition. I went along with it because the kids seemed to want the competition so badly. Also, this silly game seemed to motivate them to work hard on academic tasks all morning.

"I did the most work of anyone," Chaz called out from his desk at the other end of the room.

"No way!" countered Johnny. "You don't even do spelling. I did a whole unit."

Quickly, the voices were flying from everywhere.

"Mr. D! Pick me! I did my homework every day this week."

"Sherry can't go first 'cuz girls come after boys."

"OK, gang, everybody quiet so I can make my decision." The room went silent. All eyes were on me as they awaited the official naming of the line leader. As I opened my mouth to speak, I was interrupted by Chaz. Anticipating the fact that he would not be first, he pushed his math book onto the floor and groaned, "Ah, it's never me. This whole thing isn't fair."

Then, Johnny, seeing that Chaz was defeated, shot his competitor a whispered dig, "You'd win if this was a stupid contest." I caught Johnny's eye, giving him a "cut it out" look. Chaz hung his head in silent defeat.

I walked to the door to call the students to the lunch line. "Line leader today is . . . Sherry. She worked very hard on some very difficult. . . ." My words were drowned out by a flurry of disagreeing gasps, "oh mans," and "no ways." I then called the next best student—Johnny—followed in order by Reggie, Danny, Lloyd, and the last-place Chaz.

Once all six students were lined up, we started down the hallway toward the cafeteria. I quickly noticed that Johnny was walking backwards and teasing the down-and-out Chaz. When Chaz kept his head down and didn't respond to the teasing, Johnny taunted, "I bet your Momma always rides last on the city bus."

This comment about Chaz's mother struck a raw nerve. Chaz's mother, unbeknownst to Johnny, was in prison at the time on drug charges. Chaz missed her terribly. He was living with his grandparents for the 9-month sentence. Chaz lashed out in anger at Johnny, leaping forward to push him against the wall. Chaz generally wasn't much of a fighter. He usually kept to himself, a solitary and gloomy loner. Chaz was all mouth. He was rapid fire with the words, insulting and annoying as could be.

The two boys flew across the hallway. Chaz quickly pinned Johnny to the wall by the shoulders. I jumped in. "Enough! Enough!" I pushed the two apart with my hands. They separated easily.

"He's calling my mother names!" Chaz whined. He began to pace about in anxiety and anger. Tears flooded down his face. He turned his back so that his classmates couldn't see.

"He's the one stupid enough to always come last," Johnny replied.

"Quiet!" I shouted. "Sherry, lead the rest of the class down to the cafeteria. I'll walk behind with these two." Sherry and the others walked ahead, leaving me and the two would-be fighters standing in the hallway. I put my hand on each boy's shoulder. "Now we're going to walk quietly down to the cafeteria.

I don't want a word out of either of you. You'll get your food and I'll put you each at your own table. You'll sit by yourself, away from the group, away from each other, and eat quietly. You hear?"

"It's his fault for being so dumb, Mr. D," Johnny continued. "If—"

"Enough! Case closed! Not another word!" I barked out forcefully.

"OK, OK." Johnny looked at me with exasperation. Chaz was brooding in silent withdrawal by now. We walked down the hallway. The boys did as I had directed, each eating his lunch alone.

After finishing their lunch, the students carried their trays into the tray return area at the far end of the cafeteria. I noticed that Johnny and Chaz had gone to the tray return area at the same time. A caution light went off in my head, but I was too far away to do anything but watch. I could see them exchanging words. Their lips were moving. Then Chaz just blew up. He picked Johnny up—a boy the same size as he was—and stuffed him rear-end first into the big yellow trash barrel. He followed this with a hale of fists. I ran to the other end of the room to break up the fight.

In the weeks to come, I kept Johnny and Chaz far apart. I placed their desks at opposite ends of the room. I made them play separately on the playground. To me, they were fire and gasoline, a problem waiting to happen. I "solved" the problem by not letting them interact.

One day, I was out sick. I had the flu and was running an ugly fever. A substitute took my place. I hated to miss a day of work. I felt like the kids needed me to be there, and I didn't want them chewing up some naïve sub.

When I returned the next day, I found out that Chaz and Johnny had a big fight on the playground. Chaz ended up with six stitches above his eye from a rock with which Johnny hit him. The sub hadn't kept the two boys apart.

ANALYSIS OF "DIVIDE AND CONQUER"

The social context of this story consists of both cooperative and competitive elements. Additionally, and most important, we see me, the teacher, dealing with a conflict between two students with authority and avoidance rather than discussion and negotiation.

Cooperation was probably most common in the way the group played together. In that class, we worked hard and we played hard. Three specific social and play activities brought about lots of cooperation. The children loved to build with Legos®. We had an enormous set of Lego® blocks, and the students often worked in pairs and trios on large-scale building projects. Our recreation therapist had an incredible array of arts-and-crafts materials for the students. They did solo projects, but they also worked together on large murals and group crafts. Finally, the group spent 20 to 30 minutes each day giving one another back rubs. We did this each day after lunch. The group spread out some tumbling mats across the floor, and they took turns giving each other back massages on the floor. This activity was a wonderful way to build trust and connection between the students. Cooperation existed at the most basic, physical level. This was an especially great accomplishment with the many students who had histories of physical and/or sexual abuse. Trusting others to touch their bodies in safe and comforting ways was a great step forward.

Competition came in many forms in this class. In this story, we can see them battling to be top student so they can lead the lunch line. They also competed on the playing field and in the various games we played in the classroom. On the playground, they played basketball. In the class, the students often competed at marbles. The recreation therapist taught them how to play an old-fashioned game of marbles, and the group took the game very seriously.

Also, in this example, I allow the competition to be line leader to occur because I am so pleased that the very thought of possibly leading the line motivates my students to do academics all morning. The group would turn the academics into the arena for a macho competition. Unfortunately, I feed right into that competition. I am so pleased that the competition keeps the students working hard all morning that I fail to notice how the same competition is tearing the group apart.

My approach to dealing with the conflict between Johnny and Chaz does not allow them the opportunity to solve it through conversation and mutual understanding. I assume that my teacher authority must be used to squelch conflict, to keep it from happening. This only leads to further and more pronounced conflict. The unresolved issue between the two boys festers and grows. When my authority is unable to hold the two apart, the situation turns violent.

SPEAK WITH ME: AN EXAMPLE OF CONSTRUCTIVE CONFLICT

This incident occurred during my (Danforth) first year working with students considered E/BD. I was an untrained teacher's aide in a small high school for E/BD–labeled students. We had four classrooms and taught 38 boys and 2 girls. I was the only male staff member.

The students often entered the building in the morning in a sleepy, silent daze. They came on lengthy bus rides from six surrounding counties. Many waited for the bus in the early morning darkness, fell asleep on the ride, and awoke when the driver called out, "We're here!"

That morning was very different from the usually silent rows of zombies stumbling off the buses and into their homerooms. The hallways erupted with shouting and scuffling. I don't know what I was doing, but I recall sticking my head out into the hallway to see a group of teachers separating Edgar and Nate. Edgar quieted down pretty quickly. Nate paced back and forth, waving his arms, roaring on and on about something. Sally Hearn, a teacher, motioned for the other teachers to take the boys down to the conference room. Sally grabbed me by the arm and whispered, "Feel like trying something new? I could use a hand."

I was new. I didn't know any better. I said, "OK."

Sally and I walked down to the conference room. The two boys were sitting in chairs in opposite corners of the room. Both boys looked pretty upset. Edgar seemed sad, sullen, withdrawn, and dark. Nate was still very anxious and agitated. He moved around in his seat and occasionally mumbled under his breath.

Sally took charge of the meeting at this point, explaining to all of us how we would handle this. "OK, now, fellas. I see that you're prepared to sit at the table and work this problem out. Am I right?"

Edgar gave a silent look of agony. I wondered what he was thinking. He seemed so uncomfortable in his own skin, but I had no sense that he would become loud or nasty. Nate, on the other hand, was not so amenable to whatever it was we were about to do. He was popping with anger.

"He called me a faggot and I ain't letting that slide," snapped Nate.

"OK, Nate," Sally continued. She walked over to his side of the table and motioned for me to walk over to Edgar's side. "I know you are angry at Edgar. We're going to talk about this and work this problem out. I will help you and Mr. Danforth will help Edgar. OK?"

"As long as he ain't callin' me a faggot. I ain't no faggot," replied Nate.

"There'll be no name-calling. We're going to talk," Sally explained calmly. I found myself taken in by the confidence of her voice. I had no idea what we were about to do, but I felt like Sally knew what she was doing. I wondered if the boys felt the same way.

"I want you two guys to sit across from each other at the table. Mr. Danforth and I will stand behind you with our hands resting on your shoulders. He will stand behind Edgar. Nate, I'll stand behind you." We arranged ourselves according to her directions. I set my hands softly on Edgar's shoulders.

"OK, here's how this works. Edgar, when you have something to say, you whisper it to Mr. Danforth. He'll then say it out loud. Nate, when you want to say something, whisper it to me, and I'll be the one who says it out loud. We're going to talk about what happened on the bus that led to the fight. Edgar, you start. Tell us what happened."

Edgar looked at Sally awkwardly, as if the rules of the game were strange and cumbersome. I dipped down so that my ear was close to his face, making it easy for him to whisper to me. I was almost surprised when he did.

"He bugs me every day on that bus. I'm just sleeping and he's never leaving me alone. If he bugs me again, I'll kick his ass," Edgar whispered into my ear.

I looked up at Nate to see if he had heard the part about getting his ass kicked. The expression on his face told me that he hadn't heard it. I spoke. "Edgar says—"

"I . . . I . . ." Sally corrected me.

"I . . . I don't like it when Nate bugs me on the bus. I want to sleep and he won't leave me alone. That makes me really mad." I looked down at Edgar to see if my translation was acceptable. He seemed to be OK with it. By now, Nate was busy whispering to Sally. He cupped his hand over her ear to create greater privacy. Sally listened intently, then she spoke in an animated fashion.

"I'm really mad because Edgar called me a name. I don't like that. I don't want him calling me names."

Upon hearing this, Edgar reached up quickly and tugged on my neck, pulling my ear toward his mouth. He definitely had something to say. He whispered to me. Then it was my turn to speak.

"I called him a . . . *that* because he was tugging on my pants to wake me up. I was sleeping and he was grabbing the front of my pants."

Nate reached up and pulled Sally's head toward his mouth. He whispered in urgent tones. He was getting excited. Sally had trouble understanding him, so she whispered a question back to Nate. He jumped up on his knees so that he could better whisper to Sally. Then she spoke.

"I thought you were awake. I saw your eyes open. So, I thought you were just fooling around, making believe you were asleep."

Nate reached up one more time, tugged Sally's ear to his mouth, and whispered an addendum to his message.

"And I'm no fag just because I thought you were awake."

Edgar whispered to me and I replied for him, "My eyes were closed the whole time. I was sleeping until you woke me up."

To this, Nate/Sally responded, "I saw your eyes. I thought you were waking up a little."

Edgar and I replied, "Well, you were wrong. I was sleeping. I just wanted you to leave me alone so I could sleep on the bus."

At this point, Nate sat still. He didn't know what to say. Sally whispered a suggestion to him. He seemed a little embarrassed or weak in his commitment to the idea. She whispered in his ear again and he nodded OK. "Go ahead," she said, "you can say it."

Nate spoke directly to Edgar, "How about if I let you sleep tomorrow? I won't bug you. But you can't be calling me names."

Edgar spoke directly to Nate, "OK."

Nate replied "OK" back to Edgar.

Sally then spoke to both boys, "That was very good. How about we seal this deal with a handshake?" The boys sheepishly reached across and shook hands.

As we walked back to class, Sally complimented me on how well I did. I thanked her for including me in the whole thing. I marveled at the process. These two street-tough teens who had wanted to tear each other's heads off only minutes before had spent 10 minutes whispering into our ears just because we asked them to do it. I was amazed that Sally could guide them simply and confidently through this rather odd little ritual and bring about a peaceful resolution. During the rest of that school year, I watched Sally do many creative and fascinating exercises with the students. In each one, she asked the students to trust her, and she, in turn, trusted them.

ANALYSIS OF "SPEAK WITH ME"

Unfortunately, this school did not do enough to cultivate a cooperative context. Students competed for points, levels, and prizes. Academic lessons were rarely organized in cooperative groups. Mostly, the students worked individually on packets of worksheets. The general goal of the teachers was to keep the students separated and quiet so that conflicts could be avoided. Obviously, Sally Hearn worked from a very different philosophy. She was far more therapeutic, humanistic, and relational. She had built tremendous trust with these students before this incident.

Perhaps the most striking piece of ingenuity in this story is the way that Sally set up a context of cooperation by teaming up each boy with an adult in the whispering game. From the start, each boy was asked to rely on and work together with a partner. This arrangement required a degree of trust and interdependence. If I was to effectively speak Edgar's words and intentions, he had to trust me to remain true to what he had whispered in my ear. This cooperative teaming arrangement greatly influenced the boys toward the possibility of cooperating with one another by first asking them to cooperate with the adults. Personally, I felt pressure to live up to Edgar's trust, to represent him well. When I did so, I think that our unity as a team grew and his emotions calmed and stabilized. Also, this allowed Sally and I to do a little teaching, to show the boys how to talk through a disagreement in a reasonable way.

If there is a weakness in this example, it is the superficiality of the discussion. The process attends only to the problem at hand, never touching on deeper issues about these two boys' emotions, their lives, and their relationship to one another. This can be one of the weaknesses of conflict resolution processes that proceed in a fairly formulaic, structured, step-by-step way. Dealing with the immediate conflict often requires a narrowing of the scope of discussion, an ignoring of larger issues in order to deal with a specific disagreement. The very narrowing of the topic that helps bring about a compromise agreement between the two disputing parties limits the therapeutic depth of the conversation.

SEVEN BASIC PRINCIPLES
OF PROBLEM-SOLVING NEGOTIATIONS

Now we turn our discussion to formal processes of conflict resolution, those rituals or procedures designed explicitly to solve interpersonal problems in fair ways. If you turn on your television during the day, it is likely that you'll see any one of a number of television court programs (e.g., *The People's Court*). Disputants present their stories to a judge, who, frequently after admonishing one or both sides for being ignorant and morally despicable, pronounces a verdict. After the trial, a court reporter interviews both parties outside the courtroom to find, to no one's surprise, that the victor is satisfied and feels that justice has been served, while the loser inevitably calls the proceedings a travesty. This is a win-lose settlement. One side won. One lost. No one learned anything about responsibility and cooperation.

When teachers or schools set up and maintain formal processes of problem-solving negotiation, frequently called *mediation* or *peer mediation,* the goal is to create a standard procedure that ends in a win-win result. The procedure follows the same basic steps each time that it is used, bringing either two students or two parties (groups) together to discuss the issue and work out a compromise agreement that will guide behavior from that point forward. After completing the mediation, each side should walk away feeling that he or she has gained some or all of what he or she needs and wants. It is very likely that walking away with a partial "win" required some degree of compromise, some giving up and giving in, some acceptance of less than what was originally wanted.

Teachers who manage mediation procedures or who teach students to mediate conflicts for their peers have much to keep in mind. The standard steps of the process will be outlined in the next section. Before outlining those steps, we will extract seven crucial lessons from the work of Johnson and Johnson (1991, 1995a, 1995b, 1996), vital lessons for teachers to take to heart as they set up and manage mediation procedures in their classroom or school.

1. *Most conflicts require no formal mediation.* Most problems in the classroom are more like minor bumps in the road than major problems, calling merely for "smoothing" (Johnson & Johnson, 1995a, p. 34). If the issue is not highly important and emotionally pressing to both parties involved, humor or a simple apology can be used to smooth out the situation, normalizing things enough to go on. Additionally, it is often true that students who learn how to compromise via a formal mediation procedure tend to use those negotiation skills to solve problems in less formal ways at other times.

2. *The more important the relationship, the more likely a conflict will benefit from a formal mediation.* Students who hardly know one another or who spend small amounts of time together often are less likely to have sufficient emotional investment in their relationship to motivate them through a formal mediation. When a long-term or invested relationship is on the line, students are more likely to participate fully and meaningfully in the mediation.

3. *Focus on the shared problem, not on the individuals.* It is tempting and even habitual among some teachers to view an individual student as the problem that needs to change or be changed. A mediation process is only useful if the problem is viewed and spoken of as mutual, as something shared by the two parties.

4. *Construct the problem as small, specific, short-term, and "here and now" instead of large, multiple, vague, and sweeping.* It will be far easier to reach a resolution if the problem is framed in simple and finite terms that can be discussed directly rather than in terms of large theoretical principles. Don't change the world. Improve one little concrete corner of it.

5. *Have angry and hostile students cool down before doing mediation.* There may no uglier feeling than when you realize that a student who is too heated up and mad turns the mediation process into a verbal assault exhibition. A crucial part of supporting students' efforts to improve themselves, their lives, and their connections with others is our obligation to not place our students in unreasonably difficult situations for which they are obviously unprepared. A student who uses mediation very smoothly when calm can find the process unbearable if his or her blood is boiling. The general goal is to mediate a conflict as close in time as possible to when that conflict occurred (so that the conflict still matters). Teachers have to use good judgment in providing time and opportunity for students to cool down and calm down before entering a mediation. A variety of cool-down techniques are possible, such as talking to a teacher, talking to a peer, taking deep breaths in a quiet place, listening to calming music, or talking a walk.

6. *View each mediation session as an opportunity for students to learn new attitudes and skills.* The content of the learning is the specific conflict at hand, but the lesson operates on many levels at once. While the disputing parties are attempting to figure out how to work out a single problem here and now, they are also building a sense of themselves as cooperative problem solvers; as able peacemakers; and as people who can speak their position, listen, and compromise. As the old therapeutic mantra goes, the medium is the message.

7. *Stick to the ground rules.* Mediation, like any other process or strategy, relies on a sense of order produced by adhering to a few basic rules. Johnson and Johnson (1995a) recommend that students agree to the following ground rules:

A. Agree to solve the problem in the mediation
B. No name-calling
C. No interrupting
D. Be honest
E. Agree to abide by the agreement produced in the mediation
F. Maintain confidentiality, telling nothing about the mediation to anyone

FORMAL PROCEDURES USED IN PROBLEM-SOLVING NEGOTIATIONS

A wide variety of structured mediation programs are designed for use in public schools. Many follow a similar format of steps that guide disputing parties toward a final compromise agreement. These negotiation formats may be led by a teacher, counselor, or other qualified adult. They also may be led by a student or pair of students who have been trained to direct mediation. Because the goal is to support students in solving their own problems to the greatest degree possible, training students to conduct peer mediation is the path of choice. We recognize that this is not possible in all situations.

Rather than provide an overview of the many school mediation programs (see Crawford & Bodine, 1996; Girard & Koch, 1996), we are going to describe a generic series of steps that is common to most, if not all, conflict resolution programs.

1. *Ask both students or parties to tell their side of the story.* The conflicting students each get a chance to tell what happened in their own words. Typically, they then explain how they feel about what happened and what they want. When students give their side of the story, they often feel like they and their perspective are valued by others. Also, it is crucial that students tell what they want. This must be specific and related only to the current issue or problem at hand. Additionally, some mediation programs go a step further by asking the students to listen to the other student's side of the story and then summarize their adversary's feelings and wants. This is an advanced step that asks students to be empathic and understanding of their adversary.

2. *Ask both students to name some specific ways to resolve the conflict.* Students should be encouraged to suggest options that create a win-win situation, benefiting both students in some way. This step builds on the prior statements about what students want.

3. *Jointly choose one best solution and agree by shaking hands or signing a contract.* Students and the mediator(s) discuss possible options and agree on one. It is best to seal the agreement in a formal way. This may mean shaking hands. Often, it is a good idea to write out a formal contract and have the students and mediator(s) sign. In addition to the terms of the agreement, the contract should specify a date for evaluating the success of the contract, when the mediator(s) or the teacher checks with the disputing parties to see if the agreement has been upheld. If it has not been upheld, a new mediation may be in order.

In the final pages, we will hear a firsthand experiential account from a teacher who uses conflict resolution processes every day. Jeanine Legg teaches youngsters experiencing social, emotional, and behavioral difficulties in a regular elementary school.

THINKING AHEAD: RELATING TO THE STORIES

The purpose of the teacher account in the following section is to flesh out the main concepts and practices of this chapter within a particular teacher's practice and a specific situation. The concepts and practices play out quite differently depending on the situation, the students involved, and the teacher. As you read the teacher stories, it will be helpful to keep a small list of questions in mind.

1. In what ways do you think this story enacts the main themes or ideas of this chapter?

2. Putting yourself in the teacher's place, what do you think you might have done differently? The same? Why?

3. What troubles you about this story?

4. What brings you hope in this story?

5. What surprises you?

6. What insights, values, beliefs, and processes do you think the author was trying to convey through this story?

7. What stories of your own does this story remind you of?

JEANINE'S STORY

Getting Things Started

We began a program to help children with emotional, social, and behavioral issues within an elementary school, working with both students labeled BD and any "regular" education students whose teachers or parents requested the services. We were staffed with a classroom teacher, a paraprofessional, and a part-time social worker (with a mental health background). We provided academic as well as emotional/social support in the form of "clubs," which were social development, support, and skill-building groups. One of the groups we started as a way to teach problem-solving skills was a conflict mediation club. We specifically trained our students, as well as students from the regular classrooms, to become conflict mediators for the whole school.

We approached the middle school in our district because it had a successful mediation program that had been operating for several years. They sent us their handbook that they had produced, called RAPP—Resolve All Problems Peacefully. They also gave us the name of a gentleman who worked for the St. Louis Bar Association and spent his time traveling to school districts to train middle and high school students in peer mediation. He was a little skeptical when we approached him about training elementary school students, including a core group of "behavior disordered" students. We discussed with him what we wanted our students to get from the training: an improved ability to problem solve and negotiate their differences with peers; an increase in their self-esteem; a positive peer group to which to belong; an increase in their feeling of competence; an opportunity to practice their problem-solving skills without being involved directly with the problem; a chance to work cooperatively with peers who could model the problem-solving skills; and, most of all, empowerment of students to believe that they could begin to negotiate their own problems without an adult's assistance. He agreed to work with us.

We used a six-step process:

1. Introducing and explaining what mediation is, and the rules

2. Telling the story (both parties tell their side of the story, mediators summarize both parties' side of the story to make sure they understand the conflict)

3. Understanding the problem/identifying facts and feelings (have parties try to see the conflict from the other person's point of view, understand their feelings)

4. Searching for solutions (everyone thinks of solutions, all of them are written down, check off the solutions to which both parties can agree)

5. Reaching an agreement (using only the solutions to which both parties agree, then writing up a contract and having everyone sign it, with copies given to both parties and to adult supervisor)

6. Following up and saying thank you (set a time with each party to check to make sure agreement is okay, then thank people for letting the mediation team help them)

Training and Procedures

Mediation training was an ongoing process during the entire year. Initially, we had a 6-hour training that was conducted for 2 hours once a week for 3 weeks. During that time, we taught the students each of the six steps involved—what they looked like and what they sounded like. We used a visual checklist with the steps for the students to follow as we did lots of practicing. Students practiced as both the conflict mediators and the parties having the conflict. After the initial training, we met as a "club" for 1 hour every other week to practice our skills, discuss situations that had arisen that presented problems for the mediators, and build our sense of camaraderie. As a part of team building, we also took several field trips to the school district's outdoor campsite to participate in specific trust-building and team-building activities.

Mediation was available every day from 2:30 p.m. to 3:00 p.m. Exceptions were made in emergencies at the request of the principal or counselor. This late-afternoon time worked well for several reasons. It gave time for students to cool off so that they were able to tell their side of the story and remain calm. It also encouraged students to work cooperatively with the mediators as school began dismissing at about 3:10. Mediators were encouraged to keep students on track so a resolution could be reached if possible without dragging out the process. Often, by 2:30, what seemed like a huge insult at recess was only a minor incident.

Designated conflict mediators (students) were assigned a partner for the month, and a schedule was made for the month assigning teams for the day. They reported to our classroom area to pick up mediation referrals that students or adults had filled out earlier in the day. They were in charge of picking up the students from their classrooms for the day's mediation and beginning the mediation process. The social worker, paraprofessional, and I rotated days to oversee the mediation process. Our job was just to be present in case the conflict became heated and an adult needed to intervene. That was rarely the case. After the conflict mediators were done, the adult would also take time to discuss any concerns the mediators had with the process or review steps with the mediators. Notes were kept about skills that we needed to continue to work on and situations that we could practice. The conflict mediators considered themselves to be fairly independent and yet able to hear constructive criticism from peers and adults.

An Example of Peer Mediation

A typical mediation was as follows:

Mediator: "Hi, my name is Sarah G. and this is Tom. We are your mediators today."

Tom: "Mediators are not judges—we don't decide guilt, innocence, or punishments. You will both have the chance to tell your side of the story, and we will try to help you work out a solution to your problem that you both can agree to. We will not take sides. We do have some rules to follow."

Sarah: "Mediation rules are:

1. Respect each other (no name calling or put-downs).

2. Do not interrupt each other.

3. Remain seated.

4. Work toward a solution.

5. Be as honest as you can.

6. Keep it confidential (what is said in this room, stays in this room).

Do you both agree to follow the rules?"

Mike & Marty: "Yeah."

Tom: "Who would like to tell his side of the story first?"

Mike points to Marty and says he can go first.

Marty: "I was talking about Mike this morning to my friends and then Mike started cursing at me."

Sarah: "So you were saying things about Mike to your friends and when Mike saw you or heard you, he started cursing at you."

Marty: "Yeah, that's right."

Tom: "Okay, Mike, tell us your side."

Mike: "Well, when I was getting off my bus this morning (a Special Education bus), Marty was teasing me about being a retard. Then he told his friends that I was retarded. So I cussed at him."

Tom:	"So when you got off the bus this morning, Marty began teasing you and telling other kids you were retarded. You got angry and started cursing at him."
Mike:	"Yeah!"—he's always teasing me about riding that special bus and I'm getting sick of it. He's lucky I didn't punch him out!"
Tom:	"You're so angry about his teasing that you want to hit him."
Mike:	"Yeah!"
Sarah:	"Let's try putting yourself in the other person's shoes. Marty, how would you feel if you had to ride to school on a special bus and kids were teasing you and calling you names when you got off?"
Marty (looking aghast):	"I'd hate that! Everyone thinks only retards ride special buses! I wouldn't want kids calling me names."
Sarah:	"So you'd be mad and angry if kids were teasing you and calling you stuff when you got off your bus."
Marty:	"Yeah, I guess so."
Tom:	"And Mike, how would you feel if someone was cursing at you?"
Mike:	"Well, I wouldn't like it, but they would deserve it if they're calling people names!"
Tom:	"So you wouldn't want anyone cursing at you?"
Mike:	"Yeah, I guess I wouldn't."
Sarah:	"So now let's make a list of possible solutions and see if you both can agree on anything. What do you guys want to have happen?"
Mike:	"I want him to stop calling me names every morning."
Marty:	"I want him to stop cursing at me."
Mike:	"I want him to stop telling kids I'm a retard. I want to not have to ride a special bus."
Marty:	"I want Mike to stop saying he's going to beat me up."

As Mike and Marty offer suggestions, the mediators are writing down all the suggestions. If students have difficulty coming up with possible solutions, mediators may offer suggestions, but we generally discourage this. Young students often need some assistance in the process. Then, they go back over the suggested ideas individually to see if the boys can mutually agree on some solutions. Students have the right to say they don't or won't agree with a solution.

Sarah:	"So, Marty, you agree not to tease Mike anymore about his bus and not tell people he's retarded, and Mike, you agree to stop cursing and threatening Marty. Is that correct?"
Mike & Marty:	"Yeah."
Tom:	"Okay, we've written that down, and I need both of you to sign this agreement. Marty, you've agreed to stop teasing Mike about the bus he rides and calling him names. Mike, you've agreed to stop cursing and threatening Marty. I'm going to make you both a copy of this agreement."
Sarah:	"You will both get a copy of this agreement. I will come to your classroom next Wednesday to see if your agreement is working. If it isn't, we can come back to mediation if you want. Thank you both for coming to mediation and working to settle your problems peacefully."

Mediators walk students back to their classes and then return to our room where we can discuss how the processes went.

Common Problems for Mediation

Other common problems that come to mediation at the elementary level are the following:

1. Arguments about missing school supplies

2. Arguments about missing lunch money

3. "Your mama" arguments

4. Name calling/teasing

5. People being left out of games at recess

6. Cafeteria issues, such as places in line, taking food, and so on

7. Problems with students who share a locker

8. Shoving/pushing problems, if they didn't escalate into fights

9. Bus problems

Classroom teachers were encouraged to have the mediators handle those pesky classroom squabbles that could easily take up their whole day. The principal was very supportive, sending students with their problems to student mediators.

The Benefits of Conflict Resolution

The benefits of teaching students with emotional and behavioral issues how to be conflict mediators are immeasurable! Teaching conflict mediation skills to students who have behavior problems is a proactive approach. It's the perfect opportunity to teach them real problem-solving skills. Too often, we deal with the troubled students after they have blown up at someone and then try to put the pieces back together. These students can be trained to help mediate conflicts with others and, in the process, gain some valuable problem-solving skills that they will begin to internalize.

Teaching conflict mediation skills gives your students an opportunity to learn the specific steps involved in problem solving. It also gives them a place for guided practice in a structured setting. Because a group is learning, the students don't feel singled out as if they are the only ones who lack the skills.

Problem-solving skills are a must for any student, but they are a critical skill for students struggling with emotional and social problems. Typically, if that student was capable of solving his or her problems with others in appropriate ways, he or she probably wouldn't have been identified as behavior disordered. This population of students must have social problem-solving skills if they are to have an opportunity to be successful in school and as adults.

Conflict mediation training and meetings allow the students with behavior problems to observe and work with the other mediators, using their skills as we practice role-playing situations. The students with strong social skills serve as models and teachers for the less skilled students.

Being chosen as a conflict mediator is an excellent way to improve a troubled student's self-esteem. The student begins to receive recognition from other staff members in a more positive manner and begins to reframe the way he or she thinks about him- or herself.

The troubled students often consider themselves to be the only ones who have problems/conflicts with others. Being a mediator gives them the opportunity to be sitting on the other side of the table, helping someone else solve his or her problems. When we finish our initial training, we always have a celebration, which includes a little speech from the principal about the important role they will be filling for the school, plus photographs and refreshments.

The students also gain a better sense of responsibility. Usually, these students are never chosen for anything. Now, the school is counting on them to help the other students (especially the younger ones) settle their differences peacefully.

Asking the BD students to serve as conflict mediators with other, "regular" students helps to build their sense of belonging and identity. Emotionally troubled students are often social outcasts because of their poor social skills. Now they belong to another group of students (with "fair" social skills) with whom they can begin to build positive relationships.

I think that it's very difficult for many students with behavior disorders to be able to join in groups because they are often rejected for their poor social skills, poor judgment, and poor problem-solving skills. When they train as mediators, they gain immediate acceptance into a positive group, and hopefully, this will transfer into their everyday school lives.

A good conflict mediator has to have good communication skills. We often train students who don't have strong communication skills with the hope that all the practice will improve their communication.

The experience of training to be a conflict mediator is an excellent vehicle to help students improve their cooperation and trust-building skills. Again, positive experiences in a structured, supportive setting will enable those students to have more positive experiences in less structured settings. As a part of our conflict mediation training, we often do several trust-building activities to promote that sense of teamwork. Many of our students don't trust others easily, which makes it hard for them to gain acceptance into groups.

Being trained as a conflict mediator also meets the troubled student's sense of fairness. Often, these students think that anything that happens to them "isn't fair." The training allows them to reframe what "fair" looks like or sounds like for different people. It allows them to see that problems and incidents often have a lot of gray areas—not everything is white or black, wrong or right.

The steps in conflict mediation that require students to put themselves in the other person's shoes is very powerful. My students don't often feel empathy for others. With conflict mediation training, they begin to develop a sense of empathy—how someone else must feel when they do something. Empathy is difficult to teach because it isn't concrete, so it doesn't have steps. It is only something a person feels. A lot of students with emotional/behavioral issues don't like to experience, express, or admit to having feelings. It would make them too vulnerable and would result in additional pain. Mediation helps them face and deal with their feelings and the feelings of others.

But the single most important benefit of training students to be conflict mediators is in their self-empowerment. With the training, this population of students is given the power to make better choices for themselves with regard to solving their own problems. By learning how to be an active listener, think of alternate solutions, and negotiate a solution with others, they gain the control they so often seek in inappropriate ways. These students learn that the power they used to seek outside of themselves is really on the inside, waiting for a chance to blossom.

We always have students come to meetings, shaking their heads at younger students who are making lots of social mistakes, saying "I used to do that, but I don't anymore." There's nothing more satisfying than teaching a child a skill that will allow him or her to grow and become more independent. Too often, teachers tend to want to make students more dependent on adults by solving their problems for them or making decisions for them. I think all students need the opportunity to become more diverse and independent thinkers, because that is what we will expect of them when they are adults.

Drawbacks, Obstacles, Needs

Along with all of the benefits of using conflict mediation with students come some drawbacks. I wouldn't necessarily consider them weaknesses, but rather obstacles that occur and require some planning to accommodate.

Probably the most important obstacle to overcome is staff support for the program. Your administrators need to be fully behind the students and willing to let students handle conflicts as they arise. A meeting with your administrator will be necessary to discuss which conflicts will be handled by student mediators and which conflicts will be automatic office referrals. This becomes a problem when you train and use conflict mediators, and then you get a new administration who doesn't use the student mediators. You also need the support of other staff members. They have the power to allow students to seek mediation or just settle the problem in the classroom. Teachers like power, but they have to be willing to give some of it up if they are going to use conflict mediators. I'm sure some staff members in your school will think conflict mediators are a great idea, and others will think it's a waste of time. To implement a conflict mediation program in your school, you will need to sell it to the staff—convince them how it will make their jobs easier.

Another drawback to consider when implementing a conflict mediation program is the supervision. You will need at least one staff member available at a specific time to supervise the conflict mediation. Older students may work without supervision, but we found that with the elementary school students, you will always want to have adult supervision. The supervisors have to keep that mediation time slot open on their schedule. They also need to be able to remain uninvolved in the process. It would be very tempting for the adult to jump right in and settle the problem immediately rather than go through the six steps of mediation. The supervising adult must let the mediators do their job to the best of their ability with little or no interference.

You also need a consistent place or room for the mediators to meet. It is most helpful if the rules can be posted and conflict mediation forms can be kept in that central place. This room also needs to be private. Keep in mind, the mediation confidentiality rule that states whatever is said in this room, stays in this room—you do not want others to overhear the students in mediation. It is becoming harder and harder to find empty spaces in our school buildings, but conflict mediation requires one.

The students you train as mediators need to have adequate language skills. Students with receptive or expressive language deficits will have problems as conflict mediators. The process of summarizing what others have said will be very difficult for them.

Some of the students who come to mediation will have problems as well. Kindergartners and first graders usually have difficulty remembering what problem they had earlier in the day. It is also very difficult to have them put themselves in the other person's shoes. They often just don't get it. We usually refrained from involving those younger students in mediation.

A final drawback is the amount of time a staff member needs to commit to making the conflict mediation program work. You have your initial hours of training. You can hire someone to do your training if you have the budget. But you also want to make the time to meet regularly with your team of mediators. The meetings are used to practice role-playing and mediation skills, discuss how people are doing, answer their questions, participate in some cooperation and trust-building activities to improve the concept of "team," and inject some fun into the conflict mediation job. Without the commitment of staff members to supervise the training and frequent meetings and to supervise the actual conflict mediations, your mediation team will not succeed. A successful conflict mediation program will draw in students—students will seek out the opportunity to be heard by their peers and get assistance in solving their problems peacefully.

DIGGING IN: MAKING THE STORY PERSONAL

Perhaps the most powerful lessons we can take from a story occur when we allow ourselves to reflect and connect in a deeply personal and emotional way with what happened. We can often do this by placing ourselves in the roles of the teacher or the students, connecting those roles to the rich experiences of our own lives.

1. In Jeanine's story, elementary-grade students serve as conflict mediators for their peers. Have you had any experiences with children in those grade levels? What would you imagine might be some of the challenges and/or opportunities in using peer mediation with elementary-age students?

2. Jeanine and her colleagues started their peer mediation program by seeking expertise both within their district and in the local community. Where (or to whom) would you turn for help in getting a conflict resolution program started?

CONCLUSION

The greatest foe of attaining the peacemaking attitude that Deutsch speaks of, the optimistic dedication to teaching peace with students often trapped in lives rife with conflict and turmoil, is the limiting belief that *we can't do it because they can't do it.* We teachers can't do this wonderful, hopeful practice because these students can't realistically rise to this level of empathy and self-control.

Quite simply, those who do not believe that skilled and caring adults can teach peace will have little success, and their nonbelief will be justified by their unsatisfactory experience. We have provided stories from two teachers in an effort to show that not only is a belief in teaching peace to troubling students warranted, but it can become a mundane, taken-for-granted fact of everyday life. Jeanine used conflict resolution processes on such a regular basis that no one would even consider doubting the social usefulness of the practice or the ability of students to learn to be peaceful. Seeking peace, living peace, and teaching peace have become unremarkable habits of daily professional practice. It is simply what teachers like Jeanine do. And it can be, with work and struggle and learning and collegial support, what many more teachers do every day.

SUMMARY

In this chapter, we have provided a summary of pertinent theory and research; practical advice about doing conflict resolution; and some experiential stories from teachers who use conflict resolution with students dealing with emotional, social, and behavioral issues. We consider this chapter to be merely an introduction to a vast field of professional knowledge and skills.

Deutsch (1949, 1973, 1990, 1994; Deutsch et al., 1992) has stated that effective conflict resolution requires that professionals develop three interwoven qualities: knowledge, skills, and attitude. In this chapter, we have addressed the knowledge component by summarizing the research and theory on constructive and destructive conflicts. Constructive conflicts are resolved by way of negotiation and compromise so that each participant comes away with some portion of what he or she wants and needs. A destructive conflict is handled in a way that attempts to provide for the needs and wants of one party at the expense of the other party. This typically requires coercion, threats, and even violence.

Different kinds of social climates tend to support or not support the constructive resolution of conflicts. Competitive settings tend to work against constructive conflict resolution. Cooperative settings tend to work in favor of constructive conflict resolution.

Formal processes of constructive resolution, such as peer mediation, often involve a structure whereby students describe their own perspective on the problem, ask for what they want, and then negotiate a shared agreement. Mediation processes can be effective in teaching peaceful attitudes and habits on a classwide and schoolwide basis.

Finally, in this chapter, we have taken a look at the practical skills of facilitating peaceful mediation by outlining the basic steps of conflict resolution processes and by listening to the firsthand stories of teachers in action. We should note that each of these teachers has developed his or her skills over years of teaching practice, experimentation, reflection, and experiential learning. Additionally, as Jeanine notes, each has developed his or her craft with the support of talented colleagues who have also embraced a pedagogy of peace.

8

Implementing the KEYS Program for Students With E/BD

Scot Danforth, Natalie Thomas, and Terry Jo Smith

In many schools, teaching and counseling are completely separate activities. Teachers with little counseling expertise work in classrooms with students. Counselors are isolated in offices away from the real action of the classroom. Meanwhile, the emotional and social needs of many students remain undersatisfied and undersupported. What if teaching and counseling weren't separate activities and separate professions?

In this chapter, we will provide an in-depth look at one innovative program designed to address the needs of students experiencing social and emotional problems in school. The Keeping Every Youth Successful (KEYS) program is a unique venture of Greenland School District of St. Louis (MO) County. The KEYS program consists of a wide and flexible array of support services for students in grades K–12 experiencing emotional and social difficulties, helping them remain in the general education building. Most of the students receiving

KEYS services are labeled E/BD, but the program is flexible enough to work with any student who needs additional support. Students need not have an Individual Educational Plan (IEP) to receive KEYS services.

In this chapter, we will provide an overview of the KEYS program, including policy foundations, philosophy, goals, and structure. We will also move in closer for some narrative snapshots of KEYS staff members and their students in action. Our hope is to give the reader an inside glimpse at the actual activities of KEYS staff members and their students, for it is in the interactions between teachers and students that the key to KEYS lies. The broader goal is to provide readers with insight into one solution—one way of supporting and including students experiencing social and emotional difficulties—that teachers in one location have created.

LIMITATIONS OF TRADITIONAL PROGRAMS

The primary way that public schools attempt to address the needs of students we have described in this book as "troubling" occurs with special education programs for students labeled "emotionally/behaviorally disordered" (E/BD). Public school-based programs for students identified with emotional and behavioral disorders are frequently criticized as ineffective (Dryfoos, 1995; Durlak, 1995; Grosenick, George, & Kauffman, 1987). Programs often emphasize external, authority-based control of behaviors while failing to offer adequate mental health services and academic instruction (Knitzer, Steinberg, & Fleisch, 1991).

Traditional models employ behavior modification as a conceptual base (Peacock Hill Working Group, 1991). Teachers describe student actions and prescribe interventions. They view student actions in isolation from the variety of social environments and relational contexts that envelope the student. Adherence to rules, and clear consequences and rewards, are fundamental principles. Teachers or authority figures set the rules and expectations for students. In response, student behaviors are observed, recorded, and rewarded or punished. Teachers employ significant external controls, such as restraint, time out, suspension, and segregation from peers (Coleman, 1996).

Educators tend to view community agencies providing mental health or social support services as separate institutions with distinct goals and responsibilities (Flaherty, Weist, & Warner, 1996). Social service and mental health support for students considered E/BD are typically provided through referrals to these external agencies. Unfortunately, conventional educational approaches for students considered E/BD relegate essential services to community-based service organizations rather than providing necessary services within the context of the educational program.

Traditional approaches to students considered E/BD have produced limited educational growth and behavioral improvement. Students labeled E/BD are highlighted as a growing population of concern within schools. Instead of their performance improving within general or special education settings, these students often deteriorate (Koyanagi & Gaines, 1993). Students labeled E/BD who participate in traditional special education services fail more courses and are more likely to be retained in grade than any other students with disabilities. Only 42% of this population earns a high school diploma, compared with 50% of all students with disabilities and 76% of youth in the general population (Chesapeake Institute, 1994). Eighteen percent of youth considered E/BD go on to some form of advanced training, including vocational training, short-term training programs, or academic classes, as compared to 22% of all students with disabilities (McLaughlin, Leone, Warren, & Schofield, 1994).

Students who have been educated in traditional E/BD programs have difficulty maintaining jobs. Although approximately 75% are employed, at least part time, at the time they leave school, only 44% still have jobs 5 years later (McLaughlin et al., 1994).

About 20% of all youth considered E/BD are arrested while in school, and 58% are arrested within 5 years of leaving school. Of the students considered E/BD who drop out of school, 73% are arrested within 5 years of leaving school (Chesapeake Institute, 1994).

Their social lives and potential for positive peer interactions are extremely limited (Koyanagi & Gaines, 1993). Nationally, students considered E/BD are more likely to be segregated from nondisabled peers than are students with other disabilities (Koyanagi & Gaines, 1993). In 1993, 19% were educated outside of their local school building, compared with 6% of all students with disabilities (U.S. Department of Education, 1993).

Considering only the students labeled E/BD who are educated within their local schools, fewer than 19% are educated in general classrooms. These data are in stark contrast to 40% of all students with disabilities (U.S. Department of Education, 1993). The remaining students considered E/BD are educated in placements away from their nonlabeled peers. Twenty percent of students identified as E/BD are placed in schools exclusively serving students requiring special education, separate facilities such as juvenile justice sites or homebound/hospital settings. This contrasts with 3% of students with other disability classifications.

When IEP teams decide that segregated classrooms or schools are appropriate educational settings, their emphasis is on controlling students' behavior instead of providing therapeutic support and academic instruction (Koyanagi & Gaines, 1993; Sugai & Horner, 1994). Frustrated by the lack of meaningful services within the school, the students' families struggle to find appropriate services in the community. Fewer than one in three children with serious emotional disturbances receive appropriate mental health services in schools (Koyanagi & Gaines, 1993). Despite the existence of specialized settings, national data indicate that students considered E/BD do not improve in segregated settings (Koyanagi & Gaines, 1993). Years later, these children become adults who can require significant psychiatric services and, at times, continuous residential care. Long-term care might be avoided if students receive appropriate services during their school experiences.

Without question, students considered E/BD do not perform well in the standard special education programs. A task force commissioned by the Office of Special Education Programs (OSEP) examined these issues and asserted that "the educational problems experienced by students [considered E/BD] were often indicators of problems with educational programs" (McLaughlin et al., 1994, p. 14).

The task force offered insight into possible flaws in E/BD programs.

The focus of many school interventions has been on specific behaviors through a major emphasis on behavior management. Frequently, a focus on management or compliance can overwhelm other aspects of a student's education, resulting in sparse attention to academic . . . development. Even exemplary programs over-emphasized behavior management and behavior control and provided limited academic and vocational opportunities for the students. In addition, despite students' alleged lack of social skills, few programs provided positive opportunities for these students to socialize with non-SED [Seriously Emotionally Disturbed] peers. (McLaughlin et al., 1994, p. 15)

This is the challenge addressed by the KEYS program—a climate of continuing failure within E/BD public school programs that are marked by social segregation, weak academic instruction, and poor integration of mental health services. How can teachers do a better job of supporting all students who struggle with emotional, social, or behavioral difficulties?

KEYS: AN ALTERNATIVE APPROACH

Educators and mental health service providers have looked for strategies to improve service options for children with significant educational, emotional, and social needs. Schools are ideal sites for delivering the services that can meet the emotional and mental health needs of students. Students and their families can participate when services occur within the education environment. School-based mental health programs can offer services and support at early points for students who exhibit significant emotional difficulties. Staff with training in psychology, social work, and counseling can assist the educational staff in working with the entire family. Mental health providers can assist children and their families at times of crisis to prevent relatively minor problems from becoming persistent issues (Petersen, Compas, & Brooks, 1993).

Researchers and theorists not only identify schools as a viable location for mental health services, but they also call for specific approaches that acknowledge the complexity of the world in which children exist and function. Ecological perspectives have emerged within service system reform efforts (Franklin & Streeter, 1995; Swap, Prieto, & Harth, 1982). Ecological theory shifts our focus from the individual as the location of the problem and the primary focus of intervention to the network of relationships that surround the individual. This theory holds that individuals live and learn within a number of social systems, such as family, classroom, and neighborhood. These systems affect the individual's emotional well-being and behavioral patterns (Rhodes, 1970).

Some social systems are supportive of the child developing his or her potential, and some deter and block that growth. The goal of an ecological approach is to arrange and build systems of social support, love, understanding, and encouragement in the child's life. Strengthened relationships between the child and parents, teachers, friends, and other important persons lead that child to a strengthened sense of self and an increased comfort in the world.

Ecological Approaches

Ecological approaches

1. bridge preventive efforts and/or interventions across settings, such as classroom, school, home, and community

2. link interventions with youth and their families to changes in environment and systems

3. alter processes in the system by involving multiple change agents (i.e., youth, teachers, parents, classmates, school-based team)

4. conceptualize individual and family functioning in terms of interactions between and among the broader social environments (Dunst, Trivette, & Deal, 1988; Garbarino, 1992; Hawkins & Catalano, 1992; Henggler & Borduin, 1990).

The KEYS program embraces an ecological model and combines mental health providers and educators within the same system. Instead of dealing with the many challenges of interagency collaboration, staff with varying backgrounds work together to provide services for troubling students within the school. Staff backgrounds include special education, counseling, psychiatric social work, school psychology, and psychiatry.

The KEYS program integrates mental health services with education services within a general education building. This service delivery model is a comprehensive approach to address the educational needs of students with severe emotional and social concerns within the general education setting. The students enrolled in the KEYS program generally attend school for the full day. In a few instances, students who cannot tolerate a full day in a public school participate in community-based settings and internships for portions of the day. Each student is assigned to the KEYS program and a grade-appropriate partner classroom within the general education building. KEYS services are provided throughout the school day in a variety of locations. In addition, after-school activities, family events, and home visits occur during the school day and in evening hours.

Students with special education labels other than E/BD or students without IEPs can receive KEYS services. Teachers, parents, or the students themselves can access specific KEYS services, including social skills development, through a process called clubs, social coaching, and classroom consultation. Thus, KEYS is an option for students considered E/BD and for other students at risk for greater difficulties. This approach allows for prevention activities as well as reactive services.

The KEYS program goals are as follows:

1. Provide educational services for troubling students that result in academic and behavioral progress

2. Provide necessary services for troubling students with special education labels to demonstrate progress toward goals and objectives identified in their Individualized Education Programs

3. Provide necessary services for students with special education labels such that the student increases time and participation in general education with nonlabeled peers

The KEYS program consists of one special education teacher and one teacher assistant in each of three sites within a single suburban school district. The three sites are an elementary school, a middle school, and a high school, providing a developmental ladder of support that is available to students as they move through the grades. Additionally, the program employs the services of a therapeutic social worker, a school psychologist, and a consulting psychiatrist, who each work across the multiple sites.

Having framed the KEYS program as existing at three specific locations, we should refine our description by explaining that the three locations are programmatic hubs where the staff members are housed. In each of the three sites—Highmont Elementary School, Greenland West Middle School, and Greenland West High School—the intensity and breadth of the services provided by KEYS is greatest. However, the staff members at each site also travel to other schools in the district to provide the same support services for students that they provide within their own schools. By providing the services where students attend, the KEYS staff can support the students' social systems and staff within the school, as well as build new social relationships within the school community.

THE PHILOSOPHY OF KEYS

The philosophy that informs the KEYS work is a lived philosophy, a set of ideas that is more alive in action than on paper. The KEYS staff members share a common set of ideas about the best ways to help children and adolescents:

Building a nurturing environment—the focus of support work is not so much to change an individual as to creative a social environment around the child that supports that individual's emotional and social well-being

Creating a community of caring individuals around each student—problems of behavior and emotion in the experience of one student are challenges to educators to strengthen the caring character of the classroom and school community

Providing instruction and support for students to gain behavior and social skills in an environment where they can continually practice with peers and deal with expectations of "general school staff"—the goal is to provide what is needed within the general school building so that students are not sent off to separate special education schools

In the following sections, we will zoom in on the KEYS activities taking place within the elementary and middle school settings. These examples are snapshots of the kinds of work occurring across all KEYS locations.

KEYS—HIGHMONT ELEMENTARY SCHOOL

Our purpose in this section is to look closely at the kinds of support that the KEYS teachers at Highmont Elementary School provide for students who experience social, emotional, and behavioral difficulties. Although the KEYS staff is flexible and innovative, always devising new ways to help kids, we'll zero in on two specific kinds of interventions or activities involving the KEYS teachers: the support visit and the Club. Neither a visit nor a Club seems like a particularly extraordinary thing. The key to KEYS lies in the way the teachers do what they do.

The Support Visit

Ms. Clay can make you smile just by looking at you. She is a short, solid, African American woman with a smile that she wears as fully in her eyes as across her mouth. On a regular basis throughout the day, her entire face bursts into a joyous, radiating sweep that can't help but affect those around her.

Ms. Clay is the teacher aide. She is joined at Highmont by Ms. Lindsey, a KEYS teacher, and Ms. Manetti, the KEYS therapeutic social worker who is shared across the elementary, middle, and high school sites. At 8:20 a.m., Ms. Clay hurriedly tries to straighten up the KEYS classroom, a smallish room that holds two tables, three adult desks, and too much equipment. Many, but far from all, of the KEYS services take place in this room. Ms. Clay finishes straightening up and races off to see Bryan for some "deadheading." The day has begun.

The standard joke among the KEYS staff is that they spend their time playing checkers with kids, an activity that hardly deserves professional attention. Indeed, if one ponders the notion of serious psychotherapeutic work, the mind conjures up images of white lab coats and mysterious psychological instruments that quantify the depths of the psyche. One imagines pseudo-magical-medical therapies occurring behind the secrecy of large, closed doors—treatments that somehow transform the mad, infirmed, and incorrigible into well-scrubbed, pleasant children. The KEYS staff knows that what they actually do with children definitely does not seem as official or medical or magical as one might imagine. It seems like play. And although no one would pretend to be administering magic (although they do conduct a number of Magic Clubs for kids), they will firmly defend the fact that this isn't just playing with kids.

Ms. Clay stops by Bryan's first-grade classroom to check on him. This is something that occurs at various moments throughout the day. One of the KEYS staff members will say that he or she is going to check in on Willamina or Fred or Justin. Usually, such a visit includes a quick check with the teacher and the student to see how the day is going. The visit may involve a prolonged stay in the classroom, allying the KEYS teacher and the general classroom teacher in a variety of instructional arrangements. Often, the goal is provide a little anxiety relief to either the adult or the child. Typically, the teacher has spent the entire day in the classroom dealing with the continuous flow of issues and concerns that arise. If it has been a tough day, the chance to talk for even a few minutes to a concerned and helpful adult can often break the teacher's level of tension and ease his or her frazzled nerves. If it has been a good day, then the teacher can pause to notice the success and celebrate for a moment with a trusted colleague.

The focus is similar with the individual child. If the day has been frustrating or difficult, the KEYS teacher pulls the student aside or perhaps takes the child out for a relaxing, comforting walk around the building. As they walk, the teacher and child might directly discuss the problems encountered by the child. Or, they might take a short emotional vacation by talking about something completely different. For students who are struggling, these relational booster shots can occur three or more times per day. And when the child is having a successful day, the KEYS teacher's visit provides an opportunity for recognition, a pat on the back, a few compliments that have usually been few and far between in this youngster's experience. Recognizing and accepting new success can be a lesson in itself.

This morning, Ms. Clay drops by Bryan's classroom. He is a first grader who joined the KEYS program the year before. He had a very difficult year in kindergarten. His behavior was pretty bizarre. He often stayed separated from his peers, wandering away from the group, seemingly caught up more in his own imagination than in the concrete realities of the social context. He would talk out at odd times and occasionally throw very dramatic tantrums, writhing angrily on the ground in a way that frightened his classmates and teacher. His kindergarten teacher feared and did not like him. She wanted him removed from her classroom. A parent of one of Bryan's classmates made a serious effort to have Bryan removed. She hired a lawyer to investigate legal means of forcing Highmont School to pull Bryan from the regular kindergarten in order to secure the safety and well-being of his classmates. The Highmont administration kept Bryan in the regular class and trusted the KEYS staff to work with him. The kindergarten teacher muddled her way through a difficult year and then retired from teaching.

This year, Bryan is in a first-grade class with a teacher who likes him and sees him in a positive light. She values Bryan's sense of humor, imagination, curiosity, and energy. The KEYS staff notes that Bryan's self-esteem and sense of emotional security have improved greatly this year. He feels safe, accepted, and loved. It is amazing what a difference one teacher's attitude can make on a child.

One of the main goals of the KEYS program involves working to transform teachers rather than children. When the general classroom teachers view a student in a positive and loving way despite the odd or disruptive behavior of that child, the child typically thrives and improves in that room. When a teacher thinks of the child as evil, bad, sick, or crazy, then the child typically struggles and does not improve. Often, the KEYS teachers try to gently coax the teachers into seeing the wonderful or fascinating child behind the weird or oppositional behavior.

For instance, Ms. Clay tells the story about a girl named Sally whose teacher called in Ms. Clay for a discussion about Sally's behavior. The teacher was very concerned because Sally was "terrorizing" a boy in the room, following him around, bothering him frequently, bumping and pushing him, and making funny faces at him. To the teacher, this was a recent addition to a long list of negative behaviors that this "disturbed" child had committed. Ms. Clay listened to the teacher's very complete description of the behaviors and then said, "I think Sally has a crush on him. She's making kissy face at him." The teacher paused, thought for a moment, and smiled with a sigh, "Oh, I never thought of that. You're right!" Suddenly, the behaviors had been "normalized," cast in a different light, interpreted within a more positive way of seeing Sally and her childhood development.

Back to deadheading with Bryan. A useful strategy that Ms. Clay and Mrs. Johnson have devised is an early morning walk to calm Bryan down and help him ease into his day. They noticed that he often started the day like a whirlwind, a spinning storm of anxiety and tension that caused him problems in the first hour. Typically, a few minutes of walking or gardening with Ms. Clay would help to comfort him and orient him to the classroom setting.

Surprisingly, this morning, Bryan asked if Jake can join him for deadheading. Ms. Clay and Mrs. Johnson raised their eyebrows in curiosity. Jake and Bryan, although friends of a sort, often fought one another. Last thing the adults knew, these two kids were at war with one another. Ms. Clay, Bryan, Jake, and Ms. McGee, the classroom aide, stroll merrily down the hallway to the garden outside. It is surprising and enjoyable to see the boys walking arm in arm down the hall with Bryan explaining to his friend/foe what deadheading is.

"You cut off the tops of dead flowers. It's like giving the flowers a haircut," Bryan explains. Everyone laughs at this metaphor. Ms. Clay asks him to explain further. Bryan replies, "Well, I get my hair cut when it is too long, when I'm starting to look like a girl." Everyone laughs again as the group walks out into the morning sunshine. They spend 5 minutes chopping the tops off of flowers that have already bloomed and turned south. Ms. Clay and Ms. McGee carefully instruct Bryan and Jake on picking the right flowers to chop, leaving the active blooms alone. Jake and Bryan work side by side, discussing which flowers to cut and which to let live. At one point, Ms. Clay crouches down next to Bryan to ask him a few orienting questions about his day ahead.

"What do you have to remember today, Bryan?"

"To be quiet," Bryan replies as he reaches his scissors to another dead head.

"And look around the room to see what others are doing?"

"Yeah," Bryan agrees.

"And do you talk when Mrs. J. talks?"

"No, I wait my turn."

Ms. Clay rubs his back between the shoulder blades. Then Bryan walks over to join his gardening pal Jake, who is working on some little purple flowers.

After a few minutes, the deadheaders head inside. The boys and Ms. McGee return to their class. Ms. Clay tells Bryan that she will check in on him later. She plans in her mind two times later in the day when she will drop in to see him.

Ms. Clay then walks off to see a boy named Tim. He is often very anxious and easily upset. He tends to somaticize his emotions, turning his fears and worries into physical symptoms. He frequently asks to go to the nurse's office. Ms. Clay is trying to encourage Tim to come to the KEYS classroom to talk with her, Ms. Lindsey, or Ms. Manetti when he feels overwhelmed rather than going to the nurse's office. So far, he isn't buying it. Later in the day, Ms. Clay overhears Tim in the hallway talking to a little boy who is crying. Tim advises the classmate to go to the nurse's office to have his temperature taken.

A Club or Activity Group

A Club is what counselors call an *activity group,* a small group of children facilitated by one or two adults who do activities together as a way of organizing therapeutic interactions working toward goals of relationship building, social skill development, and the development of self-esteem. Ms. Clay explains it like this: "You have to remember what the goal is, what the lesson is *behind* the activity." On the surface, the Club might be building birdhouses, making a quilt, or planting and tending a garden. This activity is not insignificant, for it is the process through which the therapeutic work—the lesson *behind* the activity or the lesson *in the midst of* the activity—develops. As the children work together on the activity, the possible psychosocial benefits are numerous. They are finding a social group within the school where they are fully accepted and loved. They take on a new activity that is often challenging and frustrating, thereby providing an opportunity for students to learn to handle their own frustration and support other students in doing the same. When the project is successful, the individuals often feel a sense of pride and a bolstered sense of their own competence.

Additionally, there are many positive developments because of the fact that the projects are cooperative group tasks in which the students share and work toward one goal. This means that individual achievements are cast in the collaborative light of the group's common goal. Although individuals feel proud of what they are able to do, the scene is not one of competition for a prize. The group works to create something valuable together, to build a success that is shared among the participants. Students who may have few or no friends develop supportive bonds with other students and caring adults. Students who are often psychologically defended or keep themselves socially isolated feel that they are part of something good that goes beyond their fragile, lonely selves. Students who find limited success in academic endeavors find themselves amazed at what they and their classmates are able to create.

The choice to participate or not is crucial to the Club process. Often, public school students, especially students considered E/BD, have little choice in the activities they do all day. Choosing to attend and participate is vital to building the commitment to the Club, the child's personal investment in the project and in his or her peer group. It is a truism of psychotherapy that a powerful ingredient in the improvement of an individual's mental health and social well-being is the decision to enter into the therapeutic process. Forced psychotherapy is notoriously ineffective. The act of choosing to involve oneself in an activity for one's own benefit is a powerful decision that takes the first step toward personal improvement, a step that no one else can take for that individual.

Ms. Lindsey and Ms. Manetti are co-leaders of two Magic Clubs. The Magic Club idea is based on a program called *Counseling Kids: It's Magic* (Gilroy, 1998). The program comes with magic tricks and instructions on how doing magic with kids can help them build self-esteem, improve self-awareness, and improve social skills. The two Highmont Magic Clubs are practicing in preparation for performances in front of large groups of kindergarten and first-grade students. The Club members have about 7 weeks to prepare. We'll take a close look at one Magic Club meeting to get a flavor of what this activity group is all about.

Edgardo, John, Edward, and Rick enter the room. They each exchange greetings with Ms. Manetti and Ms. Lindsey. Ms. Manetti is wearing a black magician's cape and holding the magic wand. The boys excitedly ask questions about the activity. "What trick are we doing today? Can I wear the cape? Are you gonna do magic?" Ms. Manetti answers their questions and directs them to sit in the semicircle of chairs facing the make-believe stage area. The boys quickly sit down. They do not sit still, and they do not completely stop talking, not at the beginning of the group nor throughout the entire activity. They are attentive and fully involved, but they are also continuously wiggling, jiggling, and commenting aloud. Their motion and running commentary to one another hum like an engine in the background of the lesson.

John is noticeably more hyped up than the other boys. At times, he seems overwhelmed by the excitement, by the energy moving through his body. His limbs flip and flop in different directions, and comments pop impulsively from his mouth.

Phil, a tall boy with an awkward grin, enters a little late. Something is obviously going on between Phil and the other boys. Edgardo and Edward jump up and change their seats to move away from where Phil sits. They shoot Phil a look of disapproval. Although John and Rick don't seem to be involved in this conflict, their body language and facial expressions mimic those of Edgardo and Edward. It must feel to Phil like a full-force cold shoulder from the group. He seems uncomfortable, as if he knows that something is wrong, but he copes as best he can. He immediately faces and looks up at Ms. Manetti, who is standing in front of the group about to begin the lesson. He'd like nothing more than to just get started.

Ms. Manetti introduces the lesson: "Today, we're going to learn how to give advice without hurting somebody's feelings. It is important to be able to tell someone how they could do better, but we have to watch out not to hurt that person's feelings. I know that my feelings have been hurt before when someone gave me criticism in the wrong way. How can we tell someone that they made some mistakes and help them do something better without hurting their feelings?" All the boys' hands fly up. Ms. Manetti calls on Phil.

"You can smile when . . . uh . . . you talk."

"OK, you can have a smiling face," Ms. Manetti repeats. "But you mean a friendly face, not laughing, right?" The boys shake their heads. Somebody says, "Not laughing!"

"You stupidhead!" says John.

"John." Ms. Lindsey's voice is serious yet calm. She knows that he was caught up in the excitement and spoke impulsively, but she enforces the rule firmly. "We have a group rule about no put-downs. We can't be insulting the other group members with names." John looks at her in acknowledgment of what he has done. The other boys look for a moment at John. Insults are a serious violation of the group's rules. The first activity the group completed, before they embarked on developing themselves as junior magicians, was to agree upon a list of group rules. The rules are posted on the wall and signed by all the boys.

Ms. Manetti continues, "OK, remember, no laughing, because laughing can hurt someone's feelings. What else?" All the hands go up. She calls on Edward.

"You gotta talk nice, in a nice way, so they don't think you're picking on 'em."

"That *is* important," Ms. Manetti agrees. "Say it nicely so the person won't feel picked on. Anything else?" She calls on Edgardo.

"Uh. . . . you can't call 'em names or anything."

"No name-calling. Good, Edgardo. Name-calling just makes people feel bad. OK, now I'll do the coloring book trick first. Then, you'll tell me what I did well and what I could improve on. We'll take turns so that everybody gets a chance to do the trick and receive the feedback from the group."

Rick's hand goes up. Ms. Lindsey calls on him. "Can I go first?"

"I'll go first so you can see how it is done," Ms. Manetti explains, "then everyone will get a turn."

Ms. Lindsey points to an enormous poster board pinned to the wall. "Does everyone remember the list we made? The things to keep in mind while performing a magic trick?" Hands go up. She calls on Edgardo. He reads the list aloud—stand straight and tall, speak clearly, look at the audience, and so on. The list was created by the group in an earlier meeting in order to provide guidance to the students when they perform.

"Good, Edgardo," comments Ms. Manetti. "Remember to watch me closely to see if I do these things."

Ms. Manetti executes the coloring book trick. She reads from cue cards that a student holds. The magic trick itself relies on a special coloring book that has blank pages if you open it up in one corner and brightly colored pages if you open it in another corner. The magician displays the blank pages of the book, turns the pages magically to color, and then finally restores the pages to their original blank form. The whole trick takes about 90 seconds. During the actual moment of magic transformation, the magician calls one member of the audience onto the stage to wave a magic wand over the coloring book. With a few waves of the wand and some carefully selected magic words (Allacazam), the magician turns the book from colored to blank to colored again. The hardest part for the magician is remembering how to flip the pages so that the book changes in the right direction and so that the audience can actually see the pages.

As Ms. Manetti is about to start the trick, she suddenly pauses and smiles as if she has just remembered something. "Oh, wait. First, before I start, does anyone remember our agreement?" Hands go up. Ms. Manetti picks John.

"We have to keep it a secret."

"Yes," Ms. Lindsey chimes in. "Last year, someone in the Magic Club told other students how the magic works. Then, when we did the show, it wasn't as good because some of the audience knew the tricks. If we want it to be magic, we can't tell anyone. OK?" The boys agree.

At this point, Phil has shifted his chair to sit closer to Edgardo. He swings a kick at Edgardo. Ms. Manetti sees this and pauses the group. She corrects Phil directly, but in a very gentle tone: "Phil, I don't think we should be kicking each other."

Ms. Lindsey comments, "I think that sometimes some people in the group are participating while others are picking on each other." Her words are of a different nature than Ms. Manetti's correction. Whereas Ms. Manetti directly pointed out to Phil that his kicking a group member was a problem, Ms. Lindsey's comment tells the group that some negative interactions are going on that go beyond Phil's kicking. She simply points this out, setting the information in the students' laps, bringing what had been hidden to the forefront of awareness. At some level, all the boys knew that a conflict was brewing involving Phil, Edgardo, and Edward, and maybe the others. Ms. Lindsey has decided merely to tell everyone that she sees the elephant in the living room, that the supposedly hidden and subtle conflict the boys are carrying on with their facial expressions and body language is actually out in the open. By doing so, she offers the boys a chance to become more aware of what they are doing.

Ms. Lindsey and Ms. Manetti pause for a moment to see if the boys begin to talk about the issue or if they decide to pull themselves together to continue the magic lesson. The boys are silent. The movement of their bodies slows for a moment. The silent message is that they want to do the magic trick instead of picking on Phil. Ms. Lindsey and Ms. Manetti read the silence—one of a million split-second judgment calls that teachers make—and decide not to pursue a full discussion about this. That would have been one way to go, stepping out of the magic lesson to create a new lesson, a new discussion based on the conflict among the boys. But the room seems suddenly less tense. Even Phil seems a little more relaxed. Ms. Lindsey's simple act of calling the elephant an elephant is enough for now. The conflict is not solved, but it has been set aside by the boys in favor of working together as a cooperative group on the magic activity.

Ms. Manetti then works her way through the coloring book trick, performing very carefully for the group, reading the cue cards that carry her step by step through the performance. Then, she asks the boys to start by telling her what she did well.

"You stood tall and straight."

"You spoke loud and clear."

"You looked at the audience."

Ms. Manetti accepts the compliments graciously. Then, she asks the boys to give her advice on what she can improve. The hands fly up. John goes first.

"You looked around, but you didn't look at everyone."

"You're right, John. I didn't," Ms. Manetti agrees. "And you gave me that advice in a very friendly tone of voice." She calls on Edward. He is grinning.

"Didn't speak loudly." He giggles and drops his head in Edgardo's lap. Edgardo playfully pushes his friend's body away.

"I think you are right, Edward," Ms. Manetti responds, "but I'm feeling like you're laughing at me. Remember what we said about laughing."

"No laughing when giving advice," comments Rick.

"Right," agrees Ms. Manetti, "because we want to help our friend improve, so we don't want to hurt her feelings. OK, next up is Phil."

Phil hops up eagerly, and Ms. Manetti helps him put on the black magician's robe. He holds the coloring book against his chest and begins to read the first cue card. His eyes and body are tight with concentration. He is trying so hard to get this right.

In addition to the social skills lesson about compliments and criticism, this activity (and the entire Magic Club program) places the young magician in a pretty intense situation that repeatedly challenges each student's competence and confidence. Most of these boys have never been involved in a complicated public performance requiring rehearsal. Standing up in front of a group for practice and eventually a large audience to perform magic tricks requires a combination of skills: reading, public speaking, and showmanship. The magicians are learning poise, confidence, self-control, patience, and teamwork as they prepare for the big show.

When it comes time for Phil to choose a member of the audience to come on stage to wave the wand over the coloring book, an event that comes up twice in this trick, Phil selects Edgardo and Edward. He is doing all he can to move back into their good graces.

Phil concludes the performance, and the boys give him a round of applause. He bows with a proud smile. He remains on the stage to hear his reviews.

"What did Phil do well?" asks Ms. Lindsey.

"He stood straight and tall."

"He talked loudly."

"He didn't rush."

"Is there anything Phil can do to make the presentation better?" asks Ms. Lindsey.

Ms. Manetti softens the moment for Phil, the first boy to receive criticism, by commenting, "Remember that we're practicing to get better for the show. We all practice to get better, and our friends can help us. I know that I've been doing this trick since last year, and I still can improve." The boys provide advice.

"He was doing like this [wiggling legs]."

"He didn't look around at the group."

"Showing the book to everyone is hard," Ms. Manetti comments. She stands behind Phil and puts her arms around him to help him hold the coloring book in front of his body. "Phil, open the book and try flipping the pages for all to see." Ms. Manetti and Phil turn their bodies on an axis as Phil flips the pages. He does better than he did during his performance. This is a sticking point that will plague all of the performers, ruffling the pages slowly and in each direction.

The activity moves along smoothly, with each boy taking a turn at presenting the trick. The level of excitement remains high throughout the lesson as each boy joyfully and nervously takes the stage. The date of the performance for the kindergarten classes is 6 weeks away, a very long time in the minds of 10- and 11-year-old boys. But they seem to feel the urgency and the tension of performing in front of an audience, even if that audience is only their fellow group members.

At one point after Edgardo's performance, Ms. Lindsey notices that Phil's zipper is down. "Phil, I'm going to be the nicest I can while giving you this advice. Pull up your zipper." Phil smiles bashfully, and the boys laugh. It is a silly moment when the lesson of advice-giving becomes real. The boys' laughter could be harsh and demeaning to Phil, but the group is gentle in their teasing. Phil takes it well.

As the group's time draws to a close, the boys take turns trying on the magician's hat and cape. They talk excitedly about giving a performance to a live audience. Then, Ms. Lindsey says, "Time's up," and the boys scurry out the door and head back to their classrooms.

KEYS—GREENLAND WEST MIDDLE SCHOOL

The KEYS program at Greenland West Middle School consists of Ms. Deberg, a teacher assistant, and Ms. Strickland, a teacher. Also, Ms. Manetti spends a portion of her time at this site. They have a small room positioned at the corner of a busy crossroads in this suburban middle school. The KEYS ethos and practices are remarkably similar at each location. Every step Ms. Deberg and Ms. Strickland take is in complete harmony with the practices of Ms. Manetti, Ms. Lindsey, and Ms. Clay at Highmont.

"The goal of our work," explains Ms. Strickland, "is to build a relationship with a kid, because then you'll be in a better position to help him." Of course, this is easier said than done. In this section, we'll offer some insight into two specific forms of support provided by the Greenland West Middle School KEYS teachers: the drop-in talk and the activity group. Sometimes, students need someone to talk to. The KEYS teachers are available for students experiencing social conflicts and difficult-to-handle emotions to drop in and talk. The activity group we'll describe is a girl's group, one of many groups run by Ms. Deberg and Ms. Strickland.

A Drop-In Talk

It is 7:45 a.m. when the phone in the KEYS classroom rings. Ms. Strickland has been working with Mike on his social studies. The phone call is about another boy named Mike. She speaks briefly to Mike Number Two and invites him to come to talk to her.

Ms. Strickland returns to tutoring the first Mike while waiting for the second. He soon arrives. He is an extraordinarily small boy, looking more like a third grader than a sixth grader. His pale face and deep, dark eyes are partially hidden beneath the hood of a brown sweatshirt. Ms. Strickland smiles softly and invites him to sit down next to her. He sets his binder on the table and sits down. His entire body seems to sigh with deep relief. It is as if he has come home. His tense face and shoulders relax. This place and this relationship with Ms. Strickland are obviously a haven for this small boy in the complex, adolescent world of the public middle school.

Ms. Strickland finishes what she is doing with Mike Number One and turns to her hooded friend in need. The two speak softly.

"What's going on?"

"I hate the stuff we're doing in first period . . . and second period. I hate all of it." Mike's complaint is highly emotional and, in adolescent style, seems to include not just what is bugging him but his entire school experience. Ms. Strickland asks him a series of questions, calmly helping him focus on the source of his anxiety: second-period chorus.

"I hate it," says Mike. "I just want to get out of there."

Ms. Strickland listens. She has some understanding of Mike, his patterns of behavior and emotion, and his ways of coping with difficult situations. He is often emotionally defensive and anxious. He seems to have a low sense of his own worth. His size is a particularly sensitive issue. He is taking prescription growth hormones to try to gain more height and weight. Also, being viewed as very intelligent is a frequent goal. Mike is in the gifted program. Mental acuity and academic ability are evident areas of strength. Nonetheless, he often grandstands in class, trying to answer simple questions with lengthy intellectual diatribes that touch upon the subject only remotely. He also becomes easily frustrated if the teacher does not call on him often enough, as if losing the spotlight for too long infringes upon his need to show his intellectual talent. Often, Mike simply refuses to participate in a lesson or activity. He rejects the work outright and says that he doesn't like it.

After talking, Ms. Strickland and Mike decide that he is ready to go to his next class, the much-dreaded second-period chorus. Although this decision seems completely sound at the moment, it is only 20 minutes later that Mike is standing outside of his classroom. He didn't like the activity, so he refused to do it. The chorus teacher allowed him to step outside to wait for Ms. Strickland to come get him. She rounds him up and brings him back to her room. At times like this, the KEYS room seems like a behind-the-front-lines M.A.S.H. unit where the emotionally wounded fall back and receive care, a place for temporary respite before returning to the front lines of the regular classroom.

Mike hangs out for the remainder of second period, pretending to do some homework while Ms. Strickland and Ms. Deberg work with other students. When the bell rings, he goes off to his next class. He is able to remain in the rest of his classes that day.

Ms. Strickland theorizes about this fascinating and challenging student: "He is such a mixture of intelligence and fear. He tries to use all of his brains to cover all of his fears. And he gets very demanding. He's the kind of kid that you see and wonder if the school can be flexible enough for him to make it. That's part of our job, in KEYS, to make things more flexible for kids like this. He's a great kid with loads of talent, but he doesn't accept the way the school is. It just doesn't fit him.

"One concern I have is dependence. He comes here and he feels comfortable. His anxiety drops. He uses us as a safety valve, a home port. But sometimes, he may lean on us too much. Maybe he'd learn to deal with more out there [in his classes] if he couldn't flop here so easily. So, I wonder about that, but I know that if we make an error, it is better to be too supportive, too helpful."

The Girls' Group

As we wait for Samantha, Allison, and Karla to arrive for the Girls' Group, Ms. Deberg gives me a quick preview on the girls and the group's work so far. The group has been meeting twice per week for 3 weeks. By comparison to most groups, the progress so far has been very slow. Samantha, Allison, and Karla have battled for control, squabbling and jockeying for position. Each girl has difficulty making and keeping friendships. Their interactions so far in the group offer a brief microcosm of these difficulties. The purpose of the group is to provide an opportunity for the girls to build valued friendships with other girls while also confronting the obstacles that keep them friendless, the habits and attitudes that maintain social isolation for each.

Karla is a social outcast. She has been diagnosed with a language impairment. She has difficulty carrying on a discussion. Her statements seem very concrete and immature for a middle school student. Emotionally, she is very dependent. In the group, she tries to imitate and follow Allison because Allison has money and flashy clothes. She doesn't seem to notice that Allison doesn't have any friends either. Karla comes from a very poor family, so she looks up to Allison for her possessions and wealth.

Allison attends special classes for gifted students. She works very hard to impress her peers while she misses out on more authentic friendships. She is flamboyant and self-conscious, a Rose Parade strolling the hallways of the middle school. Her outfits are very colorful, stylish, and daring. She often looks like a young girl trying too hard to use clothes and makeup to look like an adult. In her home life, she is very much the focus of her mother's controlling attentions. It often seems like her mother is living out her life through her daughter. She and Allison try to create Allison as a well-financed socialite. Two years ago, they staged a lavish birthday party, and very few of her invited peers showed up. Last year, she was redeemed when a large crowd showed up for a similar event.

Samantha is obsessive, angry, and depressed. She seems like she is brooding under a dark cloud, trying so hard to get everything just right so that the cloud will break. She talks a lot about God and Jesus, taking emotional refuge in dogmatic absolutes. She also has a romantic obsession with a boy in her neighborhood who went out with her for a short time before dropping her. She continues to fixate on him. For instance, he is of Vietnamese descent, so, during a free moment at school, the teachers can often find Samantha sitting at the computer, looking up information on Vietnam on the Internet.

Samantha has an additional problem that haunts her. She has a bad reputation because of an incident last year when school officials found that she had composed a list of students she planned on killing. In the wake of the Columbine violence, this led to a lengthy suspension from school. Samantha is back in school this year, but she is known throughout school as the crazy girl with the plan to kill.

The girls spent the first three meetings working on what typically takes one meeting—writing group guidelines (or rules) and trying to come to some agreement on a community service project on which to work. So far, the girls have engaged in everything but the kinds of compromise, negotiation, and friendship building that Ms. Deberg and Ms. Strickland have encouraged and hoped for. It has been every girl for herself. The tempers and voices have run high as each girl has staked out her territory and attempted to push her own needs and wants on the group. The girls seem to have little understanding or appreciation for basic concepts of sharing and doing things together in a collaborative way. The squabbles have led to a number of hardened stalemates, moments of communication shutdown when all three sat with arms crossed and foreheads steaming.

Ms. Deberg recalls that last year's girls' group went through a similar period of conflict, defensiveness, and selfishness. The nature of the group can change in a single activity, a single watershed meeting. Last year, that transformation occurred when the group created a large mural of an ocean scene. Suddenly, the group jelled in a new way. Defenses were set aside. Each girl trusted herself and one another as they all worked out a plan for colors and materials. The tensions and fears that had kept each girl distant from one another were washed away in the moment of the unified effort, by the group's joyful focus on making something important together. Ms. Deberg has kept that mural as a reminder of how weeks of apparent non-progress can set the stage for an activity when the girls all come together. She pulls it out now and again to remind herself to be patient. She hopes that, Allison, Karla, and Samantha will come together in this way soon.

The girls have come to three agreements that may set the stage for further growth. Whatever moments of unity can be cultivated in these early sessions are appreciated by Ms. Strickland and Ms. Deberg as groundwork, early experiences of coming together that may lead to greater and fuller bonds in the days to come. First, the girls hashed out a list of group guidelines. They wrote this on a large of piece of paper posted on the wall. The six guidelines (in the girls' own words) are as follows:

1. You listen to us, we'll listen to you.

2. Do unto others as you would have them do unto you . . . in other words, treat people the way you want to be treated.

3. Anything said in this room stays in this room.

4. Take on roles and stick with your responsibilities.

5. Talk through your disagreements.

6. Respect each other and yourself.

At the bottom, it reads: "I agree to these guidelines and will follow them to the best of my ability." All three girls have signed in agreement.

The second agreement seems minor, but it may spark some sense of group unity. Ms. Strickland and Ms. Deberg asked the girls to create their own set of symbols that substitute for each letter in the standard alphabet. This will be the secret alphabet of the group, a form of modern cuneiform that only they understand. The girls did this fairly easily. Their strategy was to divide the 26 letters into thirds, assigning a set for each to match with a new symbol. This wasn't the most collaborative method of doing this, but at least they all agreed on the final set of symbols. They wrote the set down on a master sheet and then made copies for each to carry.

The third agreement is more functional than impressive. The girls squabbled at length about choosing a project to do. Ms. Strickland and Ms. Deberg presented a wide range of options, all community service projects designed to help the school or a disadvantaged group in the local area. For example, they could make quilts for a local homeless shelter. The girls battled over every option presented and reached no agreement at all. Finally, Ms. Deberg and Ms. Strickland staged a ploy to jolt the group out of the starting gate. They arranged for Mr. Ship, a much-beloved assistant principal, to ask the girls to serve as a "social committee" for the school. The social committee's job would be to make birthday cards and present them to teachers on their birthday. As expected, all three girls eagerly accepted Mr. Ship's offer to make birthday cards.

The next group meeting was the first day selecting designs for cards. Ms. Strickland had gathered a number of card catalogs and books on card-making. The goal for the day was to choose the best designs and begin making the first cards. Additionally, there was an organizational task to be accomplished. They would have to make a calendar of teacher birthdays for the year so that they could make and distribute the cards in a timely fashion.

As the three girls enter the room, Ms. Strickland hands each a decoder sheet. On the board is written a secret message in the group's symbolic code, a series of squiggles, squares, and half moons. The girls eagerly pull out their decoder sheets and begin to decode the secret message.

As they work, Karla says to Samantha, "Your dress looks nice." Samantha seems to hear, but she says nothing and looks away. This moment of failed connection hangs heavy in the air. Then, the moment passes as the girls work intently on the coded message.

This moment of caring offered but not received, this extension of a hand of friendship that fails to reach far enough, has greater significance as the clock ticks through the next 45 minutes. During that time, until a brief final exchange between Karla and Allison, the girls do not talk to one another. All words spoken by the girls in that time are spoken to either Ms. Strickland or Ms. Deberg. The group's activity is reminiscent of the phenomenon of parallel play among very young children. Each will work on her own card, and each will seek out approval and support from the adults as if the adults are the sole font of love and relationship in the room. Although the girls will tolerate one another's presence, they will exist not in a mutual way but side by side, each separately seeking the love of the two adults. Ms. Strickland and Ms. Deberg will make various efforts to cultivate interactions and connection between the girls, but the girls today are each focused on moving along a solitary row.

The two joined tables are covered with paper of various colors, scissors of all sizes and types, and books with examples of cards. Each girl selects a card from one of the books and starts working. Allison and Karla seem quite content and relaxed in this task. Samantha is frustrated, angry, and struggling. She can't decide on a card to make. Her facial expression is intense and overcast as she shuffles quickly through the books. She seems to half give up before she reaches an obstacle. One gets the sense in watching her that she is fixated on failure and angry at the world for her failing situation. Both Ms. Deberg and Ms. Strickland make suggestions. Finally, Samantha selects a frog card and begins to work. Ms. Deberg observes aloud that Samantha has selected a very complicated pop-up card that will be a challenge to make. Samantha seems unfazed by Ms. Deberg's warning.

Ms. Strickland works closely with Karla. She has decided to make a card with a big picture of a bumblebee on it.

Allison has paused from her card to deal with a crucial matter—her makeup. She tips her purse upside down and dumps all of her cosmetics out on the table. She then lines up three tubes of lipstick.

"I have pictures next period. I want it to be just right." Allison provides running commentary even though no one has asked her what she is doing. She seems like she wants to be on stage, in the spotlight. She looks into a small, handheld mirror and touches her lips. "I have three shades of lipstick and I can't decide on one."

"Allison, why don't you do that at the end of the period? Otherwise, the lipstick will just fade. It'll be fresher if you do it later."

Allison agrees. She puts all of her cosmetics back in her purse. Karla watches this with great interest, almost as if she is taking mental notes. Samantha ignores this with great disinterest, as if her mind couldn't be bothered with such nonsense.

"Can we make popcorn?" Allison asks.

"In a few minutes," replies Ms. Strickland. "Let's get rolling on our cards, then I'll make some."

"I'd rather have some now," Allison states. Ms. Strickland patiently repeats that she'll make some in a while. Allison accepts this.

Over the next half hour, Samantha and Ms. Deberg engage in a little dance. Samantha repeatedly becomes frustrated and angry. She complains about not having the right scissors or about how the card is too tough for her to do. Ms. Deberg watches her closely and looks for opportunities to help. Samantha seems to be undecided about whether to accept some help. She also seems pretty firmly decided that she doesn't want to lose Ms. Deberg's assistance and interest. This dynamic makes for an interesting two-step. Ms. Deberg offers advice at various points. Sometimes, she backs up, leaving Samantha to stew for a while in her own bubbling cauldron. At one point, the two tussle back and forth. Samantha seems stumped. She stares an angry hole into the pages of the card book. Finally, she starts cutting. Immediately, she drops the scissors to the table in frustration.

"We don't have the right scissors for this," Samantha complains bitterly.

"Here. Use these straight-edge scissors. Those pinking scissors won't work for that," advises Ms. Deberg.

Samantha picks up the straight-edge scissors, begins to cut with them, and drops them to the table. She sighs and pushes herself back from the table.

"Do you want help?" Ms. Deberg asks from across the table.

"I don't care," says Samantha without looking up.

"OK, well, tell me when you care and I'll help you," Ms. Deberg responds. She's frustrated. Samantha's frustrated. At this moment, this is what they share. This is what bonds them, a shared sense of frustration. Samantha pauses for about 30 seconds, sitting silently and brooding. Then, she asks for help in a soft voice. Ms. Deberg explains that Samantha should use the regular scissors because the pinking scissors will cut edges that zig-zag. Samantha complains that she wants pinking scissors but that they don't have the right ones. Finally, Samantha takes the straight scissors and begins to cut.

Despite this exchange and Samantha's ongoing sense of frustration, the general tone of the room is light and jovial. Ms. Strickland carries a steaming bag of hot popcorn from the microwave and a bunch of paper towels over to the table. She pauses as she reaches the table. She looks around for someplace to put the popcorn and towels on the cluttered table.

"There's no room for popcorn," Ms. Strickland says, hinting for someone to clear a space. Ms. Deberg pushes some books aside to make room.

"I know where there's room," Allison says with a big grin. She pours herself a large helping on a paper towel and begins to munch.

"Where?" asks Ms. Deberg.

"In my stomach!" Allison laughs.

Ms. Strickland laughs. She warns everyone about being careful to not get the popcorn oil on their cards. She gives Karla a look—want some?—and Karla nods. Ms. Strickland pours her a towel-full. Samantha says aloud that she doesn't like popcorn.

"I don't need scissors," comments Karla as she takes the popcorn.

"Why not?" asks Ms. Deberg.

"To eat?" Karla asks with a piece of popcorn on her lips.

"You need scissors to eat?" Ms. Deberg responds in confusion.

"No, I don't need scissors to eat," Karla replies in mild exasperation.

"Oh, I was gonna say," quips Ms. Deberg with an exaggerated expression of disbelief, "I wanna watch if you're gonna eat with scissors." Karla smiles.

Mr. Ship, the assistant principal who christened the girls as the social committee for the school, enters the room. His eyes are wide as he looks at the cards the girls are working on. "Wow. I know I picked the right group for this job."

"Hey, Mr. Ship!" All three girls greet Mr. Ship by name. Even Samantha brightens up for the moment. This administrator is obviously well liked.

"Well, I think that maybe our social committee might just get a 'Pillar of Greenland Award.'" Greenland is the name of the school district.

"What's the Pillar of Greenland?" asks Allison.

"Yeah, what's that?" chimes in Karla.

Mr. Ship pauses for a moment. He is thinking. "Gee," he says with a rather befuddled look, "I don't really know." Everyone laughs.

Mr. Ship sweeps back out of the class as quickly as he swept in. If not for the obvious respect that the girls and teachers give to him, we would say that he was a visiting clown, a jokester who wanders from classroom to classroom spreading silliness and cheer.

At the end of the period, everyone scrambles to clean up the table. Allison pulls out her lipstick and mirror. She chooses a shade and carefully applies it while looking into her mirror.

"Allison, I'm going to get the yearbook and see your picture." This is the first direct comment from one of the students to another since the beginning of the period.

"It's gonna be good," Allison replies. Satisfied with her appearance for her photo session, she is putting away her cosmetics.

"Mine last year was bad. The year before was bad." Karla thinks back through her years of school photos. "Year before that was OK."

"Mine last year . . . my hair was down to here." Allison touches her shoulder. "And now it's up to here." She points to her current length halfway down her neck.

Allison and Karla go on to discuss hair and how hard it is to avoid being fat. Samantha listens but does not comment. As the bell rings and the girls rush out, this exchange stands out as the most mutual and friendly of the entire period.

Ms. Strickland and Ms. Deberg know that the group has a long way to go. The girls show little indication that they are developing friendships with one another. What Ms. Strickland and Ms. Deberg have succeeded in doing is creating a social context of humor, support, flexibility, and acceptance. In each session, they set the stage for further developments by making it repeatedly clear that each girl is valued and that the social space is safe for the expression of emotions. The girls are beginning to relax and let down their vigilant guards. Like farmers who have carefully prepared the soil and planted the crop, Ms. Strickland and Ms. Deberg work and wait patiently. They know that the harvest will come in its own time.

The KEYS program is a unique model. It draws on the strengths of human relationships. Each staff member holds the student's personal success and achievement as the ultimate goal. Staff members gently guide students toward productivity, competence, and social engagement. They consistently assist students in protecting their own pride even when faced with extremely difficult situations. The staff builds insight and judgment with the students who receive services. Coincidently, students' academic achievement grows as their social competencies develop. Finally, the staff moves to less active roles with students as the students increase their own ability to negotiate social situations, set and achieve goals, and succeed in school settings.

WHAT NOW? CURRENT AND FUTURE CHALLENGES FOR KEYS

The KEYS staff developed a well-oiled operation that assists students to develop social competency, academic status, and progress in the public school settings. Although the staff, students, and families associated with KEYS are pleased with the capacity of the program, there are still important questions to answer and methods to develop.

The KEYS service model assists approximately 40 students throughout the Greenland school district in eight different locations. The new challenge is to expand the program's philosophy, strategies, and success to reach more students. To accomplish this new goal, the KEYS staff now turns attention toward developing the capacity in other educators to implement KEYS services with support and eventually continue the services independently.

CONSTRUCTING PERSONAL MEANINGS

1. Conduct a survey of public school E/BD programs in your area, focusing on the philosophy of the programs and the kinds of services offered. How many of them fit the traditional behavioral approach? How many of them look more like the KEYS program?

2. Investigate the children's mental health system in your area. What services are available to students and families with private health insurance? What services are available to economically disadvantaged students and families? To what extent and in what ways do these service providers coordinate their work with the public schools?

3. Investigate opportunities for professional development in your area. What opportunities are available for teachers to develop their skills in supporting troubling students?

Working With Families

Susan Perez, Scot Danforth, and Terry Jo Smith

"Wrong environment and stupid parents are responsible for the unfortunate behavior of children."

Ethel Sturges Drummer, child mental health pioneer, 1920

"For every problem child a problem parent."

Helen Leland Witmer, child guidance researcher, 1940
(Jones, 1999, p. 174)

Federal law and the current educational research advise teachers and public schools to work closely, equally, and respectfully with parents and families. Public Law 94–142 and the various revised versions of the Individuals with Disabilities Education Act contain a provision for parents of students labeled handicapped to be actively involved in their child's educational planning. Educational researchers are in agreement that parent involvement is essential to school success (Bauer & Shea, 1985; Becher, 1984; Comer, Haynes, & Joyner, 1996; Seeley, 1989). Yet parents of troubling students often have very little involvement in the schooling of their children. Schools complain that they can't even get parents to show up for IEP or disciplinary meetings, an apparent indication that "the parents don't care." Parents complain that the only thing the school wants from them is to pick up their kid when he's been misbehaving. They say that they are blamed for their child's misbehavior and judged for their child's special education label.

In this chapter, we will closely examine this problematic situation and seek answers to how we educators can improve school-family relations and work in a collaborative way with parents to support the education of their child. Most of this chapter will be devoted to hearing the biographic stories of parents of troubling students. Listening fully to the words of parents offers us an opportunity to connect to parents with empathy and understanding. We will start by looking at some of the educational research on the relationship between parents and schools. We will learn about the benefits of and obstacles to developing an effective, collaborative relationship. From there, we will listen to the biographic stories of Ellen, Stephanie, and Carlos, three parents of middle school students. These stories are excerpts of a larger ethnographic study completed by Susan Perez. These narratives will teach us not only about these parents' experiences in dealing with public school systems and parenting a labeled or troubling child, but also about their lives, their hopes, and their pain. We will conclude this chapter by describing what we consider to be the best approach to working with parents—an approach of equality, collaboration, and empowerment.

PARENT INVOLVEMENT: A VIEW FROM ACADEMIC RESEARCH

Educational researchers agree that parent involvement is closely related to school success (Bauer & Shea, 1985; Becher, 1984; Comer et al., 1996; Seeley, 1989). Henderson (1987) reviewed 19 studies involving parent involvement to find that when parent involvement in public education occurred, there was generally increased success in student performance. More recent studies have supported these findings, asserting the influential role that parent involvement plays in supporting student learning in many subject areas (Faires, Nichols, & Rickelman, 2000; Green, 2001; Hara & Burke, 1998; Keith et al., 1998) Comer et al. (1996) believed this so strongly that Comer developed "Comer Schools," in which he worked on getting all parents involved in school life. According to Bauer and Shea (1985), the question is no longer whether parents should be involved in education, but rather, how to get them involved.

Yet despite this research mandate for parent involvement, both teachers and parents tend to remain resistant to the idea of parent involvement (Mullins, 1987), leaving considerable social distance between schools and families (Lightfoot, 1978; Powell, 1991).

There are two major reasons cited for educators' resistance to parent involvement in schools. One is a belief that school and home have different roles to play in the life of a child. Mixing them together interferes with the work of educators, who, as trained professionals, are expected to educate and socialize students to become individual citizens and workers in society. The other is the belief that parents of troubling students, especially those labeled E/BD, are to blame for their children's behavioral problems (Friesen & Wahlers, 1994; Mickelson, 2000).

Parents indicate that their major resistance to working with schools is a reaction to the educators viewing them as the root of their child's emotional or behavioral problem (Swap, 1993). Rather than being included as knowledgeable contributors and advocates for their children, parents say they feel discounted by educators who communicate with them only when there is a problem at school.

PARENTS AS THE ROOT OF THE PROBLEM

There is a wealth of educational and psychological research stating that "dysfunctional families" produce "dysfunctional children." Professionals tend to see parents as hostile, indifferent, uninterested, uncooperative, and the source of their children's problems (Leitch & Tangri, 1988).

The belief that parents are incompetent and the cause of a student's emotional disorder or school misbehavior has a long history. Before World War II, the child guidance clinics operated under the assumption that parents (specifically, mothers) were to blame for the behavior difficulties of their children (Jones, 1999). Researchers after World War II came to the same conclusion, that parents were the root of the emotional disability of their children. Studies focused on the causal relationship between the maladaptive behavior of the parents and the dysfunction of the child. Findings suggested that children tended to mimic, learn, or take on behavior modeled by their parents (Bandura & Walters, 1963). Becker, Peterson, Hellmer, Shoemaker, and Quay (1959) reported that children with aggressive behavior tended to have parents who were explosive, inconsistent, and maladjusted. Numerous studies by Glueck (1953; Glueck & Glueck, 1950) said that juvenile delinquents often came from inferior families and unfit parents. Rank (1949), Despert (1951), and Bettelheim (1967) forwarded the idea that parents of autistic children were incapable of establishing an intimate, caring relationship because of their own emotional dysfunctions. Through linkages found between children's emotional difficulties and parents' characteristics, researchers promoted the belief that parents were responsible for their children's disorder.

Recent studies indicate that this foundational belief in parents as the root of their child's emotional disability or school difficulties remains steadfast. Teachers view parents as the source of their children's problems and believe that the parents are in need of help themselves (Bailey, Buyssee, Edmonson, & Smith, 1992; Friesen & Wahlers, 1994; Mickelson, 2000). Additionally, teachers tend to view minority culture parents through biased eyes that lead to misunderstanding. Yet in their study of African American, Hispanic American, Native American, and European American parents, Geenen, Powers, and Lopez Vasquez (2001) found that the culturally and linguistically diverse parents were active in special education transition planning activities. In some instances, their level of reported participation surpassed that of European American parents. Despite this, professionals described those parents as less involved than European American parents.

Parent Resistance

Because the public schools and researchers have often cast parents as the dis-ordered fall guys, it is not surprising that parents of troubling students have often avoided involvement with the schools or openly opposed many of the schools' efforts. Their protective and resistant stance stems understandably from their belief that teachers blame parents for their children's emotional or behav-ioral difficulties. They often don't feel their input is valued or desired. They report feeling unwelcome or unneeded in the schools (Leyser, 1985). Parents state that the majority of their communication with schools occurs when there are problems (Sonnenschein, 1981; Swap, 1993; Swick & Graves, 1993).

Parents often feel blamed by the schools, as if the goal of special education and other special programs is to undo the harm that they, as parents, have caused. Parents often feel they are not really wanted at school unless there is a problem. If their child gets in trouble, they are called in to be judged, but they are not valued as meaningful partners in their child's education.

Additionally, professional jargon and entangled bureaucratic systems con-fuse and silence parents. Parents are often baffled by the school system and the theories, philosophies, and jargon used by educators. Parents report feeling that teachers and administrators treat parents condescendingly or with contempt, handling the parents as they handle the child, highhandedly manipulating them out of their rights. Parents frequently feel excluded because they do not understand the language or the protocol. The use of behavioral terms, bureau-cratic anachronisms, and institutional policies often serve as barriers that leave parents unable to understand the proceedings (Williams & Hartlage, 1988). Parents also express resentment toward the formality of school meetings and the limited time allotted for them to participate. They feel that the structure of the meetings minimizes their input, demonstrating that the educators don't really value what they have to say (Swap, 1993).

When parents are unable to attend meetings at school, they often feel that educators interpret their absence as apathy rather than evidence of the many pressing demands that parents must juggle in order to survive (Leyser, 1985). Many parents lack reliable transportation, child care, or the financial resources necessary to allow them to attend meetings at school (Harry, 1992; Leyser, 1985; Singer & Powers, 1993). When educators assume that this inability to get to school is actually a lack of interest, parents feet hurt and misunderstood.

THINKING AHEAD: RELATING TO THE STORIES

In the following three sections, we will hear directly from Ellen, Stephanie, and Carlos, parents of middle school boys labeled E/BD in rural Florida. Their personal stories provide rich and often troubling insight into their lives and their experiences with schools. The purpose of these stories is to help us understand more deeply the lives of parents and students. As you read these biographies, it will be helpful to keep a few questions in mind.

How does getting to know these parents' personal stories affect your thinking about their relationships with their children and school personnel?

What might you do to get to know the families of your students at more personal and trusting levels?

In these stories, what do you think are contributing factors to the difficult relationships between the parents and the public school systems?

ELLEN

I (Susan Perez) first met Ellen through her stepson, Jeff. I had come to know him as one of the students labeled severely emotionally disturbed in the school to which I was assigned as part of my graduate assistantship responsibilities. When I spent time in his classroom, I would see him bundled up in his camouflage jacket, his collar pulled up around his ears with his long brown hair providing a curtain for his face. It appeared as though Jeff were trying to be invisible while standing out like a sore thumb.

During the next school year, I coordinated a grant aimed at bringing together parents of students considered emotionally disturbed in order to learn to become advocates for the needs of their own and others' children. My first task was to create a parent advocacy group that might come to lead others in learning how to identify these needs.

I invited Ellen to join me as a charter member. Jeff was supposed to enter high school that year, but he never went, and no one from the high school ever came looking for him. He was a 15-year-old at home, without school or job, which left him aimless and restless. Ellen was miserable. She wanted Jeff to have some kind of training and independent living, but felt she had exhausted all the possibilities available. She seemed the perfect parent to begin to give our group focus, for she seemed to have a clear idea of what she thought older students like Jeff needed.

Over the course of many interviews, I learned that Ellen grew up in a poor family. Her family lived in a wooden shack in Michigan, where they were cold much of the time. As a young girl, Ellen was responsible for hauling heavy pieces of wood to the house to provide warmth and fuel for cooking. The cold and the weight of the logs left her with joint problems later in life.

At 14, she became pregnant by a 20-year-old man who lived not far from her home. When her father found out, he gave her the choice of marriage or being sent away to a home for unwed mothers. She married, and by the time she was 20, she had five children and an abusive husband who drank up what little money he earned.

I remember her telling me one evening over a hot cup of tea how she begged the doctor to tie her tubes when he delivered her third child. He refused, saying she was too young. Two more children followed.

Ellen met Larry years later, when all of her children were finally in school. Larry was young and full of life. He took her away from an abusive, demanding husband and offered her the adolescence of which she had been deprived. And then, after 5 years together, came Jeff.

Ellen tells her own story in these words:

I guess I want people to know what our life has been like with Jeff. It was 15 years ago that we got Jeff. We were living in Florida, not far from where his biological mother lived. We knew he'd been born, but we had never seen him. I had known his mother back when Larry was dating her.

I was in Michigan with my own daughter, who was having her first baby when HRS (Florida Department of Health and Rehabilitative Services) contacted Larry and wanted to know if he wanted his son. He said, "I have to talk it over with my wife." So he called me up there in Michigan. I talked to my daughter, and she said, "Oh, go on, Mother, you got lots of love to give." So I called Larry back and told him I thought we should take him. Two weeks later, I was back in Florida and we were going to get Jeff. He was nine months old.

We met with Jeff's caseworker. She said he had malnutrition, scabies, and an infection, the whole nine yards, when HRS got him. They put him and his half-sister in the hospital until they got them all healed up. Then they were put in shelter care. That's when they contacted Larry. She showed us a letter from Jeff's biological mother saying she hoped that "the little bastard died." She didn't want to see him again. In an effort to abort him, she had drunk a mixture of quinine and turpentine when she was 6 months pregnant. She told Larry's sister, "I thought I killed the little bastard. It didn't move for a month."

My oldest son had to drive us to the HRS office because we didn't have a car. We had just gotten electricity turned on in the house. We had been living without electricity because we didn't have the money. I didn't figure we would get Jeff because of me being 12 years older than Larry, because we were so poor, and because we were barely making it on our own. But the worker drove us to the courthouse, where she talked to the judge for 5 minutes and he gave us temporary custody of Jeff.

The caseworker drove us to the shelter, where we picked up Jeff. He didn't have no clothes, he had four scroungy cloth diapers that were more gray than white, full of holes. He had one plastic pair of pants, no shoes, no socks. He didn't even have his own baby bottle. His hair was all scraggly, but other than that, he looked healthy enough.

But he was so frightened. He had been shoved around, and there was no expression, no matter what we did. I would try to love him, and he would just look at me, like "What is she going to do, what is going to happen to me now?" And I knew right then and there, there was going to be problems because he was so different.

It was always a fight to get his clothes put on him, and he didn't want to be held. You couldn't put a belt on his clothes, you couldn't tuck in his shirt or he would go berserk on you. He just couldn't be confined or contained in any way. It made you think of an animal, so to speak.

He was scared to death of water. The first bath I gave him I knew we were in for big-time trouble. I would put probably two inches of water in the bathtub because he was a baby, and I made it just lukewarm. But as soon as those little feet hit the water, he came unglued. He would kick and bite and scream, totally out of it. So every day, it was a battle to give him a bath. And he wouldn't keep anything on his feet. Couldn't even stand to have the covers on him in bed. He would throw the covers off at night no matter how cold it was. So we went and got him those sleep pajamas with the feet. I told Larry, I said, "Well, if he kicks the covers off, at least he won't be too cold." He hated those things. He come unglued on me again. He stuck his feet in his mouth and chewed the ends out of the feet so he could put his toes and feet through.

Then it got when I couldn't keep him in his crib anymore. He was so little, but he would climb up, lay on the railing, and let himself drop to the floor to get out of it. And then he would be off and running. He would play with the stove, get into the pantry. We only had enough to eat, you know. It was terrible.

Finally, I told Larry we had to have some relief 'cause you couldn't hold him, you couldn't pin him up, and you couldn't constantly run, run, run. I mean, he never stopped. He had a real sunny bedroom, so we took everything out but the toys and his bed, and Larry took a piece of plywood and put it across the door so he couldn't get out, and he fastened the door open so he couldn't close it. And I would go in and get him and change his diaper, and I would feed him and wash him. And he could see us, look out the window and everything, but he couldn't get out.

But then he got to the point where he could climb over the board, and so then the trouble got worse when he got that freedom. HRS said they were going to keep an eye on the situation for 6 months. I knew we had all these problems. I told Larry, "Gosh, if he acts terrible when they come out, they are going to take him away from us. And we don't want that, so let's hope he'll be on his best behavior." We'd be so nervous when the lady would come. We'd put all his favorite toys in the living room, we would put something across his bedroom door so he couldn't get in there and in our room and what have you. And so he stayed in the living room with his toys and she thought he was just a happy little child.

We were afraid she would take him away from us. We were afraid that she would think that we were doing something wrong. It put a terrible strain on us.

After the 6 months was up, I had to report to the HRS downtown every month. Well, that meant taking Jeff with me. What a nightmare.

They had no idea what a hardship that was for me. He couldn't stand to be held. He didn't mind too much if you were walking, if you were in motion, but if you stopped, he wanted down, away from you and your hands off of him.

Sometimes, I'd have to sit in the lobby for ages waiting to see the caseworker. There was no way I could hold him, so I'd have to turn him loose. It was awful. He would pull the other kids' hair or bite them. And he would pick everything up off the floor and put it in his mouth. When they would call my name, I would pick him up off the floor, brush him off, and in the office we'd go. But of course he wouldn't sit on my lap. And I would be so worried about what to do because I knew he would tear up the office, but what could I do? I would have to turn him loose. He would scream and bite me until I did.

Once I saw the caseworker, we were in and out. All that for a few minutes of paperwork. Who knows, maybe back then if I had let them know there was a problem, but I kept thinking our love for him would help him outgrow it. I knew he didn't have love in the past, and I kept thinking it would change. But it didn't. It only got worse.

It was about then he started talking and he wanted outside, outside, outside all the time. Well, I didn't feel like I could sit outside with him all the time, and I couldn't keep him off the highway we lived so close to, so I thought well I'm going to put a little harness on him and attach it to the clothesline. I figured that way he can go the full length of the clothesline and I could get some things done of my own. But when he reached the end of the line he would start screaming, biting, and just get hysterical. The neighbor woman popped her head out the door like I was killing him. I was afraid she would report us. I thought I'd go crazy. I couldn't find anything to give me some peace.

At two and a half, it was just unreal what we were going through. I would have to go to bed with him and physically hold him in the bed until he was asleep, and this would go on until one or two in the morning before he would finally exhaust himself, and in the meantime, I had to keep him from biting me.

There was so much frustration, I didn't know what to do. I didn't want to give up, I kept hoping well, maybe when he gets older, when he can think, that maybe he will understand and maybe we can do something more. It's a wonder that I had the patience to do anything, because I'm not that long on patience. But at the age of two and a half, it was just overwhelming. So I told Larry, "We are going to have to take him to the doctor to do something." I said, "I just can't continue."

I didn't know who to take him to, so I just took him to a pediatrician. To be honest, what I did was hold him just to frustrate him that much more. I held onto him while I waited for the doctor to come in. When she came in the door, I turned him loose, and I mean those feet and hands were everywhere. And she said, "Oh, honey, you're not supposed to do that." But Jeff, you know, he never listened, and she looked at me and said, "Is he like this all the time?" And I said, "Yes ma'am." And she said, "Well, he's too young to put on medication, so the only thing I can tell you is to strap him in a chair."

So we took him back home and strapped him in a chair. It was horrible. He broke through an inch-wide leather belt. And this was when he was two and a half. And he would just claw at his eyes. I had to hold his hands. So then he started this thing where when he would get angry, he would run, jump up in the air and come down on his butt and slam his head back on the ground. It was getting to the point where I would go to bed and cry because I didn't know what to do with him. I was so tired all the time, and I just didn't know what more to do.

We moved from Florida to Texas when Jeff was four. We took him to a behavior specialist that had been recommended by HRS. It was a 2-hour drive, which was a strain on us because we always had problems with old cars and money for gas. When we got there, the behavior specialist tried to give Jeff time-out. She wanted to show Larry how to do this. But Jeff went into a rage, and she called the hospital to see if they had a bed in their residential program.

We couldn't see him for a month because they said they wanted to get him under their control and get him over the homesickness. I worried that he would think we had abandoned him, but they said they would handle him. When we got to visit him, it near broke my heart. We were sitting in his room watching him play, and he come and sat in my lap and put his arms around my neck. That was very unusual for Jeff. He said, "Momma, I wish you could be here with me." I sat there with a grapefruit in my throat. They told me not to cry in front of him. It took all I had to hold back my emotions.

After 2 months, they said they were going to discharge him. I was nervous, I was happy, I was scared about how things were going to be 'cause it had quieted down at home. I had gotten adjusted to him being gone. We had him for 2 months, and he regressed right back. In fact, I think it got worse. So we had to call and they took him back. They kept him for another 5 months, and when they discharged him, they said they wouldn't take him back again. That kind of scared me.

We had to go down there and spend the weekend before he was discharged. They showed us how to use the point system, put him in time-out in the chair, and how to restrain him. They told us in so many words that it was our job to follow through and gave us the impression that it was our fault that Jeff was acting the way he was. They said we weren't consistent and firm enough. That hurt real bad. I thought of all the things we had tried, and they were acting as if we hadn't tried all those things before. I told them that I had raised five kids just fine, and they said this was a stepchild and that was part of the problem. That hurt me something terrible. What kind of a mother was I that I would be a "stepmother"?

We brought him home, and it worked for a while, but it got to where he wouldn't do chair time for me without physical restraint, and then that meant more anger, more screaming on his part, more frustration on ours. 'Cause the older he got, the stronger he was, the harder it was to confine him. The last time I took him down, he was 7 years old, I weighed 200 pounds, and in the scuffle, he scooted me all over the room. And he would get vicious. They showed us how to do it where you would hold his wrists, you had to hold them far enough back because he would curl his hand and dig you until it bled, and you didn't dare turn him loose 'cause you didn't get hold of him again.

Nothing has really changed since then. Oh, we'd get our honeymoon periods when I'd sit and play dominoes or cards or take walks with him. They'd be happy times. And then one morning, he'd wake up and you'd see that you had that other boy again. And you could count on it being hell.

Jeff started school in Texas in a special class. The school ordered a CAT scan to see if his brain was normal, and it was. But he was difficult to control. He was aggressive toward the other kids. From the very beginning, it was always a problem keeping Jeff in school.

When he was in the third grade, he went for about 2 weeks, and then they put him on homebound. Imagine being sent home in the third grade.

In the fourth grade, they sent him to a special school for kids like him, but the teacher wound up not putting up with him. She was pregnant. I didn't know it until later, and that it was her first child. She would come to school in high heels and dresses, and I thought, she's not really prepared for these kids. She made Jeff angry right off the bat by calling him by another boy's name. You could tell she was nervous. Well, that lasted for about 2 or 3 weeks, and Jeff was put on homebound again. They sent out a tutor. Some days he would cooperate with the tutor, and sometimes he wouldn't. The rest of the time I just had him.

Jeff couldn't keep friends because he would be mean to them. He always wound up hurting kids who would play with him. It was awful frustrating for me. I used to feel a lot of time like I was locked up in a prison. It was just me and him all day long.

At this point, I was talking to everyone that had anything to do with these types of children, trying to get helpful ideas. One counselor told me to take a book and go in my room, lock the door where he couldn't get at me, and read. She said, "You need some time away from him for yourself." I tried that. Jeff screamed and banged on the door with his head. I could only take so much of that. I couldn't read. I would just go and unlock the door. Another counselor told me that I needed to ignore Jeff. She told me to tune him out. But he would always find a way to get to me.

Every time I'd go to see someone for help, they'd tell me something different. It always sounded like I wasn't doing the right thing; I should be doing something different. It made me feel like they thought Jeff's problems were my fault.

You know, when Jeff got put on homebound in the third grade, I began to wonder why these school people thought I could handle him when they couldn't. I mean, he was in a special program and all. If they were sending him home to me, saying they couldn't do anything with him, how did they expect that I could handle him any better? Even in that residential place. They had all those staff to take him down, restrain him, put him in time-out. At home, it was just me most of the time, and I couldn't take it anymore.

We came back to Florida from Texas in 1989, when Jeff was almost ten. My sister was living here at the time. I had to start all over again trying to seek help for Jeff. It seemed like everyone would listen and recognize I had a problem, but they would pass the buck and tell me I needed to talk to this one or to so and so.

So I talked to everyone, hoping they would listen. But it was so discouraging that because we had moved, I had to begin the search for help from scratch. It was as if the whole situation had just begun, when in fact, it never seemed to end.

Two years ago, when Jeff was 13, we got so desperate and so frustrated that we packed up Jeff's clothes and things and took him to HRS to give him away. We brought Jeff back feeling worse. They lectured us on our responsibility as parents. And so, we went home feeling there was no hope left. We just didn't know where to turn. We felt as if we were at the end of our rope. Believe me, it's not easy to take your child and tell someone that you want to give him away. As a mother, this is the most awful nightmare. But for years, we've lived in a nightmare.

Then, I called the head man of child abuse and told him I was going to beat the hell out of our child, hoping they would come and take him somewhere to protect him. Desperately hoping for help, I was devastated when all I got was another lecture about myself being the adult and him being the child, and how we were supposed to be in control at all times. He said if we beat our child, we would go to jail. We already knew that. It was just another desperate plea for help.

Jeff got in trouble when he started at the middle school by attacking two staff members. We had to go to court several times on that assault charge. It was dropped to a misdemeanor, so Jeff got a little bit of probation, a little bit of a lecture from the judge, and that was it. To me, it was all wrong. I felt he needed a stronger message than a slap on the hand. He left bragging that nothing happened to him. I felt that made things worse.

I was so disappointed at how things were going. Since Jeff was a toddler, we had been in and out of so many places, so many programs, and we had seen so many professionals. But I have felt terribly let down by the system of services. Each time you go somewhere, they ask you everything that has happened since birth. And then they make their own judgments about what to do. Almost always, they tell us we need parenting classes or counseling, as if it will make a difference, as if it will help. But I know, because I have been through it so often, that it is just another [bandage] for a hemorrhage. I'd try and tell them we've done that, we've done that, we've done that, and they'd look at us like obviously we didn't do it right because none of those things worked. They just had no idea what day-to-day living with Jeff was like for us.

I can't tell you how many meetings we've sat in at schools. They'd get a whole table full of professionals in the room telling us how unmanageable Jeff was at school, as if we were supposed to have the answers of how to get Jeff to behave in school and follow the rules. Hell, we couldn't get him to do it at home. Why did they keep thinking we could get him to do it at school? It would make me so mad. I wanted to say to them, "Why do you keep calling us up here about problems in school?" He was in EH (emotionally handicapped) and SED (seriously emotionally disturbed) classes. He had specially trained teachers, they told us that when we first signed the papers for him to be in those classes. They said they had teachers that were trained in behavior management, and he would do better in a structured environment. But then they would always call us up and say "Jeff doesn't follow rules." I wanted to say, "No kidding, what do you think we've been telling you all these years?"

And sometimes I did. But the response was always the same. Jeff would be punished for his behavior at school by being sent home. The school problem became our problem.

How come I couldn't banish him to school for 10 days when he was impossible to live with at home? It's not right!

As I talk to you now, Jeff is 16 years old, he refuses to attend school, the school has never called since he stopped going, he sleeps all day, he roams most of the night, and responds aggressively to our attempts at setting limits.

We have pursued every avenue of help we know to explore. We have been told he is too severe for placement, he is not severe enough for placement, there is no money available to help him, there are long waiting lists for services. He has been Baker Acted (involuntary commitment to a psychiatric hospital), kept for 24 hours and then released back home, where he returns angrier and more volatile than when he left. The law has been involved time and time again. They say he don't have enough points, he hasn't been caught in the act, they can't do anything about threats, he hasn't done something severe enough.

He is threatening. He has destroyed so many things in our home, and he has started using drugs and alcohol. My husband and I have a padlock on our bedroom door so we can sleep with some feeling of safety. I don't know how severe things have to get before some program, with the necessary money and an available bed, can step in before me and my family are splashed across the newspaper as another tragedy that slipped through the cracks.

"I think sometimes, the hardest thing to live with is the feeling of hope. I can't tell you how many times Larry and I have been down this road to go to meetings for Jeff. We went to a FSPT (Family Service Planning Team) meeting one time where they decided to refer Jeff to the CRC (Case Review Committee). I knew coming to this committee meant a shot at getting real placement. I knew that the CRC could "okay dollars" to put Jeff in a program that might teach him a trade and how to become independent. I was so hopeful. I was all prepared to present my information to the committee members. I had all my paperwork in a folder that Larry had got for me, just for this meeting. "Can't go with that old weathered one," he said when we got the notice of the meeting.

I had my hopes up that we were going to get something to help Jeff and give us some space between us. Things were very volatile. All we had back then was our old gray pickup. We weren't sure we would make it over there to the meeting and back, but we were determined. Unfortunately, they were doing construction on the roads, so we got all turned around, and we were a little late getting to the meeting. We were so frustrated that we were late because we didn't want anything to go wrong. We opened up the door to where the meeting was being held. We were out of breath from rushing. We were met at the door by a woman who said, "You can't come in here yet. We'll call you when we're ready."

Larry and I looked at each other and wondered why we weren't allowed in the room. Jeff was our son. We knew him best. But we had to wait outside in the hallway. Finally, they called us in and told us they decided to put Jeff on their waiting list for placement. They said they had openings for three children at this residential treatment program, and that Jeff would be third on the list.

I never had a chance to show them anything that I had put together to take over there. We were in there about 5 minutes, no more. I was so angry and upset, but I held on to the fact that Jeff had been approved for placement and was third on the waiting list.

A whole month went by and we heard nothing. A social worker called me and asked me if we had heard anything, because she said she hadn't. So I started calling around.

Finally, I heard back from the social worker. Jeff was still third on the list, but the slots at the treatment program had been filled with three adolescents who came with a "different pot of money." Jeff was going to be funded under "special needs money," while the other boys had been funded under "juvenile justice money."

I found out later that funding for Jeff's list would come around the beginning of the next financial year, which was 8 months away. I went into such a deep depression. I couldn't stand to be around Jeff, or Larry for that matter. I wanted to crawl into a dark corner and never come out. I had seen that list in my head, and I believed that Jeff was going to be placed. They never said anything about pots of money at the meeting. They never said there was more than one list, each with kids like Jeff who needed more help than they could get at home or at school. They never said it could be another 8 months. They said he was third on the list for a program that had three openings.

I think that's when hope became a dangerous feeling.

DIGGING IN: MAKING THE STORY PERSONAL

Perhaps the most powerful lessons we can take from a story occur when we allow ourselves to reflect and connect in a deeply personal and emotional way with what happened. We can often do this by placing ourselves in the roles of parents, connecting those roles to the rich experiences of our own lives.

Have you had any experiences in your own life that would help you to empathize with the challenges of raising and educating Jeff? If so, what are the similarities and differences between your experience and Ellen's?

If you are lacking experiences that would help you empathize with Ellen and Larry, what might you do to gain some experience and insight?

Why do you think Ellen and Larry were treated the way they were in schools? What assumptions do you think influenced the professionals' actions?

What role do you think fear plays in this story?

In what ways do you think experts' knowledge helped and hindered Jeff and his family?

STEPHANIE

Stephanie had three children: Sally, Bruce, and Kevin. Sally was the youngest and the only girl, who tried to play mother to her brothers when she could. Stephanie felt this was a result of her reliance on Sally during her own dark periods of depression and agoraphobia. Sally was a good student in the fourth grade.

Bruce was 13 and the least appreciative of Sally's mothering. Often sullen and argumentative, he reacted strongly to Sally's frequent reminders and warnings about what he should be doing, or not doing, for that matter. He was a failing middle school student in special education.

Kevin was the oldest. He was 16 and attended school sporadically. He had been living with his father for 6 years and had returned to live with his mother, brother, and half-sister a year ago. Both Bruce and Kevin had many friends who drifted in and out of their duplex home, often presenting a disappointing view of school. Kevin's friends, who were usually between schools, judicial, or mental health placements, painted pictures of school as a context incompatible with their very being.

In our interview, Stephanie talked about her experiences growing up. She started by talking about school:

I had trouble in school as a child. My father sent me to Catholic school for the first grade. What a nightmare. I wasn't ready for it, and they held me back and said emotionally I wasn't ready. I cried all the time like a baby. It was like a nightmare. The nuns were mean. I just wasn't ready for school. I was afraid, I was timid. I was the baby. I felt like an alien at school. I felt like everyone was the same except for me.

At home, things were not going good. My parents were getting divorced right when I started school. It was very traumatic for me. My father was going to leave, and my mother was so mean. She was such a cold fish. She was not a nurturing mother. She never gave me any attention, any affection. My father and I were very close, and I think she was jealous of that. My mother was crazy. She drank a lot. My father was very outgoing. I didn't know he was drunk all the time, but he was. My mother was very depressed. I never saw her smile. There was always doom and gloom around her. My mother actually had it harder than my father, but he had a personality, and when you have a personality, kids are very forgiving. My father played with us and smiled with us and had fun with us. He was like Santa Claus, but he was very dysfunctional. He liked knives and would hold them against my mother's throat and make us watch him, so he was really no better. I forgave him, but I couldn't forgive my mother. It isn't fair, I know it isn't fair, but I still do it.

I remember we had homework piled up on us in the first grade. And my mother would make me sit at the table with all this work to do, and she would never help me. I cried all the time. She would sit across the room and give me cold stares and be very distant. And at school, I would get in trouble because my homework wouldn't be finished or it wouldn't be right.

After my father left, my mother went off the deep end, and things got terrible. We weren't being fed properly. I still have so much guilt about that today. Because I was the youngest, I often got the little bit of food there was. I hated myself at the time for eating it, but I was so hungry I couldn't bring myself not to do it. My brother, who was 6, and my sister Teresa, who was 10, often ate out of the Dumpsters. Teresa was being raped by the man who lived across the apartments from us. Nobody said that, but I knew it was happening. He would call her over and bring her inside the apartment. My mother was so depressed, she didn't seem to know. Most of the time, I felt like I had to be the mother. I was trying to watch my brother because he would wander off, and I wouldn't be able to find him, and I would be scared to death because I felt he was my responsibility even though I was younger than him. So they put us in foster care.

We were hauled away in a big black car to this home where there were so many kids. The home was okay, but it was so emotionally upsetting because when you went to a home in those days, I don't know how they do it now, you had to be put in with your age. And so my brother and sister and I were separated from each other.

We went back to our home, but we were taken away again. We were taken from my mother several times, and then she just gave us up to this lady in the neighborhood. Strange, huh? That was when we went to live with Mrs. Todd. That's when the nightmare really began.

Mrs. Todd was a very domineering woman. She was just so powerful. A manipulator. She was evil, and it was so easy to talk about her. I mean, I have pushed away things that are just too painful. It was a terrible way to live. I hated Mrs. Todd, and I had to live with that every day. She's dead now. She died a few years ago.

I had a nervous breakdown at 14 'cause she not only physically abused us, the verbal abuse was so strong that I still have a hard time with it today, and I am 40. Those years were so terrible for us all. Particularly my sister, Teresa. Mrs. Todd had three older sons who lived on their own. One of them used to come over and rape Teresa in the woods behind the house.

Waking up in the morning was like waking up in a concentration camp. It was not that bad, of course, but I think I can relate to the Jews. I really can, about mental torture. And verbal abuse. Because you have to understand when we opened our eyes up on the morning, it was gray and black. It was so doom to gloom. And I always had this nervous condition as a child. I was real high strung, very nervous. In my stomach, I'll never forget it, I would wake up with a knot in my stomach. We had to wake up at 5:30 in the morning every day, you could never sleep in. Just imagine lying in bed, opening your eyes and hearing beer cans snapping off, snapping off, snapping off. She was drunk by seven thirty in the morning. Drunk and ready to fight. I remember one morning, I didn't say good morning to her. She said good morning and I just ignored her. She grabbed the broom and hit me so hard on the top of my head with the stick part that it almost knocked me out and I said, "Good morning."

And we had to eat every single thing she put on our plate. We could never leave anything on our plates. That's why I don't make my kids eat everything, and I let them have choices. After breakfast, we would go to our work detail. Every day, seven days a week. It was always the same.

We loved to go to school because we were so glad to be out of the house. Even though we never had the proper clothing. She always picked out our clothes; we couldn't ever be ourselves. And then we would come home from school and that's when things would begin.

We would stand at the front door, and Teresa and I would look at each other 'cause we never knew what we were going to face. We never knew what mood she was going to be in. And most of the time, it would be a crazy one. I was terrified of everything.

We'd head straight to our bedrooms after school. We couldn't just walk through the house like children, like children do, or run or yell or scream. You would die if you did that. I remember hiding in the room so much, in the corner, just hiding from her. Hiding from her wrath. But when she was drunk, which was always, she would yell for me. "Stephanie, do this, do that." And she would hit on me constantly. And when she would go into her rages, that was real hard, we always got beat when she went into her drunken rages.

And she would make Teresa and I fight. Sometimes, she would go outside and get switches off the trees. And she would braid them together and make us fight each other. She'd give us each a switch and say, "Go on, now, let me see you fight with each other." And I'd say, "No, I'm not going to hit my sister," and she would beat me and say, "You're going to do it, or I'll beat you again." And she did. And then I started beating up Teresa.

When I was 15, I wanted my bangs to grow out, and she got real drunk and she cut my bangs up to here (pointing to the very top of her forehead). I pushed her. I was getting so fed up. I didn't hit her. I just pushed her and she went crazy. And we ended up in the bathroom, and she was choking me. She choked me, and I remember feeling like I was passing out. I remember thinking, "Oh, thank God, I can't take this anymore." I wanted to die then. When I came to, she had my head stuck down in the toilet. I was in shock. I couldn't tell you what happened after that. There is so much blocked. And some things, I wish I could forget.

We used to have to stay home a lot from school because we had bruises so bad on our bodies. And she would be reported by the neighbors because they could hear screams, but she would sober up and they would investigate and she would be this polite woman. That's why I don't trust people. She was so nice, I even liked her when she was sober. We were so starving for love, so starved for love, that we got attention those few days. And she would tell us to be quiet when the people came or we would be taken away. And we did. We did everything she told us to do because we had nowhere else to go, and if we told them, they would take us away and we might be separated again. Teresa and I agreed that we would not say anything because at least we were together. We figured we could take the beatings and all the craziness if we could at least be together. So that's how we lived. We worked from sunup, or really before that, to sundown running the house. We washed the floors, which she carefully examined. Everything we did had to be perfect because she would look it over, and if it wasn't right, she would hit you and make you do it again.

I ran away when I was 16, and I had nowhere to go. But I knew that whatever the streets were, I could survive. I had survived Mrs. Todd. So

I went to school the next day and just left with the clothes on my back. A really good friend at school let me stay in her garage in the back of the house. Her boyfriend even fixed it up for me. I stayed there about 3 months, and then I was just out on my own.

I met a guy named Robert, whom I had known in the eighth grade, and I started meeting other kids who were runaways. I started huffing glue, then I went to gasoline, which I know is stupid because it destroys your lungs. And then I met people who were doing acid, LSD, and it all started. When I look back, I didn't have money. I stayed high for so long, I have a hard time remembering a lot of my life 'cause I stayed high. You have to understand that coming out of a place that was like a concentration camp, the only exposure I had to humans was going to school. We were not allowed to go out on weekends. We were kept in. We weren't allowed to go skating, we couldn't have friends over, we couldn't have phone calls, and there were times when she deliberately wouldn't let me study. So it was a whole new world out there. I was a victim, and I didn't even know it because I was so naive about people. It's important that you have experience with people. That's what makes you grow, and as children, we didn't have friends. I still have a lot of trouble making friends, and it's even harder to keep them.

At a later interview session, Stephanie is filled with anxiety. Bruce had just been suspended from school . . . again.

I'm too worn out. I'm too tired. What do I say? Do I say I hate the system for constantly suspending Bruce? Do I say I hate Bruce for being such a problem in school? What is the point, I mean how does that change the screwed-up family with a screwed-up system?

Well, I could talk about suspension. I could say how I am tired of having Bruce suspended. What good does it do him? It does him no good. What is the point? He goes to school in a special class, and they send him home every time he does any stupid thing. Why the hell is he in this special program if all they can do is send him home over and over? I mean, how are we training these teachers? It makes me so damn mad.

Bruce can't stay on task, he doesn't stay on task, he laughs out of turn. He just doesn't follow the classroom rules. He doesn't do violent acts. Bruce is irritating. He disrupts the whole classroom at times. He doesn't bring his work in. He drives the teacher crazy. They always want to suspend him, and there is no real solution. He is a problem child. He's a problem person. He does not follow the rules, and they don't know how to deal with him. And you know me, I let my anger out at the teacher 'cause she can't deal with him either.

There are a lot of children like Bruce who are very stubborn children. They are very set in their ways and right there, wow, that is a challenge. Most teachers see it as the kids being rebellious, but I just think it is their stubbornness to survive. They have struggled to survive. But I don't think they mean to be rebellious. When you have to survive, you learn to be, well, stubborn. To survive. I know they have to learn rules, but they haven't learned them the way we have been teaching them. The kids, they see things differently. But when the teacher sees it as rebellious, that's what hurts the child, because the child feels misunderstood.

Then, these kids like Bruce start to act out because they are frustrated because they are misunderstood. And it is a lot for the teacher. Because I'm not saying it is easy to teach kids like Bruce. It is not an easy job, they are not easy to teach. But it could be easy, it could be simple, if the teachers learned to look at these kids differently. Teachers think these kids are demanding. They don't mean to be, but they take what attention they can get. They are survivors, yes, they are. Even though they may go to school and hardly get any education, somehow they survive.

And they don't mean to demand. It's just such a strong need. It's an inner thing. I know, I have it myself. The parents, as well as these kids, are starving inside. We are all like little kids inside, searching for attention.

But they see them as rebellious. They say they need to learn consequences, they need to follow the rules, they need to be disciplined. I'm not saying that my son or the kids that have behavior problems should be allowed to get away with murder, no. What I'm saying is that these kids know discipline. My God, they have been overly disciplined all their lives. They have been beaten. They have been mentally abused, so they know, if anybody does, about discipline. And that's what doesn't work about our system for these kids. Teachers think we want them to get away with murder, but that's not what I am saying. I've been very hard with Bruce. You know that. I have been an abusive mother. Educators feel that children like Bruce have no respect for authority. They've had authority shoved down their throats all their life. People who abused are very authoritarian. They are controlling. I have been very controlling, so picky, and Bruce has had to live with that. The last thing Bruce needs is someone being as picky with him as I have been. And school is like that. They pick at the kids for everything. Don't wear a cap, pull up your pants, turn around, sit still, do your work, sit up, don't slouch, stop talking. It's like being at home, only at school. The kids like Bruce never get a break.

It's not like he carries a gun or a knife, or that he beats up other kids. You know Bruce, he's just aggravating in school. He says smart-ass things and acts crazy to make the kids laugh. Bruce is funny. He has a good sense of humor, and he loves to perform. But in school, it gets him in trouble. Around here, Bruce has a lot of friends, the other kids like Bruce. He has a great personality. But in school, they suspend him all the time for all these things that Bruce is always going to do. Bruce can't be Bruce in school.

So he gets sent home for 5 days or sometimes 10. That's 2 weeks of Bruce away from school. And he is not allowed to do any work. He gets points off his final grade when he gets suspended, and it is all so punishing, and it makes me so mad. Every time he's suspended, he is not allowed to go back until I go for a conference. The conference only lasts, I swear, about 4 minutes. And in each conference, it is the same thing. You have to sit and listen to what your kid did wrong. Parents are lined up waiting to go in. The principal says, "Well, we are aiming to get the parents involved."

I hate going up to school because I always feel I am being blamed for Bruce's problems in school. I get so angry. Every time I go up there, I am going for a battle. I don't want to, but I get so furious. I react with so much anger; I know they think I'm barbaric. But when I go up there, I always feel I am being blamed for Bruce's problems in school. They focus so much on Bruce's behavior. What they don't understand is that by the time I have to go in there, I'm all fired up because I am very aware of Bruce's behavior, and I'm frustrated and I'm at a loss. They are sick of Bruce, and I am sick of Bruce. When Bruce gets criticized for acting out, I feel bad. I feel bad inside. So I feel damaged and misunderstood just like Bruce does.

When I go to the school, I don't feel that they are talking *to* me. I feel that they are talking *at* me. I feel like they are looking at me and saying, "You made this kid this way. It's all your fault that he acts this way and you can't get him to act right in school." And I act like a monster. I'm getting better. I am better, but that monster is always a part of me, and school brings it out. And sometimes, they make me so mad at school, I act just like those kids in Bruce's class. I snap and I am nasty and I curse the teachers, the principal, anybody. I feel like the whole time, I'm the one getting punished like Bruce for being bad. For not being able to get my son to behave in school.

In the past, I would bring Bruce home from those meetings and I would be so mad at him for acting up in school. I hated having to go up there to school because I always came home looking like a monster. So I would get all over Bruce. I would yell at him, scream at him, say terrible things to him, throw things at him, threaten him, make him feel like crap. I was tired myself of feeling that way at school, and I didn't want to go back. I just wanted him to behave. And then I hate myself when I am like that.

And now I have to go up to school again for this last suspension. I am trying to meditate and get myself in a calm place to be able to go up there. I don't want to look like a monster. I don't want to start cursing everyone out. I don't want to lose my temper. I know that I don't want to do that. I see now that when I do that, it reinforces their view of me as a monster. They help me turn myself into a monster.

I think it is because I feel like such an outcast. I feel like I don't fit in. I want to someday feel like I'm not an outcast. And I know I have to start with me, I think. Deal with my own way of thinking, but it sure would be nice not to feel that way anymore. I feel that way because I think I let these people get to me. I always feel inadequate. Because when I go to school, I feel like I'm an outcast.

I try to be real fair here from being in therapy and having done some reading to improve my mind and my behavior. I don't think it is all me, but I think a lot of it is me. When I look at teachers, they just fit right in, and they feel secure and they just fit into the system. And I would like to feel that way, too.

Now that I am talking about this, I see poor Bruce getting it from both of us. He is fighting me, and he is fighting the teacher. There is a battle between me and him and the school. How can kids grow up in this world of battling without battling back? I look at Bruce, and I just don't know how he does it. I guess I taught my kids good how to survive. I taught them this was a dog-eat-dog world and how to survive it. That's what I had to do.

At the end of last year, I took Bruce out of school. I was afraid that he was going to get suspended again. I was all over him about not getting in trouble. I was yelling at him, "Bruce, it's almost the end of school." And then one day, I was sitting there and I thought, no, I'm not gonna drive me and Bruce crazy. I just didn't want to worry about if Bruce was going to get suspended again. So I called the school and told them I was taking him out early. He flunked the year anyway, so what was the point of him going to school?

Bruce is just different. Or the school is just different. They teach a certain way, and not every kid can learn the way they teach. They have a very traditional, standard way of teaching. It doesn't fit every child, and that's been the problem for many years. The kids need some kind of discipline, but it has to be done differently.

Bruce had three teachers that I thought knew how to be with him. His first-grade teacher was a black teacher and she was a dancer. She had a very strong personality. She was outgoing. She really brought Bruce out. She and her aide were very loving toward the kids.

Then there was this teacher from New York. She was a Jewish woman. She was very positive, very loving, very caring. She would get upset some days because she had a lot of boys in her class. And she would call me sometimes and tell me, "I've had it." But it was more like she was sharing herself with me, not complaining about the kids. I knew what she meant.

In the fifth grade, he had Mrs. Navarro. She is the only teacher other than you that I thought felt comfortable with these kids and their families. You could look into her eyes and you could talk with her, and you got the idea that she really knew what she was doing. She had her own way. She worked through things with the kids. And when she would have a conference, she would talk about the good things about Bruce.

And she was human, too! There were times when she would have it with Bruce. She would get fed up and she would punish Bruce. She wouldn't let him do something. But she would give him lots of chances, warnings. Not like a traditional teacher, who would say one, two, three and that's it. She was very patient with these kids. And with me. She would come up and hug me. And that was weird. You don't see that. Never. Never, never, never. I learned a lot from her about myself. She knew I was a little crazy or very angry or very something. I think she knew all that. She was a very intuitive kind of woman. But she knew how to put things in words so I could listen to them. I didn't fly off the handle with her.

She cried at the end of the year. She got very attached. You don't see many teachers cry over these kids unless it is cries for joy. And she had the tough kids. And you know it was the roughest, hardest ones that didn't want leave her class. They came back to see her. I could see they had become very sentimental.

I wanted Bruce to stay with her another year and she wanted to keep him, but they wouldn't let him stay. The principal said she wished it was possible because she felt it took at least 2 or 3 years to really turn these kids around. This is why I get so upset with our system of education. The teacher, the student, the parent, and the principal want a kid to stay where they think he is really doing good, but he can't because the system doesn't work that way. If it isn't what's best for the kid, what is it then?

But I wouldn't have wanted him to stay with his third-grade teacher. Oh, third grade was just awful. She was so critical and judgmental. The kids had a terrible year. And so did the teacher. Half way through the year, she couldn't even talk rationally. She just screamed. It was abuse in the classroom. This damages the kids. They don't learn.

I'll never forget the time she really went over the edge. I think those kids made her insane. It had to be insane for her, I know, because I have done insane things. It had to be insane for her to write all those crazy things Bruce did down on paper. Hour after hour, she took all this time to write down every little thing he did. I almost laughed. I mean, it wasn't a laughing matter because he was driving her crazy. He'd really gotten to her.

She should not have been teaching this class any more than I should have been abusing my children. Children need to be protected from that at school as well as at home. School says it's about the kids and the family, but it is rare when that happens. They say one thing but they seem to do another. I am always confused by schools.

For example, one time when Bruce was suspended, I called the teacher and asked her if she would drop off his work at the office so I could get him to work on it while he was home. "I am not going to bring his work up to the office," she said to me. I didn't know why, but I said that I would come to the room and pick it up. And she said, "If you want to do that, fine, but you are just hurting your child." And I said I didn't see it that way. She told me, "Bruce has to grow up now. He has to show some responsibility for his actions." I had no idea how she thought it would be hurting Bruce for me to bring his work home from school. One of their complaints is, he never finishes his work. Maybe I could get him to do some at home.

It's things like that that I don't understand. Like at Sally's school. I've been in the lunchroom with the first graders. And I just can't stay in there. They have these mean ole women who write the names down of these little kids, and they make them cry while they are eating because they don't sit still or they get up too much. They said that was necessary to keep order. But I think that's looking at the whole situation wrong with children. They are first graders. I think they need to move around and be kids.

And then Kevin's teacher, who was complaining that Kevin was missing too much school. So Kevin started making an effort to get there, but sometimes, he got there late. The other day, his teacher told him he shouldn't bother to come to school when he is late. He said he had already been counted absent. So Kevin doesn't want to go back. I called the school and talked to the teacher and the principal. They told me how it was Kevin's responsibility to get to school on time. I said at least he was going. For a while, until he got the hang of it again, couldn't they tolerate late? I told them I thought the point was to get Kevin back into school. Why couldn't his teacher have told Kevin he was glad he was making an effort to be there?

I'm not saying it is all the teacher's fault, either, because Bruce is a hard individual to teach. In the traditional way. I don't know how they are training the teachers to become teachers, but I wonder if they are dealing with how kids are coming up. Times have changed. I think kids are fighting back because they are smarter from having to survive a rejecting existence while trying to find love and acceptance.

I think we are making such a mistake with these behavior problem children. They are very gifted. They have had to be to survive. The teachers don't realize this because these kids don't do good with tests. These kids are so far ahead of the other kids in a different, smart way. My kids bring all the rejects over here. You know, birds of a feather stick together. Rich, poor, all different colors, and these kids are not dumb. They are intelligent in different ways. They had to grow up in an adult world, and it is so frustrating that the teachers don't give them credit. They don't realize what they have had to endure as a child. I know I was robbed of my childhood. Who is to say these kids aren't smart? They have survived. Teaching in the school is not everything. I mean, education is the whole problem with education. It is as if what they have learned outside the classroom was not learning at all.

I think male students like Bruce are sick of women teachers. That is, women like me. When they get a woman, someone who is very hard on them. When they get a woman like me who has nagged them all their lives, it is another abusive situation. And that's when Bruce starts getting suspended.

"I have been confused since day one about the whole school system. Maybe I'm naive and that's why I have a hard time in this world of education. But what goes on there doesn't make sense to me so much of the time. If we are ever going to stop punishing the children and the families, we are going to have to look for different things in teachers so they can look for different things in kids. It has to be a positive person. A person who understands their way of thinking and won't interpret it as being wrong from the standard way of thinking. It has to be someone who is very positive so the kids can come back and be able to admit their mistakes, to apologize for their misbehaving. If it is misbehaving.

Teachers have to be genuine. They have to be genuine in their feelings. That's what I learned to pick up as a child. I can feel that from my past experience. I can feel genuine caring and concern.

Teachers have to be patient. They must feel comfortable with the students and be patient with them. And they must be loving. It takes this kind of a personality to understand that both the students and their family are in distress, and they need someone who will join with them and help them so they can all help themselves. But it has to be genuine. It has to be real. I can't feel like an outcast.

DIGGING IN: MAKING THE STORY PERSONAL

Perhaps the most powerful lessons we can take from a story occur when we allow ourselves to reflect and connect in a deeply personal and emotional way with what happened. We can often do this by placing ourselves in the roles of parents, connecting those roles to the rich experiences of our own lives.

In what ways do you think Stephanie's history of abuse affects her relationship with educators?

Stephanie describes Mrs. Navarro, Bruce's fifth-grade teacher, as being comfortable with these kids and their families. Do you think you will be (are) comfortable with troubling students and their families? To what do you attribute your comfort or lack of comfort?

What might you do to become more comfortable with your students and their families?

Why do you think suspension is such a common practice in schools? Do you think this is effective practice?

Stephanie sees her son and students like him as misunderstood survivors, and she thinks teachers often see them as stubborn and rebellious. After reading Stephanie's story, what do you think accounts for these differences in interpretation?

CARLOS

One afternoon in February, I happened to be in one of the E/BD classrooms when Carlos arrived. The seven boys in this sixth-grade classroom ranged in age from 12 to 15 and had a difficult time getting along. The boys were sitting at four tables arranged in the shape of a squared-off letter U with the open end facing the board. They were in the process of bantering with one another as Mrs. Girrard tried to begin her lesson.

I had been told earlier in the morning by one of the staff that the special education teachers were going to try to get parents to come and spend time in the classroom so they could see how terribly their kids behaved. This staff member told me that Carlos was scheduled sometime that afternoon. I remember asking the staff member, "What makes you think Carlos doesn't already know what Victor is like in school?" He responded, "Well, maybe if he sees it, he will do something about it."

As I sat with Carlos that day, Mrs. Girrard was struggling to present a lesson on social skills that required the students to pay attention to what was written on the board. However, the boys were more interested in talking among themselves and with Carlos than in paying attention to the lesson. Despite Mrs. Girrard's attempts to bring the attention of the students back on task, Victor's peers spent time telling Carlos horror stories about what Victor had done in school. David looked across the table at Victor's father and said, "You know, Victor is always running out of class and up and down the halls. He bangs on the doors or he opens them and yells curses inside. He runs up to the office and acts crazy. He's really bad."

"Poppi, that's nothing," Victor said. "The other day when we were having lunch, Mrs. Girrard told David to pick up all the peas he threw across the room." Victor jumped out of his seat and mimicked David bending over to pick up the peas. "And each time he bent over he farted," Victor said, laughing and making fart sounds as he bent down pretending to pick up peas. The other kids began laughing, except for David. "He stunk up the whole place," Victor continued, laughing. James made a fart sound by cupping his hand in his armpit and squeezing down. David growled.

"This is the way they are," Mrs. Girrard said to Carlos. "They don't want to learn a thing."

Later, as Carlos, Victor, and I left the school building, Carlos shook his head and said, "Those students are so rude and disrespectful. My own son is no better. I'm ashamed of him. I don't know how that teacher can teach. I feel sorry for her. I don't know why he acts like this in school." He turned to Victor and said, "Why would you talk like that in the school in front of people like Ms. Perez?"

"I hate school and school hates me," Victor said with both hurt and defensiveness in his voice.

"Because of the way you act," Carlos said to him.

"I hate being there. Everyone hates being there. Even Mrs. Girrard."

"I hate being there some days myself," I said to them, "because the room is filled with too much meanness."

"They don't want me, and I don't want to be here," Victor said and headed toward the passenger side of the van.

"It was nice to meet you, Ms. Perez," Carlos said as he offered his hand, and we shook.

"See you again," I said.

"Yes," he responded with a nod.

Two years later, as coordinator of the grant to involve parents in advocating for the needs of their children, I met Carlos again. A meeting had been called at the school regarding Victor's disruptive behavior, so I drove out to see Carlos. I thought maybe he would like me to go to the meeting with him as a source of support. I sensed he felt more comfortable using Spanish in conversation, and I wanted to offer to arrange for a Spanish-speaking person to be at the meeting in case he wanted clarification.

Victor opened the door when I arrived. He had been suspended from school until after the scheduled meeting. He walked me through the living room and kitchen to the back door and out to his father's work area. "Poppi," he called, "It's Ms. Perez."

Carlos looked up from under the hood of the van and waved. "Hello, Ms. Perez," he said with a musical ripple to his voice. "How are you? It's nice to see you. I got your message that you were coming out today. How have you been?"

I brought him up to date and described my new role at the school. I told him I wanted to know if there was some way I could be helpful to him at the meeting next week. I told him I would be happy to go with him if he would like me to.

He looked apologetic and said, "Ms. Perez, I'm not going to that meeting next week. I don't like to go to meetings at school. They are always talking in English, and I think better in Spanish. I don't always understand what these people are talking about. I don't like how I feel at school. I know that the school does not want my son there, and I don't want to drive all the way over there to have them tell me this again."

"But you should have a say in the decisions made about Victor. Your voice should be heard. I can arrange to have someone there who speaks Spanish," I said.

"What can I say to them? He behaves bad at school."

"What would you like to happen at this meeting?" I asked him.

"What can happen? It's always the same. They suspend him, they don't want him. He's a pain."

Victor came out the back door and joined us at the hood of the van. "Besides," Carlos said to me, "I am getting ready to run away. As soon as Victor is 18 years old, I am going to go back to Puerto Rico, and I am not telling any of my kids where I am. If they know where I am, they might follow me, and I can't be around them because they give me too much trouble. I am in court so many days. The judge, she knows me well. I hate to be in court all the time. The judge talks about my business with everyone there. Nothing is private about my life. My oldest son is in jail. My daughter is not married, and she has a baby she doesn't want to take care of. My other son, Sam, doesn't listen to me. And Victor gets suspended from school all the time. He's 15, so in 3 more years, I am just going to disappear, and they all will have to take care of themselves. I am too tired to keep getting them out of trouble. I told my oldest son if he got in jail again, I would not visit him. He keeps calling the neighbor to tell them to tell me to come and see him, but I can't go anymore."

Victor stood quietly. It was rare that I saw Victor this still. "You know," his father continued, "I know that they resent the fact that their mother left them when they were babies. My own mother left us when we were little. But I did not get my family into trouble. I worked. I worked hard to make money to help my aunt and uncle, who took us in when my mother left Puerto Rico to go to Chicago. We didn't have much to eat, and I worked hard as a little boy milking cows. Today, my hands are strong and tough from all the work I did as a child. Sometimes, I cried, sitting all alone except for the cow I was milking. I was so tired, and the work was so hard for me because I was little."

I glanced at Victor as his father began to tell us about his life growing up. I wondered how much of this he had heard before. He seemed to be captivated by his father's account.

"I think it was such hard work at such a young age that did something to my back and leg. Anyway, when I was 10, I was sent to a hospital for them to operate on my leg. I was all alone there. I had no one. And they did a bad job. They had to do the operation two more times, and I had to stay in the hospital. As you can see, I am crippled now. They cut the wrong nerves in my leg and I had to learn how to use a brace, how to walk again. After 2 years of being in the hospital, the social worker came to me and said, "You haven't had a visitor in over a year. Who can you live with?" My aunt and uncle lived very far from the hospital, and they were very poor, so I think they only came to see me one time. I told her that I didn't have anyone because my aunt and uncle already had too many to take care of and now my leg didn't work right.

"The social worker found this man who had a factory, and he gave me a job. I was just a young boy, but he gave me a job and taught me how to work on furniture. I had to sand it to be ready for stain. It was expensive furniture. And I learned well. I had a little room that I stayed in by myself. I got enough money that I could go into a shop and get food. Ever since I was a tiny little boy, I have had to take care of myself."

Victor looked pained. "Poppi, I have helped take care of things while I have been home on suspension. I cleaned and swept the house. I washed the clothes and hung them outside."

Carlos acknowledged his efforts and went on. "I didn't see my mother until I was a young man and I came to Chicago. I stayed with her for a short time, but it didn't work out. I didn't know anyone else there, so at times, I slept in cars, or found a room I could stay in. Chicago was so cold. I got very sick one time because I did not have enough to eat and I could not get warm. I had an old car I was sleeping in at the time. I would drive it around the block or to a different spot on a regular basis so I would not be arrested for loitering. I came to Florida because I couldn't stand to be so cold."

Nodding in Victor's direction, he said, "When he turns 18, I am going to go back to Puerto Rico. I don't have anybody here. I am going to go back home."

Victor jerked alive like a marionette whose strings were suddenly pulled. "I will follow you," he said, pointing his whole arm and finger straight at his father's soulful expression. "I will watch you day and night, and I will go to Puerto Rico with you when you go. Watch. I'll bet I go with you."

"They don't think I will really go, Ms. Perez, but I will. I will wash my hands of the whole bunch and go where they will never find me."

"Poppi, you wouldn't leave Venus. You wouldn't leave your own grandchild. You are the one who takes care of her. What would happen if you left and Elaine had to take care of her all the time?"

"Oh, Ms. Perez," Carlos said to me, "Victor makes me sound like a villain. I love my granddaughter, but she is here all the time. I thought I was finished with raising children. I love my granddaughter, but her mother should take care of her." He turned to Victor, "I am leaving you all. You and your brothers take care of her. All of you take care of her. You are her family."

In what seemed to me an attempt to break the evil spell of this image of abandonment, Victor suddenly pointed under the hood of the van and said, "You can't go anywhere. You have bad pistons!" He danced around the front of the van, laughing and pointing to the engine.

Carlos showed me the ruined pistons. He demonstrated a special tool he had creatively designed to pull the pistons up so he could remove and replace the springs underneath them. "You know how to fix cars, Ms. Perez?" Carlos asked in a way that felt like an invitation for me to learn.

"No, I don't. But I sure wish I did!" I said, carrying around the sting of all the times I felt ripped off by a car mechanic. "Show me."

Victor jumped up and down with glee as I leaned over the side of the van into the engine. "Ms. Perez, you think you can replace a spring in the piston? Wow, that's funny. Poppi, look at her."

"How about you, can you change a spring in a piston?" I said, tossing out an invitation to him.

"I can help," he said.

Under the tutelage of his father, Victor and I spent the next half hour working together under the hood on what was a difficult job. As I got in my car to drive off with the fresh smell of grease on my hands, Carlos said, "Ms. Perez, thank you for coming out to talk to me today. I will go to the meeting next week. I would like for you to be there, too."

"Oh, I'd be glad to," I said, suddenly remembering why I had come in the first place.

A week later, I met Carlos and Victor in the parking lot of the school. It was time for the meeting. "Good morning, Ms. Perez," Carlos greeted me as he stepped down from the van.

"Good morning to you. Looks like working pistons to me," I said, pointing toward the hood of the van.

"Oh, yes," he said, "I had some expert help with this. It runs very nice now."

Victor seemed edgy. He walked straight to the school front door. As we entered the conference room, Carlos manipulated his brace so he could sit down at the long rectangle table with tapered corners. Already seated around the table were the assistant principal, two of Victor's teachers, two behavior specialists, the school (police) resource officer, a teacher aide who spoke Spanish, and the supervisor of special education.

"Good morning," the assistant principal said. "I am glad we could all get together to be able to talk about Victor. And I appreciate that you could be here with us to talk about Victor's behavior, Mr. Quiles. I think you know that we have tried everything we know to keep Victor working in school, but he refuses to obey the rules and he is disrupting the entire school. Teachers who don't even have him in class say the school has a calmer atmosphere when Victor is not here."

Victor came to life from a slouched position. "What teachers? How can teachers who don't have me in class know about what I do? That's bull!"

The assistant principal turned to Victor. "If you can't behave appropriately in this meeting, then you will have to wait outside. You can't sit in here and talk like that, Victor."

Victor was up in a flash and at the door. "Fine, who would want to sit and have to listen to all this bull?" He left the room.

Carlos paled.

"You see what we're talking about?" said the supervisor of special education.

"That's why I don't see how we can keep Victor in school all day, Mr. Quiles," the assistant principal went on. "He causes too much disruption. You know, Mr. Quiles, we have been working for 2 years with Victor, so you know that we are committed to helping him, but first he has to want to help himself. And right now, there is no evidence that he is ready to cooperate."

"What we would like to suggest," she continued, "is that Victor come to school for just the mornings. Just until about 11:30." She looked over at the teacher and behavior specialists and said, "Isn't that what you all tell me, that he is fine until about 11:30, and then he begins to lose it?"

"Yes," said his teacher, and the assistant principal picked up on her words. "So I guess what would be best is if Victor could leave school at 11:30. If you could pick him up by then, we could put him on kind of half-day schooling."

Carlos looked stunned. "I can't pick him up every day," he said. "I have to be in court so much, and my van doesn't always work. I can't say I will be able to pick him up every day."

The school resource officer (SRO, a police officer) spoke up. He leaned across the table, which made his thick leather belt squeak. "Mr. Quiles, surely you have family that could help you out. Surely Victor has aunts and uncles who can pick him up if you can't."

Carlos turned to the imposing figure across the table. "I don't have anyone who can pick him up every day."

The SRO adjusted his belt and said, "You mean you don't have anyone at all who can come and pick him up? You don't have any family here of any kind that can come over here and pick Victor up?"

Carlos told him again that he could not make an agreement that Victor would be picked up at 11:30 every day. He said he knew he could not keep such an agreement.

The supervisor of special education spoke. "Well, Mr. Quiles, I can understand if you can't pick him up. I think in this case what might be better would be to put Victor on homebound status, and that way you wouldn't have to be concerned with transportation."

There was a flurry of talk from the teachers. They did not want Victor to be put on homebound. Certainly, it was too early in the year. They were all now just getting to know him, and they felt much of his problem had to do with Victor's inability to read. They wanted him at school.

But the supervisor of special education was already preparing the changes on the IEP (Individualized Education Plan) for Carlos to sign. She said, "We will place Victor on homebound instruction, and if you can work out something for transportation, we can meet again and make changes." She moved the papers and a pen in front of Carlos.

"I don't think this arrangement is in the best interest of Victor. I don't think we should send him home," I said.

Carlos did not reach for the pen.

"Mr. Quiles," said the supervisor in a soft, sing-song voice, "You can take us to court and we can go to court but . . ." and her words trailed off. She nudged the papers and said, "Being on homebound means a teacher will come out twice a week for 3 hours. An adult will have to be home while the teacher is there. The teacher will come after school hours from about 3 o'clock to 6 pm. It will take us a while to get that set up, but in the meantime, maybe you can work on getting transportation worked out. We would much rather have Victor at school."

When Carlos picked up the pen and signed the IEP, I was stunned. I didn't know what to say. I had been led to believe by the school administrator that the meeting was to discuss ideas to help Victor be successful in school.

The room cleared, and I walked Carlos out to the lobby, where Victor joined us. Together, we walked out to the van. "What did they say?" Victor asked.

"They said you are a pain in the neck, and they don't want you here anymore. You curse, you yell, you can't sit and have a conversation. So you have to stay home and have a teacher come out to the house to teach you," his father said.

"Well, they can send someone, but I won't be there," Victor said and hopped into the van.

Carlos turned to me with an outstretched hand. "Thank you, Ms. Perez, for coming to the meeting with me. But now you know why I don't come back. That officer made me look bad in there. I don't like how I feel now."

I felt ashamed. I felt as if I led him to slaughter. "I didn't think it would go that way, Carlos. I'm really sorry. I guess I had more faith that the school wanted to work with parents in helping the kids. That was not a helpful meeting. I feel terrible about the role I played."

"You mean good, Ms. Perez. Take care," he said as he pulled himself into the driver's seat.

I walked back into the school feeling angry and confused. I went straight to the assistant principal's office. She was standing behind her desk watching me come down the hall. As I entered the room, she said, "Don't you ever undermine the school system again in front of a parent!"

"How did I undermine the school system?" I asked, stunned at the amount of anger she seemed to be holding back. "I was expressing my concern for removing Victor from school after only the first 3 weeks of this school year. His teachers hardly know him."

"Evelyn Wilson (the supervisor of special education) came in my office after the meeting and told me she was very upset by your comment. I'm sure she will be calling you herself."

"Are you saying I can't express my opinion?"

"I'm saying that you don't use your opinion in front of a parent to undermine the school system. And now I am very busy," she said, dismissing me.

I left her office full of fury. I had a small taste of how I thought parents often felt after coming to a meeting at that school.

DIGGING IN: MAKING THE STORY PERSONAL

Perhaps the most powerful lessons we can take from a story occur when we allow ourselves to reflect and connect in a deeply personal and emotional way with what happened. We can often do this by placing ourselves in the roles of parents, connecting those roles to the rich experiences of our own lives.

Victor's teacher had Carlos come to school to see how terrible his son was in school. Do you think this is an effective way to involve parents in their child's education? Why or why not?

Victor and Carlos believed that the school did not want Victor there. How do you think this belief affected their relationship with the school?

How do you think Carlos's experiences as a child and as an adult affected his relationship with professionals at Victor's school?

What effect do you think it had when the supervisor of special education told Carlos, "You can take us to court and we can go to court but . . ." ?

Why do you think the school personnel thought Ms. Perez was undermining them by agreeing with Victor's father in the meeting?

THREE APPROACHES TO WORKING WITH PARENTS

After immersing ourselves in the stories of Ellen, Stephanie, and Carlos, we emerge with an intense awareness of the complexity, dignity, suffering, struggle, hope, and sometimes hopelessness of parents of labeled or troubling students. Hopefully, we can allow that awareness to increase our shared humanity and connection with these parents and families. Hopefully, we can understand that these poignant and painful biographies are not just narratives about "problem families" but stories about the tenuous and often tumultuous state of family life in the United States, particularly for those families living in poverty or on the margins of dominant Anglo culture. These are stories of human hardships that affect so many of us as we try to survive, make a living, and love our loved ones. These are stories of economic inequality, alcohol and drug abuse, physical and sexual abuse, cultural dislocation and racism, unemployment and underpaid employment, violence and crime, government bureaucracies and insensitive school professionals, and inadequate social welfare and mental health systems.

It is too easy for us to read these stories as tales of disordered kids being raised by disordered parents. It is too easy for us to fall into the old diagnostic habit of psychology, psychiatry, and special education. Rather than using these stories for the purposes of erecting that traditional hierarchy of normality and abnormality, of mental health and mental disorder, we invite you to comprehend these narratives and hear these parents' words on a plane of equality. These are persons neither greater nor lesser than you or me. These are persons who have undoubtedly suffered from a variety of hardships. Our task is to hear them as fellow humans who, like you and me, suffer as surely as they breathe the air. Like you and me, these are people who need love, support, understanding, food, shelter, and health care. Like you and me, they need to be heard, valued, and taken seriously.

If we are to be respectful of the struggles and dignity of parents of troubling students, refusing to climb on a high horse to judge them or blame them, how should we work with these parents and families? The remainder of this chapter will be devoted to this question. We will look at the three basic approaches to parent involvement that schools have used: parents as recipients, parents as participants, and parents as empowered individuals. Although each serves some purpose within education, we will promote the third approach, a model of empowerment, as the best approach.

Parents as Recipients

The *parents as recipients* approach assumes that parents lack sufficient knowledge and skills to properly raise their children. The school professionals have the necessary knowledge and skills. The educators must provide advice and training to parents in need of education in raising their children (Ascher, 1988; Dunst & Trivette, 1987; Greenwood & Hickman, 1991; Heath, 1987). The goals for parent education from this focus are aimed at increasing the parents' understanding of the skills, behaviors, and attitudes necessary for their children to succeed in school. Teachers are seen as having an expert role in helping parents develop the skills necessary to be effective in preparing their children for school (Schaefer, 1991). For parents of troubling students, this often means that parent involvement is an attempt on the part of educators to teach parents how to manage their child's behavior.

This approach can produce positive benefits for parents. Undoubtedly, some parents can gain new knowledge and skills from school professionals. This is especially true when school professionals are parents themselves and can relate firsthand to difficulties faced by the students' families.

Yet this approach is very limited. Parent involvement in this mode tends to perpetuate the very things that have kept many parents away from schools. Parents and families are targeted as the reason for and source of the behavior problem. They are assumed to be incompetent or lacking in an expertise that the professionals are assumed to have. Professionals are placed in the powerful position of knowing what parents should do and should have already done. This arrangement tends to perpetuate the blaming of parents and the rejection of the parents' and families' knowledge about their own lives.

Parents as Participants

The *parents as participants* approach assumes that parents should be involved beyond the role of recipient of training. From this approach, parents are expected to be actively involved in school activities. Parent involvement programs focus on increasing parent participation through attending sports events and PTA meetings, volunteering in the schools, and working on committees (Cervone & O'Leary, 1982; Hoover-Dempsey & Sandler, 1997; Williams & Chavkin, 1989).

This model of parent involvement differs from the recipient approach in that parents are expected to come to school and actively take part in a variety of ways to support the school effort rather than come to school as someone needing help. Being involved can mean anything from serving on the school planning committee to working the concession stand at sporting events. Because parents are expected to be more active and visible in schools, teachers are expected to work at establishing interactions with parents in a number of positive ways (Epstein, 1988).

There are many obstacles to success in this approach. For parents of troubling students, the feeling that schools blame them for their child's behavior or label may preclude this kind of participation. Bursuck et al. (1999) emphasize the need for educators to maintain open, clear communication with parents. Open communication is obviously a good idea, but this approach typically does not address the blame that is often already felt by parents of troubling students and the belief on the part of educators that parents are to blame for their children's emotional problems. The tension this feeling creates is a powerful barrier to parent involvement that cannot be ignored.

A variety of other obstacles stand in the way of parent participation in this model. Many low-income parents work multiple jobs or have difficulty finding transportation to school events. Many simply have no one to take care of their other children so that they can be freed up to participate in school activities. Educators using this approach to parent involvement need to consider how they might provide funding, transportation, and other support services to help parents attend and help them feel that they are not misunderstood and blamed.

Other social and cultural barriers to parent involvement may exist. Parent groups such as Parent Teacher Associations may be dominated by middle-class parents, parents of certain ethnic or racial groups, or parents of students who achieve academically and conform behaviorally. If this is the situation, families of students from other racial or ethnic groups, or families of working-class backgrounds may feel uncomfortable. Parents and families of students who are known in the school or community as troublemakers might not be received with open arms. Negotiating the political terrain of parent groups can be very difficult for teachers who wish to cultivate a climate of acceptance.

Parent Empowerment

The *parent empowerment* approach frames parent involvement as an equal and respectful partnership or collaboration between parents and educators (Comer, 1980; Comer et al., 1996; Seeley, 1989; Swick & Graves, 1993). The notion is that parents and teachers each bring expertise and competence to the relationship and the ongoing dialogue. Whereas teachers may understand more about school matters such as curriculum, instruction, and school policies and procedures, parents bring to the relationship a deep, experiential wisdom about their child and a love and concern for the well-being of their child. Each has something necessary to offer. The goal is to construct a collaborative relationship between teacher and family that allows each to contribute fully.

Parent involvement is seen as a process in which parents and educators work together to find ways to increase the academic performance and social well-being of students. Critical to this kind of parent involvement is the acceptance of the idea that parents must have a sense of choice, a feeling that they are powerful and valued, and a sense of ownership of the process and the results.

There is a reciprocal nature in the relationship between parents and educators that sets this view of parent involvement apart from the others. Seeley (1989) refers to this collaboration as a "dynamic relationship" between parents and educators in which real-life interactions occur when different "factions" come together to work collaboratively to bring about change.

Perhaps best known for developing the empowerment model of partnership with parents is James Comer (1980; Comer et al., 1996). In 1968, this professor of child psychiatry headed a team of professionals and entered two urban elementary schools in New Haven, Connecticut, to put into practice a theory of the necessity of valued and full parent participation in their children's schools. The children came from financially poor, racial minority families. Academically, the students were generally performing at least 2 years behind their grade level.

Comer (1980) believed that the cultural and social gap between home and school created the most detrimental effect on the poor academic standing of the students. "I began to speculate that the contrast between a child's experiences at home and those in school deeply affects the child's psychosocial development and that this in turn shapes academic achievement" (p. 3).

Comer immersed the two schools with parents in a variety of ways. Some parents were paid for their involvement, which gave them income while allowing them to become part of the school community. Other parents volunteered in different capacities that brought them into the school community as contributing, functioning members. Still other parents were considered collegial members in decision-making groups that gave the school direction.

Accepting and arranging for parents to be full members of the school community did not occur without misunderstandings and conflict.

> In the first year teachers and administrators could not agree on clear goals and strategies, so we had a difficult school opening. Some new teachers tried to have open classrooms, but the children soon became uncontrollable. Teachers blamed the administration for not providing adequate resources, and parents became angry, angry enough to march on one of the schools. (Comer, 1980, p. 4)

From a collaborative stance, Comer considered this rift between educators and parents as "a spectacular deterioration" because "it illustrated the social dynamics, something that would otherwise have taken us many years to perceive" (Comer, 1980, p. 6). It was a necessary and useful moment of apparent failure that set the stage for future success.

> It became obvious that we would make no progress until we had reduced the destructive interactions among parents, teachers and administrators. We invited parents from among the group that had protested against us in the first year to join the team and with their input we developed a program. (Comer, 1980, p. 6)

In this way, parents had a forum to be heard and understood. Their words were angry and critical, but the fact that the school professionals heard the critique and took the parents' words seriously made all the difference. From there, parents and educators worked collaboratively to create a school focus.

Academically, the "performance at the two New Haven schools surpassed the national average, and truancy and disciplinary problems declined markedly" (Comer, 1980, p. 2). The success in these two schools spurred Comer to develop more "Comer" schools. These schools continue to focus on closing the gap between home and school in order to nurture the psychological development of students needed to achieve success in their academic performance.

Another example of a collaborative, empowerment approach to parent involvement is illustrated by Cryer (1989), a principal of a California elementary school. In response to an influx of multiethnic families that dramatically changed the demographic nature of the student body, Cryer turned to parents for help. He invited parents into the school as knowledgeable individuals to become partners with educators in bringing about an understanding among the different cultures. Parents taught educators the unique ethnic values and traditions of their cultures. They became involved in translating and communicating school information into the various new languages. Reciprocally, educators provided support and assistance to families in their efforts to get established in the community. It was this mutual respect for personal knowledge and ethnic beliefs, along with a care and concern for one another, that caused Cryer to call his school a "therapeutic community."

What does it take for parents of troubling students to become involved with educators in a way that supports the academic success of their children in school? Many, or perhaps most, parents of labeled or troubling children want to be involved with schools, but the feelings of judgment or misunderstanding that emanate from schools make them resistant to crossing the schoolhouse door.

An empowerment model offers a distinct advantage over the other two models in the notion that parents and educators have equal voice. Their relationship is built on working together to bring about collaboratively decided change. Both Comer (1980) and Cryer (1989) give examples of how, in the process of establishing relationships, parents and educators worked through conflicts that arose between and among them. This suggests that the issue of blame can be addressed as part of the relationship that is being worked and reworked between parents and educators. The dialogue between school professionals and parents is open to discussions of everything from feelings of blame and judgment to questions of curriculum and problems on the school bus. Such a dialogue requires teachers to share power with parents and open themselves to equal conversations and relationships with persons who are often from different cultural backgrounds and social class. Our challenge as educators is to engage in deep listening—a valuing of the kinds of wisdom that come from places beyond the school, our professional knowledge, and our experience. This is the challenge of working with parents in a collaborative and empowering way.

TIPS FOR TEACHERS

Build a relationship with parents or guardians from the very start. Too often, the first (or only) time that parents and guardians hear from a teacher is when their son or daughter is in trouble. Initiate an early discussion with a parent or guardian in which you introduce yourself and ask questions about what that parent wants for his or her child.

When you arrange meetings with parents or guardians, be open to a variety of possible meeting times and places. Some parents prefer to meet in their home. Some feel comfortable coming to the school. Another option that is often good for parents who do not feel comfortable going to the school building or inviting school personnel into their home is a neighborhood setting such as a community center, public library, or a church.

Be aware of and sensitive to linguistic differences. Even if a parent or guardian speaks conversational English, that doesn't necessarily mean that she or he feels able to discuss complex topics in English. Find and use interpreters whenever possible.

Limit the number of school personnel attending meetings with a parent or guardian to the lowest number possible. For many parents, meeting with a group of five or eight professionals is intimidating.

SUMMARY

The educational research clearly supports the value of the participation of parents in the schooling of their children. Around the country, special and general educators usually agree that parent involvement dramatically increases a child's chances for school success. Yet parents of troubling and labeled students and schools frequently do not work in productive collaboration. Resistance to the formation of such an equal, respectful, and beneficial relationship occurs on the part of both schools and parents.

Researchers cite two reasons for educators' resistance to parent involvement in schools. One is a belief that school and home play different roles in the life of a child. Educators view themselves as trained professionals who educate and socialize students to become individual citizens and workers in society. Mixing this job with the family's task of child rearing only interferes with the work of the professionals. The second is the common belief among teachers that parents of troubling students are to blame for their children's behavioral problems.

Parents of troubling and labeled students, on the other hand, often feel disrespected and silenced by the schools. The three parent stories we have seen in this chapter are rich with examples of public school personnel failing to value the experiential knowledge of parents. The special education label stigma projected onto the students is also often projected onto the parents, creating a major obstacle to a respectful working relationship.

The three models of working with parents view parents in very different ways. Parents may be seen as the recipients of training from school-based experts; as participants in schooling activities; or as empowered and valued educational colleagues, knowledgeable co-partners with schools in the many tasks of raising and educating children. This third approach—the empowerment model—offers the most hope and opportunity for schools and parents alike.

CONSTRUCTING PERSONAL MEANINGS

1. Many towns and cities have formal parent advocacy networks that assist parents of students receiving special education services. Contact a local advocacy network and invite one or more advocates to meet with the

class. Or, you could conduct interviews with advocates to understand their perspectives and their work.

2. A second idea that is similar to the first is to work through a local parent advocacy network to access parents of students labeled E/BD (or another disability category). Either interview these parents or invite them to come to your university class for a conversation about their experiences.

3. Interview your own parents to understand the challenges, hopes, successes, and failures that they went through within your own family.

4. Many school districts provide programs of support and/or education to parents and families. Contact local school districts to find out what kinds of services they provide to parents. Are there specific services for parents of students who receive special education services? Are there specific services for parents of students struggling with emotional or behavioral difficulties? Is there an effort to reach economically poor and minority culture parents and families?

5. Contact a local mental health service that works with children, adolescents, and families. Invite administrators or therapists to discuss their experiences working with families with the university class.

10

Considering Inclusive Education

Perhaps rather than always contemplating inclusion, we should flip the binary and think about exclusion. What does it tell about us when we systematically shut off access to public space for specific groups, marked out conspicuously as "other"? When viewed through the safe distance of history, we can look at practices of exclusion and see rather clearly that they are enactments of both fear and power together. Inclusion is a practice that involves deep learning for all involved because it entails a fundamental shift in relationship between humans. Inclusion involves an opening up, a making of space, an engagement in dialogue.

In this chapter, we examine inclusive education as a social ideal that we seek to fulfill in our lives as democratic citizens and as a complex, practical effort within school settings. We will explore the moral and philosophical underpinnings of inclusive education in the vision of democratic community held by John Dewey. Then, we will examine the complexities and practicalities of trying to live that ideal within real lives and within real schools. We will look at obstacles and possibilities for inclusion of students with emotional, social, and behavioral issues.

Troubling students are frequently excluded from general education settings. The most common special education label for students considered troubling is

Emotional/Behavioral Disorder (E/BD). Students labeled E/BD frequently are not included in general education classes. As inclusive educational efforts have increased the number of students with all disabilities educated in general education classrooms, students labeled E/BD seemingly have been untouched by the inclusion trend (U.S. Department of Education, 1994, 1999). In 17 states, including California and Florida, less than 20% of all students labeled E/BD are included in general education classes (U.S. Department of Education, 1999). Instead, they are placed in segregated schools, residential programs, or sent home for "homebound instruction."

Why has the inclusion of these students been so slow and difficult? Our answer is fear, fear, and fear. We will take a close look at fear in three dimensions: (a) a general fear of people whom we believe to be different from ourselves; (b) the fears of teachers, who often prejudge and stereotype E/BD-labeled kids; and (c) the fears of previously segregated students as they attempt to cope with general education environments that are often unfamiliar and filled with academic and social booby traps.

As we examine each of these three dimensions of fear, our primary message will be that understanding, compassion, and communication are the best ways to allay these many anxieties and build school communities where students can feel like they belong. We will include experiential stories that flesh out the complexities of these fears and the hopeful possibilities that reside in understanding and communication with students and teachers. We will provide two examples of inclusive practices with students labeled E/BD as a means of addressing the complexities and possibilities of practice.

INCLUSION AS DEMOCRATIC COMMUNITY

Inclusive education is a moral and political movement that seeks the instruction and socialization of students with disabilities side by side with their nonlabeled peers. The goal is the creation of public schools that accept and support students of all stripes, patterns, and sizes. The goal is one of building a democratic and caring community within schools as well as beyond schools (Kliewer 1998a, 1998b; Lipsky & Gartner, 1996).

What is a democratic community? John Dewey described democracy as a lived ethic that must be made each and every day by citizens, created and recreated in our actions and our attitudes. It is a way of life that we make together (Dewey, 1916, 1920, 1925, 1927, 1929, 1930, 1939; Gouinlock, 1994; Ryan, 1995; Westbrook, 1991). The ideal way for young people to learn about this way of life is by doing, by participating in schools and classrooms that make equality a daily priority.

We'll narrow down our discussion to two notable themes that recur in Dewey's many writings on democratic community: (a) the creation of equality in mundane, daily activity; and (b) the need for an equal, inclusive dialogue among the diversity of community members.

The Daily, Communal Making of Equality

"Equality . . . is not a natural possession but is a fruit of the community."

(Dewey, 1927, p. 151)

Dewey viewed democratic community as a shared way of life that makes equality happen. Equality is something we can put *in* our activities, something we can make in the face-to-face conversations and interactions of common folk. Two neighbors lean against the fence that divides their properties, each standing at the edge of his or her own self, his or her own identity, the partial weight of each set in equal proportion against opposite sides of that common fence. As the neighbors lean, they talk about interests and concerns that are inevitably shared by persons who live side by side. It is in that discussion that occurs daily in side yards, marketplaces, houses of worship, and schools where the equality of persons can be made and remade. In this sense, equality thrives not within abstract statements of natural rights but through the actions taken each day by citizens who carry on this "common narrative" (Edgar, 1998, p. 162) called democratic living.

Equal and Inclusive Dialogue

John Dewey also felt that democratic living depends on open and free communication. The democratic community is a multicolored mosaic where many views and perspectives are invited and accepted. A shared culture of equality and freedom is created in the dialogue of varied, disparate, and even opposing voices.

The goal of public dialogue is not conformity, not a uniformity of opinion or belief or action. In fact, to Dewey, conformity occurs only when democratic dialogue is halted, when discussion is stagnated. "Conformity is the name of the absence of vital interplay; the arrest and benumbing of communication" (Dewey, 1930, pp. 85–86). The only consensus required by democracy is the general agreement to accept differences of belief in order to maintain the civil space of dialogue. What is shared is the valuing of the equal opportunity to speak one's mind, contribute what one can to the community, and offer forth words arising from one's experience and cultural background.

The purpose of this inclusive and diverse dialogue is moral. When citizens (or students and teachers) converse over the specific issues and dilemmas of the day, we ask ourselves moral questions: "How shall we all live together with peace and justice?" There are no certainties or absolutes regarding the outcome of the moral dialogue. There is no program or step-by-step recipe for making this work. The distinctly moral dimension is enacted not in the surety of the results but within the cooperative process of inclusive conversation itself.

Essential to this process of discussion is the attitude of critique (see Patton, 1998), the vigilant awareness of and opposition to the ongoing prevalence of social inequalities within the structures and habits of groups, organizations, professions, and the economic marketplace. Schools and society alike tend to create hierarchies of value, elevating some with wealth, high status, and power while degrading others with poverty, low status, and powerlessness. Dewey continuously championed the need for marginalized groups to have the status of full participation in all aspects of American society. He was aware that these groups often bring an otherwise unnoticed critique of the status quo, of the assumed fairness of doing business as usual (see Ryan, 1995; Westbrook, 1991). A truly inclusive dialogue allows for the unique perspectives of the downtrodden and undervalued to contribute critique of the customary practices of dominant groups, thereby providing for opportunities for the correction of those habitual practices and the greater equalization of power.

We believe that inclusive education is a worthy and just goal because it is one way of attempting to create schools that are democratic communities that value equality, diversity, and dialogue. In saying this, we also acknowledge that understanding the democratic ethics of inclusive education and making inclusion work within public schools are not synonymous. Action is far more difficult than understanding. Now we will turn to the many reasons why living up to that social ideal of inclusion is so difficult within the public schools. As we noted earlier, we will focus on fear, fear, and fear.

TEACHER ATTITUDES AND FEARS

Let us start with the way that many teachers and administrators often view troubling students, especially those considered E/BD. The following reflection by Terry Jo Smith (second author) on the comments school personnel have made about students labeled E/BD is not an isolated phenomenon.

> It was my first day at my new school. My position was as a behavior specialist. I would be working with the students and teachers in the four E/BD classes. I was excited about starting my new job and arrived early on the first day of teacher planning. A woman about my age came up as I was opening the door to my office. She extended her hand and introduced herself: "Hi, I'm Kathy Miller," she said. "I am the eighth-grade reading teacher. My classroom is two doors down. You must be the new behavior specialist."
>
> I confirmed her guess, and she launched into a 5-minute diatribe about the students in the E/BD classes. She said, "I feel sorry for you having to work with those kids. Anytime you need a shoulder to cry on, I'm right down the hall. Last year was absolutely crazy in this hallway. Those kids were forever disturbing the whole wing. They have no respect for anyone! I don't know why anyone would want this job! No one stays more than a year, and who could blame them when they have to work with children that act like animals."

Had I been a novice teacher, I think I would have been surprised by her words of contempt. But I had that rude awakening more than 5 years earlier in my first teaching job when the principal told me that she didn't think the E/BD kids belonged in the school, and if she had her way, they wouldn't be there. She assured me that even if they didn't say so, most principals felt the same way. And over the course of my teaching career, there have been many, many other examples of teachers, parents, and administrators who have voiced their scorn and loathing for the students considered E/BD. So I sighed a tired sigh and told Kathy that I loved working with E/BD-labeled students, that in ways I thought they were the most honest and wonderful kids in the school. The warm and welcoming look disappeared from her face as she said, "I can tell you one thing, I would never allow my own children to attend a school with an E/BD program in it. I would pay for them to go to private school first. I don't think anyone should have to put up with those kids' rude behavior! It is just not fair to the students who behave appropriately and are here to get an education."

With that, she turned on her heel and headed down the hall. I walked into my office feeling very sad, the excitement of the previous few moments crushed. I had forgotten how despised E/BD kids often are in schools and how even their teachers are treated with contempt, especially if they advocate for their students. Here was a woman who did not even know me yet, but felt compelled to make her position clear in our first meeting. She was willing to be kind to me if I despised the students too, then she'd offer comfort. Later on that day, one of the teacher's aides in the E/BD department told me that she hated some of the kids. She described one boy as "plain white trash."

The students in the E/BD program were very aware of how they were perceived. During the first week of the school year, the assistant principal of the same school was talking to a boy named Jose. He was one of the few Hispanic students in the school. She was very kind to Jose, giving him a hug and telling him how happy she was to see him. That looked promising, but Jose balked at her attempts to be friendly. Once she left, I asked him why he had been rude to her. He told me that she hated him and didn't want him in the school. He said that what I had just seen was an act put on for my benefit. I defended her and her intentions and asked Jose to give her a chance. "You'll see," Jose said with certainty. And I did. Two months later, I sat at a staffing where this assistant principal put Jose on homebound instruction, which meant he was being pushed out of the school altogether. She refused to allow him to attend the staffing and spoke to his father with equal disdain. She did seem to hate him, and it was evident she did not want him in the school. And that was no secret to anyone.

In our teaching careers with troubling students, and in the endless stories brought into our university classrooms by teachers, we have heard these kinds of stories time and again. These strong negative reactions affect and confound efforts toward inclusion. Students labeled E/BD and their teachers often become reclusive in their excluded classrooms and programs. They do not want to read the derision others feel for them in their eyes, detect it in their tone of voice, or hear it spoken freely in their words of condemnation. It's just too painful. Although students who bear other labels of disability are often discriminated against in schools, they tend to evoke pity in those around them. Pity, like disdain, often provides invisible roadblocks to inclusion, but allows the person feeling pity to feel righteous in his or her patronizing attitudes. Attitudes toward students labeled E/BD, however, are often blatantly scornful. Students labeled E/BD are often treated as if their disability or disorder is a result of poor moral fiber, poor parenting, and poor self-control. Students with stigmatizing labels are often judged and blamed on the basis of their categorical label.

In our experience, this kind of negative, fearful stereotyping is common. The inclusion and exclusion of troubling students involves their often despised and feared identities within schools. Placing a child into a general education classroom in which he or she is viewed as a pariah and shunned, punished, and ostracized may be called inclusive, but it can also be a particularly cruel situation. Anyone who has ever felt like an outcast in a group or who has felt lonely in a crowd knows that inclusion involves more than simply sharing space.

Often, students considered E/BD are openly feared and scorned within schools. They are seen as threats to order and thereby impinging on other students' right to learn. In order to work effectively toward an authentic, inclusive school community, these underlying factors must be carefully addressed. The roadblocks to the inclusion of nonconforming students involve human fears; values; judgments; and the often unquestioned assumptions of classroom practices, curriculum, and behavior modification. In light of all of these elements of inclusion, we need to create safe spaces for the development of deep dialogue, critical reflection, and negotiation.

EXCLUSION AND FEAR

The enemy within can at last be hunted down on the outside.

(Miller, 1990, p. 11)

Many teachers do not admit the fear that some students evoke in them. The fear of being responsible for educating and controlling the behavior of students whose very presence is often experienced within the school with aversion is not often acknowledged. Rather, exclusion and other practices of marginalization operate to protect teachers from those fears. Instead of admitting to and facing those fears, teachers push the feared students away. Exclusionary programs in special education provide a ready format for this activity. In *The Courage to Teach,* Parker Palmer (1998) explores how fear invades educational contexts at every level. Palmer sums up what he thinks is often at the base of our fear and how that leads to exclusion:

> We collaborate with the structures of separation because they promise to protect us against one of the deepest fears at the heart of being human—the fear of having a live encounter with alien "otherness," whether the other is a student, a colleague, a subject, or a self-dissenting voice within. We fear encounters in which the other is free to be itself, to speak its own truth, to tell us what we may not wish to hear. We want those encounters on our own terms, so we can control their outcomes, so they will not threaten our view of world or self. (p. 37)

Palmer tells us that the fear of the live encounter is composed of a whole series of fears that begin in a fear of diversity. Young (1990) contends that, at present, it is not socially acceptable to be openly bigoted, so the fears of diversity that fuel exclusionary practices often operate in more subtle and unconscious ways. According to Kristeva (1982), these fears result from a fear of a loss of one's own identity, a fear of invasion and dissolution of one's own self. In an unconscious effort to shore up one's own self-identity, there is a tendency to push people away whose differences make us uncomfortable. Special education as a segregated educational process has provided an institutional mechanism for marginalizing differences and protecting the general population of teachers and students from facing their own fears of diversity.

Rhodes (1977) explains that we use our assumed sense of normality as a defense mechanism against our deepest fears. Together, we cultivate social norms of behavior, appearance, and belief. We take on these social conventions and call ourselves "normal" as a way of shielding us from our own vulnerability in the world. Rather than question our own assumed normality, we often demonize and fear those who do not seem like us. We define ourselves as normal and call those who fall outside the social conventions "abnormal." Typically, we view those deemed abnormal as fearful characters who rightfully should be excluded.

Inclusion often brings us face to face with our unconscious fears of difference. However, if those fears are not made conscious and addressed, they will continue to operate in subtle, pervasive ways. Consciousness raising, then, is imperative in our work toward creating inclusive schools. Otherwise, we will continually reproduce exclusionary practices even if students with disabilities are educated in the same classroom as their nondisabled peers. How can we raise our consciousness? How can we attend to our own fears of the diverse "other" with compassion and open-mindedness?

One of the best ways to move beyond our own fears of students with disabilities, including students labeled E/BD, is to spend time with them. Although inclusion may bring a labeled student into our classroom, it may be difficult to get to know the student on a level that would help dispel our fears in the midst of a large group of students. Setting aside the time to get to know the student individually can be extremely rewarding and provide a foundation for trust and respect. This may mean inviting a student to have lunch with you or making a home visit.

Confronting our fears about various forms of human diversity is a lifelong endeavor. Feeling fear is not shameful; we have grown up within cultures that often pathologize or demonize difference. We learn to fear those whom we do not know. Segregation maintains those fears. Inclusive communities provide us with opportunities to engage in the work of breaking down the barriers of fear that segregation maintains. It is both a personal and a public endeavor. We need to change our social structures to support inclusion, and we need to interrogate our own fears to support the development of mutual and respectful relationships with others.

AUTONOMY AND COLLABORATION

Inclusion also poses a threat to teacher autonomy. Historically, teachers have conducted their work in isolation from other teachers. Teachers often have come to value the complete control they exercise in their own classrooms. Additionally, most teachers have become accustomed to working without another professional watching and possibly criticizing their work. Isolation, in many cases, breeds fear of other professionals discovering one's inadequacies, and fear of being exposed. Most inclusive models involve a far greater amount of collaboration; a sharing of both responsibility and authority. Teachers often go in each other's classrooms, collaborate on teaching and classroom management, and negotiate many decisions. Suddenly, teaching is not an individual job but a social and interactive job. This can be a challenge to teachers who have spent years working alone.

Some general education teachers are eager to work with special education students and their teachers. Some want no part of it. Some are willing to work with the students, but unwilling to work with teachers. Others are willing to take labeled students *only* if they are accompanied by an adult who would be responsible for their modifications and, if need be, removal. Special education teachers often complain that they feel like guests when they co-teach in general education classrooms. Some have complained of being treated like an assistant and asked to make copies and do other clerical jobs.

There are vulnerabilities involved in working out truly respectful collaborative relationships within schools that traditionally have been premised on the idea of teacher autonomy rather than collaboration. Figuring out how to share space and power with other teachers traditionally has not been a necessary talent for teachers. Of course, the possibilities for learning and personal growth are enormous. So are the possibilities for anger, hurt feelings, and misunderstandings. This is a very human endeavor, and the intensity that often surrounds the education of students considered E/BD usually increases the pressure.

Inclusion occurs within a web of relationships. Inclusion, at its very essence, is about relationships and the ways we choose to live together.

"REASONABLE" TEACHER FEARS

Although strong psychosocial processes and deeply seated fears often come into play in relationship to the education and inclusion of students with special education labels, we do not want to imply that the difficulties all rest in the compulsive needs for control and conformity of the systems and the adults who comprise it. Students who are labeled E/BD (and many who are not) are often disruptive to school contexts and, on occasion, pose real threats to the safety and well-being of students and teachers. Often, troubling students have experienced assaults on their young lives that have left them angry, distrustful, and resistant. Some students have a tremendous amount of energy surging through their veins, some find it difficult to concentrate, some hear voices, and some are very sad. They may well confound the smooth running of a general education classroom to the detriment of other students and teachers. Or, if they are hurt, sad, confused, or angry, they may feel totally overwhelmed by the demands of a general education classroom.

It is important to understand that some children may behave in ways that are too volatile and violent for a general education classroom. In our own history as teachers, we have occasionally made decisions that led to students' placement in more "restrictive" environments, which means more restricted or segregated environments. This should always be a soul-searching endeavor, a difficult decision for professionals to make.

We might simply say that with the right supports, all children will be educated in general education settings, but we should understand that there are times when the right supports are highly unlikely. We need to move toward the social ideal of inclusive democracy while retaining a real awareness of the extreme vulnerability and violent capacity of a few children. We need to carefully and continuously evaluate the risks and promises involved with inclusion with each individual student within each setting. In this evaluation process, teachers need to be aware of their own levels of comfort and fear and how these interact in their judgments. For the vast majority of these decisions, the risks will involve only the possibility of the nonviolent disruption of a class, not fears that a child might seriously harm someone else.

The students considered troubling are as unique as all other people. Some of them simply act very immature for their age. Some children know how to be class clowns, always vying for the class's attention, often undermining the teacher's authority and classroom order in the process. Some act strangely, hear voices, show extreme variation in mood, are noticeably withdrawn, fantasize excessively, tell tall tales, have difficulty with peer relationships, and so on. Most of these students don't pose a threat of violence against other children, but they might disrupt a learning environment in various ways. They are often feared because they undermine the teacher's control and the order thought necessary to maximize teaching and learning.

We must notice the difference between fearing that violence will occur in the classroom and fearing the disruption of the norms of order and control.

Violence is obviously a very serious concern. But most of what occurs in schools and most of what teachers actually fear falls under the latter category, a loss of quiet, order, and control. We must work to be sure that fears of disorder or disruption are not inflated into unfounded fears of violence. We need to take responsibility for our contribution and always take into account that fear is as much about who we are as who students are.

What we have tried to point out thus far is that some of the barriers to the meaningful inclusion of students with E/BD or other labels exist within the psychology of teachers and institutions, not simply within the child. Strong fears come into play when children act out in angry, confused, sad, or otherwise nontraditional ways within schools. In order to promote a caring democratic community within schools where students who are experiencing social, emotional, and behavior difficulties can be supported rather than endlessly controlled and punished, teachers need to explore their own fears so that they do not unconsciously act these out on students. We need to be honest and compassionate with ourselves in order to be the same way with our students.

STUDENTS' FEARS

Like their teachers, students are not always conscious of their fears. They often mask their fears with anger, resistance, and a show of bravado. Often, troubling and defiant students seem like the least afraid students in the school, doing daring things, defying authority, or simply acting differently from what peer and institutional pressures would have them do. Frequently, these students are seen as fearless. This couldn't be further from the truth.

Many students have experienced or continue to experience some kind of emotional trauma in their lives. Often, they have not been able to control the really important things in their lives. Many of the students have lived through physical abuse, sexual abuse, or emotional neglect. Many have experienced a number of major losses in their lives. Perhaps they lost a parent or loved one to illness, violence, or drugs. Perhaps they have lived in a number of foster homes and group homes. They do not always trust easily. Troubling students are often said to have "control issues." They sometimes feel extremely vulnerable in the face of authority. And yet, it would be just as rare for a student to admit to his or her fear as it would be for a teacher.

Inclusion often seems extremely intimidating for students who have spent much time in segregated classes. Even when they complain about the isolation and stigma of special classrooms, they often sabotage efforts to include them or mainstream them into general education classes. It is not uncommon for students who are in a special program with a level system to "mess up" just before they get to a level that includes mainstreaming. We have seen this happen more often than not.

In our experience, students in segregated classes are afraid of many things. Often, they are not up to grade level academically and have learning difficulties.

Feeling exposed, the students frequently act up in order to avoid the embarrassment of having to read in front of the class. The fear of making a mistake in front of everyone may be an incredible source of worry for students who already feel stigmatized by their label, their reputation, and perhaps other issues in their lives.

Another looming source of fear for students with special education labels involves their status with their peers. Inclusion often brings more opportunity for ridicule by other students. Students are often made fun of based on their labels or reputations. Often, the students in segregated special education classes are quite well known in schools. When they get mainstreamed, most people know that this is a student in the special program. The students fear they will be taunted, and sometimes they are.

Some students also might not trust themselves when it comes to being included. Many students lack confidence in themselves, especially in schools where they have been marked out as "disturbed" and "disordered." Frequently, they cover their lack of confidence with an over-show of confidence, a bravado or machismo. They may say that they don't want to be included in a class because it is "too easy," when, deep down, they are afraid they can't do the work or they can't make any new friends. Or, students may not trust their own behaviors and don't want to get in trouble or embarrass themselves. This is often compounded by isolation. Many students have spent extended periods of time—perhaps their entire education—in small, self-contained rooms. The big general classrooms may seem strange and intimidating to them.

Sadly, teachers often react to the surface messages, the defensive behaviors and masks, and don't work with the students to recognize and face their deep fears. Students often use inappropriate behavior as a means to avoid the things they are afraid of. Usually, these students are more afraid of exposure, ridicule, loss of control, and looking and feeling stupid than they are of the school's consequences for their disruptive or deviant behavior. And if they can get out of what feels like a threatening situation by acting tough or as if they don't care, then no one will guess they are really afraid. All the while, the deeply seated fear may go unacknowledged. We have seen cases of students who, when included against their will in general education classes, worked tirelessly to get removed from those classes. That is not a difficult thing to do in most schools.

THE LEGITIMACY OF STUDENT FEARS

What we have seen through our own experiences as teachers, through our students' experiences as teachers, and through our many school visits and collaborations falls in line with Knitzer's (1990) assessment that most programs for students labeled E/BD are hyperfocused on the control of student behavior through the use of rewards and punishments. This is not to say we never come across programs that we find therapeutic. We do. The KEYS program discussed within this text is an example of an excellent program. But too often, such programs are the exceptions. Once again, we are not talking about teachers who care or don't care, but an approach to students premised on pathology and control that limits teachers' freedom to respond to students in caring and therapeutic ways.

Labeled students' fears of vulnerability within the school system are often very legitimate. They know from their own school histories that people in schools are prone toward punishing those who are not able to conform, quietly, to their social agenda. Their labeling and exclusion, and very often their treatment, has confirmed their fears of the real harm schools can do in the name of interventions and discipline. Some students live personal nightmares within their home and neighborhood lives only to come to school to be punished for their anger, distractibility, differentness, and lack of interest.

Additionally, we must acknowledge the feelings and desires of parents. An opportunity to move into the mainstream may be viewed by a parent as a loss of security, as an invitation for his or her child to encounter social problems that he or she cannot handle. The parent may fear an increase in disciplinary action from a general education system that is not sensitive to the student's individual needs. In our communications with parents, we should listen closely for both the hope of an inclusive education and the fears of failure and punishment.

SHIFTING OUR FOCUS FROM CONTROL TO COMPASSION

Strong needs to control others and to push them away from us when they disrupt our own sense of comfort and order must be addressed or practices of inclusion will mirror our underlying fear and ignorance. Inclusion involves raising our own fears to consciousness and encouraging that process in ongoing dialogue with others. Compassion, rather than control, nurtures these deeply transformative processes. Inclusion offers us incredible opportunities to learn about ourselves and others. It offers us incredible opportunities to grow.

When we realize that we, like our students and colleagues, are afraid, we can begin to interact with students from a place of compassion, a compassion for self and a compassion for others. Fear is usually amplified around the education of students who have been labeled E/BD or segregated in special programs.

The sad thing is that we rarely talk about fear when we talk about inclusion. We talk about different models, methods, and procedures. Rather than acknowledging our feelings, we act tough, resistant, professional, and official. Fear is acted out as thinly disguised bravado on both sides, students and teachers. Ignoring and repressing fears keeps them from being addressed and keeps people entrenched in defensive positions, pushing away those who threaten their safety. Exclusion and separation allow those involved to maintain their limited and limiting beliefs about others and themselves. We owe it to our students to address our own fears and to help them address theirs, rather than shield ourselves from the real sources of separation that exist inside of and between us.

NEGOTIATING INCLUSIVE SPACES

Inclusion is a way of life, a way of thinking put into action. It involves a conscious commitment to creating authentic democratic communities where diversity in all its wonderful, fascinating, and confusing forms is valued. It is not only about educating students with disabilities with their nondisabled peers to the greatest extent possible. It is about living in such a way that we face our fears of diversity and resist the all too human tendency to push away from us those who challenge or scare us.

Living inclusively means being aware and sensitized to exclusion even when it is cloaked in habits we have long accepted as common sense. Living inclusively means listening to our students when they complain that they are not being treated fairly, when they are feeling excluded. It means trying to see what they see, from their angle. Living inclusively means being awake and aware of the ways in which our school contexts and community construct various types of human diversity. Living inclusively means working toward educational aims that teach us about our connection with others, that celebrate difference rather than repress it.

The general education classroom is not the only place where inclusion can take place. We need to have our eyes open to the whole school context, looking for places that students desire to be and working with them to dislodge obstacles to their access. Inclusion is a process of creating new interpersonal connections. If it is really going to affect the kinds of social and personal transformation its proponents envision, we need to approach it in thoughtful and conscientious ways.

We need to look carefully at and evaluate the general education environments in which inclusion might take place. Many different factors and forces in individuals, schools, and communities affect this process. Institutional cultures, administrative styles, parental involvement and power, and the community in which the school resides all play important roles in determining the level of openness for inclusive community.

Inclusion involves very different things in different districts and schools. To make a broad statement of how it should proceed and what it should look like without looking at the context in which it takes place involves a naïve view of educational change. The resources available, the relative opportunities offered in special and general education, the nature of the teachers and students involved, and the overall institutional culture must be taken into consideration. Then, inclusion must be tailored to that place, with those people, in ways that genuinely benefit students.

On the practical level, inclusion involves negotiations with students and teachers to arrange new ways of interacting, relating, and learning together. In the following story, we will explore 2 years of negotiating for inclusive spaces in a public high school. This story is based on the experiences of Smith (second author) and Perez (co-author of Chapter 11).

We (Smith and Perez) came to work for Lincoln High School as a team. We were hired to teach in the new S.E.D. (Severely Emotionally Disturbed) Units at Lincoln. It was a school of mixed socioeconomic status and race, and it had never had an S.E.D. program before. All of the students in the new S.E.D. program had been educated in separate schools (called centers) for much of their educational history. In conjunction with the strong national push toward inclusion, the district decided to shut down the S.E.D. center schools. However, the students were still referred to as "center-based" students and were simply moved to the outskirts of public schools. For the most part, the schools housed the S.E.D. students as far away from the main school buildings as possible. The S.E.D. classes were held in specially designed prefabricated "portables," each with its own bathroom and time-out room. The students' breakfast and lunch were served to them in their classrooms. Initially, they were not allowed to come into any part of the school, not the library, cafeteria, or even the bathrooms.

The year we began teaching at Lincoln was the first year many of our students attended school in a neighborhood school. The students felt their own alienation, their own "otherness" in a way they had not felt at the center school. They felt conspicuous as they rode up on their special buses with only 10 or 12 students in each. They felt conspicuous as they were met by their teachers and escorted to their classrooms on the margins of the school. They felt conspicuous as the carts rolled up to the door with their food on it, the only classes in the entire high school that ate meals in the classrooms. They felt conspicuous when students from the general education classes came into our rooms bringing a note from the office or to visit one of the students. At least in their separate school, they had not felt so marked out and visible.

At first, they were terrified and deeply embarrassed. They put their heads down and turned their faces away when someone came in the door. They ran into the portables when no one was looking and sat outside the back door where no one could see them. They did not sit on the side of the portable that faced the school building. They felt exposed and naked in their labels of damnation. They spoke about this often, lamenting that they did not have access to the wide range of classes offered to other students.

Inclusion in that school was a three-way process. One part of the process involved negotiating with the school administration to get the students full access to the school. That was a gradual though steady process that involved a lot of dialogue. It usually moved forward, but sometimes hit snags. We approached administrators about our students being allowed to go to lunch, unattended, like all of the other students in the school. We agreed to take a few weeks to get to know the students better before we determined, together with the students, if they could handle that much freedom. They were used to schools that were run like prisons, and they had their own fears. We also agreed with administrators that if students had difficulties at unsupervised lunch, we would confine them to their classroom for lunch for a specific number of days as a consequence for their behavior. So we had a plan, it was agreed upon, and the students were given access to the school cafeteria.

The second part of the process involved working with the students in order to help them feel ready for more participation. So many of the students were both extremely eager to be included in various aspects of high school life and deeply afraid. Their ambivalence was palpable. One student who had complained the loudest about the initial total segregation of the S.E.D. students rarely ventured out of the classroom. As various roadblocks were removed, he had to come to terms with his own fears. Before that, he could believe the only thing holding him back was the school.

We talked to students about the responsibility that came with inclusion and always made sure that our classrooms were available to retreat to when they felt like they needed to calm down or needed someone to talk to. We worked hard at establishing classroom communities that the students came to value very much. Once they had access to the cafeteria at lunchtime, they often would go find friends from their neighborhoods and bring them back to our classroom for lunch. Through this process, many students became familiar with our classrooms at lunch, and they became the "hang out" of many general education students. Rather quickly, we became a high-status class in the eyes of many students.

Overall, our students did very well at lunch and in other areas of the school. They gained access to the library, were allowed to walk freely through school before the first bell rang in the morning rather than be escorted by their teachers from the buses, and were allowed to go in the halls between classes like all of the other students in the school. These changes occurred over a pretty brief period of time. The more administrators and other teachers saw our students around school, mixing in with other students, the less they feared them. The more our students saw themselves as part of the school, the more confidence they began to have in themselves. As they began to see their friends migrate toward our classroom and relax there with us, they began to feel less stigmatized. They stopped caring about getting on their special education buses as they began to feel like a legitimate part of the school, being just who they were.

The third part of the inclusion process occurred naturally out of these initial negotiations. As the students began to feel comfortable within our classroom and the school, they began to want to be included in general education classes. Because our classroom sat right on the physical education (P.E.) field, many of our students would sit longingly watching the P.E. classes. Unfortunately, with our small classes, P.E. did not include some of the same activities. The coach who worked with our students mostly had them play basketball. They would watch out the window and see P.E. classes playing tennis, football, soccer, baseball, and track and field. As they began to voice their feelings of being denied these opportunities, we began to talk with them about joining those classes. Once again, we were back as a team, negotiating with administrators. According to the district rules, center-based students did not have access to general education classes in their first year on a general education campus. Our administrators made an exception to the rule.

We encouraged our students to take general education classes, and several of them jumped at the opportunity. Some never wanted any general education classes, and we respected their wishes, although we worked with them to understand their reasoning and their fears. The third phase of our inclusion process involved beginning to get to know the teachers in the school and looking for good matches for our students. We began to realize, for instance, through dialogue with various coaches, that there were some coaches who liked working with our kids and others who didn't. Once we established lines of communication and learned from the various interactions our students had in their classes, we began to schedule students into classes where we felt they'd have the best chance. We also offered support to their teachers. The most important ingredient was an agreement that if the student or teacher was having difficulty, that without question or recrimination, either one of them could initiate the student coming back to our class for that period. This allowed for a level of safety, of control, for both students and teachers that definitely took some of the pressure off the process. We had ongoing dialogues.

There are many different places for students to be both included and excluded. The general education classroom is one place. School clubs, sports teams, the cafeteria and library, and even the special education classroom are other sites of inclusion. We need to work with our students, colleagues, and ourselves right where we are.

As teachers, we worked to support what the students wanted. It was a fluid, interactive process that involved much dialogue and negotiation. Working inclusively at Lincoln often meant confronting our own fears. We had to learn to let go of our students who ventured more and more into general education classes. We had to let go of our desire to protect them. In some ways, we dealt with similar issues that parents deal with as they begin to see that their children don't need them so much anymore. Often, special education teachers pride themselves on working with the "difficult" kids. When we see other teachers do it, we feel less special. These are normal human emotions and need to be addressed so that we don't sabotage our students' best interests.

In addition, working toward authentic inclusion within the school involved each of us moving beyond our own comfort zone. It meant cultivating respectful relationships with administrators, classroom teachers, and even cafeteria workers. It meant listening to our students and acknowledging the legitimacy of their feelings, and then working with them to continuously work toward opening up access to the school community. It required all of us to take chances. Sometimes, students were unable or unwilling to comply with the requirements of a specific class or opportunity. We had to deal with feelings of embarrassment and betrayal. We had to learn that things would not always work the way we wanted them to. This had to be seen as part of the process and not as a failure on anyone's part. We also needed to deal with our own anger when we felt our students were not being given the opportunities they deserved. We had to learn to keep calm and not rupture the relationships we were establishing with others in the school.

One of the things this work has done is that it taught us to be patient. Like any social change agenda, things often seemed to move very slowly. We'd work for weeks on getting the kids access to the cafeteria, assuming that once that door was opened, they'd have access to the library as well. Then we'd find ourselves answering the same questions once again and worry that we were up against a mind-set that was unchanging. However, when we looked back over the course of 2 years, the change in our students' position within the school and access to the majority of its programs was dramatic. We all learned and grew a lot.

THE IMPORTANCE OF PEER RELATIONSHIPS IN THE INCLUSION PROCESS

Peer relationships are an incredibly important aspect of inclusion for students. When they are included in a general education classroom, students with special education labels are surrounded by other students. The relationships that are established are critical for effective inclusion. Many troubling students have difficulty with peer relationships, whereas others do well with their peers at the expense of relationships with their teachers. It is important to attend to this dimension of inclusion.

The social worlds of students must be taken into account in inclusive practices. To send an adolescent student into a general education high school class with a one-on-one aide might both embarrass the student and further alienate him or her from peers. In situations like this, students may use their tried-and-true method of getting out of situations in which they don't feel comfortable: They may disrupt the situation until they are removed. It is much more advisable to collaborate with students on the types of supports they believe they need and want, or they will confound our best intentions time and again.

Sometimes, especially with younger students, teachers may pair an included student with a general education student as a coach or support in helping them be included. In the following story, we tell the story of one such arrangement. After that, we will describe the Circle of Friends approach, a process for gathering a community of ongoing support for an included student. Each of these approaches views relationships between peers as central to successful inclusion.

SAM AND MRS. FORD TEACH US ABOUT SUCCESSFUL INCLUSION

This is the story of Mrs. Ford and Sam, a third-grade teacher and a boy considered a "behavior problem" whom she struggled to successfully include in her mainstream class. This teacher believed strongly in the value of human diversity in the classroom community (Lipsky & Gartner, 1989). Her instructional methods and teaching style can be described as caring pedagogy and whole language literacy instruction based in a constructivist educational philosophy.

A blonde, buzz-haired, third-grade boy named Sam entered Blanton Elementary School in early November. He was placed into a third-grade general education class where he had two teachers, one in the morning and the other in the afternoon. Mrs. Ford taught math, science, health, and social studies in the morning, and Mrs. Blue taught reading/language arts during the afternoon.

Mrs. Ford learned of her new student through the school records clerk, who warned her, "He'll be a handful. He came from California, where he was in a special class for hyper children." Records showed that Sam had been schooled in a pull-out program for students with Attention Deficit Hyperactivity Disorder (ADHD) and Emotional/Behavioral Disorder (E/BD). He received the medication Ritalin for his ADHD. At Blanton Elementary, he was assigned to the general education classrooms of Mrs. Ford and Mrs. Blue. The school records described Sam's home environment as chaotic; he had moved frequently and attended many schools.

In the first 2 weeks, Mrs. Ford and Mrs. Blue both noticed Sam doing a variety of deviant and bizarre behaviors. He climbed up on tables and leaped to the ground in flying helicopter twirls. His other dramatic activity was nose-picking, a boyish, gross-out display done in such a public and celebratory way as to disgust his peers. Also, throughout the day, especially when he was anxious or bored, he chewed on the fabric of his shirts, leaving them with big wet spots and holes showing through to his chest. If one were to capture Sam's mood in a single word, one would have to say "anxious." He hummed with anxiety and skirted the periphery of social connections with others, apparently drawn to his peers and fearful of them at the same time.

Sam's peer relationships were marked by his verbal and physical provocation of the other children. He seemed to form no genuinely caring friendships with the other students. His social identity appeared to revolve around a continuous dance of dramatic provocation resulting in the peer responses of laughter; teasing; and, ultimately, social avoidance. He wandered the edge of the social core of the classroom, poking fun from the outside, making it ever clear that he was living on the margins of the group.

Mrs. Ford described her relationship with Sam as similarly "gamey." It lacked the demeaning nature of the students' interplay with Sam while engaging his provocative spirit on a more strategic, intellectual level. He seemed to understand that the challenge of alluring and enticing a teacher could require a greater subtlety and wit. He often left his desk to hide under tables in the remote corners of the room, his eyes and ears tuned closely to his teacher as he rested in his distant bunker. When Mrs. Ford gave him directions to return to his seat, he would smile and adjust his hiding place. If she ignored his wandering, he would move to a new spot, perhaps barricading himself behind a pile of boxes, watching her eyes to see if she saw his move.

Sam did not fare equally in his mornings with Mrs. Ford and his afternoons with Mrs. Blue. He struggled academically in each class, but he found more conflict and disciplinary trouble in his afternoon reading/language arts lessons with Mrs. Blue. During the months of November and December, he was sent to the main office for disciplinary action six times by Mrs. Blue, leading to four suspensions for violent and disobedient behavior. It was clear that Sam acted out much more in the afternoon class. It was clear that this boy who seemed so uncomfortable in school felt more comfortable and at home with Mrs. Ford than with Mrs. Blue.

Mrs. Ford had a theory about all this that she had developed by spending time with Sam in her class and by talking to Mrs. Blue about how she dealt with Sam in her class. In Mrs. Ford's mind, there were two specific reasons for the dramatic difference in Sam's behavior from morning to afternoon:

- Sam's idiosyncratic but strong bond with Mrs. Ford, his morning teacher
- Sam's strong conflict with the basal-based literacy instruction provided by Mrs. Blue

The literacy activities provided by Mrs. Blue centered on basal readers and written assignments in the accompanying workbooks. The curriculum was highly programmed and teacher-directed, offering little choice of activities and little opportunity for a creative boy to express himself or find himself meaningfully in language. To Sam, conformity to this type of dry program was all but impossible. He was often off-task, goofing around, seeking colors and interest in a curriculum that seemed dull and gray. Although his noted area of academic strength demonstrated in achievement testing was in reading/language arts, he refused to do many assignments given by Mrs. Blue.

Mrs. Ford often had close, personal discussions with Sam about his struggles and his feelings. He expressed to her his strong distaste for the basal-based program. In Mrs. Ford's words:

> I don't think he was rebelling against authority as much as against things that had no meaning. If it wasn't relevant to him, he wouldn't do it. Basal reading and workbooks didn't mean anything to him. Why should he do it?

Mrs. Ford viewed Sam as an adamantly self-directed learner who demanded that his learning activities be personally meaningful. In one sense, he was a disruptive, bizarre, acting-out student who refused to follow directions and conform to acceptable standards of appropriate behavior. That would be a fairly typical way of viewing him. In another light, he was a creative, dynamic, inquisitive child who had a strong desire to connect with a supportive adult and a fierce instinct for learning in his own way. Mrs. Ford decided to trust the latter depiction, assuming competence rather than deficit. She advocated for the creation of a general education program to address the needs of that passionate, self-directed learner.

In response to the repeated suspensions and to Sam's spoken feelings about the basal curriculum, Mrs. Ford approached Sam, Mrs. Blue, Sam's mother, and the school principal with a proposal to switch the youngster to a full-day program in Mrs. Ford's classroom. The four met to discuss this idea. Under this plan, Sam would remain in class with Mrs. Ford for the entire day, and she would be responsible for guiding Sam through his literacy activities. All agreed, and the new program was started in February.

Over much time and dialogue, Sam and Mrs. Ford developed a shared philosophy concerning his education, a way of doing things that stressed hands-on, relevant activities in which Sam found salient meaning. This philosophy was based on three premises:

- Sam enjoys hands-on activities.
- Sam must be able to find personal meaning in an activity.
- Sam should have an active role in choosing his educational activities.

Mrs. Ford and Sam created a literacy program with a daily routine for Sam to follow in a self-directed manner. His daily routine included a dialogue journal in which Sam and Mrs. Ford carried on a personal correspondence in words and illustrations. Additionally, Sam worked on self-selected reading. Sam chose to read "chapter books"—children's literature that not only was more advanced and complex than the traditional basals, but also carried immense personal meaning to Sam. During and after completion of each chapter book, he completed oral and written comprehension and creative writing activities. The third component of his new literacy curriculum was a spelling and vocabulary program in which Sam chose words to learn from his chapter book.

The last component of the literacy curriculum developed by Sam and Mrs. Ford was the expansion of creative writing to include all aspects of book writing, editing, illustration, and publishing. Sam wrote on self-chosen topics that included witty stories, science fiction, and many gory tales perhaps reminiscent of a young Edgar Allan Poe. It should be noted that in order to make the writing of stories meaningful to Sam, he was allowed and encouraged by Mrs. Ford to write about whatever topics he chose to explore. This opened the door for Sam to write some very sad and disturbing stories, including one about his own suicide.

As he wrote this story over a week's time, Mrs. Ford kept up daily conversations with Sam about the story, his life, and his feelings. She was very frightened that a third-grade boy would write about killing himself. Gradually, Mrs. Ford's fears for Sam's immediate safety were allayed, and the personal meaning of the story became evident. Sam explained to her that it wasn't Sam who was killed in the story but only a part of Sam—the "dumb" part. Now that he was doing well in school under the new arrangements, he felt that the dumb part had died and gone away. Sam described the suicide story as a tale of loss and personal growth.

With this change in curriculum and placement, Sam's grades improved markedly. Mrs. Ford approached Sam with two areas of behavioral concern (Sam had already cut out the helicopter twirling). Sam had two habits that garnered him much negative attention from peers: picking his nose and eating the front of his shirt. Mrs. Ford and Sam met one day during lunch. Mrs. Ford expressed her concern with these two specific areas and asked Sam if he wanted help in changing them. At first, he said that he didn't. He said that he liked picking his nose and eating his shirt. Mrs. Ford backed off, telling Sam that if he ever wanted help in working on these areas, he could ask her and she would help him. Two days later, Sam approached his teacher and said, "My mom says I'm running out of shirts." The teacher and student then discussed a plan to deal with both the nose picking and the shirt chewing.

"One idea I have is that we get somebody in the room, one of your classmates, to help you out. What do you think of that?" Mrs. Ford asked.

"OK," Sam replied, squirming nervously in his seat.

"Who would you want to help you out? Who's your favorite?"

"Cesar," Sam selected.

"Great. What do you like about Cesar?" Mrs. Ford asked.

"He's a good kickball player," said Sam.

"That he is," agreed Mrs. Ford. An interesting choice, she thought to herself. Cesar is one of the most popular boys in the class, but he also seemed to have a wild streak in him. Mrs. Ford saw Cesar as "Sam at his best," a child who seemed to survive great emotional struggles in order to somehow maintain himself successfully in school.

The teacher and the two boys met to figure out how Cesar could help Sam. It was important to Sam that nobody know that somebody was helping him. The boys created a secret code word ("touchdown" initially, and other words later) that would be whispered by Cesar whenever he observed Sam picking his nose or eating his shirt. Sam and Mrs. Ford met at the end of each day to evaluate the day.

After 7 weeks of peer monitoring, Cesar approached Mrs. Ford and said, "Sam doesn't need me anymore." Sam had completely stopped both behaviors. The behaviors were not observed for the duration of the school year. As Sam let go of the annoying behavior, he was more readily accepted by peers as part of the class. He still did not befriend the other students, but the social distance between him and the others decreased significantly.

How would Mrs. Ford describe her approach to teaching? Her philosophy and practices exemplify a caring pedagogy that she describes in terms of three basic ideas.

1. *Relationships among children and teachers are of primary importance in the learning community.* Relationships are not seen as secondary to the completion of instructional activities, or vice versa. Human connection and learning are intertwined and complementary processes.

2. *Instances of student misbehavior are understood and addressed within the context of the teacher-student relationship that mutually values each person.* When a student behaves in odd or disruptive ways, she asks herself: "What is going on with this student? How does this child feel? How does this look from his or her eyes? What can I do to help this student feel more comfortable and able? What can I do to improve the relationships with myself and with the peers that support this student?" The focus is on communication and relationship.

3. *Understandings of student learning, behavior, and social life are not interpreted through theories of human deficit and pathology.* The student is seen as an equal and able partner, a co-constructor of the teacher-student relationship. Student behaviors that the teacher does not comprehend or support are not seen as signs of deficit or disability. The child's emotional and instructional needs are addressed within the classroom web of relationships, the connection between the teacher and student, and the teacher's efforts to arrange for social support and individual emotional comfort.

Additionally, we note that Mrs. Ford's approach to including Sam roughly fits what inclusive educators call a "peer intervention" or "peer buddy" (Thousand, Villa, & Nevin, 1994, p. 406). Creating an inclusive classroom or school community cannot rely completely on teachers and their bags of tricks. School communities are made up primarily of children. Enlisting this student majority in the activities of building and maintaining community bonds is essential. Peer interventions occur when teachers take leadership roles in arranging for students to befriend, tutor, support, or advocate for a peer.

CIRCLE OF FRIENDS: ARRANGING FOR SOCIAL SUPPORT NETWORKS

The Circle of Friends approach is a way of planning for and cultivating social support networks in general education classes for students with cognitive disabilities (Forest & Lusthaus, 1989). Researchers and educators in the field of E/BD within the United States have tended to ignore this approach. On the other hand, our British colleagues have used this approach with tremendous success (Newton, Taylor, & Wilson, 1996).

The basic idea of Circle of Friends is that difficult behaviors are indications of weaknesses in social systems, in networks of relationships between people. Improving behavior requires improvements in the comfort, satisfaction, and level of emotional support that children experience in their relationships in the classroom. An excellent way to deal with the behavior of a student who acts in odd or disruptive ways in the general class is to directly address the need for more and better relationships between the individual and classmates.

Often, the problems of behavior and relationship operate in a self-perpetuating cycle. A student who wanders strangely away from the group during a class lesson, who pushes his books on the floor in a moment of frustration, or who curses at peers who won't do what she wants is not behaving in a way that initiates and builds friendships. Such a student is likely to be rejected by classmates and viewed as crazy, strange, or mean. Rejection by one's peers only brings about feelings of anger and sadness on the part of the individual. Often, the rejected youth will then lash out in more dramatic ways, unfortunately furthering the very rejection and isolation that hurts so much.

Newton et al. (1996) have done extensive work in using the Circle of Friends process to build social support networks that counteract this cycle. They have used this approach with students from preschool age to adolescence. They describe these students as "pupils with severe emotional and behavioral difficulties where other approaches have been tried and found to fail" (p. 45). They have much to teach us about doing the Circle of Friends for purposes of including troubling students. As you read through the process below, note that the student must be included in the general class for a period of time *prior to* this process so that classmates will know the individual well. For that reason, this is an ideal way of keeping students with difficult behavior in the general class in the first place rather than excluding them to a separate classroom.

Before initiating the Circle, we must be sure that a key teacher or other adult understands and is committed to managing and guiding the process. This person will facilitate an initial planning meeting with classmates, lead weekly meetings with the Circle of Friends, and troubleshoot as problems come up along the way. It is helpful if this person is an outsider rather than the general classroom teacher.

First, the facilitator must meet with the child who is the focus of the process (whom we'll awkwardly call the "focus child") and the child's parents in order to explain the entire process. Both the parents and the student must understand

and accept the approach. It is crucial that the child completely accept and support the process. This must be done *with* the student rather than *to* him or her.

Next, the Circle facilitator meets with the general education class (including the teacher) for about an hour. The focus child is not present for this discussion. It is important for the facilitator to gain an agreement from the students that what is said at the meeting is confidential and not to be shared outside. Also, it is helpful to acknowledge that talking about a person without that person being present is generally not respectful. In this case, we have the focus student's permission to do so. This information helps the students feel more at ease with the proceedings.

The purpose of the initial class meeting is to discuss the behavior of the focus child and ways that the classmates can help that child. The end result of this meeting is the creation of a group of six to eight volunteers who will serve as the Circle of Friends and provide day-to-day emotional support for the focus child. First, the facilitator asks the students to tell the positives—what the child does well and what they enjoy about the child. These are written up on the board for all to see. Second, the group is asked to make a list of things that are difficult about this child, what he or she does that they find troubling or problematic. Newton et al. (1996) note that classmates often hesitate at this point. Although they have feelings and ideas, they have often been taught not to openly say negative things about a peer. They may need to be encouraged with a reminder that the purpose of the meeting is to figure out ways of helping this student. Honesty about problems and difficulties is vital to being helpful.

Next, the facilitator engages the students in an examination of the role and necessity of friendships in their own lives. A visual representation of the circles of friendship is a useful aid in explaining this to children. The individual sits at the center of the picture. The innermost circle consists of the most intimate loved ones, such as parents and other family members. The second circle consists of friends—those who most enrich the individual's life. The third circle is acquaintances, who are people we know and with whom we interact but are not very close to. The outermost circle consists of people who are paid to be in the individual's life, such as teachers and doctors.

As the facilitator goes through an explanation of the rings of relationship, it is helpful to have the students completing their own representations of the rings in their own lives on a sheet of paper. Filling in the levels within their own lives makes this activity more personally meaningful and brings greater depth to the children's understanding of the emotional necessity of social relationships. Newton et al. (1996) advise that the emphasis in this activity should be on the quality, not the quantity, of relationships in each circle, on the way that these relationships make us feel instead of the total tally.

The next step is crucial to the process. The purpose is

> to elicit empathetic feeling in the group towards those who have very few people in their lives. The group is asked how they would feel if their second and third circles were empty and that all they had in their life

were immediate family and paid people. This is a powerful part of the session and a rich range of responses is always forthcoming. . . . Lonely . . . Bored . . . Unhappy . . . Embarrassed . . . Sad. (Newton et al., 1996, p. 43)

The facilitator then asks the students how they might behave if they felt all of these painful, difficult feelings. Newton et al. (1996) explain that this is often the "turning point in this whole class meeting" (p. 43). Frequently, students notice that the list of behaviors that they generate at this point bears great similarity to the list that they generated earlier describing the common behaviors of the focus child. It is common for older students to make this connection in an "a-ha!" kind of breakthrough in awareness. For younger students, the facilitator often must ask the children if there is any similarity. This moment brings the students to realize that with greater circles of friendship and support in the life of the focus child, much of the difficult behavior would be unnecessary or unlikely.

After the students have gained this vital insight, the next task is to make a list of ways that the group might be able to help the focus child. Supposing that classmates were to fill roles in the second and third rings for the focus child, what might they do to help him or her? This is the beginning of the ongoing, problem-solving process that the actual Circle of Friends will continue in weekly meetings.

Finally, the group brainstorms about what it might do that is not helpful to the child. This step of the process helps students gain an awareness of ways of behaving and interacting that are nonsupportive and rejecting. These are the things we don't want to do.

The class meeting concludes with a request from the facilitator for volunteers to be part of the Circle of Friends. The facilitator takes down all of the names. Typically, after a successful meeting, far more than the needed six or eight students volunteer. It is emphasized that only six or eight students will be selected because a group larger than that is too big to meet and work productively. It is explained that even those who are not official members of the Circle can play important roles in befriending and supporting the focus student.

Newton et al. (1996) have used a variety of methods of selecting the final Circle of Friends group, from random selection to having the classroom teacher choose from among the names. No single system is best. But these researchers advise against selecting the most well-behaved or compliant students in the class. It is important to have some students in the Circle who engage in behaviors that adults find deviant or difficult. These students often have an ability to understand the focus child, appreciate his or her situation, and contribute wisely to the Circle meetings.

The Circle itself consists of the focus child and the six to eight selected students. It meets once every week for 30–40 minutes from this point on. The original facilitator or other qualified adult leads the group in generating ways of being supportive and helpful. As with any group meeting of this nature, the group should initially produce a short list of ground rules governing the group meetings. Also, they must understand and agree to confidentiality. During the first session, the group should also give itself a name that does not include the student's name. This helps foster a sense of identity and purpose.

The group time each week is often filled with discussions of problem-solving tactics, what the student needs from his or her peers, and the actual ways that students can be supportive to the focus child. This occurs within discussions of specific instances that occurred in the past week—times when the focus child might have benefited from some help and times when classmates were actually helpful. Both the focus child and the other Circle members are able to make useful contributions to this discussion.

It is helpful to talk about both the difficult or negative experiences and the positive or satisfying experiences in the past week. When students tell about difficult experiences, such as times when the focus child behaved in ways that provoked a peer's feelings of anger, fear, or sadness, the leader should help that student express those feelings. It is important for the group members to learn the connection between actions and feelings. This occurs in two ways, in terms of how one child's behavior affects the feelings of another child and in terms of how one child's own feelings are often demonstrated in his or her actions. The central message throughout this discussion is that feelings are always natural and acceptable, whereas behavior involves choices and decisions. We do not control our feelings, but we do control our actions.

Newton et al. (1996) describe six reasons why they have found this approach to be highly successful. They conclude that

1. children gain much from the additional attention focused on them;

2. children feel more accepted and liked and this affects their behavior radically;

3. other children can be much more effective interventionists than adults. Children are more likely to take notice of each other and change their behavior as a result;

4. peer group pressure and encouragement to change is as powerful with individual group children as it is with adult groups, perhaps more so;

5. providing a framework for problem-solving, support and active intervention is the ideal way of enhancing and mobilizing a small community's impact on one of its individuals;

6. honest and open discussion with children about an individual's pain, about isolation and the lack of friends combined with the difficulties adults face in dealing with certain behavior, encourages empathy and provides a model for healthier relationships in the classroom and beyond. (p. 47)

Both the Circle of Friends and the story of Mrs. Ford and Sam direct our attention to the quality of relationships between individuals in the classroom, particularly the connections between students. Inclusion in this sense is an active process of negotiating, discussing, arranging, encouraging, and cultivating relationships that individuals who might otherwise be excluded experience as supportive and helpful. Our goal is the promotion of social support that eases tensions, resolves conflicts, creates new bonds, and helps troubling students find greater acceptance and caring in the classroom.

TIPS FOR TEACHERS

1. If you are a general education teacher, check early in the year to see if you have any labeled students included in your classes. Take the initiative to meet the student, the special educators responsible for the student's individual education plan (IEP), and the student's parents in order to express your commitment to collaborating in the student's best interest.

2. If you hear students teasing or speaking in derogatory terms about students with disabilities, address the issue directly. However, remember that fear is often the underlying cause, and rather than punish or shame the offenders, help students work past their fears and mistaken beliefs.

3. Include stories, curricula, and writing assignments about various types of disabilities in your classes, and help students critically investigate images of people with disabilities in the media.

SUMMARY

In this chapter, we have looked closely at the complex issues involved with inclusion of students with difficult behavior. We have examined the democratic ideal of John Dewey to understand why inclusion is an important social goal. We have attempted to make visible some of the important obstacles to effective inclusion, focusing in particular on the psychological and social dynamics of fear. When we acknowledge and discuss our own fears, we are more able to be compassionate and supportive to students who behave in deviant or disruptive ways.

Given the complexities of inclusion with troubling students, we believe any easy formula would only work with some students, in some places, at some times. What we have tried to accomplish in this chapter is to alert readers to the many social and emotional factors that affect inclusion efforts. We prefer to look at inclusion as an ongoing process of negotiation and relationship that is particular to each classroom and school.

We think it is important to recognize and acknowledge the attitudes and beliefs that are prevalent in schools in relationship to troubling students. When teachers, administrators, or students resist moves toward inclusion, we must address the fears that fuel that resistance. If inclusion is imposed on people, rather than negotiated with people, fears are often increased, and resistance and exclusion can continue to occur even if labeled students are physically included in general education classes. At every turn in the road, communication and negotiation are the keys to dissolving fear and opening new doors.

CONSTRUCTING PERSONAL MEANINGS

1. Write an autobiographical story about a time when you felt fear or anxiety in interacting with a person whom you found different, odd, confusing, and challenging. Often, these personal stories have to do with issues of human difference, whether physical or cultural. Reflect on how you felt and thought about this person. Look closely at your own biases and prejudices.

2. Write an autobiographical account of a time in your life when you felt rejected and cast aside. How did you feel? What were your thoughts? What did you do?

3. Interview students considered E/BD (or other labels) to find out how they feel and think about being included and being excluded. Talk to a variety of students in order to access the perspectives of those who have spent much time in general education and those who know little of general education settings.

4. Interview general education teachers to understand their thoughts and feelings about including students considered E/BD (or other labels). Talk to a variety of teachers to gain different perspectives.

11

Honoring and Developing Ourselves as Teachers

Teaching, like any truly human activity, emerges from one's inwardness, for better or worse. As I teach, I project the condition of my soul onto my students, my subject, and our way of being together. The entanglements I experience in the classroom are often no more or less than the convolutions of my inner life. Viewed from this angle, teaching holds a mirror to the soul. If I am willing to look in that mirror and not run from what I see, I have a chance to gain self-knowledge—and knowing myself is as crucial to good teaching as knowing my students and my subject. (Palmer, 1998, p. 2)

Throughout this text, we have focused on the importance of caring for, knowing, and honoring the students with whom we work. This final chapter is about caring for, knowing, and honoring ourselves as teachers. It's about learning how to care for ourselves, renew ourselves, and forgive ourselves for not being able to solve all the difficulties of our students' and our own lives. It is about finding ways to recognize, clarify, and learn from the struggles we face in our teaching.

Working with troubled and troubling students can elicit a range of strong emotions in teachers in relationship to the system, our selves, or our students. It is our hope that by addressing the social, emotional, and political complexities of teaching, we will help teachers navigate the often perilous waters involved. We know that it is possible to love this work, to learn continuously, and to experience an intense fullness. However, challenges and constraints are often inherent in working with troubling students and must be addressed head-on. Sadly, the emotional life of the teacher has not been given much notice in teacher education or in schools, and teachers are often taken by surprise by the intense emotions teaching evokes.

In this chapter, we will examine some of the possible tensions in teachers' roles. We will explore the cyclical nature of teacher development, using the life/death/rebirth cycle as a metaphor. We will delve into social and psychological reasons why troubling students often evoke intense emotions in teachers and administrators. Understanding helps us become less judgmental. We will also address ways that teachers can renew and sustain themselves. We'll explore the ways that support networks, mentors, and engaging in teacher research can help promote teacher growth. We'll end the chapter by looking at the possibilities teaching holds for transforming not only our students' lives, but our own, in a process that is as alive and vital as anything we've ever known.

CONFRONTING AND NEGOTIATING TEACHER ROLES AND IDENTITIES

We do not create our own role definitions, and they are rarely articulated. Much of what we interpret as aspects of our teaching role evolves from our own experience as students with teachers in our past and present. Confronting our roles as teachers—the sometimes unconscious, and almost always unquestioned, assumptions about how we should act with students and what we are responsible for—involves looking back at our own experiences with teachers and schooling. Tompkins (1996) describes the difficulty and profundity of this type of reflection. She describes how experiments with her teaching prompted her to reflect on her past experiences with teachers.

> Some alterations in the way I taught led to greater self-consciousness about what I was doing in the classroom. This prompted me to look back into my own past as a student, to relive the school days of my childhood. As I experimented more boldly in my teaching, and delved further into the past, my inner life began to be transformed. Remembering the past was not, as I had originally thought, just an attempt to see how I had been molded as a teacher by the teachers who had molded me; it was an exploratory mission into the depths of my formation as a person, and it put me in touch for the first time with the founding experiences of my life. (p. xvi)

Tompkins came to the difficult conclusion that in spite of school preparing her for a career in academia, it also had "stunted and misshaped" her life. She began to realize that a deep insecurity had been instilled in her as a young child who became obsessed with perfection, with pleasing the teacher, with never making a mistake. She struggled with the emerging realization that school had not been a healthy place for her as a child and that it might not be the fundamentally good experience she had always assumed. She writes:

> School was my life; it was the world. It simply never occurred to me that it might not be good at bottom. But finally it did occur to me. The early memories woke me up to who I was—a terrified performer—and to what school had been about—obeying rules. And I gained a new perspective on the fear I felt later on as an adult experimenting in my own classroom. (p. xvii)

Tompkins traces the impact that being a "good" student had on her own development as a person and a teacher. She chronicles her own transformation as she begins to re-envision her role as a teacher, to re-think and re-create the parameters of her relationships with students and subject matter. Moving beyond the unspoken and, in some ways, unconscious definitions of teachers' roles involves questioning aspects of teaching that have long traditions. Such questioning leads one to question the assumption that the harsh realities of schooling are always for "our own good." Such questioning is necessary if we are going to renegotiate and redefine our roles. This is not easy, but roads leading to greater freedom never are.

Tompkins's reflections led her to realize that schooling, for her, involved "obeying rules" and becoming a "terrified performer." She describes the unrecognized pain this caused her and how she, in turn, perpetuated this process with her own students. She speaks as someone who discovers that her own compliance came at an incredible price and that she, in her role as teacher, exacted this same price from her students. As an overachiever, as someone driven to excel at schooling, as someone who attended Ivy League universities, she is astounded by her difficult discovery that schooling, at its bottom, is about obedience.

In programs and classes for troubling students and resistant students, the fact that, at bottom, schooling is about obedience is often blatant. It screams from the angry expressions of students who are restrained in classrooms; hauled into time-out rooms; controlled through point and level systems; and, in some settings, heavily tranquilized with medications (Knitzer, 1990). It can also whisper softly through the walls of schools that have good reputations for orderliness and discipline. Tompkins embarked on a careful journey, slowly and thoughtfully examining her past for clues to her emerging dissatisfaction with her role and experience as a teacher. In many schools, teachers are confronted daily with the painful underlying assumptions that Tompkins had to so carefully dig up from the recesses of her psyche. Whether they are looking for it or not, ready for it or not, willing to recognize it or not, many teachers daily face the realization that obedience is what schooling is about, and finding ways to instill obedience in students is an expectation in their roles. Coming to terms with this realization and transcending the constraints embedded in our roles are major components of learning to love our work. Doing so requires honest self-exploration and a willingness to let old patterns and beliefs die. This is never done once and for all, but is a part of a cyclical process of deep personal learning.

THE LIFE, DEATH, AND REBIRTH CYCLE OF E/BD TEACHING

> The life/death/life nature is a cycle of animation, development, decline and death that is always followed by reanimation. This cycle affects all physical life and all facets of psychological life. Everything—the sun, novas, and the moon, as well as the affairs of humans and those of the tiniest creatures, like cells and atoms—has this fluttering, then faltering, then fluttering again. (Estes, 1992, pp. 130–131)

Often, when educators speak about teacher development, they describe a linear path. We would like to propose a more cyclical journey, one that mirrors the cycle we find in nature: the life/death/rebirth cycle. In our own experiences, we have found that learning—personal, social, formal, and informal—is more often like a spiral. A spiral contains both a cyclical dimension and a certain kind of linearity, for even while a spiral circles, it ultimately moves in a direction. It is this intersection of linear time and cyclical time that we see in the passing of each year. The year is composed of seasons that cycle again and again, whereas the year itself is gone forever once it has passed.

THE LIFE WE BRING TO OUR CLASSROOMS

In reflecting on the lives of teachers and what might be needed to sustain us in the challenging work, the life/death/rebirth cycle seems an apt metaphor. The life we bring to teaching has already had its seasons. We have learned from our experiences in life, from what we have been exposed to. When we come to teaching, we come armed with theories, experiences, and methods. Some of these have been taught to us explicitly in teacher education classes; some of our learning has come from life and from being students. Some of our learning comes from our culture, family, and the media. The life we bring to the classroom mirrors our own culture in many ways. It is full of unspoken assumptions, unquestioned family and cultural beliefs and values.

The lives teachers and students carry with them into the classroom are often informed by very different experiences, in many cases because of differences in race and social class. Teachers often need to learn that our own experiences and norms do not represent some unquestioned, privileged truth. When teachers are confronted with students' realities that are very different from our own, we can either garner our forces to try to make students comply with our own and the school's expectations, or we can open ourselves up to learn from the students about their lives. This kind of learning can be very frightening, because it may mean critical reflection on our selves, our systems, our training, our families, our cultures, and our own experiences as students. Parker Palmer (1998) explains this fear:

> We collaborate with the structures of separation because they promise to protect us against one of the deepest fears at the heart of being human— the fear of having a live encounter with alien "otherness," whether the other is a student, a colleague, a subject, or a self-dissenting voice within. We fear encounters in which the other is free to be itself, to speak its own truth, to tell us what we may not wish to hear. We want those encounters on our own terms, so we can control the outcomes, so they will not threaten our view of world and self. (p. 37)

Teachers often enter the classroom unaware of the ways in which our beliefs, cultures, training, social class, gender, sexual orientation, and experiences affect how we view and interact with students. Until these deeply personal aspects of ourselves are challenged, we may not even be aware of their prominence in our lives or the ways they have become institutionalized into our educational systems. The following reflection written by Smith (in press) reflects her own state of unknowing as she entered the classroom for the first time:

> Although my heart raced with fear and anticipation as the students whose lives I had hopes of transforming began to saunter into my classroom, I stilled those fears with the knowledge that I knew what I needed to know to teach them.
>
> But there were so many things I did not know, things I had no way of knowing on that fine August morning. I didn't know that the very "knowledge" I had thought would see me through, was actually a lens I was seeing through. I didn't know that that knowledge would often create barriers between my students and me. I didn't know that my white working-class background separated me from my students in ways that were invisible, yet pervasive. I didn't know I had entered into a war zone in which knowledge and worldview were coveted resources that were protected and defended. I didn't know I would defect and join sides with my students. I didn't know how feared or despised my students would be within the school, nor did I know I would be feared and despised by my association with them. I didn't know that *my life* would be transformed by my relationships with my students and by my experiences as a teacher. I didn't know how much I'd cry, nor how much I'd laugh or love. There were whole worlds of things I didn't know, and didn't know I didn't know. (pp. 103-104)

DYING A THOUSAND DEATHS

The life we bring to teaching—its beliefs and assumptions—will certainly be tried and tested in our work with children. Some of our beliefs and assumptions might need to die in order for new beliefs and assumptions to emerge. This can be a scary and painful process. Even many of the theories and methods we learned in our own teacher education may not survive our first year. We may feel angry when we realize teaching is not nearly as simple as we have been taught. We may also have to deal with the insecure feeling of not knowing exactly what to do in some situations, and this is particularly frightening because we are, by virtue of being teachers, always supposed to know what to do.

Often, the first year in the classroom or the first year in a different school brings out things in teachers we never knew existed. Coming to terms with many of the realities of our own lives, our students' lives, and the realities of the systems in which we work is often experienced as a series of disappointments or small deaths. For new teachers, this can feel overwhelming. It is easy to see how teachers might easily move toward trying to "manage" behaviors and "structure" the school environment in order to gain some semblance of control. Often, it is not just the outer world of the classroom we are struggling to gain command of, but our inner worlds as well.

The first year or two in a teacher's career are particularly intense. It is like suddenly and unexpectedly entering into another world. It is a world where we have been conferred with the role of teacher and given a systemically supported and sanctioned position of authority in our classrooms. We are often expected to teach students who question the authority of the system and the sacredness of its norms. If we do not learn to question ourselves, our systems, our traditions, our training, and our practices, then we may perpetuate the cultural imperialism embedded in our systems, educational training, and popular culture.

Smith, in her personal journal, describes the social/personal learning in which she engaged as a new teacher:

> As the realities of my students' lives began to come into focus, some of the realities of my own did as well. The racism, classism, sexism, and ableism which had been invisible in my own life, family, community, school and media began to become apparent. I found myself questioning the use of derogatory terms, especially by my family and friends. I remember arguing with one of my friends when he made the statement that I was wasting my time trying to teach them "niggers," "spics," and "criminals." I tried to explain to him that once you got to know the kids they were wonderful. He saw them and theirs as the source of the country's problems. He thought they should be locked up. He felt I coddled them. I told him I thought the hatred and ignorance he was expressing was the source of the country's problems. The argument that ensued got very ugly and angry. We never worked things out and did not remain friends.

I confronted limiting beliefs in myself on a daily basis. When I looked back on my first year teaching I could see that I had feared the kids, thought they were very limited intellectually, and felt an aversion to them on a deep, unconscious level. I can remember punishing students for speaking Spanish in class, telling them this was America, and we spoke English here. I can remember thinking many of the kids were physically ugly at first only to see them later as beautiful. I can remember mistaking students' dialects and limited English skills as indicative of low intelligence. I can remember thinking their parents, some of whom had become cherished friends, were low-lives who didn't love their children.

These are difficult life lessons. If we are changed by our experiences with students we may not fit so easily into our families and cultural groups. We may find friends, other teachers, and even family members speaking disparagingly about the students we have come to love. Beyond this, we may begin to see the theories and methods we have been taught in our own teacher education classes and within our school cultures as limited or even harmful. As we begin to get to know our students' life stories and understand the contexts in which they live, it becomes much less certain whether it is right to try to coerce them to conform to a school culture in which they are not afforded respect nor dignity. As we begin to allow our students to teach us about themselves and the logic of their behaviors, it becomes much less appealing to think of these students in terms of derogatory labels.

In all of these personal upheavals, myriad emotions can be felt. In this very process of coming to terms with the realities of others' lives, with the constraints of the "system," our own histories, and the limitations of many educational theories and methods in relationship to marginalized students, we can find a thread that connects us to our students. If we are willing to be changed by our experiences in our classrooms, we can ask students to join us in this exploration.

Unless we have experienced many of the things our students have experienced, it is difficult to understand their "behaviors." When we begin to let go of some of our notions of what it means to be a student, a teacher, and a "normal" person, we can allow our students to become our best teachers. We need to stop thinking we have the answers to "fix" them and realize they have a tremendous amount to teach us. This is much more vulnerable than being an "expert" or a behavioral "technician." However, once we begin to let go of some of the "life" we bring to the classroom, once we begin to let parts of ourselves "die," we can pave the way for an entirely different sort of classroom, where not only our students, but our "selves" can be transformed by our experiences. This is risky business, but as Kohl (1994) describes, it is essential to good teaching:

Risk taking is at the heart of teaching well. That means that teachers will have to not-learn the ways of loyalty to the system and to speak out, as the traditional African American song goes, for the concept that everyone has a right to the tree of life. We must give up looking at resistant students as failures and instead turn a critical eye toward this wealthy society and the schools it supports. (p. 32)

Without disillusionment, without confronting hard truths about social oppression, inside and outside of schools, it is difficult to break through and find ways to engage with students in struggles toward solutions.

THE REBIRTH STAGE: MOVING FROM DISILLUSIONMENT TO HOPE

The rebirth part of this cycle involves teachers who are no longer naive about power, the controlling nature of schooling, and the unacknowledged social and political roles schooling plays. This involves shifting from an authoritative, expert stance to learning with and from our students, their parents, other teachers, and administrators. Something incredible can happen when teachers begin to learn from and with our students. An authentic learning community can be born in our classrooms.

Once we let go of those beliefs that separate us from respecting and authentically interacting with our students, we have the opportunity to be changed in a process of deeply meaningful learning.

Kohl (1994) describes what was necessary for him to move to the "rebirth" stage of the teaching cycle. He describes his own process as one of learning to "maladjust" to the system. This is an interesting twist, because the children who maladjust are often the ones who end up with labels.

I had to maladjust myself to the notion that the demands and structure of schooling were normal and the students were problems if they did not adjust. This meant examining the nature of the life I was supposed to live as a teacher and sorting out what was sensible and beneficial to my students from procedures meant simply to keep them under control. It meant learning to recognize practices or texts that were racist or sexist, as well as coming to understand the mechanisms for tolerating professional incompetence and for marginalizing children who are outspoken or different. This had to be done while I was figuring out how to teach well, and I had to be creative about it if I wanted to keep my job.

For me an understanding of the need for creative maladjustment is not a rejection of public education, but an affirmation of its possibilities. (pp. 133–134)

Kohl is certainly not the only teacher-author who has come to this conclusion. One teacher autobiography after another echoes this very theme. From Sylvia Ashton-Warner's (1963) classic *Teacher* to the more recent works by LouAnne Johnson (1993, 1995) on which the movie *Dangerous Minds* was based, we see that teachers who are changed by the experiences of their marginalized students often find themselves at odds with the dictates of the system. It is then that we begin to recognize our own marginalized status, with the understanding that if we are not to lose hope in the possibilities of education, we must maladjust to the dictates of a system that has often gone awry.

Although this is not without its risks, neither is the opposite path. Teachers who blindly follow the constraints of a curriculum of control never clear the space for new life in the classroom. Rather, they find themselves engaged in an impossible task: attempting to control other human beings. We believe that teachers who enter into blind compliance with a system of control often leave the field because they spend much of their days facing the resistance of students. They wear down, burn out, and move on to other careers. Or, perhaps worse, they remain teachers for long careers of bitterness and rigidity.

Teacher autobiographies allow us to see that it is possible for teachers to find ways to work with children who are alive, vibrant, and worth the struggles it takes to get beyond the curriculum of control, beyond the objective of managing others. Ashton-Warner (1963) describes her journey. It is certainly one that has its cycles of disillusionment. But she tells of something else, the "wide and happy fields," and this is what new teachers need to be able to imagine.

> You've got to be either brave or desperate to take this road, even though in the end it leads to wide and happy fields. And I'm not brave. But I've got to the wide and happy fields. I'm all too aware that they are noisy fields, since my teacher's mind has been set by the past into the tradition of silence. But they are the only fields that I can trust or believe in, I being so simple—and even if the price is professional isolation and inerasible, inescapable and corrosive guilt, here we stay. (p. 91)

Ashton-Warner's story is one of transcendence, of moving beyond the curriculum of control. Yet she is still haunted by the "tradition of silence" into which she was socialized. She stories life in the classroom "with the lid off" and gives us a vision of an educational experience bursting with life. She also stories her loneliness and poor evaluations by the headmaster, who holds to traditional values of silence and discipline. But she has found something more compelling than a high evaluation on a misguided evaluation. She has found what she calls the organic life of the classroom.

> Yet, I'm a disciplinarian. It's just that I like the lid off. I like seeing what's there. I like unpredictability and gaiety and interesting people, however small, and funny things happening and wild things happening and sweet, and everything that life is, uncovered. I hate covers of any kind.

I like the true form of living, even in school, I'm in love with the organic shape. (p. 93)

Once teachers begin to realize and recognize some of the obstacles (both internal and external) to teaching well, they can either become overwhelmed and "burn out," or they can begin to understand how really important this work is. For the teachers who find the "wide and happy fields," like those about which Ashton-Warner speaks, they have connected with something incredibly alive and well worth the struggles. The obstacles, the many children who are harmed in the name of education, and the simplistic and often cruel ways children who are suffering are treated in schools become the fuel for teachers who want to work toward change—their own, their students', and the systems'.

SPIRALING UPWARD

Once we have experienced the seasons a few times, we can begin to anticipate the continuous change that life brings. This is also true of the deep, transformational processes that are possible in teaching. This process is never done once and for all. After all, at its base, this cycle describes the learning process. We bring a life to the classroom that is full of what we have learned from the world. So do our students. As we learn together, much of what we brought with us is challenged, and some of it dies away. In its wake, we come to new understandings and possibilities. We have learned.

The joy of teaching for someone who loves learning is that the possibilities of our own and our students' transformations is endless. We become much more adept at recognizing when our beliefs are being challenged, and we begin to trust the process. We know, after living through a number of winters, that spring will come and new life with it. It is these insights that come with time, that allow us to begin to flow with the cycles of learning in the classroom, the small deaths, the new lives.

Teaching marginalized students requires teachers to unlearn much of what they have learned in and about education. Students who resist us and the systems we are supposed to represent evoke deep learning in us. They draw us out. They challenge us to reflect on our own meanings. The opportunity this affords us for personal learning is incredible. The possibilities for personal and educational change rest in embracing the life/death/rebirth nature of teaching. Conflict, uncertainty, fear, anger, pain, and all of the other so-called negative emotions are an important part of the learning process. When we experience these emotions or observe them in our students, we will not run so quickly to repress them or avoid them. If we can engage in this type of authentic learning, we can encourage it in our students.

Once we recognize and embrace the life/death/rebirth cycle of teaching, we will still need to find ways to survive the winters, the storms, and the droughts. The second half of this chapter speaks to practical ways to sustain ourselves in this challenging but very worthwhile vocation.

CREATING AND RECREATING BALANCE IN OUR TEACHER LIVES

Teaching, even in the best of situations, is an emotionally, physically, spiritually, and intellectually demanding job. It is important for teachers to find ways to replenish themselves. If part of how we envision our work with students involves helping them to find healthy and peaceful ways of being in the world, it is important that we can do the same. A teacher who is emotionally wrung dry, who is not in touch with nor at peace with his or her own emotions, will not be able to help students find their own calm place. Likewise, a teacher who does not nurture his or her own love of learning will have a hard time imparting enthusiasm to students about the adventure of ideas.

If we envision teaching and learning as a process of relationship that occurs between whole people, then who we are and how we are as people is perhaps the most crucial ingredient in effective teaching. However, this is not to say that teachers should be superhuman and live perfect lives. Actually, the unspoken image of the "saintly" teacher, the perfect person who never gets angry or sad, or ever dislikes anyone, works against honest reflection on our work with children. If we are going to learn to love and accept our students for who they are, we must do the same for ourselves. What this requires is openness to the process of learning, a willingness to reflect, to learn from ourselves as well as others, and a means to continue to move and grow, rather than get stuck when we come upon obstacles, fears, and difficulties.

Taking care of ourselves is a prerequisite for caring for students. If we envision ourselves as physical, spiritual, emotional, social, and intellectual beings and recognize that we take all of who we are into the classroom, replenishing ourselves involves attending to these many dimensions of our lives. In the remainder of this chapter, we will examine these dimensions. We will discuss ways to work toward achieving a healthy balance, even in the midst of a challenging career.

NURTURING OUR PHYSICAL SELVES

We begin with a very brief mention of taking care of our physical selves. There is a tremendous amount of literature on this subject, and we don't pretend to be authorities. However, teaching can be a stressful endeavor. One way to release the stress is through physical exercise, whether that means a walk in the park, working out at the gym, yoga, tennis, or jogging. When we feel stressed, it is sometimes easier to have a glass or two of wine at the end of the day than to take a walk. Teachers must be careful to attend to their stress in healthy ways, or they run the risk of developing habits that only add to their stress. Exercise and proper diet are important factors in maintaining physical and emotional health. This is particularly important for people who are in professions that elicit a lot of strong emotion, but offer little in the way of physical activity or outlet.

In times of stress, our need for physical release increases, but often these are the times we feel overwhelmed and stuck. Exercise can help us move both physically and psychologically. If we are used to making connections between our bodies and our feelings, we can help students do the same. It is possible to incorporate physical activity in the daily routine of the classroom as well. Sitting for long hours in classrooms is an unnatural practice for students and teachers. Taking a walk or jog around the PE field at the end of a class when tensions are building can work wonders for students and teachers. Relaxation techniques can also be employed in the classroom. Stress that gets built up in our bodies can make us sick and angry. Movement is often curtailed in schools, and finding ways to transcend this limitation can only help us and our students to live more balanced, healthy lives.

NURTURING OUR SPIRITUAL SELVES

Spirituality is a difficult concept to write and talk about in relationship to educational practice because we have rarely found a way to talk about spirituality that doesn't offend some group in some way. And yet, in spite of this taboo, a focus on spiritual dimensions of education have begun to make their way into educational literature (Elkind, 1998; Palmer, 1998). What we refer to as spirituality involves a wide range of beliefs and practices that involve the deeper mysteries of life and death.

What we want to acknowledge is that many teachers have spiritual beliefs and engage in spiritual practices, either alone or in community, and these beliefs and practices affect their view of teaching and learning, moral development, and ideas about discipline. Often, spiritual beliefs and practices bring hope, peace, and comfort to those who embrace them. Working with children who are living difficult and sometimes painful lives can lead us to deeper questions than our university training prepares us for. How, for instance, does one deal with the death of a student? How does one make sense of the abuse some of our students have endured? How do we deal with the pain some students bring into the classroom? The following story involves one of Smith's spiritual lessons in relationship to her teaching.

Learning the Importance of Life in the Classroom

Billy saw his father beaten to death with a baseball bat when he was 10. There was a deep sadness in this boy's eyes, and a deep anger and violence that erupted over and over again in his behavior. By the age of 13, he had been convicted of 23 felonies. His mother was going through her own grieving and was quite immersed in drugs and alcohol. Billy pushed everyone away. In my work with him over a 3-year period, slowly, and with a good deal of testing, conflict, regression, and persistence, we bonded. He came to trust me, and he began to attend school regularly and excel academically. A loving child often peeked out at me from behind his hardened exterior. He often made me little presents and played like a small child in the class. I watched Billy relax and be a kid. I watched him learn and produce beautiful writing and artwork. In my eyes, his transformation was a "miracle" of sorts, a resurrection of an innocent child within a life so brutalized that the child had hidden away for safety.

In spite of his remarkable progress in the world of our classroom, Billy was involved in other worlds that did not go away just because he settled down in ours. He was in a street gang, and in spite of his incredible progress in school, he continued to place himself in very dangerous situations. Often, he participated in violent, antisocial acts.

I wrote in my journal during my second year teaching him that I thought Billy flirted with death, each time trying to prove he wasn't a coward. I believed that Billy blamed himself for not preventing his father's death. He had hidden behind the couch when his father was murdered and somehow, in his child's mind, believed he should have been able to save his dad. This deep shame and guilt played out over and over as Billy tried to prove he wasn't afraid. He set up situations where he had the power to kill, trying to come to terms with what he had experienced. The situations escalated, and his daring became more and more dangerous. He'd pick fights with a group of boys rather than one. He fired BBs into a school bus. He hurt and killed small animals.

Dealing with the range of emotions evoked in me in relationship to Billy was difficult. Most teachers were afraid of him. In their fear, they pushed him away, and in their anger, they punished him. His school career was a long record of suspensions, detentions, loss of privileges, and physical restraints. This fueled his anger and his pain. His cruelty to small animals sent chills through my body. I had to constantly remember what he had experienced, his own feelings of helplessness and anger. I had to learn to love Billy as he was— sometimes, a brutal child. I drew on my own spiritual beliefs that healing rather than punishment held the potential to help Billy come to terms with his grief and anger.

By age 15, Billy was sentenced to the most restrictive juvenile program available in the state. He was released when he was 16, having mastered the levels and demonstrated all the behaviors the program required. Billy returned to his street life immediately. A year later, he was shot in the heart in a gang-related incident. I deeply loved this child. His death came right before the beginning of a new school year. The sadness I felt at his passing was paralyzing for me at first. I struggled with the possibility of teaching again. How could I? Billy was a child with whom I felt I had been incredibly successful. I felt sure, if asked, that he would name me as the best teacher he'd ever had and maybe the best friend. I had watched him come to trust me and settle down in the classroom. I had watched him take great pride in his learning, rewriting his assignments for neatness, decorating them with cartoon figures, putting them up on the bulletin board. We had talked through difficult times, found ways to negotiate power in the classroom. What did it matter? Where was he now? These were not questions with scientific answers.

No longer living in Billy's hometown, I missed the funeral. A week later, I took the trip to sit by his grave. I must have sat there for 3 or 4 hours crying, thinking, praying in my way, and talking to Billy in my mind. During those hours, I had some insights that brought me some peace and allowed me to continue teaching. Why Billy's life had been so full of sadness, I did not know. Why it ended at the age of 17, I did not know. Why so many children suffer, I did not know. But what I did know was that for 3 years when I was his middle school teacher, Billy knew he was loved. I knew that 3 out of his short 17 years on this earth were spent in a classroom community that he loved and cherished. I know that Billy had fun, felt loved, learned a tremendous amount, and felt a part of our family. I knew when I sat at Billy's grave that the time he spent in our classroom was some of the happiest, safest, and most cherished moments of his life. I know, because Billy told me this in letters when he was incarcerated, and he told it to me in his willingness to trust me and to honor our classroom agreements. I know because I lived it with Billy. I saw it in his smiling eyes, in the gifts he gave me, in the ways he settled down with his classmates, and in the love and joy he brought to that place.

As I sat at Billy's grave, I thought about the spoken and unspoken logic in education that what we do in the classroom prepares children for the future. Often, extreme punishments are justified by saying, "This is how it is in the real world, and if kids don't learn now, the lessons will be harder in the future." I thought about how cruel education can be, because we don't look at the time in the classroom as being important in its own right, as being a rich experience of life, rather than a separate training ground for life. In the midst of my sadness, I realized that rather than question what else I could have done to save Billy, those golden moments we had shared made up a large portion of his short life. They were important moments for themselves, right then, right there. I had been socialized in my educational training and in school culture to discourage kids from having fun in school, from laughing and joking and playing. But I loved those aspects of learning, loved how healing and hearty they were, and so did the kids. Sitting at Billy's grave, I felt a deep peace with how I worked with kids, with the fun we had, with the importance I placed on community and relationship. What Billy's death taught me was to cherish the life that spontaneously bursts forth in classrooms.

Spiritual Insights

The insights gained at Billy's grave were spiritual. They evolved out of questions not only of the meaning of teaching, but of the meaning of life. Reading inspirational writing or engaging in spiritual practice or exploration may help some of us deal with the deep questions in our work. Teachers often encounter situations that rock us to the core. We may need to draw on our deepest sources to help us be the best teachers we can be. Our spiritual practices are as diverse as we are and are often a source of strength and kindness.

NURTURING OUR INTELLECTUAL SELVES

Nearly everything we ever live or learn affects who we are as teachers. Our formal education and professional training are, collectively, only one source of meaning we bring to our work. One way for teachers to nurture their intellectual selves is to be active, lifelong learners. Formal education should be only a starting point for a teacher's learning. Once graduated, we can choose what we read and seek out the types of texts that are alive for us. Broadening our scope to read broadly in the social sciences in relationship to our areas of interest allows for an expansion of interpretive frames, as does reading good literature, and arts. Continuing to learn from a variety of sources helps us move beyond the narrow scope of professional training and begin to consider the complex communities of schools and classrooms from wider and more diverse perspectives.

Learning About Students and Schooling From the Social Sciences

Anthropologists and sociologists offer very different conceptual frames for understanding marginalized students. For example, Harry Wolcott (1994), an educational anthropologist, has written some pieces about a young man named Brad, whom he discovered living in a hut that Wolcott had constructed on a remote area of his property. Through writing about and offering interpretations of Brad's life, Wolcott questions the educational and social service systems that offer him close to nothing. Wolcott does not address Brad through a series of deficit theories, as educators are sometimes prone to do, but through a more relational scheme. He is amazed at the resourcefulness, seeming honesty, and personal code of values by which Brad lives and through which he interprets the world. He does not romanticize the portrait of Brad but fills it with the complexity and contradictions that real lives are full of.

Wolcott (1994) has written another piece, based on his field study in a Kwakiutl village in British Columbia, Canada, called "The Teacher as Enemy." This piece unravels the unspoken belief that teachers are held in high regard by all students and their families. Wolcott writes his way into those unspoken beliefs by using descriptions of the resistance the "native" children have toward him and anything he teaches. He looks beyond the context of the classroom at the history and politics of the community, the legacy of white supremacy and domination of the native peoples, and concludes that teachers would be much less surprised, hurt, and angered by the resistance and anger of marginalized students if we'd only realize that, in some ways, we may be perceived as "enemies." Although this may seem like a very contrary piece, it is actually hopeful because once underlying power relationships are identified by the teacher, they can be both acknowledged and addressed. Nonrecognition leads to a stalemate and, often, the assumption that resistance in students is pathology rather than logical and legitimate political struggle.

Reading books by psychologists, physiologists, educators, counselors, political theorists, feminists, cultural theorists, philosophers, and writers of fiction can help us expand our notions of students and schooling. They can prevent us from becoming too narrow in our approaches to students and to our roles as teachers. They can help us to make connections between our work with students and larger social, emotional, and political realities. This broadening of perspective gives us richer, deeper wells from which to draw than if we define our work within the constraints of one "field."

Teacher Autobiographies

There is a wonderful collection of teacher autobiographies that can be read to connect with the fullness of teachers' lives. Some examples of excellent autobiographical writing are Sylvia Ashton-Warner's *Teacher* (1963); George Dennison's *The Lives of Children* (1969); Torey Hayden's *One Child* (1980), *Somebody Else's Kids* (1981), and *The Tiger's Child* (1995); LouAnne Johnson's *Girls at the Back of the Class* (1993) and *My Posse Don't Do Homework* (1995); Herb Kohl's *36 Children* (1968), *I Won't Learn From You, and Other Thoughts on Creative Maladjustment* (1994), and *The Discipline of Hope: Learning From a Lifetime of Teaching* (2000); and Vivian Paley's *White Teacher* (1979), *The Boy Who Would Be a Helicopter* (1991), and *Kwanzaa and Me: A Teacher's Story* (1995). Teacher autobiographies offer an extremely rich source of inspiration and insight into real, complex worlds of teaching. We experience and live our roles as teachers through whole, dimensional lives. Reading about education only through books that focus on theory and methods leaves many important aspects of *being* a teacher unaddressed, unrecognized, and unnamed. Teacher autobiographies look at school through the complexity of a life, and so the social, emotional, political, and relational aspects of schooling can be included naturally.

Teacher autobiographies allow us to confront the moral dilemmas of our own teaching in relationship to the teachers whose stories we read. Sylvia Ashton-Warner's classic autobiography *Teacher* is still as pertinent today as it was in the 1960s when she wrote it. The issues she identifies are issues teachers still face daily. Smith (in press) has written a critical auto-ethnography highlighting her experiences as a teacher for students labeled E/BD. She focuses on both the world inside of her head and the world of schools. She makes many of the tensions in E/BD teaching visible as she addresses issues of power, theory, and pedagogy.

Torey Hayden's books show us the inner struggles of a caring teacher as she negotiates her relationships with students, families, and administrators. We can read about her triumphs and her discouragements and identify with her. In the process, we gain insight into how these teacher authors resolve or learn to live with the major tensions in their lives in schools, and we benefit from their wisdom and experience. In a very real sense, these teacher authors become mentors to the teachers who read their books.

Engaging in Teacher Research as a Means of Having Voice and Bringing Change

Teachers who base their work on critical constructivist values and principles and work with marginalized students may run into opposition with administrators or other teachers (Zaragoza & Scardina, 1998). It may take a while for others to see the benefits of a constructivist approach. When teachers are silenced and don't find ways to break that silence, we can become angry and hopeless. For our own sanity, we need to work diligently at having our voices heard within the schools in which we work, and we need to explore the process with our students as well. Writing our interpretation of schooling and sharing our versions with others are powerful ways to have voice, even in the most oppressive settings. Writing our stories is a very powerful form of teacher research—one that can break through the myths that hold us hostage.

We spoke about journaling in Chapter 8. Here, we would simply like to add that teacher journals are a powerful data source for teacher research. Writing down our experiences, values, beliefs, insights, questions, joys, and fears allows us to look back on them and then to carefully construct stories that help others understand our teaching and learning within a real context, from within a real life.

In our university teacher education classes, we encourage our students to write about their experiences in classrooms and to carefully look at their own stories as a means of reflective practice. Often, the teachers with whom we work are amazed at how healing the process of writing their stories becomes. Sharing stories with other teachers, students, parents, and administrators allows us to begin dialogues about our work with others. Beyond that, writing our stories helps us to know them and to clarify what we think, feel, believe, hope for, and fear.

Engaging in teacher research allows teachers who are working for school change to have a voice even when they are silenced within school doors. It allows feelings, ideas, and interpretations to flow through us, rather than get stuck. It allows us to feel the power of the pen, of the story, of telling how we view schooling and all it entails. It allows us to transcend the narrow confines of our roles, which often include an unspoken assumption that we will defer to authority even when we don't agree.

NURTURING OUR SOCIAL AND EMOTIONAL SELVES

Nurturing our social and emotional selves is critical for teachers. Our work is very demanding. The students with whom we work have a lot of energy, a lot of emotion, and, often, many emotional needs. Teaching can be an emotionally exhausting experience if we do not build effective support networks. These networks can take different forms. Creating and nurturing friendships with co-teachers and other colleagues allows us to build supports and establish allies. Finding mentors is invaluable. Beyond our own schools, we can often develop friendships and informal supports with teachers we meet at conferences, workshops, and college courses. Teachers may also meet in various groups to discuss work-related issues in our lives. This may evolve out of our work contexts or from other sources. There are also Internet communities of teachers. And finally, there are times when a counselor or psychologist might be a necessary and helpful source of support. We will discuss these various options below.

Developing Rich Collegial Friendships

Collaborative Teaching

Often, teaching is seen as solitary work. However, in many cases, teachers co-teach, work with another teacher in an inclusive classroom or as a teaching assistant, and collaborate with other professions in the classroom. It is very important that we nurture our relationships with the people with whom we work most directly. Developing respectful relationships and open, honest communication can make our lives so much easier and richer. When we work effectively as a team, we benefit from two people's insights, working styles, and talents. We also have someone with whom to talk about our work. We limit the supportive possibilities of our collaboration if we consciously or unconsciously discount the perspectives and insights others bring to the classroom. The possibilities for support, creativity, reflective dialogue, and teamwork in collaborative teaching are incredible. So are the possibilities for feeling silenced and disrespected.

Many teachers have been socialized to work alone, and collaborative work requires different types of communication and people skills. We need to consciously develop these relationships by having dialogues about roles, responsibilities, methods, and values. Dialogue allows for negotiation and understanding. If the school day does not afford us an opportunity to talk with our colleagues as much as we would like, scheduling time outside of school to have coffee to get to know one another, to plan, or to work through some difficulties is a good idea and well worth the investment.

Administrators

Nurturing our relationships with administrators is extremely important. Because administrators hold more power in the system than teachers do, they can be a powerful detriment or a powerful source of support for teachers. Troubling students often have a knack for continued involvement with administrators, and so, more often than not, teachers who work with these students find themselves interacting with administrators on a regular basis. When teachers and administrators don't see eye to eye, or at least don't deal constructively with that difference of opinion, teachers and students can lose out.

The opportunity for our relationships with administrators to become adversarial, whether overtly or covertly, is constant. It is easy to become discouraged and to communicate less rather than more. However, this tactic will never bring change, but leave us feeling hurt and angry. Beyond this, our students suffer when we have adversarial relationships with administrators. Setting appointments with administrators to talk about our work with students, to develop plans for working together, and to learn about and negotiate how our students fit into the overall culture of the school is a very good idea.

Sharing insights about our students or the impact of a school policy on their education can help administrators gain the benefits of our close relationships with students. This sharing can happen in dialogue, through sharing narratives or stories we've written, through sharing research or books we've found useful, or through sharing students' work or writing. It is important that we learn to be advocates for ourselves and our students in the larger school community. Working respectfully with administrators is one of the best ways to do this. Often, administrators bring a lot of experience to their position. There are times when they can be excellent mentors and guides. No matter what the case, purposeful and respectful communication enhances the possibilities of our working well together.

The Broader Community of Teachers

When we teach graduate courses in education, we share in the opportunity to participate in a dialogue among teachers around issues, experiences, and theories. This is almost always interesting and educative. Both the similarities and the differences in perspective and experience are illuminating. These conversations allow teachers to locate themselves within a broader community. They can compare their experiences with others, finding out if what they are experiencing is common or not, and learning about how other teachers navigate the various challenges and opportunities that teaching brings. Teachers share resources in class, ideas, advice, and, at times, heartaches.

Personal friendships among teachers that extend beyond the school doors can provide support, comfort, and enjoyment. Sharing our teaching experiences with nonteachers can sometimes become overwhelming for them. There may be too many things that they do not understand. However, another teacher has insider knowledge that allows us to talk more freely and sometimes with more depth. Taking a class or enrolling in a graduate program is one way to find other teachers with whom to talk about our work. Workshops, seminars, and conferences offer other possible arenas in which to talk with teachers. Joining teacher organizations where we can become active in working with others for social change is an excellent way to build community and support. In addition, Internet communities and groups of teachers allow communication across the country and the world. Finding those of like mind and heart allows us to feel less alone in the world and provides opportunities for lasting friendships.

Mentors

The various supports we have discussed thus far involve a mutual and reciprocal type of learning and support. However, there are occasions when we recognize another teacher, administrator, or other person who we believe typifies the type of teacher we would like to become or who otherwise stands out as someone from whom we believe we can learn a lot. When we come across such an individual, we are wise to seek out that person as a mentor. Volunteering or being asked to mentor a less experienced colleague is both an honor and a responsibility. However, most caring teachers/professionals see it as part of their professional and ethical role to mentor others.

Sometimes, first-year teachers are assigned mentors through the school system. At times. these prearranged mentor relationships work very well, and other times, they don't. It is important to have an open mind and heart toward an assigned mentor, but also to recognize when there are sometimes differences in values or philosophies that are too broad to span. Because the expectation in a mentoring role is that the learning is sometimes unilateral, being assigned a mentor whom one does not respect poses a problem. It is important that new teachers actively explore the school for teachers from whom they would like to learn, and pursue these individuals. Keeping one's eyes open for talented educators and seeking them out to learn from them is one of the best ways to continue to develop as a teacher.

Counselors or Psychologists

In many other helping professions, it is recognized that working with individuals who are experiencing social and emotional difficulties is an extremely demanding profession. Clinical psychologists, counselors, and social workers engage in "clinical supervision," where they regularly talk about the impact of their work on themselves. Teachers rarely have this kind of support built in, even when they work with the most troubled students. The lack of clinical support for teachers denies and neglects the inner lives of teachers. Much of this stems from the prevalence of behavioral approaches in education. In a behavioral scheme, a teacher is conceptualized as a technician, and a "professional" distance from students is encouraged. The need for teachers to have clinical supports to help them work through their own social and emotional challenges is not acknowledged. The belief is that once teachers become good technicians, the students will be changed and the struggles in the classroom will be extinguished. It is no surprise that behavioral programs don't focus on supporting teachers' social and emotional needs when they don't focus on students' social and emotional needs either.

However, from a dynamic psychological or counseling perspective, the work of teachers is seen as much more complex. When we enter into close relationships with students who are experiencing a wide range of social and emotional tensions, we cannot help but be affected by their lives and their worlds. Working with students who are sad, angry, withdrawn, confused, and resistant brings up a world of emotions in us. Often, these emotions are tied to our life histories and bring to the surface memories and feelings that may have been repressed. These feelings can surprise us, confuse us, or even shut us down if we do not find ways to work through them. Help from a caring professional can be extremely beneficial.

The work of Alice Miller (1986, 1990, 1997) makes clear the importance of confronting our own hurt and anger in order to work effectively with students. She describes the deeply unconscious beliefs and feelings that are often evoked in adults when they are confronted with angry children. Unless we have confronted the ways our own anger has been silenced and repressed, we may very well insist that students conceal their feelings. We cannot tolerate in others what we cannot tolerate in ourselves. Being a good teacher requires a great deal of personal learning. Coming to know ourselves and finding ways to process and learn from our own emotions are important. We will not be able to help our students in their journeys toward greater joy and emotional health if we are stuck in our own anger, fear, or sadness.

It is natural to go through a whole host of emotions in teaching. At times, it can be overwhelming. Seeking out a professional who can help us navigate these feelings can be a very healthy move. It is important that we find someone whom we respect and who shares similar values in regard to our work. It is important to understand the theoretical background of a counselor or therapist to make sure it is compatible with our own beliefs and values. Plus, it is important to find someone with whom we can speak easily and whom we trust and respect. This may not happen at first, but it is important to continue to seek out professionals until we find someone with whom we work well.

Although we may feel that seeking this kind of help shows some weakness in us, we must remember that this type of support is often built in for other helping professions. We cannot help our students if we are struggling too much ourselves. We owe it to them, as well as to ourselves, to get the type of support we need. In this intense line of work, the support we need may well mean therapeutic support. It is important to honor our inner lives and attend to our hearts if we are going to have the strength and insight to help students do the same.

As critical constructivist teachers, we are often passionate about our work with students and enter our classrooms as whole, authentic people. If teaching is an extension and an enactment of whole selves, then attending to, nurturing, and developing our selves are essential to good teaching.

A Case in Point: Curriculum Research Group

The following portrait of a teacher researcher group shows one instance of a group of teachers coming together to learn and grow together. Smith (second author) is a member of the teacher research group described below, and the account is written from her perspective.

More than 4 years ago, I asked four of the teachers who had been my university students to work with me in a teacher research group. William Rhodes, my mentor and close friend, had developed a constructivist curriculum that needed to be researched and developed further by teachers. I chose four teachers who showed interest and insight into constructivist pedagogy. Rhodes was a member of the group as well. Our work together has taken many forms. The group has met monthly for the past 4 years. We discuss our lives in and out of schools, curriculum, school politics, and the sorrows and joys of teaching. We also read and discuss articles and books. Our meetings often run for several hours, and we never feel like we get to say all we want to say. We have an Internet "classroom" where we post our research journals and respond to one another. We present at conferences, share research with colleagues, and are in the process of writing up our research for publications. We support each other, learn from each other, and care about each other.

On an occasion when Bill Rhodes and I visited one of the teachers' classrooms, I realized that there were four generations of students and teachers in the room. We had a lineage of sorts. In every teacher-student relationship along this lineage was a two-way street. Students were teachers and teachers were students. There was a mutuality based on a constructivist philosophy of education, education that occurs in relationships between whole human beings. It made sense that four generations of constructivist teachers and students would be present in one place. We worked through enduring relationships, and here they were in one room. It was beautiful.

In anticipation of writing this chapter, I asked the teacher research group to talk about what sustained them as teachers. I asked them why they were still enthused and hopeful about their work in education when teachers were dropping like flies in this field. Our dialogue went as follows:

Terry: I'm writing a chapter on teacher renewal. Do you have any thoughts on what sustains you, what allows you to thrive in a field that has so many casualties?

Greg: This group for one. I know I'm not alone. In my school, I feel alone sometimes, like the only one who is seeing things this way. But knowing I'll get to talk with others about what I'm thinking and doing is comforting. I also read things to renew me. Books like Tatum's (1997) *Why Are All of the Black Kids Sitting Together in the Cafeteria?*, ethnographies like *There are No Children Here* (Kotlowitz, 1991), and teacher autobiographies. Your dissertation (autobiography) and other teacher stories were also important. Plus finding mentors, both on the job and in the university. I studied with Bill Ayers at UIC (University of Illinois–Chicago), I researched him, followed him around. I wanted to learn all I could. Plus, writing, doing teacher research. And seeing things work with kids, watching kids change. That is amazing.

Becky: You also have to come to understand the politics of schools. You have to learn when you have to play the game. If we are going to learn to be political agents, we have to be smart about what we do.

Greg: When you first start out, you try to control everything. Then you realize you can't.

Becky: Yes, and there are a lot of emotions to deal with. At first, I thought the kids were so ungrateful and manipulative. I felt like, I do all of this for you, and you don't even care.

Greg: And sometimes it's really hard. Once I found out one of my students at Briarwood killed a couple of people. That was a tough one.

Becky: Yes, you have to come to terms with the limits of our love. That lesson comes early. You have to believe that you do make a difference. You have to believe that. But you also have to know that that may not carry on forever to every single area of their life. So you have to realize that the moment also matters for itself. We don't have the power to save them, but we do have power.

Craig: Yes, it's humbling to realize you are just a person—not a miracle worker.

Becky: The high is in knowing there is a possibility for connecting, for creating a place of belonging for kids who rarely feel like they belong anywhere.

Craig: Yes, we have the power to give them some moments in life.

Greg: In the light of the tragedy, we can look and see that each moment matters. But we can give them more than the moment. We don't know what we give, but it does make a difference later, too. Contradictions, that's what you have to come to terms with. There was one kid who tried to make me hate him. I was sure he hated me. I could see it in his look. Later, another teacher asked him to write a list of the people in his life who had the biggest impact on him. He listed me first. Wow. You never know the impact you have. You never know when you are getting through.

Craig: Yes, you connect with them and bond whether you or they like it or not. They bring you out. They make you see parts of yourself you've never seen.

Becky: That's why some people run. But when you're teaching and it works, that's the high.

Craig: The students do give to us. They reach out.

Greg: Yeah, once the kids pooled their money and bought me a pair of socks. It was the best pair of socks I've ever owned.

Becky: I remember once when I was out for the day. When I came back, there was money in our candy jar. The kids collected it when I was gone for more candy. They did this themselves.

Greg: Or when they have a day off high school and they stop by to see you. Some of last year's students came by, and the security stopped them and wouldn't let them in. I happened to see them and let them know it was OK. You know that you've made a difference when they come back to see you.

This dialogue, like most of our dialogues, was very affirming to me. This group sustains me as a college professor and keeps me grounded in the lives of schools. We are friends and fellow researchers. The group received a Practitioner Research Communication and Mentoring Grant from the Spencer Foundation that supported our work together for 2 years. It allowed us to attend national conferences, communicate with other teacher researchers, and purchase texts and journals that support our work. This grant validated and supported our work; however, we met for 2 years without this support. It has been very helpful, but not necessary.

Any group of teachers can create a teacher research group. There are numerous books and articles on conducting teacher research or support groups. We need to research and honor the whole lives of teachers and students. In order to change this state of affairs, teachers need to begin to tell their stories, to create another kind of research that is grounded in real contexts and real lives. The icing on the cake is that engaging in this kind of research, especially in relationship and collaboration with other teachers, not only helps to work toward meaningful transformation of our teaching, but also our personal transformation as educators and human beings.

WHAT IS POSSIBLE?

Sometimes, one of our university students asks us why someone would enter such a complex and socially, emotionally, and politically charged field. Wouldn't it be easier to work with the well-behaved kids? Wouldn't it be easier to just flow with whatever policies and procedures the school system suggests? After all, this is just a job, isn't it? Who can expect teachers to work so hard on themselves and the systems in which they work, in addition to teaching students? We rarely have to answer this question when it arises. Other teachers do.

Many of the teachers who end up working with troubling kids are very passionate about their work. They come to love their students and want the very best for them. Often, these teachers feel limited by the constraints of the system and by limiting theories that simply try to change students' behaviors rather than help students understand themselves and the worlds in which they live. We see this situation in dire need of change. Working toward social change and greater social justice is important work and, as such, satisfying in a deep, soulful way.

The secret to teacher renewal is not contained in this book. It is in your classrooms, smiling, frowning, laughing, loving, and screaming out at you from the lives of children—children, whose learning and development is your "work." It just so happens that all of them are wonderful, alive, funny, creative, and smart. Some of the students you will teach may initially conceal some of their incredible talents and gifts from you. Your job is to discover them with the child. And this, of course, is not a mechanistic process, but a very human one.

In Chapter 2, we used an ink blot as a metaphor for constructivist pedagogy. We wrote:

> In the process of interpreting an inkblot, there is conscious recognition of our "projection" onto it. We know, in part, that we are making with our mind what we are finding in the blot. Constructivist theories of learning and knowing assume that reality is much like this inkblot; the meaning is not inherent in the "world," but in the interaction between our minds and the "stuff" we project meaning onto.

The meanings we apply to our students' lives are like all other meanings—socially constructed. What we see in them is as much our own making as what is "there." When we see students as problems—disordered, disturbed, delinquent, and disabled—we participate in the construction of their social identity as such. Our seeing is a product of our own socialization, including our professional training. In order to discover the possibilities of each child, we need to have "eyes to see." This may mean learning to see things differently. And this is, after all, the essence of learning.

When we let our students bring their whole selves into the classroom, we must allow for some sadness, anger, and fear. When we accept our students as whole, we accept all the emotions they bring as legitimate, and we provide them opportunities for expression through writing, artwork, conversation, and learning. Students also bring laughter, joy, creativity, passion, and love to our classrooms. They bring their wholeness; everything they need is there. We have to develop a space where kids can grow, develop, express, and simply be. When we do, we, too, are invited into a place of transformation.

It is a great privilege to watch a group of students that is often scared, hurt, and angry begin to settle down, trust, grow, learn, and heal. We have the great opportunity to touch and be touched by students' lives, to learn from our students, and to grow right along with them. Who could ask for a more meaningful, interesting, and fulfilling job? Once we begin to experience the magic of a classroom community, our efforts don't feel like a burden. Challenges are a necessary and important part of the process. For those who take this journey, an incredible adventure in human relationships, ideas, self-discovery, social justice, and creativity awaits. We can think of nothing finer to do with a life.

SUMMARY

In this chapter, we have focused on the lives of teachers. We began by examining teacher development in relationship to the life/death/rebirth metaphor to describe a process of deep, personal learning. We approached teacher development this way in the hope that teachers view the challenges in their work with children as important aspects of transformation, as keys to learning. We particularly want new teachers to understand that they may experience many situations in which they need to let go of what they have learned in life, and some of what they've learned in school, in order to be open and free to learn from their students. This is not an easy process at first, but once we embrace it, we have an opportunity to be transformed along with our students.

In the second half of the chapter, many different ways that teachers might work toward sustaining and renewing themselves as teachers and people were explored, along with suggestions for personal renewal. This may include engaging in exercise, engaging in spiritual training, or engaging in teacher research. It should involve a commitment to lifelong learning and seeking out and developing friendships and collaborations with other teachers. Teachers who attend to their own physical, spiritual, intellectual, and social and emotional needs have a much better chance of remaining in the classroom and supporting their students' learning and growth. Taking care of ourselves, seeking the supports we need, and continuing to actively learn and grow are essential to being a good teacher.

In-Vocation

For those of you who enter this extremely important work, we wish you the greatest joys and fulfillment. We have given you our best advice and insights on how to replenish yourself and balance the demands of being a critical constructivist educator. However, the most important source of renewal comes from students. It begins with the realization that these wise children are our greatest teachers. This insight is essential to constructivist teaching and opens us, as teachers, to the vitality and creative energy of our students. Once we have made this vital connection, we create a space together for learning, growing, and living. There is something sacred that occurs when people learn together in meaningful and authentic ways. The classroom comes alive—children light up when they walk in the door, and there is a sense of adventure and accomplishment. This doesn't happen overnight, but when it does, the great quantities of love and respect we bestow on students begin to come back to us in their smiles, their laughter, and their learning. There is nothing more powerful than this.

References

Abeson, A. (1972). Movement and momentum: Government and the education of hand-icapped children. *Exceptional Children, 39*, 63–66.

Addams, J. (1972). *The spirit of youth and the city streets.* Urbana: University of Illinois Press.

Addams, J. (1981). *Twenty years at Hull-House, with autobiographical notes.* Franklin Center, PA: Franklin Library.

Albom, M. (1997). *Tuesdays with Morrie.* New York: Doubleday.

Anderson, W. T. (1995). Introduction: What's going on here? In W. T. Anderson (Ed.), *The truth about the truth: De-confusing and re-constructing the postmodern world* (pp. 1–11). New York: Penguin Putnam.

Ascher, C. (1988). *Improving the school-home connection for low-income urban parents* (ERIC/CUE Digest Number 41). New York: ERIC Clearinghouse on Urban Education.

Ashton-Warner, S. (1963). *Teacher.* New York: Simon & Schuster.

Ayers, W. (1992). Teachers' stories: Autobiography and inquiry. In E. W. Ross, J. Cornett, & G. McCutcheon (Eds.), *Teacher personal theorizing: Connecting curriculum, practice, theory, and research* (pp. 35–52). Albany: SUNY Press.

Ayers, W. (1998). Forward popular education—Teaching for social justice. In W. Ayers, J. A. Hunt, & T. Quinn (Eds.), *Teaching for social justice.* New York: The New Press and Teachers College Press.

Bailey, D., Buyssee, V., Edmonson, S., & Smith, B. (1992). Creating family-centered services in early intervention: Perceptions of professionals in four states. *Exceptional Children, 58*(4), 298–309.

Baker, H. J., & Traphagen, V. (1935). *The diagnosis and treatment of behavior-problem children.* New York: Macmillan.

Bandura, A., & Walters, R. H. (1963). *Social learning and personality development.* New York: Holt, Rinehart and Winston.

Baritz, L. (1960). *The servants of power: A history of the use of social science in American industry.* Middletown, CT: Wesleyan University Press.

Bauer, A. M., & Shea, T. M. (1985). Parent involvement: The developmental capital of special education. *Techniques, 1*(3), 239–244.

Becher, R. M. (1984). *Parent involvement: A review of research and principles of successful practice.* Washington, DC: National Institute of Education.

Beck, M., & Malley, J. (1998). A pedagogy of belonging. *Reclaiming Children & Youth: Journal of Emotional & Behavioral Problems, 7*(3), 133–137.

Becker, W. C., Peterson, D. R., Hellmer, L. A., Shoemaker, D. J., & Quay, H. C. (1959). Factors in parental behavior and personality as related to problem behavior in children. *Journal of Consulting Psychology, 23,* 107–118.

Beers, C. (1907). *A mind that found itself: An autobiography.* New York: Longmans, Green.

Bennett, W. J. (1995). *The children's book of virtues.* New York: Simon & Schuster.

Bentley, J. E. (1936). *Problem children.* New York: Norton.

Berger, P. L., & Luckmann, T. (1966). *The social construction of reality.* New York: Anchor.

Bettelheim, B. (1967). *The empty fortress: Infantile autism and the birth of the self.* New York: Free Press.

Beyer, L. E. (1992). The personal and the social in education. In E. W. Ross, J. Cornett, & G. McCutcheon (Eds.), *Teacher personal theorizing: Connecting curriculum, practice, theory, and research* (pp. 239–256). Albany: SUNY Press.

Block, A. (1997). *I'm only bleeding: Education as the practice of violence against children.* New York: Peter Lang.

Borgmann, A. (1992). *Crossing the postmodern divide.* Chicago: University of Chicago Press.

Bowles, S., & Gintis, H. (1976). *Schooling in capitalist America: Educational reform and the contradictions of economic life.* New York: Basic Books.

Boykin, A. W. (1983). The academic performance of Afro-American children. In J. T. Spence (Ed.), *Achievement and achievement motives: Psychological and sociological approaches* (pp. 321–371). San Francisco: W. H. Freeman.

Brantlinger, E. A. (1993). *The politics of social class in secondary school: The views of affluent and impoverished youth.* New York: Teachers College Press.

Brendtro, L. K., & Wasmund, W. (1989). The peer culture model. In R. D. Lyman, S. Prentice-Dunn, & S. Gabel (Eds.), *Residential and inpatient treatment of children and adolescents* (pp. 81–96). New York: Plenum.

Bretherton, D. (1996). Nonviolent conflict resolution in children. *Peabody Journal of Education, 71*(3), 111–127.

Brown, D. G. (1972). Behavior modification with children. *Mental Hygiene, 56*(1), 22–30.

Bruner, J. (1986). *Actual minds, possible worlds.* Cambridge, MA: Harvard University Press.

Bunker, B. B., & Rubin, J. Z. (1995). *Conflict, cooperation, & justice: Essays inspired by the work of Morton Deutsch.* San Francisco: Jossey-Bass.

Bursuck, W. D., Harniss, M. K., Epstein, M. H., Polloway, E. A., Jayanthi, M., & Wissinger, L. M. (1999). Solving communication problems about homework: Recommendations of special education teachers. *Learning Disabilities Research & Practice, 14*(3), 149–158.

Canada, G. (1995). *Fist stick knife gun: A personal history of violence in America.* Boston: Beacon Press.

Carrier, J. G. (1983). Masking the social in educational knowledge: The case of learning disability theory. *American Journal of Sociology, 88*(3), 948–974.

Cervone, B. T., & O'Leary, K. (1982). A conceptual framework for parent involvement. *Educational Leadership, 40*(2), 48–49.

Charles, C. M. (1996). *Building classroom discipline: From models to practice.* New York: Longman.

Chesapeake Institute. (1994). *National agenda for achieving better results for children and youth with serious emotional disturbance.* Washington, DC: U.S. Department of Education, Office of Special Education and Rehabilitative Services, Office of Special Education Programs.

Christensen, L. (1998). Writing the word and the world. In W. Ayers, J. A. Hunt, & T. Quinn (Eds.), *Teaching for social justice* (pp. 39–47). New York: The New Press and Teachers College Press.

Chunn, E. W. (1987). Sorting black students for success and failure: The inequity of ability grouping and tracking. *Urban League Review, 11*(1–2), 93–106.

Cochran-Smith, M., & Lytle, S. L. (1993). *Inside/outside: Teacher research and knowledge.* New York: Teachers College Press.

Coleman, M. (1996). *Emotional/behavioral disorders: Theory and practice.* Boston: Allyn and Bacon.

Comer, J. P. (1980). *School power: Implications of an intervention project.* New York: Free Press.

Comer, J. P., Haynes, N. M., & Joyner, E. T. (1996). *Rallying the whole village: The Comer process for reforming education.* New York: Teachers College Press.

Coontz, S. (1992). *The way we never were: American families and the nostalgia trap.* New York: Basic Books.

Cooper, J. E. (1991). Telling our own stories: The reading and writing of journals and diaries. In C. Witherall & N. Noddings (Eds.), *Stories lives tell: Narrative and dialogue in education* (pp. 96–112). New York: Teachers College Press.

Crawford, D., & Bodine, R. (1996). *Conflict resolution education: A guide to implementing programs in schools, youth-serving organizations, and community and juvenile justice settings: Program report.* Washington, DC: Office of Juvenile Justice and Delinquency Prevention; Office of Elementary and Secondary Education, U.S. Dept. of Education.

Cremin, L. A. (1970). *American education: The colonial experience, 1607–1783.* New York: Harper & Row.

Cremin, L. A. (1980). *American education: The national experience, 1783–1876.* New York: Harper & Row.

Cremin, L. A. (1988). *American education: The metropolitan experience, 1876–1980.* New York: Harper & Row.

Danforth, S. (1997). On what basis hope? Modern progress and postmodern possibilities. *Mental Retardation, 35*(2), 93–106.

Danforth, S. (2000). Resistance theories: Exploring the politics of oppositional behavior. *Multiple Voices for Ethnically Diverse Learners,* pp. 13–29.

Delpit, L. D. (1993). The silenced dialogue: Power and pedagogy in educating other people's children. In L. Weis & M. Fine (Eds.), *Beyond silenced voices: Class, race, and gender in United States schools.* Albany: SUNY Press.

Dennison, G. (1969). *The lives of children: The story of the first street school.* New York: Random House.

Despert, J. L. (1951). Some considerations relating to the genesis of autistic behavior in children. *American Journal of Orthopsychiatry, 21,* 335–350.

Deutsch, M. (1949). A theory of cooperation and competition. *Human Relations, 2,* 129–152.

Deutsch, M. (1962). Cooperation and trust: Some theoretical notes. In M. R. Jones (Ed.), *Nebraska symposium on motivation* (pp. 275–319). Lincoln: University of Nebraska Press.

Deutsch, M. (1973). *The resolution of conflict: Constructive and destructive processes.* New Haven, CT: Yale University Press.

Deutsch, M. (1990). Sixty years of conflict. *International Journal of Conflict Management, 1*(3), 237–263.

Deutsch, M. (1994). Constructive conflict resolution: Principles, training, and research. *Journal of Social Issues, 50*(1), 13–32.

Deutsch, M., Mitchell, V., Zhang, Q., Khattri, N., Tepavac, L., Weitzman, E. A., & Lynch, R. (1992). *The effects of training in cooperative learning and conflict resolution in an alternative high school.* New York: Teachers College, International Center for Cooperation and Conflict Resolution.

DeVries, R. (1997). Piaget's social theory. *Educational Researcher, 26*(2), 4–17.

DeVries, R. (1998). Implications of Piaget's constructivist theory for character education. *Action in Teacher Education, 20*(4), 39–47.

DeVries, R., Haney, J., & Zan, B. (1991). Socio-moral atmosphere in direct-instruction, eclectic, and constructivist kindergartens: A study of teachers' enacted interpersonal understanding. *Early Childhood Research Quarterly, 6*(4), 473–517.

DeVries, R., & Zan, B. (1994). *Moral classrooms, moral children: Creating a constructivist atmosphere in early education.* New York: Teachers College Press.

Dewey, J. (1916). *Democracy and education.* New York: Macmillan.

Dewey, J. (1920). *Reconstruction in philosophy.* New York: Holt.

Dewey, J. (1925). *Experience and nature.* Chicago: Open Court.

Dewey, J. (1927). *The public and its problems.* Denver: Swallow.

Dewey, J. (1929). *The quest for certainty: A study of the relation of knowledge and action.* New York: Minton, Balch.

Dewey, J. (1930). *Individualism, old and new.* New York: Minton, Balch.

Dewey, J. (1938). *Experience and education.* New York: Macmillan.

Dewey, J. (1939). *Freedom and culture.* New York: Capricorn.

Dewey, J. (1993). *The political writings.* Indianapolis, IN: Hackett.

Dewey, J. (1994). *The moral writings of John Dewey.* Amherst, NY: Prometheus.

Dryfoos, J. (1995). Full service schools: Revolution or fad? *Journal of Research on Adolescence, 5,* 147–172.

Dunn, L. M. (1968). Special education for the mildly retarded: Is much of it justifiable? *Exceptional Children, 35,* 5–22.

Dunst, C. J., & Trivette, C. M. (1987). Enabling and empowering families: Conceptual and intervention issues. *School Psychology Review, 16*(4), 443–456.

Dunst, C., Trivette, C., & Deal, A. (1988). *Enabling and empowering families: Principles and guidelines for practice.* Lexington, MA: Lexington Books.

Duplass, D., & Smith, T. (1995). Hearing Dennis through his own voice: A redefinition. *Behavioral Disorders, 20*(2), 144–148.

Durlak, J. (1995). *School-based prevention programs for children and adolescents.* Thousand Oaks, CA: Sage.

Dybwad, G., & Bersani, H. (1996). *New voices: Self-advocacy by people with disabilities.* Cambridge, MA: Brookline.

Edgar, E. (1998). Where does weather come from? A response to "Behavioral disorders: A postmodern perspective." *Behavioral Disorders, 23*(3), 160-165.

Elkind, D. (1998). Behavior disorders: A postmodern perspective. *Behavioral Disorders, 23*(3), 153–159.

Elliott, J. (1991). Changing contexts for educational evaluation: The challenge for methodology. *Studies in Educational Evaluation, 17*(2-3), 215-238.

Epstein, J. L. (1988). How do we improve programs for parent involvement? *Educational Horizons, 66*(2), 58-59.

Estes, C. P. (1992). *Women who run with the wolves: Myths and stories of the wild woman archetype.* New York: Ballantine.

Faires, J., Nichols, W. D., & Rickelman, R. J. (2000). Effects of parental involvement in developing competent readers in first grade. *Reading Psychology, 21*(3), 195–215.

Fine, M., Powell, L. C., Weis, L., & Mun Wong, L. (1997). Preface. In M. Fine, L. Weis, L. C. Powell, & L. Mun Wong (Eds.), *Off white: Readings on race, power and society.* New York: Routledge.

Flaherty, L., Weist, M., & Warner, B. (1996). School-based mental health services in the United States: History, current models, and needs. *Community Mental Health Journal, 25,* 341–352.

Forest, M., & Lusthaus, E. (1989). Promoting educational equity for all students: Circles and maps. In S. Stainback, W. Stainback, & M. Forest (Eds.), *Educating all students in the mainstream of general education* (pp. 443–457). Baltimore: Paul H. Brookes.

Fosnot, C. T. (1996). Constructivism: A psychological theory of learning. In C. T. Fosnot (Ed.), *Constructivism: Theory, perspectives, and practice* (pp. 8–33). New York: Teachers College Press.

Franklin, C., & Streeter, C. (1995). School reform: Linking public schools with human services. *Social Work, 40*(6), 773–783.

Fraser, N. (1987). *Social movements vs. disciplinary bureaucracies: The discourse of social needs* (CHS Occasional Paper No. 8). Minneapolis: University of Minnesota, Center for Humanities Studies.

Freiberg, H. J. (Ed.). (1999a). *Beyond behaviorism: Changing the classroom management paradigm.* Boston: Allyn and Bacon.

Freiberg, H. J. (1999b). Consistency management and cooperative discipline: From tourists to citizens in the classroom. In H. J. Freiberg (Ed.), *Beyond behaviorism: Changing the classroom management paradigm.* Boston: Allyn and Bacon.

Freire, P. (1970). *Pedagogy of the oppressed.* New York: Continuum.

Freire, P. (1973). *Education for critical consciousness.* New York: Continuum.

Friesen, B. J., & Wahlers, D. (1994). Respect and real help: Family support and children's mental health. *Journal of Emotional & Behavioral Problems, 2*(4), 12–15.

Funk, R. (1987). Disability rights: From caste to class in the context of civil rights. In A. Gartner & T. Joe (Eds.), *Images of the disabled, disabling images* (pp. 1–30). New York: Praeger.

Garbarino, J. (1992). *Children and families in the social environment.* New York: Aldine de Gruyter.

Gardner, H. (1983). *Frames of mind: The theory of multiple intelligences.* New York: Basic Books.

Gaston, L. (1990). The concept of the alliance and its role in psychotherapy: Theoretical and empirical considerations. *Psychotherapy, 27,* 143–153.

Geenen, S., Powers, L. E., & Lopez-Vasquez, A. (2001). Multicultural aspects of parent involvement in transition planning. *Exceptional Children, 67*(2), 265–282.

Gergen, K. (1995a). The healthy, happy human being wears many masks. In W. T. Anderson (Ed.), *The truth about the truth: De-confusing and re-constructing the post-modern world* (pp. 136–144). New York: Penguin Putnam.

Gergen, K. J. (1995b). Social construction and the educational process. In L. P. Steffe & J. Gale (Eds.), *Constructivism in education* (pp. 17–40). Hillsdale, NJ: Lawrence Erlbaum.

Gilligan, C. (1977). In a different voice: Women's conceptions of self and of morality. *Harvard Educational Review, 47,* 481–517.

Gilligan, C. (1982). *In a different voice: Psychological theory and women's development.* Cambridge, MA: Harvard University Press.

Gilligan, C. (1988). Remapping the moral domain: New images of self in relationship. In C. Gilligan, J. V. Ward, J. McLean Taylor, & B. Bardige (Eds.), *Mapping the moral domain: A contribution of women's thinking to psychological theory and education.* Cambridge, MA: Harvard University Press.

Gilroy, B. (1998). *Coulseling kids: Its magic—manual of therapeutic uses of magic with children and teens.* Therapist Organizer.

Girard, K., & Koch, S. J. (1996). *Conflict resolution in the schools: A manual for educators.* San Francisco: Jossey-Bass.

Giroux, H. (1983). *Theory and resistance: A pedagogy for the opposition.* South Hadley, MA: Bergin and Garvey.

Glueck, S. (1953). The home, the school, and delinquency. *Harvard Educational Review, 23,* 17–32.

Glueck, S., & Glueck, E. (1950). *Unraveling juvenile delinquency.* New York: Commonwealth Fund.

Goodman, N. (1978). *Ways of worldmaking.* Indianapolis, IN: Hackett.

Gouinlock, J. (1994). Introduction. In J. Dewey, *The moral writings of John Dewey* (pp. xix-liv). Amherst, NY: Prometheus.

Green, R. S. (2001). Closing the achievement gap: Lessons learned and challenges ahead. *Teaching & Change, 8*(2), 215–224.

Greenbaum, P. E., Dedrick, R. F., Friedman, R. M., Kutash, K., Brown, E. C., Lardieri, S. P., & Pugh, A. M. (1998). National Adolescent and Children Treatment Study (NACTS): Outcomes for children with serious emotional and behavioral disturbance. In M. H. Epstein, K. Kutash, & A. Duchnowski (Eds.), *Outcomes for children and youth with behavioral and emotional disorders* (pp. 21–54). Austin, TX: Pro-Ed.

Greenwood, G. E., & Hickman, C. W. (1991). Research and practice in parent involvement: Implications for teacher education. *Elementary School Journal, 91*(3), 279–288.

Grob, G. N. (1983). *Mental illness and American society, 1875–1940.* Princeton, NJ: Princeton University Press.

Grob, G. N. (1994). *The mad among us: A history of the care of America's mentally ill.* New York: Free Press.

Grosenick, J., George, N., & Kauffman, J. (1987). A profile of school programs for the behaviorally disordered: Twenty years after Morse, Cutter, and Fink. *Behavioral Disorders, 12*(3), 159–168.

Gross, M. (1987). *The psychological society.* New York: Random House.

Group for the Advancement of Psychiatry (GAP), Committee on Child Psychiatry. (1966). *Psychopathological disorders in childhood: Theoretical considerations and a proposed classification* (GAP Report 62). Dallas, TX: Author.

Hara, S. R., & Burke, D. J. (1998). Parent involvement: The key to improved student achievement. *School Community Journal, 8*(2), 9–19.

Harris, I. M. (1996). Peace education in an urban school district in the United States. *Peabody Journal of Education, 71*(3), 63–83.

Harry, B. (1992). *Cultural diversity, families, and the special education system: Communication and empowerment.* New York: Teachers College Press.

Harry, B. (1994). The disproportionate placement of African American males in special education programs: A critique of the process. *Journal of Negro Education, 63*(4), 602–619.

Hawkins, J., & Catalano, R. (1992). *Communities that care.* San Francisco: Jossey-Bass.

Hayden, T. (1980). *One child.* New York: Putnam.

Hayden, T. (1981). *Somebody else's kids.* New York: Putnam.

Hayden, T. (1995). *The tiger's child.* New York: Scribner.

Healy, W. (1915). *The individual delinquent: A text-book of diagnosis and prognosis for all concerned in understanding offenders.* Boston: Little, Brown.

Heath, P. A. (1987). Developing parent education courses: A review of resources. *Family Relations, 36*(2), 209–214.

Heck, A. O. (1940). *The education of exceptional children: Its challenge to teachers, parents, and laymen.* New York: McGraw-Hill.

Henderson, A. T. (1987). *The evidence continues to grow: Parent involvement improves student achievement: An annotated bibliography.* Columbia, MD: National Committee for Citizens in Education.

Henggler, S., & Borduin, C. (1990). *Family therapy and beyond: A multisystemic approach to treating the behavior problems of children and adolescents.* Pacific Grove, CA: Brooks/Cole.

Hernandez, A. (1997). *Pedagogy, democracy and feminism: Rethinking the public sphere.* Albany: SUNY Press.

Hobbs, N. (1982). *The troubled and troubling child.* San Francisco: Jossey-Bass.

hooks, b. (1994). *Teaching to transgress.* New York: Routledge.

Hoover-Dempsey, K. V., & Sandler, H. M. (1997). Why do parents become involved in their children's education? *Review of Educational Research, 67*(1), 3–42.

Horn, M. (1989). *Before it's too late: The child guidance movement in the United States, 1922–1945.* Philadelphia: Temple University Press.

Horvath, A. O., & Greenberg, L. S. (1994). *The working alliance: Theory, research, and practice.* New York: Wiley.

Horvath, A. O., & Luborsky, L. (1993). The role of the therapeutic alliance in psychotherapy. *Journal of Consulting and Clinical Psychology, 61*(4), 561–573.

Horvath, A. O., & Symonds, B. D. (1991). Relation between working alliance and outcome in psychotherapy: A meta-analysis. *Journal of Counseling Psychology, 38*(2), 139–149.

Howard, G. S. (1991). Culture tales: A narrative approach to thinking, cross-cultural psychology, and psychotherapy. *American Psychologist, 46*(3), 187–197.

Johnson, D. W. (1991). *Human relations and your career* (3rd ed.). Englewood Cliffs, NJ: Prentice Hall.

Johnson, D. W. (1993). *Reaching out: Interpersonal effectiveness and self-actualization* (6th ed.). Needham Heights, MA: Allyn & Bacon.

Johnson, D. W., & Johnson, R. T. (1989). *Cooperation and competition: Theory and research.* Edina, MN: Interaction.

Johnson, D. W., & Johnson, R. T. (1991). *Teaching students to be peacemakers.* Edina, MN: Interaction.

Johnson, D. W., & Johnson, R. T. (1994). Effects of conflict resolution training on elementary school students. *Journal of Social Psychology, 134*(6), 803-817.

Johnson, D. W., & Johnson, R. T. (1995a). *Reducing school violence through conflict resolution.* Alexandria, VA: Association for Supervision and Curriculum Development.

Johnson, D. W., & Johnson, R. T. (1995b). *Teaching students to be peacemakers* (3rd ed.). Edina, MN: Interaction.

Johnson, D. W., & Johnson, R. T. (1996). Teaching all students how to manage conflicts constructively: The peacemakers program. *Journal of Negro Education, 65*(3), 322–335.

Johnson, D. W., Johnson, R. T., & Holubec, E. J. (1993). *Cooperation in the classroom* (6th ed.). Edina, MN: Interaction.

Johnson, J. L. (1968). Special education and the inner city: A challenge for the future or another means for cooling the mark out? *Journal of Special Education, 3*(3), 241–251.

Johnson, L. (1993). *My posse don't do homework.* New York: St. Martin's.

Johnson, L. (1995). *Girls at the back of the class.* New York: St. Martin's.

Jones, K. W. (1999). *Taming the troublesome child: American families, child guidance, and the limits of psychiatric authority.* Cambridge, MA: Harvard University Press.

Katz, M. B. (1971). *Class, bureaucracy, and schools: The illusion of educational change in America.* New York: Praeger.

Katz, M. B. (1996). *In the shadow of the poorhouse: A social history of welfare in America.* New York: Basic Books.

Kauffman, J. M. (1976). Nineteenth century view of children's behavior disorders: Historical contributions and continuing issues. *Journal of Special Education, 10*(4), 335–349.

Keith, T. Z., Keith, P. B., Quirk, K. J., Sperduto, J., Santillo, S., & Killings, S. (1998). Longitudinal effects of parent involvement on high school grades: Similarities and differences across gender and ethnic groups. *Journal of School Psychology, 36*(3), 335–363.

Kelly, U. A. (1997). *Schooling desire: Literacy, cultural politics, and pedagogy.* New York: Routledge.

Kincheloe, J. L. (1991). *Teachers as researchers: Qualitative inquiry as a path to empowerment.* Philadelphia: Falmer.

Kliewer, C. (1998a). The meaning of inclusion. *Mental Retardation, 36*(3), 317–321.

Kliewer, C. (1998b). *Schooling children with Down syndrome: Toward an understanding of possibility.* New York: Teachers College Press.

Knitzer, J. (1990). *At the school house door: An examination of programs and policies for children with behavioral and emotional problems.* New York: Bank Street College of Education.

Knitzer, J., Steinberg, Z., & Fleisch, B. (1991). Schools, mental health, and the advocacy challenge. *Journal of Clinical Child Psychology, 20,* 102–111.

Kohl, H. (1968). *36 children.* New York: New American Library.

Kohl, H. (1991). *I won't learn from you: The role of assent in learning.* Minneapolis, MN: Milkweed.

Kohl, H. (1994). *I won't learn from you, and other thoughts on creative maladjustment.* New York: New Press.

Kohl, H. (2000). *The discipline of hope: Learning from a lifetime of teaching.* New York: New Press.

Kohlberg, L. (1967). Moral and religious education in the public schools: A developmental view. In T. R. Sizer (Ed.), *Religion and public education.* Boston: Houghton Mifflin.

Kohlberg, L. (1984). *The psychology of moral development.* San Francisco: Harper & Row.

Kohn, A. (1993). *Punished by rewards: The trouble with gold stars, incentive plans, A's, praise, and other bribes.* Boston: Houghton Mifflin.

Kotlowitz, A. (1991). *There are no children here: The story of two boys growing up in the other America.* New York: Doubleday.

Koyanagi, C., & Gaines, S. (1993). *All systems failure: An examination of the results of neglecting the needs of children with serious emotional disturbance.* Washington, DC: National Institute for Mental Health and the Federation of Families for Children's Mental Health.

Kreidler, W. J. (1984). *Creative conflict resolution: More than 200 activities for keeping peace in the classroom.* Glenview, IL: Scott, Foresman.

Kreisberg, S. (1992). *Transforming power: Domination, empowerment, and education.* Albany: SUNY Press.

Kristeva, J. (1982). *Powers of horror: An essay on abjection.* New York: Columbia University Press.

Kugelmass, J. W. (1987). *Behavior, bias, and handicaps: Labeling the emotionally disturbed child.* New Brunswick, NJ: Transaction Books.

Kunc, N. (1992). The need to belong: Rediscovering Maslow's hierarchy of needs. In R. V. Villa, J. S. Thousand, W. Stainback, & S. Stainback (Eds.), *Restructuring for caring and effective education: An administrative guide to creating heterogeneous schools* (pp. 25–39). Baltimore, MD: Paul H. Brookes.

Kysmissis, P., & Halperin, D. A. (1996). *Group therapy with children and adolescents.* Washington, DC: American Psychiatric Association.

Lagorio, J. (1993). *Life cycle: Classroom activities for helping children live with daily change and loss.* Tucson, AZ: Zephyr.

Lavin, G. K., Trabka, S., & Kahn, E. M. (1984). Group therapy with aggressive and delinquent adolescents. In C. R. Keith (Ed.), *The aggressive adolescent: Clinical perspectives* (pp. 240–267). New York: Free Press.

Laycock, S. R., & Stevenson, G. S. (1950). Parents' problems with exceptional children. In N. B. Henry (Ed.), *The forty-ninth yearbook of the National Society for the Study of Education: Part II, the education of exceptional children* (pp. 117–134). Chicago: University of Chicago Press.

Lee, V. E., & Bryk, A. S. (1988). Curriculum tracking as mediating the social distribution of high school achievement. *Sociology of Education, 61,* 78–94.

Leitch, M. L., & Tangri, S. S. (1988). Barriers to home-school collaboration. *Educational Horizons, 66*(2), 70–74.

Lesiak, C., & Jones, M. (Producers). (1991). *In the whiteman's image* [Motion picture]. Available from PBS Video, Alexandria, VA.

Leyser, Y. (1985). Parent involvement in school: A survey of parents of handicapped students. *Contemporary Education, 57*(1), 38–43.

Lightfoot, S. L. (1978). *Worlds apart: Relationships between families and schools.* New York: Basic Books.

Lipsky, D. K., & Gartner, A. (1989). *Beyond separate education: Quality education for all.* Baltimore, MD: Paul H. Brookes.

Lipsky, D., & Gartner, A. (1996). Inclusion, restructuring, and the remaking of American society. *Harvard Educational Review, 6,* 762–796.

Long, N. J., & Morse W. C. (1996). *Conflict in the classroom: The education of at-risk and troubled students* (5th ed.). Austin, TX: Pro-Ed.

Long, N. J., Morse, W. C., & Newman, R. G. (1965). *Conflict in the classroom: The education of emotionally disturbed children.* Belmont, CA: Wadsworth.

Long, N. J., Morse, W. C., & Newman, R. G. (1971). *Conflict in the classroom: The education of emotionally disturbed children* (2nd ed.). Belmont, CA: Wadsworth.

Long, N. J., Morse, W. C., & Newman, R. G. (1976). *Conflict in the classroom: The education of emotionally disturbed children* (3rd ed.). Belmont, CA: Wadsworth.

Long, N. J., Morse, W. C., & Newman, R. G. (1980). *Conflict in the classroom: The education of emotionally disturbed children* (4th ed.). Belmont, CA: Wadsworth.

MacLeod, J. (1995). *Ain't no makin' it.* Boulder, CO: Westview.

Martin, R. (1996). Self-advocacy and the International League. In G. Dybwad & H. Bersani (Eds.), *New voices: Self-advocacy by people with disabilities* (pp. 63–68). Cambridge, MA: Brookline.

Martinez, Y., & Smith, T. J. (2000). Cultural constructions of life and meaning in the classroom. In J. L. Paul & T. J. Smith (Eds.), *Stories out of school: Memories and reflections on care and cruelty in the classroom* (pp. 65–88). Stamford, CT: Ablex.

McFadden, A. C., Marsh, G. E., Price, B. J., & Hwang, Y. (1992). A study of race and gender bias in the punishment of school children. *Education and Treatment of Children, 15*(2), 140–146.

McLaren, P. (1985). The ritual dimensions of resistance: Clowning and symbolic inversion. *Journal of Education, 167*(2), 84–97.

McLaren, P. (1993). *Schooling as a ritual performance.* New York: Routledge.

McLaren, P. (1994). Multiculturalism and the postmodern critique: Toward a pedagogy of resistance and transformation. In H. A. Giroux & P. McLaren (Eds.), *Between borders: Pedagogy and the politics of cultural studies* (pp. 192–219). New York: Routledge.

McLaughlin, M., Leone, P., Warren, S., & Schofield, P. (1994). *Doing things differently: Issues and options for creating comprehensive school linked services for children and youth with emotional or behavioral disorders.* College Park, MD: Westat, Inc., and University of Maryland.

Mickelson, J.-R. (2000). *Our sons were labeled behavior disordered: Here are the stories of our lives.* Troy, NY: Educator's International Press.

Miller, A. (1986). *For your own good: Hidden cruelty in child-rearing and the roots of violence.* New York: Noonday.

Miller, A. (1990a). *For your own good: Hidden cruelty in child-rearing and the roots of violence* (2nd ed.). New York: Noonday.

Miller, A. (1990b). *Thou shalt not be aware: Society's betrayal of the child.* New York: Meridian.

Miller, A. (1997). *Breaking down the wall of silence: The liberating experience of facing painful truth.* New York: Meridian.

Miller, D. (1993). Sexual and physical abuse among adolescents with behavioral disorders: Profiles and implications. *Behavioral Disorders, 18*(2), 129–138.

Morse, W. (1993, Spring). Fritz Redl for today. *Journal of Emotional and Behavioral Problems,* pp. 53–55.

Mullins, J. B. (1987). Authentic voices from parents of exceptional children. *Family Relations, 36*(1), 30–33.

Nasaw, D. (1979). *Schooled to order: A social history of public schooling in the United States.* New York: Oxford University Press.

National Rural Research and Personnel Preparation Project. (1980) *A national comparative study regarding rural special education delivery systems before and after passage of PL 94–142.* Murray, KY: Murray State University, Center for Information and Development.

Newton, C., Taylor, G., & Wilson, D. (1996). Circles of friends: An inclusive approach to meeting emotional and behavioural needs. *Educational Psychology in Practice, 11*(4), 41–48.

Nice, S. (2003). *On our shoulders: Supporting children's social, emotional, and behavioral development.* Unpublished doctoral dissertation, National-Louis University, Evanston, IL.

Noddings, N. (1984). *Caring: A feminine approach to ethics and moral education.* Berkeley: University of California Press.

Noddings, N. (1991a). Stories in dialogue: Caring and interpersonal reasoning. In C. Witherall & N. Noddings (Eds.), *Stories lives tell: Narrative and dialogue in education* (pp. 171–192). New York: Teachers College Press.

Noddings, N. (1991b). Stories in dialogue: Caring and interpersonal relationships. In C. Witherall & N. Noddings (Eds.), *Stories lives tell: Narrative and dialogue in education* (pp. 157–170). New York: Teachers College Press.

Noddings, N. (1992). *The challenge to care in schools: An alternative approach to education.* New York: Teachers College Press.

Oakes, J. (1985). *Keeping track: How schools structure inequality.* New Haven, CT: Yale University Press.

Oakes, J. (1990). *Multiplying inequalities: The effects of race, social class, and tracking on opportunities to learn mathematics and science.* Santa Monica, CA: RAND.

Paley, V. G. (1979). *White teacher.* Cambridge, MA: Harvard University Press.

Paley, V. G. (1991). *The boy who would be a helicopter.* Cambridge, MA: Harvard University Press.

Paley, V. G. (1995). *Kwanzaa and me: A teacher's story.* Cambridge, MA: Harvard University Press.

Palmer, P. (1998). *The courage to teach: Exploring the inner landscape of a teacher's life.* San Francisco: Jossey-Bass.

Patterson, G. R. (1965). An application of conditioning techniques to the control of a hyperactive child. In L. P. Ullmann & L. Krasner (Eds.), *Case studies in behavior modification* (pp. 370–375). New York: Holt, Rinehart and Winston.

Patton, J. M. (1998). The disproportionate representation of African-Americans in special education: Looking behind the curtain for understanding and solutions. *Journal of Special Education, 32*(1), 25–31.

Paul, J., & Smith, T. (Eds.). (2000). *Stories out of school: Memories and reflections of care and cruelty in the classroom.* Norwood, NJ: Ablex.

Pavlov, I. C. (1906). The scientific investigation of the physical faculties or processes in higher animals. *Lancet, 1*, 911–915.

Peacock Hill Working Group. (1991). Problems and promises in special education and related services for children and youth with emotional or behavioral disorders. *Behavioral Disorders, 16*, 229–313.

Petersen, A., Compas, B., & Brooks, G. (1993). Depression in adolescence. *American Psychologist, 48*, 155–168.

Philips, E. I. (1968). Achievement place: Token reinforcement procedures in a home style rehabilitation setting for predelinquent boys. *Journal of Applied Behavior Analysis, 1*, 213–223.

Piaget, J. (1963). *The origins of intelligence in children.* New York: Norton.

Piaget, J., & Inhelder, B. (1969). *The psychology of the child.* New York: Basic Books.

Platt, A. M. (1969). *The child savers: The invention of delinquency.* Chicago: University of Chicago Press.

Powell, D. R. (1991). How schools support families: Critical policy tensions. *Elementary School Journal, 91*(3), 307–319.

Rank, B. (1949). Adaptation of the psychoanalytic technique for the treatment of young children with atypical development. *American Journal of Orthopsychiatry, 19*, 130–139.

Redl, F. (1966). *When we deal with children: Selected writings.* New York: Free Press.

Redl, F., & Wineman, D. (1951). *Children who hate: The disorganization and breakdown of behavior controls.* Glencoe, IL: Free Press.

Redl, F., & Wineman, D. (1952). *Controls from within: Techniques for the treatment of the aggressive child.* Glencoe, IL: Free Press.

Rhodes, W. C. (1970). A community participation analysis of emotional disturbance. *Exceptional Children, 36*(5), 309–314.

Rhodes, W. (1977). The illusion of normality. *Behavioral Disorders, 2*(2), 6–11.

Rhodes, W. C., & Tracy, M. L. (Eds.). (1975). *A study of child variance*. Ann Arbor: University of Michigan Press.

Richardson, J. G. (2000). *Common, delinquent, and special: The institutional shape of special education*. New York: Falmer.

Richardson, J. G., & Parker, T. L. (1993). The institutional genesis of special education: The American case. *American Journal of Education, 101*(8), 359–371.

Richardson, T. R. (1989). *The century of the child: The mental hygiene movement and social policy in the United States and Canada*. Albany: SUNY Press.

Ridenour, N. (1961). *Mental health in the United States: A fifty-year history*. Cambridge, MA: Harvard University Press.

Ross, D. (1991). *The origins of American social science*. New York: Cambridge University Press.

Rossow, L. F. (1984). Administrative discretion and student suspension: A lion in waiting. *Journal of Law & Education, 13*(3), 417–440.

Ryan, A. (1995). *John Dewey and the high tide of American liberalism*. New York: Norton.

Ryan, W. (1971). *Blaming the victim*. New York: Pantheon.

Schaefer, E. S. (1991). Goals for parent and future-parent education: Research on parental beliefs and behavior. *Elementary School Journal, 91*(3), 239–247.

Schniedewind, N., & Davidson, E. (1983). *Open minds to equality: A sourcebook of learning activities to affirm diversity and promote equity*. Boston: Allyn & Bacon.

Schniedewind, N., & Davidson, E. (1998). *Open minds to equality: A sourcebook of learning activities to affirm diversity and promote equity* (2nd ed.). Boston: Allyn & Bacon.

Schön, D. A. (1983). *The reflective practitioner: How professionals think in action*. New York: Basic Books.

Schön, D. A. (1987). *Educating the reflective practitioner: Toward a new design for teaching and learning in the professions*. San Francisco: Jossey-Bass.

Schön, D. A. (1991). *The reflective turn: Case studies in and on educational practice*. New York: Teachers College Press.

Seeley, D. S. (1989). A new paradigm for parent involvement. *Educational Leadership, 47*(2), 46–48.

Sergiovanni, T. J. (1992). *Moral leadership: Getting to the heart of school improvement*. San Francisco: Jossey-Bass.

Shorter, E. (1997). *A history of psychiatry: From the era of the asylum to the age of Prozac*. New York: Wiley.

Siepker, B. B., & Kandaras, C. S. (1985). *Group therapy with children and adolescents: A treatment manual*. New York: Human Sciences Press.

Simpson, R. L. (1990). *Conferencing parents of exceptional children*. Austin, TX: Pro-Ed.

Singer, G. H. S., & Powers, L. E. (Eds.). (1993). *Families, disability, and empowerment: Active coping skills and strategies for family interventions*. Baltimore, MD: Paul H. Brookes.

Skiba, R. J., Peterson, R. L., & Williams, T. (1997). Office referrals and suspension: Disciplinary intervention in middle schools. *Education & Treatment of Children, 20*(3), 295–315.

Skinner, B. F. (1971). *Beyond freedom and dignity*. New York: Knopf.

Skinner, B. F. (1989). *Recent issues in the analysis of behavior*. Columbus, OH: Merrill.

Slawson, J. (1926). *The delinquent boy*. Boston: Gorham.

Smith, F. (1998). *The book of learning and forgetting*. New York: Teachers College Press.

Smith, T. J. (1997, April). Storying moral dimensions of disordering: Teacher inquiry into the social construction of severe emotional disturbance. Paper presented at the annual meeting of the American Educational Research Association, Chicago.

Smith, T. J. (in press). *Teaching the children we fear: Stories from the front*. Cresskill, NJ: Hampton Press.

Sonnenschein, P. (1981). Parents and professionals: An uneasy relationship. *Teaching Exceptional Children, 14*(2), 62–65.

Stone, L. (1992). Philosophy, meaning constructs and teacher theorizing. In E. W. Ross, J. Cornett, & G. McCutcheon (Eds.), *Teacher personal theorizing: Connecting curriculum, practice, theory, and research* (pp. 19–34). Albany: SUNY Press.

Stullken, E. H. (1950). Special schools and classes for the socially maladjusted. In N. B. Henry (Ed.), *The forty-ninth yearbook of the National Society for the Study of Education: Part II, the education of exceptional children* (pp. 281–301). Chicago: University of Chicago Press.

Sugai, G., & Horner, R. (1994). Including students with severe behavior problems in general education settings: Assumptions, challenges and solutions. In J. Marr, G. Sugai, & G. Indall (Eds.), *The Oregon conference monograph* (pp. 102–120). Eugene: University of Oregon Press.

Swap, S. M. (1993). *Developing home-school partnerships: From concepts to practice*. New York: Teachers College Press.

Swap, S., Prieto, A., & Harth, R. (1982). Ecological perspectives of the emotionally disturbed child. In R. McDowell, G. Adamson, & F. Wood (Eds.), *Teaching emotionally disturbed children*. Boston: Little, Brown.

Swick, K. J., & Graves, S. B. (1993). *Empowering at-risk families during the early childhood years*. Washington, DC: National Education Association.

Tarlow, B. (1996). Caring: A negotiated process that varies. In S. Gordon, P. Benner, & N. Noddings (Eds.), *Caregiving: Readings in knowledge, practice, ethics, and politics* (pp. 56–82). Philadelphia: University of Pennsylvania Press.

Tatum, B. D. (1997). *"Why are all the black kids sitting together in the cafeteria?" and other conversations about race*. New York: Basic Books.

Thomas, R. M. (1992). *Comparing theories of child development* (3rd ed.). Belmont, CA: Wadsworth.

Thousand, J. S., Villa, R. A., & Nevin, A. I. (1994). *Creativity and collaborative learning: A practical guide to empowering students and teachers*. Baltimore, MD: Paul H. Brookes.

Tobin, K., & LaMaster, S. U. (1992). An interpretation of high school science teaching based on metaphors and beliefs for specific roles. In E. W. Ross, J. Cornett, & G. McCutcheon (Eds.), *Teacher personal theorizing: Connecting curriculum, practice, theory, and research* (pp. 115–136). Albany: SUNY Press.

Tompkins, J. (1996). *A life in schools: What the teacher learned*. Reading, MA: Perseus.

Trent, J. W. (1994). *Inventing the feeble mind: A history of mental retardation in the United States*. Berkeley: University of California Press.

Tyack, D. B. (1974). *The one best system: A history of American urban education*. Cambridge, MA: Harvard University Press.

Tyack, D. B., & Cuban, L. (1995). *Tinkering toward utopia: A century of public school reform*. Cambridge, MA: Harvard University Press.

Tyack, D., & Hansot, E. (1982). *Managers of virtue: Public school leadership in America, 1820–1980*. New York: Basic Books.

U.S. Department of Education. (1993). *Fifteenth annual report to Congress on the implementation of the Individuals with Disabilities Education Act*. Washington, DC: Author.

U.S. Department of Education. (1994). *Sixteenth annual report to Congress on the implementation of the Individuals with Disabilities Education Act.* Washington, DC: Author.

U.S. Department of Education. (1998). *Twentieth annual report to Congress on the implementation of the Individuals with Disabilities Education Act.* Washington, DC: Author.

U.S. Department of Education. (1999). *Twenty-first annual report to Congress on the implementation of the Individuals with Disabilities Education Act.* Washington, DC: Author.

von Glasersfeld, E. (1995). A constructivist approach to teaching. In L. P. Steffe & J. Gale (Eds.), *Constructivism in education* (pp. 3–16). Hillsdale, NJ: Lawrence Erlbaum.

Vorrath, H. H., & Brendtro, L. K. (1985). *Positive peer culture* (2nd ed.). New York: Aldine.

Wagner, M. M. (1995). Outcomes for youths with serious emotional disturbance in secondary school and early adulthood. *Critical Issues for Children and Youths, 5*(2), 90–111.

Weber, M. (1958). *The Protestant ethic and the spirit of capitalism.* New York: Scribner.

Westbrook, R. B. (1991). *John Dewey and American democracy.* Ithaca, NY: Cornell University Press.

Whelan, R. (1966). The relevance of behavior modification approaches for teachers of emotional disturbed children. In P. Knoblock (Ed.), *Intervention approaches in educating emotionally disturbed children* (pp. 35–78). Syracuse, NY: Syracuse University Press.

Williams, B. L., & Hartlage, L. C. (1988, August). *Communication and retention of psychoeducational diagnostic information in parent conferences.* Paper presented at the annual meeting of the American Psychological Association, Atlanta.

Williams, D. L., Jr., & Chavkin, N. F. (1989). Essential elements of strong parent involvement programs. *Educational Leadership, 47*(2), 18–20.

Williams, P., & Shoultz, B. (1982). *We can speak for ourselves.* London: Souvenir.

Winzer, M. A. (1993). *The history of special education.* Washington, DC: Gallaudet University Press.

Wolcott, H. F. (1994). *Transforming qualitative data: Description, analysis, and interpretation.* Thousand Oaks, CA: Sage.

Yalom, I. (1995). *The theory and practice of group psychotherapy* (4th ed.). New York: Basic Books.

Young, I. M. (1990). *Justice and the politics of difference.* Princeton, NJ: Princeton University Press.

Ysseldyke, J. E., & Algozzine, B. (1982). *Critical issues in special and remedial education.* Boston: Houghton Mifflin.

Zaragoza, N., & Scardina, M. (1998). The critical transformation of a special education classroom: A beginning teacher puts theory into practice. In J. L. Kincheloe & S. R. Steinberg (Eds.), *Unauthorized methods: Strategies for critical teaching* (pp. 79–94). New York: Routledge.

Zettel, J. J., & Ballard, J. (1979). The Education of All Handicapped Children Act of 1975: Its history, origin, and concepts. *Journal of Education, 179*(3), 5–22.

Zweig, C. (1995). The death of the self in the postmodern world. In W. T. Anderson (Ed.), *The truth about the truth: De-confusing and re-constructing the postmodern world* (pp. 145–150). New York: Penguin Putnam.

Index

**CORWIN
PRESS**

The Corwin Press logo—a raven striding across an open book—represents the union of courage and learning. Corwin Press is committed to improving education for all learners by publishing books and other professional development resources for those serving the field of K–12 education. By providing practical, hands-on materials, Corwin Press continues to carry out the promise of its motto: **"Helping Educators Do Their Work Better."**